I0093391

Early acclaim for *Ecosynomics: The Science of Abundance*

"Ecosynomics translates and drives the natural phenomenon that occur within human interactions, allowing the achievement of much greater results than normally expected, on a sustainable basis. The application of Ecosynomic principles integrates nature's processes of value creation, transformation, and propagation into the space of human interactions, structured around cycles of positive feedback and growth in the outcomes and experiences desired."

~Ana Cláudia Gonçalves, economist and CEO,
Global Financial Services IT Company

"Harmonic Vibrancy is the experience that leverages the potential we experience in human interactions, in their creativity, their nature, their light, their spirit, their awareness, and their attention. Ecosynomics provides a framework for making a qualitative jump in the harmonic vibrancy experienced, transforming towards a more equitable world of opportunities, wellbeing, and happiness for all."

~Luis Paiz Bekker, director Oxfam Guatemala,
former director of Doctors without Borders Argentina

"Jim Ritchie-Dunham came to 'Impuls' for an evening and shared with us his ideas on harmonic vibrancy and Ecosynomics. It was a deeply inspiring evening for all of us. The time is ripe to bring together the pioneers of sustainable business and show the world that things can be done differently: more collaboratively, more creatively, more peacefully"

~Benjamin Kafka, co-founder and director,
Impuls, Agency for applied utopianism, Berlin, Germany

"I couldn't agree more with Ecosynomics' basic premise that Abundance is all around us. Dr. Ritchie-Dunham very successfully shows us how to find it, prosper from it, and how to play it forward."

~Prof. Ellen J. Langer, Professor of Psychology,
Director of Langer Mindfulness Lab, Harvard University

"Any kind of group, even very small ones, can achieve extraordinary things on our way towards a more sustainable society. What makes some groups so special to be able to do that? Can we learn from them for a broader and sustainable transition in society? Ecosynomics provides an appealing lens for seeing the potential of change in how and for what we currently work together."
~Prof. Dr. Martin Welp, Chair of Socioeconomics and Communication, Global Change Management, Faculty of Forest and Environment, Eberswalde University for Sustainable Development

"In its ambition to transform human agreements, Ecosynomics does not resort to oversimplification but deals with the true complexity of social interaction and value creation. In revealing the underlying structures and practices that determine how we think, feel and perform individually and as a group, it empowers people to achieve better results and get more out of life."
~Makaio Witte, advisor, financial sector development, Sub-Saharan Africa, Deutsche Gesellschaft für Internationale Zusammenarbeit (GIZ)

"We at KATE e.V. enjoyed a two-day training in Ecosynomics led by Christoph Hinske, where we explored the implications of our results from the web-based Harmonic Vibrancy survey. We found that the survey questions and results helped clarify our developmental needs, as well as the communication and decision making processes that would best support that development. We were able to then identify our shared values and how to more efficiently meet them, bringing us greater focus on the more important elements, while reducing background noise. Personally, as a director, the Ecosynomic framework helped me see the importance of expressing needs, setting clear agreements, and opening the space for the potential of the individuals and the group."
~Kerstin Wippel, director of KATE (Kontaktstelle für Umwelt und Entwicklung) e.V.

"ASAPreneurs – Shaping a Sustainable World" is an international and widely recognized program that supports young people to gain leadership and entrepreneurial competencies for sustainability. We do so by offering a one year international training cycle in close cooperation with companies and other relevant organizations. Out of years of experience in advanced leadership training and empowerment of young leaders for sustainability, we know that current economic, environmental and social challenges cannot be met by applying the solutions of yesterday. Accordingly, in future, we plan to integrate Ecosynomics in our work and training cycles. We are doing so since we are convinced that innovative management and organizational development approaches are needed to address the challenges humanity is facing. The scientific results, frameworks and tools of Ecosynomics encourage us in our work that is based on collaborative structures, innovative networks and the ability to generate a culture where each individual is invited and able to incubate and implement its own creative activities in order to support a bigger whole. ASApreneurs is part of the ASA-Program & network, which is part of the GLOBAL CIVIC ENGAGEMENT gGmbH – Service for Development Initiatives."

~Simone Zeil – Project Manager- Program ASApreneurs, GLOBAL CIVIC ENGAGEMENT gGmbH – Service for Development Initiatives.


"Last year I had the chance to experience the framework, insights and tools that Ecosynomics provides, in two different groups. However different these groups were, and my role within them, it was an amazing experience. In both cases we started the process by taking the online survey of the institute. We did so since we wanted to gain a deeper understanding of our group as a whole. The survey results reflected my individual perception of the group and myself as a member of it. Revealing the different dimensions of group performance, the Ecosynomics framework supported and empowered me and the other members to move us in an active and cooperative way forward."

~ Arun Hackenberger, FairBindung e.V.


"Both major economic theorists Keynes and Mises, who have dominated monetary policy for over 100 years, make no accommodations in human interactions for time, relationship, possibility, or awareness. Their theories tend to produce win-lose outcomes, which in turn produce a mindset of scarcity and competition. On the other hand, THORLO, Inc., in collaboration with James Ritchie-Dunham and The Institute of Strategic Clarity, has created a dynamic business model that includes all the traditional metrics as well as including the four considerations listed above. We named it "Ecosynomics." The outcome THORLO is enjoying today, after 10 years of investments, is what we call "synergistic profitability." This is the synergistic effect of the success of our strategy — Integrated Collaboration Conversations — which results in a safe environment, much like a community or extended family, which has produced an ownership perspective in most of our community. This an environment where the individual who fully engages and participates can become self-aware, self-responsible, and self-reliant, leading to a less stressful and more prosperous life, achieving superior outcomes along the way."

~ Jim Throneburg, founder and CEO, THOR-LO

# Ecosynomics

## The Science of Abundance

JAMES L. RITCHIE-DUNHAM
WITH BETTYE PRUITT

VIBRANCY PUBLISHING     VIBRANCY INS., LLC     BELCHERTOWN, MA

Vibrancy Publishing
Vibrancy Ins., LLC
65 Old Bay Road
Belchertown, MA 01007
ecosynomics.com

Copyright © 2014.  James L. Ritchie-Dunham.
Printed in the United States of America.

All rights reserved. No part of this book may be reproduced, stored in a retrievel system, or transmitted, in any form or by any means whatsoever without prior written premission from the publisher, except in the case of brief quotations embodied in critical review and certain other noncommercial uses permitted as "fair use," by copyright law. For permission request, write to Vibrancy Publishing address above, attn: Permissions Coordinator.

Cover and Design by *Nowherehouse Designs*

Ritchie-Dunham, James L.
    Ecosynomics: The Science of Abundance / by James L. Ritchie-Dunham with Bettye Pruitt.
Includes bibliographical references and index.
ISBN# 978-0-9907153-0-6 (pbk.)
    1. Ecosynomics. 2. Abundance. 3. Harmonic Vibrancy. 4. Social Learning. I. Title.

10 9 8 7 6 5 4 3 2

*For those who are finding the way
to greater harmonic vibrancy
through their everyday agreements.*

# CONTENTS

Part I

## Describing Your Experience

Part II

## Ecosynomics and Economics: Lenses for Seeing Agreements

# Part III
## Moving to Greater Harmonic Vibrancy

# Part IV
## Learning in Laboratories

# Part V

# An Ecosynomic Vision of the Future

# Appendices

# FIGURES AND TABLES

# ACKNOWLEDGEMENTS

This book addresses fundamental questions about the quality of the human experience; questions I have been pursuing for most of my life. Looking back on my life's journey, I see that teachers have always shown up to support me at key times. Among many other things, these teachers helped me to recognize and appreciate all the giants who came before. Many of those, who have helped humanity see itself in a clearer light, are referenced in this book. Most are not. But I am grateful to all of them, as it is on their shoulders that my work stands.

The two people who set me on the path to this book by launching me into my work with social systems are Javier Chavez Ruiz and Carlos Alcerreca. Javier and Carlos were my dean and department chair as a young faculty member at the Instituto Tecnológico Autónomo de México (ITAM) in Mexico City. They asked me to attend a conference on organizational learning and system dynamics because I had had some organizational learning experience. I am forever thankful they asked me to go, and grateful I went, as I found I completely jibed with the system dynamics approach. That conference started me on the path of studying human decision-making and the factors that influence it. I now see that this was the beginning of my exploration into human agreements, the central focus of this book. Many great teachers and scholars helped me in my time as a doctoral student in Decision Sciences at UT Austin. I especially thank my advisor Jim Dyer and my thesis committee, which included Doug Morrice, Ed Anderson, Fred Davis, and Sirkka Jarvenpaa. I am also grateful for all I learned from my colleagues in the System Dynamics Group at MIT and from John Carroll at the MIT Sloan School of Management, where I spent a year as a visiting scholar. I have also been fortunate enough to spend the past nine years with Ellen Langer's Mindfulness Lab in the Psychology Department at Harvard University. I thank all of these incredible academics for showing me how to work with the deeper questions of life.

Jim Throneburg, the founder of THORLO, has also helped me wrestle with those questions, while teaching me about the entrepreneurial approach to melding possibility and action. In addition, I have greatly benefited from my study with teachers of different spiritual traditions: on ritual with Malidoma Somé and Orland Bishop; on cyclical time with the Maya; on meditative practice with Sogyal Rinpoche; and on Spacial Dynamics with Jaimen McMillan. All of these teachers have influenced the ideas in this book.

The engineer in me thoroughly enjoys studying the foundations of a field and putting that knowledge into practice. I have had many opportunities to put knowledge to practice living in many different places and working in different fields. For their support and friendship in these different settings, I thank my colleagues in Azima, the Institute for Strategic Clarity (Scott Spann, Helen-Ann Ireland, Michael Puleo, Ned Hulbert, Cleon Dunham, Luz Maria Puente, Steve Waddell, Fred Simon, Andy Leaf, Orland Bishop, Annabel Membrillo, Sandy Hessler, Christoph Hinske, Luis Paiz, and Ana Cláudia Gonçalves), my colleagues around the world in the Vibrancy network, GIGAL (Susanne Cook-Greuter, Anne Starr, and Rebecca Koeniger-Donohue), the Society for Organizational Learning, GAN-Net and iScale, Spacial Dynamics IS10, my partners at SDSG/SC (Hal Rabbino, Luz Maria Puente, Jay Forrest, Annabel Membrillo, Conrado Garcia), and GEP (Mary Day Mordecai and Ned Hulbert). I am also grateful for the opportunities I have had to learn in the field with leaders from many organizations, including consulting clients, colleagues in my own organizations, and other members of the boards on which I have served. A special thank you to all of my colleagues at THORLO.

My greatest practice field is my family. Here again, I have the most magnificent teachers. Leslie is my life-partner and my foundation stone, mentoring me in every aspect of life for over two decades, and hopefully another ninety-plus years. Jackie and Conor teach me every day how to grow in my capacity to be in relationship with two of the people I most love on the planet. My parents Jane and Cleon brought me into this world, gave me everything I ever needed and most things I wanted, along with many great lessons about a life well-lived. Early on they set me on the path of cross-cultural inquiry. My brothers and in-laws make it very easy to be a member of my family. I am also very grateful to my high-school exchange family, the Diaz-Paton Porras, especially Dorita and Julian, for making me their "child living overseas." Finally, I thank the many who have supported my work, specifically in the area of Ecosynomics. The Institute for Strategic Clarity (ISC) supports this work, and the Institute's funders have allowed me to spend my time developing and testing the framework. ISC Senior Fellows Christoph Hinske and Annabel Membrillo continue to road test the framework and tools, providing groundbreaking insights along the way. Sandy Schultz Hessler emphatically urged me to take the time to develop the framework and write this book. Specific gifts that supported the writing of this book came from the James L. Throneburg Foundation, THORLO, Cleon and Jane Dunham Foundation, Ned Hulbert and Mary Day Mordecai, Steve Waddell, Ellen and Tony Alfar, and the Philip Schultz Memorial Fund of the Community Foundation of Jackson Hole. Leslie Ritchie-Dunham developed the graphics used throughout the book. Bettye Pruitt guided the storytelling in the book as my developmental editor and co-writer. Jeff Lawson, Terri O'Fallon, and Alain Gauthier helped with the initial design of the harmonic vibrancy survey and analysis. Many thanks also go to the dozens of people who have helped the survey evolve and translated it into over a dozen languages. Lastly I give heartfelt gratitude to the helpful comments on early versions of the book generously given by Mike Puleo, Ned Hulbert, Andy Leaf, Alain Gauthier, Susann Cook-Greuter, Anne Starr, Beena Sharma, Jim Throneburg, Richard Oliver, and Leslie Ritchie-Dunham.

To all of you and the many more I unintentionally missed—thank you!

# OVERVIEW

Several years ago, working with a leadership group on a transition project, I was asked this question: "If I am leading several groups that meet on a regular basis, and all the members of these groups are the same people… why is it that some of our groups are inspiring, efficient, and effective and others are draining, inefficient, and ineffective? It's the same people! So, it isn't just that…. is it me? Something I am doing as a leader… even with the same people? What is really happening?" In reviewing the groups, the contents of the different meetings and the people involved, none of the obvious answers seemed to apply. Just what *was* really going on?

What a great question. What was even more interesting about this question was that it came from a leader in a company that was considered an outlier. A company that was off the charts in all the standard economic performance metrics and that had sustained that edge for over 20 years. If he had that question, then obviously it was a good question.

I had been working with groups going through strategic transformations for over 15 years when he asked me this question. I was already working with the ideas of scarcity and abundance and with what I would now call higher vibrancy and lower vibrancy groups and had seen that some groups seemed somehow "naturally" higher in vibrancy and performance than others. With this company, I was brought in to help them sustain their high-achieving strategies during a significant leadership transition after several failed attempts. To do this I had to discover first just what those strategies really were; both as a practitioner, at the level of their company to successfully help them through the transition, and as an academic, I wanted to understand their success at a deeper level to begin to define the underlying principles of how these highly successful groups actually function.

My academic interest had already been piqued by working with several high performing groups (like a community health center in Texas, a toy store in Moscow, and a textile manufacturer in North Carolina), such as this one, and realizing that the standard set of economic measurement tools did not fully measure and explain what the successful strategies were. More often than not, when a group like this, or someone studying them, thought they had figured it out and went to implement the ideas elsewhere, they did not work as expected. It seemed that we just kept missing something. So when he asked me that question, it was the nagging tickle that caused me to go back to basics and question all of my underlying assumptions. That started me on a different path to seeing the agreements in human interactions in a new way. From that question, I have created a broader framework of underlying principles with an expanded set of tools to measure what is actually happening at all levels in these high performance, high outcome groups so that we can really begin to learn from them.

## ECONOMICS AND ECOSYNOMICS: SCARCITY AND ABUNDANCE

You prefer abundance to scarcity, yet you tend to experience more scarcity than abundance. You know the difference and yet you accept agreements that produce scarcity. You do not have to, and this book will show you why not. It will also show you how to bring abundance into your life.

As any textbook will tell you, economics is the social science of the allocation of scarce resources.[1] It is the dominant social science of the modern era. Economics touches virtually every aspect of material life through its influence on decision making in government and business at every level. Ecosynomics (pronounced ee-co-sin-nom-iks) is brand new and relatively unknown. It builds on the foundation of economics, but goes in quite a different direction by exploring what happens when we start from an assumption of abundance rather than an assumption of scarcity. The mission of this book is to engage many more people in this exploration and, ultimately, to launch a revolution of positive outcomes based on the simple yet momentous shift in perspective that Ecosynomics proposes.

Derived from the Greek roots *eco* (relationship), *syn* (together) and *nomics* (rules), the term Ecosynomics literally means the rules of relationship together, or more broadly, the principles of collaboration.[2] Thus, it is the social science

---

1   Nobel laureate in economics Paul Samuelson in his popular economics textbook (Samuelson & Nordhaus, 1995, p. 4) defines economics as "the study of how societies use scarce resources to produce valuable commodities and distribute them among different people." The top-selling economics textbook of Harvard economics professor N. Gregory Mankiw defines economics as "the study of how society manages its scarce resources" (Mankiw, 2008, p. 4).

2   The word "Ecosynomics" acknowledges and builds on the word "economics," derived from the Greek for rules of relationship, oikos nomos, which originally translated as "household management." Back 2,500 years ago, the rules of relationship for a home and a govern-

of the agreements that guide human interaction. It is also the "science of abundance" because it posits that abundance—the state of having plenty of resources, both tangible and intangible—is always available.

Ecosynomics provides a framework for recognizing and creating agreements that enable us to experience abundance in the five most critical relationships in life: our relationships to ourselves, to other individuals, to groups, to nature, and to spirit. When we experience a flourishing relationship, we have a sense of vitality, of vibrancy. The experience of flourishing in all five relationships together I call *harmonic vibrancy*. This is what operating from abundance-based agreements feels like.

In this book, I will show that you know what harmonic vibrancy feels like and where it comes from. I will also share the stories of individuals and groups who have successfully developed agreements that have a brought greater abundance and harmonic vibrancy into their lives. These people are discovering innovative ways to work with their resources and organize their interactions to create value for themselves and many others along the way. In my travels and through my research, I have encountered organizations in education, health services, manufacturing and community development that are modeling abundance-based agreements and performing at a much higher level than their peers by all measures of effectiveness and efficient use of resources. They are redefining what is possible.

Moreover, they are part of a large-scale phenomenon, involving many thousands of groups around the world experimenting with the emerging principles of abundance. Over forty-five hundred communities using complementary currencies to create value and provide for people's needs within the local economy are part of this phenomenon. Also included are thousands of cooperatives of all types, organized in over three hundred federations of cooperatives in one hundred countries. These organizations are harnessing the strength of large groups to provide their members with greater autonomy and consumer power within the globalized economy. Thousands of groups are turning to asset-based community development, mobilizing untapped cultural and relational resources to improve the lives of their families and neighbors. Over sixty global action networks, with active national organizations in over

ment of the people were seen as the same. Historian of economic thought Roncaglia suggests that, "in Greek culture we find no contrast between the viewpoint of the family administrator and the viewpoint of the government of the polis. Xenophon and Plato explicitly stated this fact," according to economic historian Professor Roncaglia (Roncaglia, 2006, p. 25). In 390 BC Xenophon, a student of Socrates, writes, "The management of private concerns differs only in point of number from that of public affairs. In other respects they are much alike." (Goold et al., 1997, p. 189).

fifty countries, are leveraging tiny operating budgets to make progress against some of the most intractable global problems, such as corruption, small-arms trafficking, and water conservation. These too are part of the phenomenon that Ecosynomics helps us see and understand.

## WHY A SCIENCE OF ABUNDANCE AND WHY NOW?

When we look at the array of problems and challenges societies face today, we typically frame the issues from an assumption of scarcity, in terms of what is lacking: time, money, jobs, natural resources, regulations, leadership, consensus, open mindedness, goodwill, or something else. In contrast, we have no broadly applicable framework for understanding success stories like the ones mentioned above, in which people have created abundance, often in contexts seemingly dominated by scarcity. Ecosynomics offers such a framework.

### THE NEED FOR A SCIENCE OF ABUNDANCE

As a framework, Ecosynomics shows how a set of fundamental assumptions and the agreements that come from them can explain the extraordinary outcomes groups are creating, based on a new paradigm of abundance. While much is being learned about this new paradigm, I believe that much more is being missed. For example, we are missing the fact that a broad phenomenon is occurring, because we are unaware of the similarities among unconnected and seemingly disparate innovations. We are missing the significance of those innovations because we don't fully understand what makes them innovative. Also because of that lack of understanding, we are missing out on opportunities to build on what these innovators are learning. We need scientific inquiry into the emerging paradigm of abundance if we are going to grasp its meaning and make the most of what it has to offer.

This is the project of science: to build on what has been learned by developing new ideas and testing them rigorously. Science is a systematic process of inquiry. It is also a framework of knowledge expressed in the form of testable explanations and predictions. These are the two goals of science, according to the classic text by Robert .Dubin. *Understanding* (explanation) focuses on the interactions among variables in a system, how they relate to each other. *Prediction* focuses on the outcomes of an intervention in the system. The first describes the world being studied and the second looks at how it will behave. Each has its own theory-building processes; together they show

how the system works. In the search to learn from and build on what people are discovering about how to experience greater levels of harmonic vibrancy and abundance, we will need to understand human agreements and how these agreements influence the experience we desire. In other words, we need both understanding and prediction.[3]

## ECOSYNOMICS AS A SCIENCE

I present Ecosynomics as a science based on four key elements. First, Ecosynomics builds on past knowledge, in particular the large base of understanding created by economics. Humanity has enjoyed great advances in material wellbeing, due in great part to the economic science of human agreements based in scarcity. The Ecosynomics framework rests on that foundation of knowledge and incorporates a great deal of economic thinking. Second, Ecosynomics, like economics and other sciences, is evidence-based. A founding father of economics, Alfred Marshall, has stated "It is the business of economics, as of almost every other science, to collect facts, to arrange and interpret them, and to draw inferences from them."[4] Just so, Ecosynomics has emerged from looking at what is actually happening, developing frameworks to make sense of the evidence and testing that framework against further data.

Third, Ecosynomics provides a framework that integrates existing evidence with previous knowledge to create lenses that enable us to see more clearly what is emerging. Without these lenses, which are a basic feature of scientific development, much of what is being learned would be lost. Finally, Ecosynomics provides a conceptual framework and a common domain of language, which enables people to compare experiences, share what they are learning, improve the framework and apply their insights to practice in different environments. This aspect is critical given the explosive growth of abundance-based agreements that to-date remain mostly unconnected and underappreciated.

---

3   UC Irvine Professor of Sociology Robert Dubin wrote a classic text on the need for theory to help human beings make sense of their unordered experience of Nature (Dubin, 1978, pp. 6-7).
4   Alfred Marshall lays out a reason for and a program of research in human agreements through the emerging science of economics in his classic book on the principles of economics (Marshall, 1890, Bk 1, Ch 3, Sec 1).

## THE IMPORTANCE OF NAMING

If, as this book suggests, there are many thousands of groups experimenting with agreements based on abundance-based principles, it is time for a naming exercise. There is a need to name what is emerging so that it can be seen more clearly and we can learn from the successes and failures. The act of naming an emerging field of inquiry has had a significant impact on human understanding on various occasions, when new fields have coalesced around a concept or theory that named what many people had been working toward independently, unaware of each other's efforts.

Perhaps the best-known 20th-century case is the quantum revolution in physics. Around the turn of the century, scientists in various branches of classical Newtonian physics were trying to explain observed phenomena that could not be explained by the axioms of their fields. Then, in 1899, Max Planck introduced the concept of the "quantum," a discrete quantity of energy proportional in magnitude to the frequency of the radiation it represents. Planck hypothesized that any system (physical, chemical, electrical, etc.) that is composed of atoms and radiates energy can be divided into some number of discrete quanta. This insight opened a door through which hundreds of physicists stepped, including such luminaries as Albert Einstein, Niels Bohr and Erwin Schrodinger. The naming of the quantum made them realize that, with different questions and different tools, they had all been discovering aspects of the same thing, quantum mechanics—a new set of axioms and rules that did not fit with classical physics but described the world from a completely different perspective. Quantum mechanics quickly became, according to physicists, "one of the three great pillars supporting our understanding of the natural world."[5]

Another relevant example is the emergence of the field of systems theory. While many people cooperated in naming this field in the 1950s, credit usually goes to Ludwig von Bertalanffy for introducing the terminology of "general systems theory" in academic lectures and publications starting in the late 1930s.[6] A biologist, von Bertalanffy found that much of the behavior he observed was unexplainable within the prevailing scientific view that living organisms are closed systems, to which the laws of physics must apply. He proposed instead a concept of open systems. Such systems, von Bertalanffy realized, operate organically rather than mechanistically, and their behavior is determined by

---

5    The naming of the field of quantum physics is described in (Cox & Forshaw, 2011, p. 1).
6    Decades later, some of the "namers" of systems thinking that stand out most for me from the 1950's, in addition to von Bertalanffy, are cyberneticist Norbert Wiener, computer scientist Jay Forrester, and operations researcher Russell Ackoff (Bertalanffy, 1950; Churchman & Ackoff, 1950; Forrester, 1990; Wiener, 1954).

the relationships among the parts, not by the parts themselves. In working to understand the dynamics of system behavior, he recognized that others were dealing with the same issues in different contexts, for example, in cybernetics, and that the systems perspective could usefully be applied to many different fields in both the physical and social sciences. In proposing a general systems theory he did not offer a single unified theory of systems but rather, in the words of Ervin László, "a new paradigm for the development of theories."[7]

This vision became reality in the mid-1950s when the formation of the Society for General Systems Research brought together leading thinkers, not only in biology and cybernetics, but also in mathematics, economics, philosophy, psychiatry, anthropology, computer science, engineering, sociology and political science. In a very short period, experts who had been disconnected from each other by their professional language, practice, methods and standards were able to create a rich, textured shared understanding of system behaviors they had all been separately struggling to understand. Through this naming of the territory where their insights converged, these new systems thinkers were able to learn from each other's innovations and apply them to their own fields, accelerating the development of understanding and applications in many arenas.

Today, as in the examples of quantum and systems theories, it appears that thousands of observers across many fields of study are noticing a new phenomenon emerging across the globe. These include psychologists looking at happiness, sociologists looking at complementary monetary systems, economists addressing poverty, and foundations dealing with network philanthropy. They are all dealing with findings that cannot be explained solely by the economic laws of scarcity and self-interest. Ecosynomics provides a model of health to begin to name the field these observers and practitioners are discovering.

For example, within the deficit-focused field of psychology that addresses mental health disorders, psychologists looking at happiness have discovered a complementary pathway beyond treating illness to nurturing human flourishing through a focus on individual strengths and virtues.[8] The Ecosynomic model of health highlights how these positive psychology discoveries are shining a light into a more complete picture of full-human health of the individual, and how this new image points the way to potential advances in understanding one's relationship to the other, the group, nature, and spirit.

---

7   From the preface to Perspectives on General System Theory (von Bertalanffy, 1975, p. 12).

8   For an overview of the research on flourishing, see (Fredrickson, 2009; Seligman, 2011) or visit the University of Pennsylvania's authentichappiness.org or the University of Michigan's centerforpos.org.

Likewise, within the global network of national monetary systems, designed as scarce, Central-Bank-based currencies, sociologists and economists looking at community health have uncovered over 5,000 examples of local currencies designed as abundance-based currencies that promote sustainable, local relationships and local development, finding creative ways to match local unmet needs with local unused resources in ways that national currencies have not.[9] The Ecosynomic model shows that one of the key innovations in the complementary currencies is the sociological framing of agreements. What most of us assume to be a given, our national currency, is actually simply a set of agreements that people can choose.

Surfacing from within an economic development, anti-poverty approach that assumes scarcity-based competition, behavioral economists have discovered the impact of the scarcity mindset on the experience of poverty and that community development based on the assets the community has, its existing strengths, leads to strong, sustainable results without the need to create long-term financial-aid dependencies.[10] Ecosynomics frames this scarcity mindset and view of a community's assets as the starting point in the core assumptions that influence one's experience and outcomes, focusing on the resources one sees as available within any group.

## RELEVANCE TO YOU

You might be asking, "Why should I care about Ecosynomics?" This is a great question because it forces me to pull everything together concisely. So, let me be clear that Ecosynomics can benefit you in two important ways. First, as I have stated, the essence of Ecosynomics is the definition of the principles of collaboration. Greater understanding of how to collaborate is valuable to anyone who is part of a group—that is, to everyone. Whether the group is a family, a neighborhood or community, a spiritual or volunteer group, a school, a team or any group you may work with, collaboration will make the group and you more effective at achieving the outcomes you aim for.

If you think of being effective in terms of being more effective than others—being competitive—collaboration will enable you to do that as well. The collaborators I describe in this book play the competitive game much better than do those who focus only on competition. By competition I mean where

---

9    For an overview of complementary currencies, see (B. Lietaer & Dunne, 2013).
10    For research on the scarcity mindset, see (Mullainathan & Shafir, 2013). For an overview of community development, see (Easterly, 2006; McKnight & Block, 2010).

rivals interact to win something at each other's expense.[11] These collaborators are more competitive, more able to win in an interaction, because they work continuously with creative possibility and are always looking deeply at the potential of everyone in their group. They can choose to develop the capacities they need when they need them and so have much greater capacities to play the competitive game. If you think in terms of competition, Ecosynomics will help you by showing you that there is a much broader game out there than just competing head-to-head with an opponent. Ecosynomics shows groups how to focus the competitive mindset internally, striving to continuously strengthen their own capacities, and striving to see how much of their own creative potential they can embody.[12]

The second great benefit of Ecosynomics is freedom, in particular the freedom to develop your full potential for harmonic vibrancy in the five primary relationships. The source of this freedom is the recognition that your experiences are shaped by agreements, whether or not you are aware of them. This means that you do not have to accept scarcity as "just the way things are."[13]

## MY VISION

In this formative stage of the field of Ecosynomics, there is one thing of which I am very clear: Ecosynomics is not replacing economics; it is building on that foundation. This path of development is one of "transcending and including," that is incorporating the best of what has been seen before while moving beyond it. Many great economic thinkers have wrestled with the difficult questions about human existence and through their deep work arrived at extraordinary insights. Because of this, humanity can see further and build a stronger future.

---

11    This definition of competition comes from (Greenwald, 1983, p. 90).

12    In particular, compare Ecosynomics with the "competition" school. Michael Porter, one of the fathers of modern strategy, coined the term "competitive advantage." Porter describes competition in similar terms, invoking the outcomes, the process, and the possibility (Magretta, 2011).

13    In reflecting on different economic perspectives on freedom, Nobel Laureate in Economics Daniel Kahneman, awarded for the impact of his psychological work on rational economics, compares the rational-man of the Chicago school and the behavioral economics school. He suggests both prize freedom, but it is more costly for the behavioralist, "borne by individuals who makes bad choices, and by a society that feels obligated to help them (Kahneman, 2011)." This is not a problem for the Chicago school, because rational people do not make mistakes.

The advances humanity has made in the era of economics have been tremendous. Yet, it is not okay that much of humanity still experiences deep scarcity, because of the agreements in which they live. They can shift those agreements. I believe that naming the emerging field of Ecosynomics, making it visible and understandable, will support the movement to higher harmonic vibrancy that is happening globally, increase its momentum and spread its benefits to a much greater portion of humankind. Said more boldly, I believe everyone deserves the opportunity to experience a higher level of harmonic vibrancy and abundance in their lives. Ecosynomics can create this opportunity by providing the means by which more people connect to and benefit from what is being learned about collaboration.

## THE PATHWAY WE EXPLORE

I would like you to approach this book as a pathway into the science of abundance. As Figure 1 depicts, I envision this pathway as a spiral. From your initial discovery of the basic principles of Ecosynomics, I hope this book will carry you along to a level of understanding from which you can move on to working with this framework and increasing the vibrancy and abundance you experience in all your relationships.

Part 1 shows you how the building blocks of the main framework for seeing human agreements are already part of your experience. We start in Chapter 1 by reviewing your experiences of groups and situations, great and awful. We will also uncover the main components of all experiences, the five primary relationships—to one's self, to other individuals, to groups, to nature and to spirit. You will see that you know the difference between scarcity and abundance, low and high vibrancy, in these relationships. You will also recognize that you prefer the high-vibrancy experiences yet seldom have them because, most likely without thinking about it, you accept agreements that produce scarcity.

In Chapter 2, we explore further this idea of agreements. You will see how, based on our perceptions of reality, we all make certain assumptions and our assumptions, in turn, determine what agreements we are likely to be living with. One way of perceiving reality focuses on possibility; another focuses on development, the processes of bringing new things into being; the third focuses on the things themselves – what currently exists. Each of these three perspectives tends to come with a distinctive sensation, which we can relate to as a familiar experience of a fundamental quality of the physical world:

light (possibility); motion (development); and matter (things). In Chapter 2, I share stories of how people describe their experiences with these three levels of reality: the abundance and high vibrancy that are available when all three are present; the medium abundance and vibrancy when the focus is on development-motion; and the scarcity and low vibrancy associated with perceiving only the things-matter level.

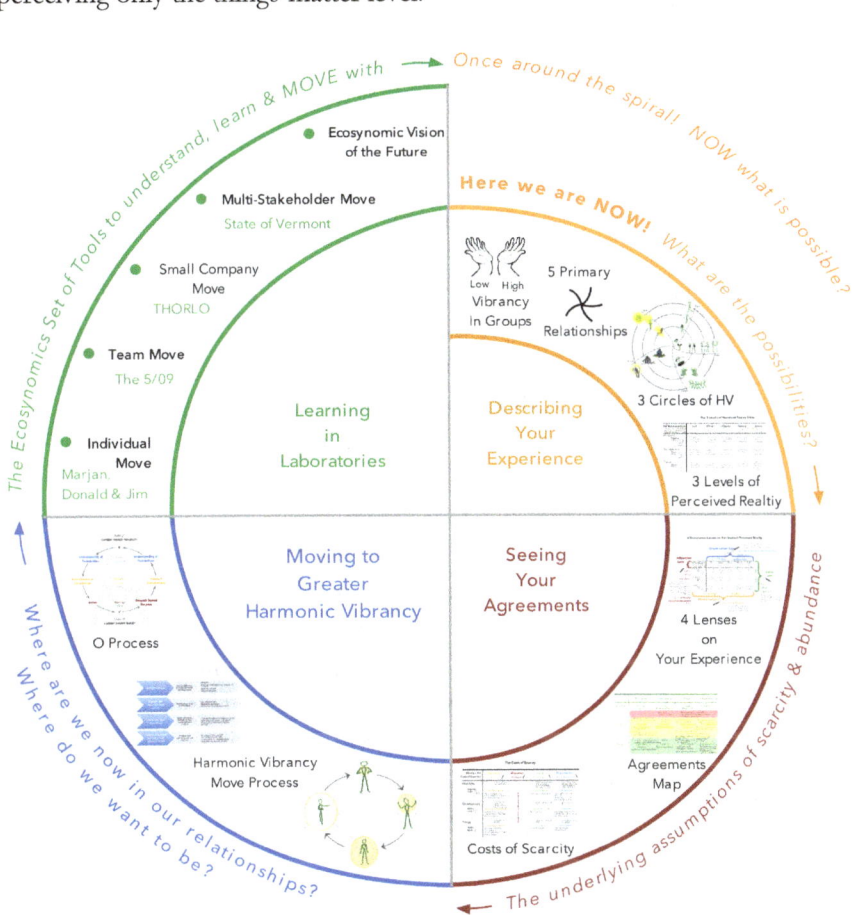

*Figure 1: The Pathway We Explore*

Since they are only perceptions of reality, not reality itself, all three of these aspects of reality are always present, whether or not we perceive them. In the same way, all five relationships contribute to our overall sense of well being whether we are paying attention to all of them or not. I will show you how we can combine the three levels of perceived reality with the five fundamental relationships, to create a map of the territory through which we must navigate our way to abundance and harmonic vibrancy. Then, we will consider different routes we may take through this terrain, each leading to different agreements and qualities of experience.

Chapter 3 examines the role of agreements in depth. It provides a bridge from looking at abundance in terms of our personal experience to a larger domain by showing that the basic principles developed so far apply to agreements at all levels. I will show you how this works with examples of interactions I have had with individuals, small groups like my family, a corporate leadership team and a school board, as well as large groups like government agencies, multi-national corporations and non-profits, and global networks.

By the end of Part 1, you will have a working understanding of the core insight of Ecosynomics: we know abundance is possible because we have experienced it directly, and we know we prefer abundance to scarcity; yet we tend to experience more scarcity than abundance because, without thinking about it, we accept scarcity-producing agreements. The remainder of the book builds on this foundation to show you how to see the scarcity or abundance in existing agreements and how to move toward agreements of abundance and harmonic vibrancy.

Part 2 refines the experience-based framework from Part 1 with lenses that sharpen your understanding of agreements. Chapter 4 looks historically at the assumption of scarcity in economics and how four major streams of economic thought—the theories of resources and resource allocation, value theory, and organization theory—influence the agreements we see and those we enter every day. We also see how different interpretations of these four areas of thought have led to five very different economic systems around the globe in the past two hundred years. The chapter concludes by considering the paradoxical nature of economics. The paradox is this: all economic systems aim to deliver abundance yet cannot succeed because they start from an assumption of scarcity and premise all of their agreements on that assumption.

In Chapter 5, I suggest that the four main areas of economic thought might more usefully be conceived as four different lenses on experiences and agreements. To make this possible, I present a framework that integrates the four lenses with the five basic relationships (self, other, group, nature, and spirit) and three levels of perceived reality (possibility-light, development-motion, and things-matter). This seems like a lot of complexity, I know. However, in Chapter 6, it all comes together in a relatively simple tool, the Agreements Map. This tool makes it possible to see the agreements underlying our experience and the costs of scarcity in those agreements. The Agreements

Map will also show you that you have choices to shift agreements to create higher-vibrancy experiences.

Part 3 continues to explore what these choices and possible shifts can look like. I start, in Chapter 7, by examining what thousands of groups around the world have already done to create abundance for themselves. I present survey data I have collected from over 1,600 responses in 90 countries. I also use the Agreements Map to compare innovations in abundance-based agreements to established patterns of agreements based in assumptions of scarcity. Chapter 8 then lays out a four-step process for identifying choices and making a shift toward abundance based agreements—what I call a Harmonic Vibrancy Move. Part 3 will help you see what outcomes are possible and how to get them.

Part 4 shares the stories of experiences I have had over the past ten years, helping groups and individuals bring about positive change using the principles and tools that have evolved into Ecosynomics. Chapter 9 presents three examples of individual-level change. Chapters 10 and 11 describe Harmonic Vibrancy Moves undertaken within a small company, first within the leadership team and then within the company as a whole. In Chapter 12, I share the story of a statewide change initiative in Vermont, USA. I call these stories "learning laboratories" because they have shaped my understanding of Ecosynomics. They also show you how change is possible in groups of all different sizes.

Chapter 13 looks ahead to the continuing development and application of Ecosynomics. I share what I see is possible as the world begins to take on abundance-based agreements on a larger scale. Finally, in the concluding chapter, I also suggest ways you can participate in achieving this vision of greater harmony, vibrancy and abundance, not just for yourself but also for everyone. This will complete our journey around the spiral and point us toward where the science of abundance may take us.

Now I invite you to step onto this pathway and move toward an experience of the possibility of abundance you desire. This experience is available, now; it is just an agreement that needs to shift. Once you know this and what to do, you can make it happen. I invite you to do just that. Along the way, I also invite you to share what you learn with others and with me at jimritchiedunham. com or at jlrd.me. Learning together we can achieve a step to a higher level of harmonic vibrancy for everyone. This is not an invitation to experience "what Jim knows," rather an invitation to join millions in the future we all prefer.

PART I

# DESCRIBING YOUR EXPERIENCE

# CHAPTER 1

# SEEING SCARCITY AND ABUNDANCE IN OUR RELATIONSHIPS

I really enjoy asking people, all over the place, about their experiences with scarcity and abundance. My various roles as a business school teacher, an organizational consultant and coach, a leader in my own organization, an academic researcher, and often just as a friend, give me many opportunities to start this conversation that I am passionate about. In classrooms, in boardrooms, in people's offices and homes, in factories and on the street, over the past three years, I have been in hundreds of conversations, from as short as fifteen minutes to hours-long, about the observations and ideas we will explore in this book.

A typical conversation, like the ones I had last week in Boston, last month in North Carolina, two months ago in Mexico City, or three months ago in Germany starts off with a simple question, "Are you experiencing the best you believe you can in your life?" So far, everyone has said that sometimes they experience the best they can, but not all the time. When I ask why, they look at me quizzically and say, "Well, that's just the way it is. I don't know." When I tell them I think they do know, they give me the look of, "Oh yeah? Show me." This is where it gets fun for me, because I know I can show them something they know to be true but often do not realize.

## EXPERIENCES OF GROUPS, AWFUL AND GREAT

"Ok," I say, "Have you ever experienced a group where you feel awful?" This usually gets me another funny look, of "what do you mean?" I suggest that they might feel bad while in the group or realize it afterward. After being with these people, they feel fatigued, tired, frustrated, and they want to change something. They want to medicate themselves. Whether it is going for a walk, watching television, or drinking a coffee or a beer they need to do something else, to get away from the feeling of fatigue from the group. At this point in the conversation, people are nodding their heads, acknowledging that they have had that experience. Some even make comments about the meetings they were just in earlier in the day: "You should see our meetings. They would kill you!"

I then ask whether they have had the opposite experience that makes them feel great, where they are stronger and more energized because they are with that group. After being with these people, they want to spend even more time with them. They nod their heads excitedly, remembering such an experience in the recent past.

In a few of my conversations, usually with people working in large organizations, I have asked people what percentage of the day they typically spend in the fatiguing experience. For many, the answers are up in the range of 70-80 percent of the time. Ouch.

At this point I suggest to the group that we have established, from their own experience, that they know when they feel awful in a group and when they feel great. They confirm this. I have also shown that they have both experiences on a rather frequent basis. So, then I ask the seemingly obvious: "Do you have a preference for one over the other?" Here I get chuckles and nodding of heads, "Of course." To be a little naughty and provocative, as well as to make my point more strongly, I suggest that the obvious preference is for the fatiguing experience. "Right?" This always gets me a laugh and a firm response, "No. We prefer the energizing experience. It has a better vibe." While this seems like hammering home the obvious, I like to anchor the conversation with a clear statement of people's preference for energizing groups.

Next I invite the group to delve into the differences between the fatiguing and energizing experiences. When I ask for details, people describe the fatiguing experience as "exhausting", "draining my energy" or "painful." Often I hear something like, "I have to work really hard to get anything done." Many people tell me that this experience feels frustrating, with a sense that they are just doing what they are told to do, with little or no creativity, even though they are trying. They even share that they are often not sure what they contribute to the group or, in fact, what anybody contributes to the group.

In contrast, when I ask about the energizing group—no big surprise here!—my conversation partners have much more positive things to say. This experience is "enlivening." They have more energy afterwards than when they started. Anything seems possible in this group. Everyone has lots of creative ideas, building off of each other, usually ending up in places they feel they would never have seen on their own, "It's really cool!" Here is where the idea of abundance starts to surface. Many people say that in this energizing group they "experience abundance all over the place." This leads me to ask, "If this is an experience of abundance, what is the other experience?" Most people respond, "Scarcity. Nothing. It is very hard. There is a much lower vibrancy to the group."

This is fascinating. The awful place is an experience of scarcity and low vibrancy, and the great place is an experience of abundance and high vibrancy. And, now, we are getting to a critical insight. "If you could live more in the abundant world, would you?" I ask. Well, duh… "Yes." I counter with, "Then why don't you?" This starts us on a new path. When people respond that it is hard to live in greater abundance in most groups, I suggest that maybe it is and maybe it is not. To see how it might become easier, however, we need to explore the differences in the two experiences in more detail.

## THE FIVE RELATIONSHIPS: SELF

As I have described, I like to draw people into the conversation about abundance and scarcity through their experiences in groups—often work groups, but not necessarily. Humans are social animals, so unless one is living as a hermit, he or she is likely to be part of a variety of groups. We all know, however, that we have more relationships than just ones to groups. Having pursued this issue extensively in the field of psychology and in various spiritual traditions, I have found a broad consensus around the idea that there are five fundamental human relationships: to oneself, to other individuals, to groups, to nature, and to spirit (which may signify different things in different traditions). For a deep dive into experiences of scarcity and abundance, I invite my conversation partners to look systematically at each of these relationships.

How do people experience themselves differently in groups where the dominant feeling is one of either scarcity or abundance? Time and again I have heard that, in the scarcity experience, it feels like the self simply does not show up. For example, a friend described, "In the awful experience, I am just there, getting the energy sucked out of me." On the other hand, he said, "In the great experience, not only am I more creative, I also experience parts of me showing up that are new and exciting. I am better for having been in that experience."

Across all my conversations, "vibrancy" is the word that keeps coming up when people talk about these experiences. So it became obvious that this is the best term to capture the different levels of energy experienced in the five relationships. I also figured out that "a picture is worth a thousand words" when it comes to communicating what people are sharing about different levels of vibrancy.

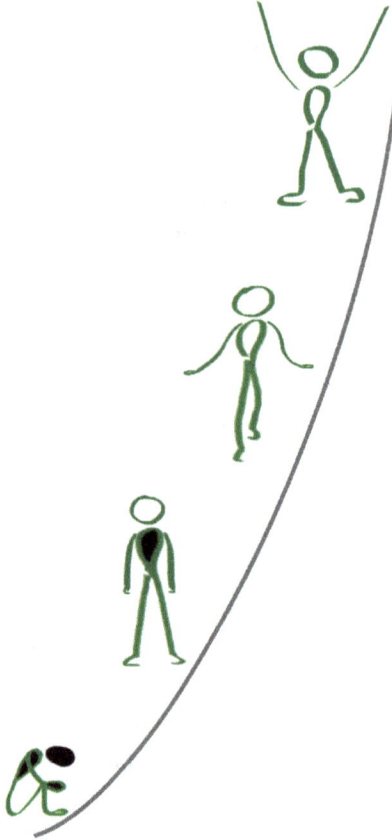

*Figure 2: Experience of One's Own Self*

Figure 2 captures the high, low, and midpoints of the experience of one's relationship to oneself. In the lower left we see a representation of when you experience your "I" as slumped over, with your head in an invisible darkness through which no light can enter. Everything is dark—from here nothing or very little can be seen. Here you experience great vulnerability, moving into the fetal position, literally or figuratively, to protect all of the core systems, such as your will, your heart, and your head.[14] This is the collapsed state in your relationship to self.

---

14   When you look at your own self, do you see great potential or a lost cause? The lost

There is another experience you often have of the "I." You experience your "I" as standing tall, acknowledging what you have to bring to the world, with the gifts, talents, and abilities you have developed over your life. This is the second individual in Figure 2.

You also experience the "I" moving through everyday life, learning, developing new capacities, and developing new relationships as you engage with the dance of life. This is the third individual in Figure 2.

The outstetched individual in the upper-right of Figure 2 represents yet another experience you have, in some places and groups, where the "I" not only stands tall, but also opens to the world, fully participating and sharing everything that you have to give and everything that might come. You experience this position of complete openness and invitation as one of great strength and happiness, with your full will, heart, head, and soul engaged. While this looks like the most vulnerable position, as everything is exposed, it is the one in which you experience the most strength. [15]

Just as you have experiences of scarcity and abundance in different group situations, chances are you have all four experiences along the continuum of your relationship to yourself. At each higher level, from the collapsed experience of low vibrancy to the fully open experience of high vibrancy, more of you becomes available. Since you experience all four levels of vibrancy in your relationship to yourself, depending on the situation you are in, they are all part of who you are. They are all available to you. This is an important point.

The suggestion I want to make here (to be developed more fully in Chapter 3) is the following: how much of your vibrant self is available in any given

---

cause in us believes that we have already learned everything necessary to do our job. It is now just a matter of doing it; getting on with life. There is nothing interesting out there, just a lot of cold, hard responsibilities. The American humorist of suburban home life, Erma Bombeck, expressed this as, "If life is a bowl of cherries, then what am I doing in the pits?" Actress Katharine Hepburn lived into this, suggesting, "Life is hard. After all, it kills you." More seriously, Bill Strickland, pulling on his 40 years of inspirational work in the poor areas of Detroit, calls this the "deadliest lie the ghetto uses to shrink your soul—that your world is the whole world; that your future and all the sorry possibilities life will ever offer you, are already right before your eyes" (Strickland & Rause, 2007, p. 28).

15    The Spanish philosopher Ortega y Gasset describes the possibility-light of the self, "Among his various possible beings each man always finds one which is his genuine and authentic being. The voice which calls him to that authentic being is what we call 'vocation.' But the majority of men devote themselves to silencing that voice of the vocation and refusing to hear it. They manage to make a noise within themselves, to deafen themselves, to distract their own attention in order not to hear it; and they defraud themselves by substituting for their genuine selves a false course of life. On the other hand, the only man who lives his own self, who truly lives, is the man who lives his vocation, whose life is in agreement with his own true self" (Ortega y Gasset, 1962, p. 180).

space or group is determined by an agreement. You agree to this, whether or not you are aware of the agreement. This also means that you can make a different agreement and step into a different relationship to yourself in that group or situation.

Think, for example, of a day when you woke up feeling negative about yourself and a bit shut down. Perhaps you felt like going back to bed, but you got yourself up and out to school or work, and maybe you congratulated yourself on "just showing up." Maybe later in the day you decided to take a risk and offer an idea or a suggestion and possibly you were rewarded with the great feeling of having your offering accepted and appreciated. Looking back on an experience like this, you can see that your choices have an impact on your relationship to yourself. This is what I think of as making different agreements. Being able to see the scarcity or abundance in our relationships is the first step toward changing agreements to bring greater vibrancy into our lives.

## THE FIVE RELATIONSHIPS: OTHER

Your relationship to the other is how you experience another human being. The other is the "you" that your "I" experiences—someone who is also having an "I" experience. The quality of the relationship rests largely in your ability to see the "I" that uniquely expresses the identity of the other person, as well as in his or her ability to see the "I" that is a unique expression of you.

In my inquiries about how people experience scarcity and abundance in the groups they are part of, I often hear that in low energy groups that they do not experience anything of the other group members as individuals. The other individuals in the group are just there, perhaps neutral or possibly a source of annoyance or disturbance. In contrast, in the descriptions of groups where energy is abundant, I hear that the experience is one of seeing and appreciating all of the different people who are part of it, and even sensing that together you can see further and accomplish more than you could alone. As one woman in a recent conversation shared, "Everyone is really creative, just as I am, and we support each other in that."

From what people have shared with me, it seems that we have two possible, distinct experiences. When you see another person, do you see a brilliant soul or someone intent on disturbing you? The disturber is everywhere. He cuts you off in traffic, gives you extra work to do, makes you pay taxes, disappoints you, spoils your appetite, and hurts your feelings. She makes your life more difficult. That is one experience. In this experience, you turn your back on the other, protecting yourself from his influence. It is impossible for you to see her, and you experience that she does not see you. This is the relationship of the two, dark, slumped over, back-to-back individuals in Figure 3. This is the collapsed state of the relationship to the other.

Depending on the situation, you also have the experience of being able to stand tall and face each other, seeing him as separate from you, with his own unique talents, gifts and abilities. You too feel seen by the other for what you can do and contribute. This is the relationship of the two individuals facing each other in Figure 3.

*Figure 3: Experience of the Other*

You also experience being seen and met by the other. He is with you on the path of learning, engaging with you in the development of new capacities and new relationships. This is the third relationship in Figure 3, where the two individuals are open to each other and shaking hands.

Occasionally, you also have the experience of being seen completely by the other, both who you are and who you can be. That other person sees right into your soul, witnessing the light that streams through you, your full potential for possibility and creativity. When this happens, you feel liberated at what another was able to see in you. At the same time, you see gifts in the other that he may not even see in himself. You see his potential, and it fills you with warmth to experience this flow of light-spirit potential in another. In this relationship, the other brings lightness to your life. She makes you smile or even makes your heart overflow with joyful tears. He proves to you, continuously, how beautiful life can be. Whether it is the artist down the street, the author of your favorite book, the genius you respect, your mother, or your kid shining on stage you experience the brightness of their light shining through their offering. This is the high vibrancy experience represented by the two individuals on the right side of Figure 3.[16]

16    The scientist and playwright Johann Wolfgang von Goethe expressed this as, "If we take

To appreciate that the level of vibrancy available in your relationship to another is an agreement, consider those times when you have been able to resolve an interpersonal conflict or convert an enemy into a dear friend. What did it take to make that happen? Most likely one or the other individual took the first step, perhaps a friendly overture or an apology, but ultimately both of you had to agree to put your relationship on a more positive path. Then the door could open to mutual respect and appreciation. Similarly, with someone you feel neutral about or barely know, both people must be agreeable to greater openness and connection for a vibrant relationship to emerge.[17] At the risk of repeating myself, I like to point out the role of agreements, because if the current state of relationships is based on an agreement, it means we can also choose a different agreement—an agreement to go for greater vibrancy. This holds true for our relationships to groups as well.

## THE FIVE RELATIONSHIPS: GROUP

Your relationship to the group is how you experience the "we." It is completely different from the "I" that you can only experience for yourself or the "you" that you experience with another "I." We-ness is experienced collectively as well as individually. For example, it is the identification we have of "our" family, which in my case is the Ritchie-Dunhams. The experience of "family" is different from that of me as an individual member of the family. I am both Jim (the "I") and Ritchie-Dunham (the "we").

By the time I get to the point of talking about this relationship in my conversations, I usually find that people are pretty comfortable drawing distinctions between scarcity and abundance and high and low vibrancy, and there is always a lot of enthusiasm for sharing stories about group experiences. These are stories about immediate and extended families, communities, workplaces and places where people hang out with friends. Recently, a young man from Germany captured the essence of what many have shared about the relationship to groups as represented in Figure 4.

people as they are, we make them worse. If we treat them as if they were what they ought to be, we help them become what they are capable of becoming." Attributed to Johann Wolfgang von Goethe in (Frankl, 1986, p. 8), who lived from 1749 to 1832. Recent research supports this, finding that people who see others as fixed—not changing over time—tend to demoralize not only others, but also themselves. This research finds this fixed mindset in half of the people; with the other half open to a growth mindset where people adjust to life experiences. See the work of Stanford professor Carol Dweck and UNSW's Peter Heslin (Dweck, 2006; Heslin, 2010).

17    Jennie Jerome Churchill, Winston Churchill's mother, said, "Treat your friends as you do your pictures, and place them in the best light."

When the vibrancy in the group is low, we all act like we just want to be told what to do. It seems clear that none of me is needed, other than what I can do right then. It feels very frustrating. We are all in our little boxes, somebody has a whip, and I am submissive to the task at hand. But when I experience high vibrancy in a group, we are all looking for the unique contributions our creativity can make to the group. It's like the harmony we create when we each sing our piece. It feels like together we are able to take on anything.

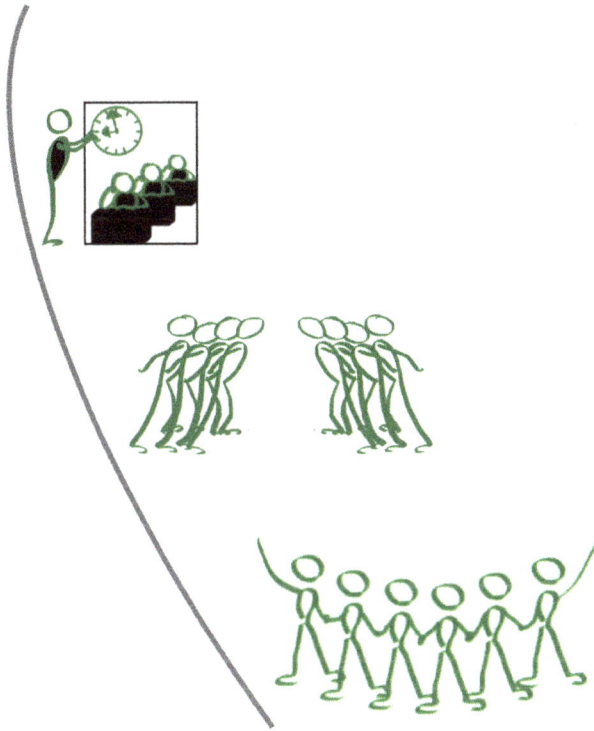

*Figure 4: Experience of the Group*

You often experience your relationship to the "we" as one of "just tell me what to do." This is an experience many of us have at work or in a community where we have no voice. It can also be the experience we have when everyone talks but no one ever listens. These exhausting groups bore us, increase our fatigue, and always ask too much of us ("yet another endless meeting?"). In this relationship, you are clear that you make no unique contribution, as a matter of fact, many people could replace you in your job or another family could live in your house and it would make no difference. You are all just cogs in a machine and no one feels he can do much about it; the experience of alienation and disempowerment often felt in low vibrancy groups.

Chances are you have experienced another quality of relationship to the group, when you feel that you can stand tall, shoulder to shoulder with others who are all, like you, valuable members of the group. You experience your contribution as clear in this group, and the group is clear that it is stronger because you are bringing your abilities. At this level of group vibrancy, there is a positive sense of collective identity; perhaps neighborhood pride or, at work, a passive tolerance and a feeling of competing with other units or businesses. The group bets on who can make a valuable contribution to the group, bringing them in and keeping everyone else out. This is the cooperative competition of us versus them, as seen in the middle group in Figure 4.[18]

You may also have had the more rare experience of a group where the relationship was one of deep collaboration. This is the experience of "united we can," when people come together in an active embrace and find they can achieve outcomes that they previously thought were impossible. The group knows that not everyone will make a value contribution to the group, but anyone can.[19]

For musicians this is experienced as "being in the groove," when the ensemble melds fully, and a much greater possibility emerges for the group. These are moments of greatness, often experienced on sports teams, in transformational family moments, or when a country comes together to face an extraordinary hardship. In these group relationships, no matter how many hours you put in and how much effort it took, you feel invigorated afterwards. You made a contribution, which the group appreciated and engaged with, and it felt great. You are a better person because you were with them today. This is the experience of the united group at the bottom-right of Figure 4.

---

18    For an enlightening description of cooperative competition, see Co-opetition (Brandenburger & Nalebuff, 1998).

19    The relationship that we have to the group explores one's social expression of group intention; that which we give to the 'group will' and cannot achieve on our own. This is a group form of light flow, which requires a group to manifest. The inner experience of this relationship to the group manifests as one's own 'group higher purpose,' the superordinate essence to which we relate the contributions we want to make—one's relationship with self-in-group—or how I relate to the group. The self's group expression is physically observable in one's gut. It is one's will; that which one serves.  Culturally, the group supports and embraces the individual in exploring the gifts they contribute to the needs of the group. Our experience of the group nature of harmonic vibrancy is one of interdependence, which in the old French is solidaire. This culture of interdependence is supported by social structures and processes focused on the integration of interests, purpose or sympathies among members of a group—a fellowship of responsibilities and interests, such as collaborations, co-operatives, and the primary focus politically of collectivists.

Like the people in my conversations, I expect you have experienced your relationship to the group along this continuum, from the subsuming experience of low vibrancy to the uniting experience of high vibrancy. As you experience greater harmonic vibrancy along this continuum, what is present at the lower levels of vibrancy is also available at higher levels, along with new dimensions.

In the experience of low vibrancy, you are just a doer. In the experience of medium vibrancy you are now a contributor; both able to do as before, and to bring greater talents and abilities to the group. In the high-vibrancy experience you are a doer, a contributor, *and* full of a potential you may not even be aware of, all at the same time. This phenomenon takes place in all of the relationships we have looked at so far: at each higher level of vibrancy, you have access to more of your gifts, so you can make a larger contribution to the group, just as you can access more of your creativity in relationship with another individual and see more and more of the potential inside yourself.

It is usually when I get to this point in my conversations that the insight about agreements appears most powerfully. I say something like, "It seems that there is a huge difference in the experience of the low and high vibrancy groups." This statement gets lots of agreement—people are clear that they feel scarcity everywhere in the low-vibrancy experience and abundance everywhere in the high-vibrancy experience. Then I push a little. "Why is there scarcity in one group and abundance in another?" Often the first response is something like, "There just is. Right?" "Why?" I ask again. After awhile I can always count on at least one person coming forward with a statement like this one from the executive director of a non-profit research group:

"Because that's what we agree to. Or, at least, that's what I accept. What I mean is that this has something to do with me. You see, I have two very different experiences with two of the committees I lead. One is a 'low vibrancy group' and the other is a 'high vibrancy group.' One is exhausting—it is very hard to get anyone to do anything and we are stuck. The other is exhilarating— every one participates and we have made huge advances. I have assumed that this was just the reality of these two committees. Now I realize that if I am the one leading both committees, and many of the same people sit on the two committees, then there must be something in what I am doing that makes the difference. I agree to the lower-vibrancy experience and that is unnecessary."

Yes! Once we clearly see that we are experiencing different levels of vibrancy in different situations, we can begin to raise our awareness of the underlying agreements. Only then can we set about changing them to move toward higher vibrancy. Often the impetus for change comes from an external event, for example, a crisis or at work the arrival of a new leader who wants to "shake things up." These external forces can shine a light on the internal group dynamics and create an opportunity for a shift in agreements. Maybe you have also experienced a shift that was internally generated. Perhaps one or two people decided to push for change, or possibly the entire group just realized that things could be better and took steps together to achieve that. The fourth relationship, to "nature," provides an important clue as to how these shifts toward higher vibrancy and abundance can come about.

## THE FIVE RELATIONSHIPS: NATURE

We have now seen how we experience scarcity and abundance in human relationships—to the self, the other, and the group. However, from psychology and the spiritual traditions, as well as our own experience, we know that we humans have important relationships to other dimensions. I call these nature and spirit. When my inquiry takes my conversation partners and me into these dimensions, we find that there is scarcity and abundance in these relationships as well.

One way to experience our relationship to nature is simply in terms of how we relate to the natural world. Another involves seeing how we experience the nature of reality—that is, it involves giving some thought to what is real for us. These two are closely interrelated, as we shall see.

I like to enter the conversation about the relationship to nature by asking people to think of their favorite place in the whole world, the place that makes them feel the best. When I ask this question, most people tell me about a place in nature—the beach, a river, the mountains. Then I ask, "What is the essence of this place that makes you love it so much?" Interestingly, what I usually hear about then are things. For example, the beach lovers mention sun, sand, salt water, and heat. Well then, I suggest, I will give them a bright lamp, some sand, salty water, and heat, right where they are. Will that make them really happy? This usually gets me a laugh, "No, of course not." But, if it's not those things, then what is it that evokes their deep feelings of pleasure? They then begin to describe the movement of the water, the waves, the tides, the energy of the sun, and the wind moving clouds across the sky. If the setting is a river, I hear about the force of its flow, the teeming life beneath its surface, its earthy smell, and its ever-changing nature. These are descriptions of the forces that enliven the things we encounter in nature. People love the lively sense of emergence that is everywhere in the natural world.

In one of my conversation groups I was fortunate enough to have a forester, someone who has devoted his whole adult life to preserving natural habitats for people to enjoy. He captured the idea beautifully when he said it is "the experience of manifestation" that accounts for the strong positive feelings we humans have for the natural environment. The manifestation we experience most directly in nature is the transformation of infinite light-energy potential into continuously unfolding processes, and the things these processes produce. We love the strength and growth in the tree through the seasons, as much as we appreciate its fruit on a given day. At the same time, we sense the flow of energy from sunlight into the tree, then into leaves, flowers, and fruit that exist for a while then fall to the ground to fertilize the soil and nurture the tree in its continuing growth. It is this manifesting cycle of life that mesmerizes us in our relationship to the natural world.[20]

When we tease apart these three different ways we experience nature; as things that we can touch and see, as vital processes of growth and change, and as the energy that flows through all and makes everything possible, we have the basic elements for seeing how our relationship to nature is related to our perceptions of reality.[21] Sometimes we are immersed in the reality that is touchable. "If I can't touch it, it is not real," is how people express this to me. In this state, the reality of the tree is the bark, the branches, the leaves, and the apple. Reality-as-things in our daily lives shows up as food, money, a house, a car, and sometimes other people (depending on the quality of our relationship to them).

We also have the experience of reality as something more intangible, like the processes of growth in the tree. People in my groups often mention growing older and wiser, learning, practicing new skills, and getting stronger. They resonate with a positive sense of reality as a journey of growth and development, which is just as real as whatever the concrete outcomes of that

---

20    Much research has shown the importance of the human relationship to nature, in its forms of possibility, process and momentary outcomes. University of Michigan psychology professor Stephen Kaplan finds, "the natural environment is experienced as particularly high in compatibility. It is as if there were a special resonance between the natural setting and human inclinations" (Kaplan, 1995, p. 174). This is supported by recent experimental research, such as (Berman, Jonides, & Kaplan, 2008; Hartig, Evans, Jamner, Davis, & Garling, 2003).

21    Though the word "Nature" today often invokes trees, birds, sun, and streams, people use the word in common, everyday language much more broadly to describe the "nature" of their experience. Three of the definitions for "nature" from the Oxford English Dictionary describe light, verb, and noun levels of the common use of the word. Nature is the innate, inherent or essential quality of a thing or a person—its possibility-light level of potential. Nature is also the vital power that sustains mental and physical activities—the development-verb level. And nature is the sensory experience we have, as in "mother nature" and in "human nature—the things-noun level. When we look to the philosophers for a definition of nature, we find definitions similar to that of the British mathematician and philosopher Alfred North Whitehead, who said nature is that which we perceive to be real (Whitehead, 2007, p. 3).

journey might be. My son's soccer coach expressed this to the team at the beginning of the season, "Yes, I want you to enjoy the game, and it will be fun to win. And, most of all, I want you to improve as a soccer player this year. We will work to develop your skills and understanding of the game, so that you mature as a player." The kids have found this very exciting, rejoicing in both the wins and the improved skills, endurance and understanding of the game.

Building on this theme, I invite folks to recall a time when they experienced reality as that sun-like energy of limitless possibility. It is one of my great pleasures to hear the stories they offer about what it feels like to be in that experience—stories of inspiration and motivation to realize an audacious vision for a community, a family or a team. When I ask, most people tell me that they love the experience of seeing a possibility that they know they can choose to make real. The director of a continuing-education company for dentists told me, "You should see what happens when our dentist-students see, usually for the first time, that they can be health-providers for the patients, and not just highly skilled technicians. In addition to fixing problems with the teeth they can bring greater health to their patients. For example, seeing that they can address sleep apnea, a major issue for many patients, shows them a possibility they had not seen—one that enlivens their sense of purpose."

What is most interesting to me about that experience of possibility is that you know that something has become "real" long before it becomes tangible. Then you witness the development phase, as resources come together, perhaps over a long period of time, until at last the concrete outcome or product—the thing—appears. This is where I like to share my own story of experiencing nature as the manifesting of possibility. My wife, Leslie, is an architect. In the design phase of her projects, she sifts through all the possibilities of what a home might be like to come up with a vision that fits the wants and needs of the future homeowners—her clients. It is so exciting to see that moment when the image of that home materializes in the minds of the homeowner, Leslie, and all of the contractors who will work from that image for many months to develop it into a tangible reality. It is real to them at every stage in that process of manifestation, not just when the house is "done."

However, at each stage the relationship to the nature of reality is distinctive. Figure 5 captures these distinctions, using Leslie's home design projects as an example. On the lower left, the image of a light bulb with a house design in it represents the experience of the highest vibrancy in the relationship to nature, where one experiences the infinite possibility, the choosing of a vision to manifest—the dream of the house—the process of developing that possibility

*Figure 5: Experience of Nature—What Is Real*

by building the house, and the actual home. All three levels are available in the high-vibrancy experience. The joy experienced, the vibrancy, is in imagining the house, building it, and in living in it over time.

In the middle level of vibrancy in the relationship to nature, reality includes both the development of the house and the finished house. These are now fixed in the design and plans. There is no longer the possibility of an alternate vision.

At the lower level of vibrancy in the relationship to nature, the only reality is the completed house. While it may have many wonderful attributes that will make it a home for the family for which it was built, the completed house alone represents a lower-vibrancy experience of reality because it is fixed. It is a manifestation of the vision of what could be possible and the development process that realized that vision, but it does not hold their vibrant characteristics. It has become a thing.

The fact that you can shift perspectives to see reality at these different levels of vibrancy—just as you can access different qualities of relationship to self, other, and group—is a sign that what you experience in your relationship to what is real in any given group or place is an agreement. Let's come back to the experience of the leader who reflected that the same group of people in two different committees could tacitly agree to operate at high or low vibrancy under different circumstances. Now we can imagine how that might be so. When a group defines its task in an inspiring way, it may give itself permission to start from the perspective of limitless possibility, thereby creating the context for each group member to show up as his and her most creative self. In contrast, when in a different committee, work is assigned that is defined as totally detail-oriented and perhaps insignificant, the committee members unstated acceptance of this view of the nature of the task can create a context in which they also accept a low-vibrancy relationship to each other.

This is similar to the difference between the design phases in one of Leslie's projects, when she evokes creativity by inviting her clients to start by imagining their dream house without worrying about constraints. In contrast, when the house is built and the project has reached the stage of selecting among a million different drawer pulls or doorknobs, and working through a long list of details to be finished or fixed, Leslie understands that staying focused on the concrete and tangible is what she, the contractor, and the clients most need to do. However uninspiring that may feel, she agrees to operate in that mode.[22]

The point I want to emphasize is that once you begin to see these different relationships and see how you experience them differently, you have the insight and the motivation to shift your perspective and to operate from a place of higher vibrancy. You can choose a different agreement, one that will bring greater vibrancy and abundance into your life. This is the whole point of Ecosynomics.[23]

---

22    Sometimes it is useful to look to our poets, the synthesizers of human experience, to describe what we know unconsciously. The English poet William Blake, who grew up in the 2nd half of the 18th century observed of the experience of Nature, "I see Every thing I paint In This World, but Every body does not see alike…The tree which moves some to tears of joy is in the Eyes of others only a Green thing that stands in the way…But to the Eyes of the Man of Imagination Nature is Imagination itself. As a man is So he Sees. As the Eye is formed such are its Powers. You certainly Mistake when you say that the Visions of the Fancy are not to be found in This World. To Me This World is all One continued Vision of Fancy or Imagination & I feel Flattered when I am told So." This quote from William Blake can be found in his compiled work (Erdman, 1988, p. 702). Herein we see the light, verb, and noun levels of the perceived reality of our experience of our relationship to Nature.

23    Our relationship with Nature explores the manifest realm of probability, when life meets with the possible, where the absolute nature of the light-flow-Spirit expresses itself in a relative form within the human-perceived universe. Probability is when possibility meets nature, that instant when one knows something as "real," even if it is far from manifesting in a tangible form. Most of human life is experienced this way. For example, from when the design of a house is "seen" by the architect, owner, and builder, many weeks of work and resources start moving even before the house shows up. When did it become "real" for everyone involved? When it became a probability. The inner experience of this relationship to Nature is the psychic energy one experiences as life-force, intentions, feelings, and thoughts, as perceptions of the movement of light—one's relationship with self-in-Nature—or how I relate to Nature.

## THE FIVE RELATIONSHIPS: SPIRIT

In my conversations, people have shared lots of ideas and stories about how they experience the relationship to spirit. Some emphasize religion or spirituality; others speak about the spirit in a family, a community, an organization, or a team. "It's when you feel a part of a much greater whole," said a young woman in one of my business classes. "You are a part of the cosmos; you know that you are supported by something greater than yourself." However they choose to acknowledge that relationship to a greater power, the stories all convey a sense of spirit as the source of creativity. Like the sun in the natural world, spirit is the light-energy that unleashes the potential in those who tap into it.

So, what do higher and lower vibrancy look like in our experiences of this relationship? A corporate executive answered this question as follows, "In scarcity mode, there just isn't any creativity. We know what to do in this mode, because the rules are given. They are in the book. We just ask what we are supposed to do. I mean, somebody just tells us what the rules are. This is very different from the abundance place, where we never even ask, because I can see what we can do, the creativity and knowing is everywhere. The essence of the spirit of the group in this mode is that anything is possible."

Figure 6 depicts these distinctions. In many groups, you experience the light coming from a respected, well-established source. Often in the form of a book, this is the story that shows the way. At home, these may be the family standards for how things are done—the current generation's interpretation of the family traditions. At work this might be the employee handbook, the industry standards for best practices, or the code of ethics. In religions there are the books of the guiding word or the divine spirit. This relationship you have to spirit as being the light coming only from the accepted word is in the bottom-right of Figure 6.

---

The self's Nature expression is physically observable in one's sensory-perception organs of touch, life, movement, balance, warmth, taste, sight, and hearing. Culturally, the group supports the individual's balance within the ecosystem.

*Figure 6: Experience of Spirit—the Source of Creativity*

A young man living in Ohio described this experience, "When my wife and I moved here, our kids came to a new school, a school old with traditions, which we found comforting. The families in the school knew who they were and where they came from—they knew what they were doing. It was great to experience the strength of this wisdom. Until I tried to share some ideas I had about new ways to do things. Then the traditions started to feel like a constraint."

A somewhat higher vibrancy experience is one in which the creative force flows from you, as well as from the book. The light shines on all and shines through you. This is when you experience the exhilaration of creativity, the capacity to discover new truths because you are both able to work with the teachings from others and to offer your own ideas and intrepretations. This is the experience of yourself as the portal, the host, for the flow of spirit, as depicted in the middle of Figure 6. It is the creative force in you that makes others' hearts sing, your parents cry, and your friends adore you. Exploring this point, the same young man from Ohio interjected, "And this is what I experienced with our minister. While the school board would have none of my suggestions, the minister invited me to share my ideas. He said, 'You are very creative, and we can always improve on what we have done in the past.' I feel like I was standing on the shoulders of giants."

Sometimes you also experience your relationship to spirit as one in which spirit radiates from you and everything all around you—it is everywhere. In these moments, you and the people with you invite spirit to show up everywhere that it exists. You see that, and with that awareness you are actually co-hosting the flow of spirit. What makes this experience different is that you are not just an observer, as when the light is sourced from outside of you. Rather you are an active participant, bringing spirit-awarness to the flow all around you. This high-vibrancy relationship to spirit is represented in the light-energy swirl at the top-left of Figure 6. My daughter and son play in occasional jam sessions with other musicians. They love them. "Everyone is creative," they tell me. "People come up with really cool harmonies that I would never have thought of, and I get to play with them. That's chill."

The agreements in these different groups invite in different levels of spirit's presence, from received wisdom in the book, to what you can see in yourself, to what can be experienced in everyone and everything. Seeing the creativity around you or not is a choice, an agreement you accept, an agreement that you can change. The next time you are in a situation completely lacking in creativity, you can realize that there seems to be very little creativity and you can begin to look around, looking for the creativity that you know must be there. Once you begin to see it, the juices begin to flow, as you have experienced many times in your life, and you do see the spirit, the source of creativity in everything and in everyone. You can recognize this moment and shift this agreement, because you trust, you know, that the creativity is there. It only needs to be seen and invited in, which is what the people we call "creative" do all the time.

## HARMONIC VIBRANCY: FROM SCARCITY TO ABUNDANCE

At this point in the conversation, having looked at the five primary relationships, people tell me it all starts to seem like a bit much, "Five relationships experienced at three different levels—give us a break!" This is my opportunity to introduce my favorite image, "The Three Circles of Harmonic Vibrancy."

The conversation now begins to focus on describing the differences among the experiences of the inner circle, the middle circle, and the outer circle. The stories that people share as we look together at the image in Figure 7 invariably lead the group to a realization: in real life, we do not have a separate experience of vibrancy in each of the five relationships. Rather all the relationships interact and work together to produce an overall sense of more or less wellbeing. This is "harmonic vibrancy."

When people experience greater harmonic vibrancy, which is what they want, all relationships are taken care of, and through those relationships they accomplish more. Conversely, when people experience less vibrancy, which they do not want, it is hard to pay attention to any relationships. Everyone does what he can alone, accomplishing much less. Starting from scarcity, the lack of relationship in all five dimensions generates a lower vibrancy. Starting from abundance, all relationships work together to generate a higher vibrancy.

Do you recognize the experience captured in the inner circle in the figure? In one group, a school administrator jumped in: "Well, you should see our meetings; they are numbing." Everybody nodded knowingly. We have all at times felt this kind of energy-draining dreariness. The inner circle describes this experience of the lack of relationship in all five relationships, an experience of what I call "apart-from-ness"—being apart from all relationships of vibrancy.

The middle circle of the Three Circles of Harmonic Vibrancy describes the experience of medium vibrancy in all relationships. This is an experience of "next-to-ness." A Dutch engineer captured this experience of the middle circle in terms of what it feels like when outside consultants come in to work with his team. "When they are in the room," he said, "we develop new skills, see new relationships, and learn. Sometimes it's frustrating, but I see that it works. We see each other's capacities and what we each bring to the team. We get stronger, more resilient standing with each other, and we get better outcomes, both in our individual and team development, and in the things we are producing."

The outer circle describes the experience of high vibrancy in all five relationships, an experience of "one-with-ness." A Russian lady in one of my groups recognized the outer circle in an experience with her daughter in the toy store Mir Detstva in Moscow. "I was more alive, trying new activities I would have never tried before. I was doing them with my daughter, who was also shining. We each brought something new to our relationship in the way we did it together. Creativity was flowing everywhere, in both of us and in the lovely girl helping us. The possibilities were endless, we enjoyed the process, and we came out with beautiful works of art. A high level in all five relationships—all in one!"

People naturally liken this experience to music, where the songs that move us most have rich harmonies. Each voice contributes a distinctive element, yet no voice can achieve the harmony alone. My favorite image, however, is one that folks have suggested more than once in my conversation groups: ice

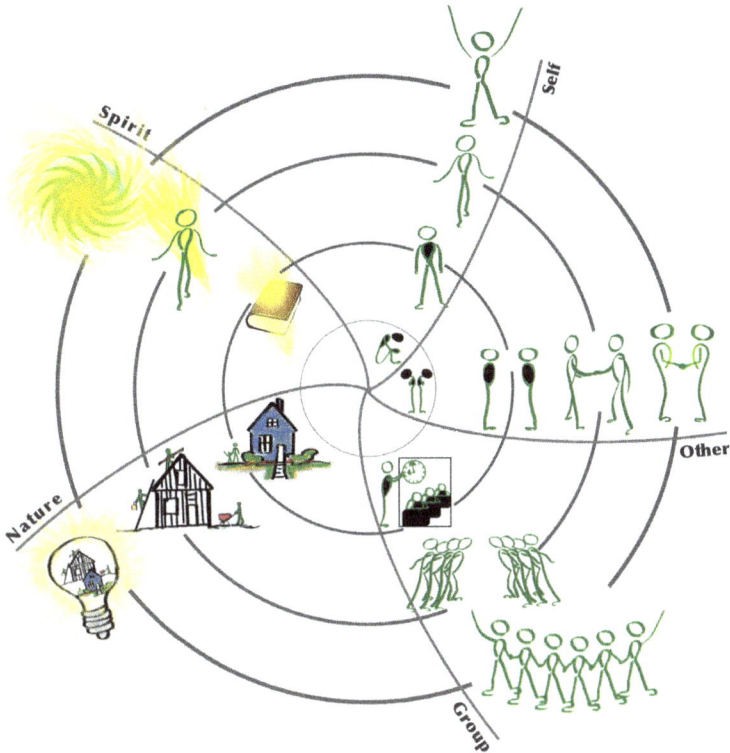

*Figure 7: Experience of Scarcity-Abundance in All Relationships*

cream! One person might notice the experience of taste ("it's all about the sweetness"); another emphasizes texture ("it's all about being both smooth and crunchy"); yet another thinks temperature is key ("it's all about being cold); while another describes appearance ("it's all about the colors of the ice cream, the cone and the sprinkles"). But, of course, nobody wants just sweet, just smooth and crunchy, just cold, or just colorful. Ice cream is about the perfect combination of taste, texture, temperature, and appearance. In the same way, our experience of harmonic vibrancy depends on the quality of our relationships to self, other, group, nature, and spirit, altogether.

Towards the end of one of our early presentations about the Three Circles of Harmonic Vibrancy, held in Mexico, a banking executive asked my colleague, "Do you have that graphic as a sticker or a magnet?" We had never been asked that before. "Why?" asked my colleague. "Because I want to put it on my refrigerator to remind me that when I am experiencing the inner circle of scarcity, that it is an agreement that I have accepted. I know the experience of abundance, and since I am often the leader, I can choose another agreement.

The graphic would remind me of this choice, what I feel like when I choose it, and the outcomes we can achieve when we live within the abundance-based agreements." Since then, hundreds have asked for that graphic. Now we have magnets.

The realization that it is our agreements that are determining our experiences of scarcity or abundance in different groups can be a rude awakening. People are choosing to experience lower vibrancy most of the time. That is the inner circle of scarcity. Why would we do that? Maybe because we are not aware that it was an agreement we were making. Could we make different agreements? Sometimes it is easy to see how to go about this, but in many situations it can seem hard to figure out how to even start. It gets pretty complicated and difficult. Or does it? I like the way Tom Robbins puts it in his novel, *Jitterbug Perfume*: "The universe does not have laws. It has habits. And habits can be broken."[24] That's where Ecosynomics comes in—to help us see our habit of accepting agreements that produce scarcity, so that we can take steps toward abundance and greater harmonic vibrancy.[25]

## SUMMARY: FOUR PRINCIPLES OF SCARCITY AND ABUNDANCE

So let's review what has emerged from my many conversations. It seems that people agree to scarcity or abundance in different situations, whether or not they are aware of that agreement. When they agree on abundance, they experience a greater harmonic and a greater vibrancy. Everyone seems to recognize that this is what he wants and that he just does not always get it. It also seems that when people experience greater abundance, there is a greater vibrancy in their relationships to self, other, the group, nature, and spirit. Conversely, when they experience greater scarcity, there is less vibrancy in all of these relationships. This seems to show something about people's ability to bring vibrancy to all of the relationships or to none of them, and that is related to the level of scarcity or abundance they experience.

Furthermore, when the group is in scarcity mode, it is very hard to attend

---

24    See (T. Robbins, 1990, p. 312).

25    Professor Damasio, a leading neuroscientist and psychologist at USC, finds that human beings are hardwired for harmony, as it is a fundamental process of consciousness. From years of laboratory research he finds that, "Optimal workings of an organism, which result in efficient, harmonious states of life, constitute the very substrate of our primordial feelings of well-being and pleasure. They are the foundation of the state that, in quite elaborate settings, we call happiness. On the contrary, disorganized, inefficient, inharmonious life states, the harbingers of disease and system failure, constitute the substrate of negative feelings" (Damasio, 2010, p. 6).

to the vibrancy in any of the relationships. In abundance mode, it just shows up in all of them. There's relationship all over the place. Specifically, in the scarcity mode, each person tries individually to do what is required to move the thing along, to keep life going. No relationship there, just a lot of everyone doing her own thing. The abundance mode is completely different. It is through the relationships that people get things done—a lot more done. And, just as important, it is not harder to get more done, rather when people experience greater vibrancy, there seems to be creativity and energy in abundance. They are in the flow, and they get a lot done. In lower vibrancy, they never have enough, and everything gets stuck.

Often, when I share this summary of the conversation, someone will speak up and say that this sounds like a set of principles—guiding principles. "Right!" I say, and here they are:

**First**, groups that start with an assumption of scarcity, experience mostly scarcity and low harmonic vibrancy, and groups that start with an assumption of abundance, experience mostly abundance and high harmonic vibrancy. It is not that scarcity or abundance is absolutely right, rather that one or the other shows up depending on which one is perceived to be the underlying basis of the agreements in the group. Having said this, I will also suggest that abundance has to exist for the whole system to work. By this I mean that the abundance is always there, it is just a matter of peoples' capacity to perceive it. When the abundance, the infinite light, is not perceived, it is kept in the dark. By keeping it in the dark, it is undernourished, underutilized, underdeveloped, and undervalued.[26]

**Second**, the degree of harmonic vibrancy you experience in any one of the five relationships is very similar to what you experience in all of the relationships. The experience of a low harmonic vibrancy in any relationship seems to be present when they are all low, and a high harmonic vibrancy in any relationship is only experienced when they are all high. This suggests that to experience abundance and greater harmonic vibrancy, one needs to pay attention to all five relationships at the same time.

**Third**, the individual and the group are better off, experiencing greater abundance and harmonic vibrancy, when all five relationships are stronger. Relationship matters, and the agreements in those relationships determine

---

26   Abundance is in possibility and in how we are in relationship with development-verb and things-noun. This is different than saying that nouns can grow infinitely, which is the pathology of current logic that ecologists so strongly attack. We CAN access infinite abundance, from possibility, by how we are in relationship with it. This is the experience of positive net flow forever, and not infinite positive feedback.

what is possible. It is a system.

**Fourth**, people prefer the experience of greater harmonic vibrancy to the experience of less, and people experience that harmonic vibrancy in all five relationships—to self, to other, to group, to nature, and to spirit.

These principles have important practical implications. High-vibrancy groups start from an assumption of abundance; low vibrancy groups start from an assumption of scarcity. High-vibrancy groups pay attention to all five primary relationships and low-vibrancy groups do not. High-vibrancy groups realize that the web of relationships makes up a system and low-vibrancy groups do not. Finally, people prefer higher harmonic vibrancy, as experienced in all five relationships. With these four principles about your experience and the five primary relationships, we have the foundation we need to see, explain, and choose healthier, freer agreements—agreements for higher harmonic vibrancy and abundance. You can paint your own world, as in Figure 8. The rest of this book will show you how.

*Figure 8: Painting the World You Agree To*

# CHAPTER 2

# PERCEPTIONS, ASSUMPTIONS, AND HARMONIC VIBRANCY

In Chapter 1, we looked at the five relationships: self, other, group, nature, and spirit, through which people experience harmonic vibrancy, as well as three circles or levels of harmonic vibrancy: low, medium, and high. We saw that people experience quite different realities in each of the three circles. Now I want to explore how our *perceptions* of reality influence which circle we find ourselves in.

We examined three distinct, though interrelated, perceptions of reality in the context of the relationship to nature. These are represented in the Three Circles of Harmonic Vibrancy graphic (Figure 7 on p. 23) as the possibility of a new house, the development of a new house, and the concrete manifestation of the house as a solid, fixed object. The different experiences of these three, equally real, versions of "house" we categorized as high vibrancy (possibility, development, and things), medium vibrancy (development and things) and low vibrancy (things). Each level of higher vibrancy works with the lower level of reality and the next level, both-and. This continuum, combined with those of the other four relationships in the graphic, captures an interesting and important phenomenon; as our perception of reality expands from seeing only the things that currently exist to including processes of development to working in the possibility realm, our experience of reality also expands, from low to medium to high harmonic vibrancy, and from scarcity to abundance.

In their national bestseller, *The Art of Possibility*, Ben and Rosamund Stone Zander tell a story that neatly highlights this power of perception:

A shoe factory sends two marketing scouts to a region of Africa to study the prospects for expanding business. One sends back a telegram saying, 'SITUATION HOPELESS STOP NO ONE WEARS SHOES.' The other writes back triumphantly, 'GLORIOUS BUSINESS OPPORTUNITY STOP THEY HAVE NO SHOES.'[27]

We can easily see that these two different perspectives on the same situation have led the two scouts to make radically different assumptions about the market opportunity, each with quite different implications for how the shoe company could proceed. We don't know for sure that diving into a new market on the advice of the second scout would lead to huge sales of shoes in the region, but we do know that following the instinct of the first scout that there was no point in entering that market would produce no sales at all. This story brings us back to the first principle of scarcity and abundance from the end of Chapter 1, which is: *groups that start with an assumption of scarcity experience mostly scarcity and low harmonic vibrancy, and groups that start with an assumption of abundance experience mostly abundance and high harmonic vibrancy.* So, our perceptions of reality shape our assumptions of what is possible, and our assumptions influence the reality we experience. Let's explore in more detail how this can be so.

## POSSIBILITY, DEVELOPMENT, THINGS: LIGHT, MOTION, MATTER

First, I want to delve into the three basic perceptions of reality we have identified. In Chapter 1, I labeled these "possibility," "development," and "things" as a way of identifying the central focus of each perspective. It is important to remember that these are "only" perceptions of reality, not reality itself. All three of these aspects of reality are always present, whether or not we perceive them. Yet, it is human nature to see what we expect to see and miss those aspects of reality we are not looking for.

To become more aware of our ways of perceiving can be challenging, especially when we are in the midst of the perception. We can meet this challenge, however, by developing awareness of how we tend to experience the differences among them. In fact, each of these three perspectives tends to come with a distinctive sensation, which we can relate to as a familiar experience of a fundamental quality of the physical world: light (possibility), motion

---

27    This story comes from (Zander & Zander, 2002, p. 9).

(development), and matter (things). By recognizing these differences among the three ways of perceiving, we can become more aware of our perception in a particular situation and more aware of the assumptions we may be making on the basis of that perception. Once again, I will draw on my many conversations to show how what I am saying is really just stuff you already know.

## POSSIBILITY-LIGHT

You experience possibility, all around you, all of the time. You may see possibility daily in mundane things such as what you will do when you wake up in the morning, what you want for breakfast, or how you will get to work, as well as in important things like how you will engage with your family or your co-workers or your school mates. You also see possibility in the creative moments of your life, when perhaps you have surprised yourself with gifts of unexpected inspiration.

When you are in that place of inspiration and seeing possibility all over the place, other people notice it, often in a particular way: "I can see the light in your eyes," or "you were glowing today." Just as in the natural world, light-energy is the source of all possibility, so in the human arena we associate light with the realm of infinite possibility, from which everything flows. When you or others notice this sense of light, you know your perception of reality is in that possibility realm. And when you are in that light-possibility realm, the assumptions you make tend to favor the idea that things will work out well, precisely because there is so much possibility for them to do so. This is how you feel when you see the possibility that you can do something you've never done before—learn a new skill or have an experience you never thought you could have. The energy flows and you decide to go for it.

A woman in Germany told me a story about how she had experienced this sense of potential with a new group of people. "Last year, as I began to form a sports team, I could see clearly how we might perform together. It was very exciting." Have you had the experience of being able to see, somewhere in the future, a group of people achieving certain outcomes and performing together, long before they ever came together? How did you know that it would work? Again and again people have assured me, "You can just see the potential. You can feel it."

In my conversations I like to draw out this experience by asking if people have ever hired someone to work for them. Many say yes. "What I want to understand," I say, "is how you decided the person you hired could do the job." A woman in a lecture in Mexico City addressed this quite logically by saying, "There are basically two different likely cases here. In one case, I hire someone who is already doing a similar job elsewhere. In the other case, I hire a person who has never done anything like this before." Other folks in the group nodded their heads, telling me that this is typical of their experience. So I dove into the second case with a question I ask in every conversation, "How do you know someone will be able to do the job if he has never shown that he can?" The response I have heard, over and over again, in English, Spanish, German, and Dutch (the last two through translators) is that, "You can just see it in him." "When you meet someone, you can see the potential. You can see it in their eyes." "There is a light in her eyes, and when I see this, I know she will fit well." Here I always push back, to check whether this is a common experience in the group. So far, most everyone agrees. "Yes, I can see this, and often I am right." Okay. So, people actually seem to know something about people before the physical evidence of it ever shows up, and they see this potential in the experience of light.[28]

This is the daily work of designers. As an architect, when my wife works with her clients, much of the initial effort brings her and the client to a place where they can both see the same end product—the home. This is purely possibility. As the seeing becomes more real, they collaboratively experience what it would be like to live in the house, making it their home. This is very real—when they reach this shared knowing of what the future building will be like, they move onto the next phase of dedicating lots of resources to building the home, another level of perceived reality.

Entrepreneurs also do this, constantly seeing new business models, ways in which they can bring greater value to someone else by organizing resources in new ways. They do this by seeing possibility in each of the five primary relationships, and seeing how to translate that possibility they see into outcomes. One form of this creativity is expressed through innovation. How common is innovation in groups today? A 2008 national survey in the USA conducted by the National Science Foundation (NSF) found that "about 9% of the estimated 1.5 million for-profit companies were active product innovators in 2006-2008. The corresponding figure for process innovators was also about 9%." [29]

Thus, it seems that many people see the potential in themselves, in others, in groups, and in many new situations. They seem to do this all of the time,

---

28    In his book Yes to the Mess, jazz pianist and management professor Frank Barrett finds that, "Human beings are at their best when they are open to the world, able to notice what's needed, and equipped with the skills to respond meaningfully in the moment." (Barrett, 2012, p. xii).

29    For the NSF study, see (Boroush, 2010, p. 1).

seeing into the potential, the possibility, and they experience this seeing as very real. So real that they make assumptions—and significant decisions—based on the potential they see. Of course, not every decision to "go for it," nor every new team or new hire, works out as well as anticipated. Nevertheless, these examples highlight our shared human experience that approaching reality from the perspective of light-possibility is how we create the possibility that good things will happen. This, in a nutshell, is how the assumption of abundance begets the reality of abundance.

## DEVELOPMENT-MOTION

Now I want to look at how we experience another way of perceiving reality. This is the perception that focuses not on limitless possibility but on the process by which a particular possibility is, or may be, realized—the perception I have named "development." We can recognize when we are looking at reality through this perspective when our predominant sense is of motion: things changing and new things, tangible and intangible, emerging. Just as I link the possibility perspective to its predominant experience of light, I like to link development with this sense of movement and change.

Sitting in the park in the Boston Commons with my class a few years ago, one of the students observed, "Looking around, at all of the people, animals, buildings, trees, and fountains, I can't see anything that isn't always changing. It is all dynamic." A fellow teacher added, "That's what I see too. That tree over there changes in size and strength, based on the net difference of what flows in to the tree in the form of nutrients and water, and of what flows out of the tree in the form of oxygen, bark, leaves, and broken limbs. The net rate of change influences how much more or less there is every day, every year. Even when it looks the same to me day after day." A kindergarten teacher in the group chimed in, "I see this in my work every now and then. The young children that come to us at the beginning of the year in kindergarten are very different than the ones that leave us to go on to first grade. Developmentally they come in as advanced toddlers and they leave ready to engage the world in the classroom."

Not all movement is in a positive direction, of course, and not all actions produce the desired results, but the energy to pursue positive change is inherent in the development-motion perspective. As with light-possibility, this way of perceiving reality leads to certain types of assumptions about oneself and others. We expect to see people and situations changing over time. We expect individuals and groups to learn, to get better at what they do—to change. We look for plans to come to fruition—houses built, new relationships established and old ones strengthened, resources assembled and strategies pursued. This is a realm of action and movement towards the realization of expectations. The agreements people tend to make based on this perspective can lead them toward the occasional experiences of abundance that we saw in the middle circle of harmonic vibrancy.

## THINGS-MATTER

The third way of perceiving reality focuses on what is here now. When you are operating in this realm, you are not thinking of many different possibilities or how things might change for the better. You are dealing with what is concrete and available in the present. This is a way of looking at reality that resonates with the old adage, "a bird in the hand is worth two in the bush."

In contrast to the predominant sense of light in possibility mode and the sense of motion and change that characterizes the development perspective, the feeling that lets you know you are working with the things-focused perception of reality is the grounded sense of knowing exactly what you have to work with. Whatever it is has volume and mass—it feels solid. For example, it is the resources you have right now, not what you might have in the future or what you can bring forth if you make an investment. It could be the capacity you have that you can apply right now. You may see and sense that you can count on the capacities others have. Whether it is an individual or a group, you know what they can do, today, here and now. This is the world of the matter-things perspective.[30]

I was working with a group of philanthropists in the US Northwest, and a young leader of a large family foundation expressed her gratitude for her experiences, "When I look around me, seeing what I really have, I feel blessed." Driving through the forest in western Guatemala, a Mayan leader told me the same thing, "Look at how fertile this land is. My people have been working

---

30   While the apparent tangibility of the here and now of the things-noun level seems to make it more real than the possibility-light and development-verb levels of reality, science is very unclear what here-now actually means. Until the quantum revolution at the beginning of the 1900s, things seemed to be real. Yet, since then physics has shown that, at the very small level of the quanta, there is nothing solid there. The social sciences have also dealt with this question, divided on whether reality actually exists or is simply created by human intention. For example, by the time you "realize" something is happening "right now," you are already looking at the past—once you see something, it already happened. Even the term people commonly use "to realize" means to make real, to convert into reality. So, what is real? Even the seemingly tangible is not.

with this land for over 5,000 years. It is part of who we are, the people of corn. We are truly fortunate."

Of course, along with solidity there is scarcity in this view of reality. You may be very energetic in making the most of what you have. If development and possibility are out of the picture, however, before long you are likely to run into a sense of constraint or inadequacy. Your assumptions have the spirit of resigned acceptance: "This is just the way things are." "There's no point in trying to change them." Agreements grounded in these kinds of assumptions tend to lock that sense of scarcity in place.

The manager of a mid-Western town told me, "When I get frustrated, feeling like I am backed into a corner, all I can see is how little I seem to have in me. Life seems so complicated. Even when it's not true, it seems that way." A colleague working in a national governmental agency agreed with him. She said, "I get so busy in my day-to-day work, that even when I feel like I am in the groove, flying, I go from one moment to the next, responding to life with whatever I have at hand. The day has passed, I have checked off dozens of things from my to-do list and answered a hundred e-mails, and I feel some satisfaction of getting lots done. And, the next day it's the same all over again. It never stops, no matter what I do."

＊ ＊ ＊ SIDEBAR ＊ ＊ ＊

# SCIENTIFIC EVIDENCE FOR THE LIGHT, MOTION, AND MATTER LEVELS OF REALITY

Physics is the science of the nature of the physical universe. With its evidence-based heritage, the power of physics as a science comes from its very precise predictions of natural phenomenon, from very, very small sub-atomic particles to very, very large universes of galaxies.[31]

---

31   The physics I will present here belongs to the class of scientific materialism; a phi-losophy that suggests the physical world is all that exists. The core philosophical question of ontology—the nature of reality—is material, from this point of view, versus ideal, the other major school of ontology. Bestselling author and physicist Brian Greene captures this mindset, "I believe that a physical system is completely determined by the arrangement of its particles. Tell me how the particles making up the earth, the sun, the galaxy, and everything else are arranged, and you've fully articulated reality. This reductionist view is common among physicists, but there are certainly people who think otherwise. Especially when it comes to life, some believe that an essential nonphysical aspect (spirit, soul, life force, chi, and so on) is required to animate the physical. Although I remain open to this possibility, I've never encountered any evidence to support it. The position that makes most sense to me is that

The whole of quantum physics now assumes that the world is one of infinite possibility. To deal with the difficulty of experiencing infinite possibility, best-selling authors and physicists Brian Cox and Jeff Forshaw clarify, "The fact that it is not something we can touch, smell, or see directly is irrelevant. Indeed, we would not get very far in physics if we decided to restrict our description of the Universe to things we can directly sense."[32]

Cox and Forshaw explain the light-possibility, motion-development, and matter-things levels. "Things happen. We wake up, we make breakfast, we eat breakfast, and so on. We'll call the occurrence of a thing 'an event in space-time.' We can uniquely describe an event in space-time by four numbers: three spatial coordinates describing where it happened and a time coordinate describing when it happened." Motion in space-time, then, is the movement from one event in space-time to another. "Don't forget that…these two distances, in space and time, are not universally agreed upon… Our aim is to find a distance in space-time upon which everyone agrees."[33] Einstein described this space-time distance, by invoking the cosmic speed limit, which happens to be the speed of light.[34] This light, now known to be quanta or particles or photons, "behaves as a wave and as a particle."[35] "Try though we may to split light into fundamental atomic pieces, it remains whole to the end."[36]

Said another way, everything is energy, which shows up as possibility everywhere, and what we observe in motion is always moving through space-time at the cosmic speed limit. A thing is an event, a specific, non-moving moment of that motion. This sounds like everything is possible, some of it is moving, and some of it we can hold still for an instant. Another description from physics of our daily experience of possibility-potential, motion, and matter comes in the form of the total energy in a system. Total energy equals

---

one's physical and mental characteristics are nothing but a manifestation of how the particles in one's body are arranged. Specify the particle arrangement and you've specified everything" (Greene, 2011, pp. 33-34). I find this materialist approach most curious given that most of these physicists have spent the past 150 years studying phenomenon that can only be seen indirectly or in the math; they have not seen directly much of the phenomena they study, such as quanta, black holes, event horizons, the Higgs boson, parallel or multiple universes, probability fields, or eleven dimensions.

32    This quote can be found in their best-selling book Why Does E=mc2? (Cox & Forshaw, 2010, p. 40).

33    Authors Cox and Forshaw describe the light, motion, and matter connections in (Cox & Forshaw, 2010, pp. 72-73).

34    "Light is not so special… Light just happens to use up all of its space-time quota on motion through space," and not through time (Cox & Forshaw, 2010, pp. 103-104).

35    See (Cox & Forshaw, 2011, p. 6).

36    Amherst College professor of physics Arthur Zajonc describes the history of light (Zajonc, 1995, p. 299).

potential energy plus kinetic energy. $E_{Total} = E_{Potential} + E_{Kinetic} = mgh + \frac{1}{2}mv^2$. The possibility in potential energy, the movement in kinetic energy, and the mass in matter. Possibility, development, and things. Light, motion, and matter.

While people usually think of light as what they see, the light shining from the sun or from a lamp, physics uses the term much more broadly, as electromagnetism. Physics defines light as electromagnetic radiation, which is energy in the form of transverse magnetic and electric waves.[37] Said another way, light is energy, and it travels very fast—at the speed of light! Furthermore, Einstein showed that everything in the universe travels at the speed of light.[38] Everything.[39] Now this gets a bit complex, so I will try to simplify. Basically, everything moves through space-time, through an interweaving of space and time, at the same speed—the speed of light. Some of it moves mostly through space and barely through time, while some of it travels mostly through time and barely through space. This is a mind twister. The relevance is that to move at the speed of light, in space-time, everything has a relationship to this speed of light.[40]

---

37    As described in ("Shorter Oxford English Dictionary," 2007). Some Physics dictionaries refer to light only in the realm visible to the human eye, electromagnetic radiation having a wavelength of 400-750nm; while this dictionary includes the invisible realm outside of the realm visible to the human eye.

38    Physicist Brian Greene describes the logic and math of Einstein's observation that everything travels through the four dimensions of space-time at the speed of light (Greene, 2003, pp. 50, 392n).

39    For a relatively easy introduction to this idea of everything moving at the speed of light, see (Cox & Forshaw, 2010). In physics, there is an understanding that everything in the universe is moving at the speed of light, which includes us. What gets tricky is how to understand what it means to travel at the speed of light through space-time. The amount of energy that this represents is mind-bogglingly huge. At the equivalent of 670 million miles per hour, when I walk at 5 miles per hour through space, all of the rest of my energy goes into moving through time. Moving through time takes a very large amount of energy, energy humans barely notice. Walking down the path to my house, Einstein suggested that I am crushing through the time dimension of space-time with most of my light-speed, and barely moving through the space dimensions of space-time. The relevance of this here is two-fold. First, an enormous amount of energy goes into the ability to move through time. You experience two forms of this energy used in moving through time, which we can characterize as horizontal time and vertical time. In horizontal time, you experience "the passing of time." In vertical time, you experience "no time." Have you ever realized that you have no idea how much time has passed? It felt like seconds and it could have been hours. Often associated with deep reflection or meditation, this is when you experience vertical time. This is what happens when you access the light levels of possibility. In vertical time, as light, everything travels at the speed of light, thus there is no time in the space-time continuum, and therefore infinite possibility is always there, as there is no time that experiences the change. If you have had this experience, I suggest you know the experience of moving at light-speed through both space and through time. You do this because you are a light-being—Homo lumens.

40    The German mathematician and physicist Theodor Kaluza saw that Einstein's general

Now I will add a second piece to what physics shows us. Science also makes another mental leap. It suggests that at the quantum level—a very, very small level—everything exists in fields of potential—they are both here and not here, everywhere.[41] To sum up and pull together these insights from physics, everything is related to light speed and exists as potential everywhere in space-time.[42] In physics terms, reality consists of light as potential, as wave, and as particle, all at the same time. This is what people said, from their own experience of seeing themselves and others—I can see the potential in the light in your eyes. You shine. And this is a driving force of being human.[43]

While the apparent tangibility of the here and now of the things-matter level seems to make it more real than the possibility-light and development-motion levels of reality, science is very unclear what here-now actually means. Until the quantum revolution at the beginning of the 1900s, things seemed to be real. Yet, since then physics has shown that, at the very small level of the quanta, there is nothing there. The social sciences have also dealt with this question, divided on whether reality actually exists or is simply created by human intention. For example, by the time you "realize" something is happening "right now," you are already looking at the past—once you see something, it already happened. Even the term people commonly use "to realize" means to make real, or to convert into reality. So, what is real? Even

---

theory of relativity connected gravity and light, by adding a fourth dimension to space—a dimension that was curled up instead of extended like the other three dimensions of space (Kaluza, 1921). By adding the fourth spatial dimension, interwoven in the space-time fabric, he showed how Einstein's theory connected Einstein's theory of gravity with Maxwell's theory of light. Physicists now refer to this as the fifth dimension, opening the way for string theory. In his national bestseller, CUNY physicist Michio Kaku, a co-founder of string theory, wonders whether this formulation hinted that, "Perhaps the secret of light lies in the fifth dimension." (Kaku, 2008, p. 233).

41    Two recent texts bring together many of the seminal papers on quantum theory (Hawking, 2011) and an interesting story of the field (Baggott, 2011).

42    Best-selling authors and physicists Brian Cox and Jeff Forshaw describe the transformation of light energy as, "This assembly of particles is able to capture the light that has travelled the 93 million miles from our star, a nuclear furnace the volume of a million earths, and transfer that energy into the heart of cells, where it is used to build molecules from carbon dioxide and water, giving out life-enriching oxygen as it does so. It's these molecular chains that form the superstructure of trees and all living things, and the paper in your book. You can read the book and understand the words because you have eyes that can convert the scattered light from the pages into electrical impulses that are interpreted by your brain" (Cox & Forshaw, 2010, p. 3).

43    Nobel Laureate in Economics Michael Spence reminds us of the important role of human curiosity in economic growth, and that, "it is a very powerful, and largely noneconomic, force (Spence, 2011, p. 38)."

the seemingly tangible is not. The relevance for our exploration is to see that the things-matter level of reality is useful, just as are the possibility-light and development-motion levels, and is just as privileged.

In his reflections on the theory of relativity, the British analytic philosopher and winner of the 1950 Nobel Prize in Literature, Bertrand Russell, put the complex science in plain terms, "Mass used to be defined as 'quantity of matter,'...the mass as measured was found to increase with the velocity; this kind of mass was found to be really the same thing as energy... The world which the theory of relativity presents to our imagination, is not so much a world of 'things' in 'motion' as a world of *events*... It is *events* that are the stuff of relativity physics."[44]

Connecting the scientific perspective of physics back to the creative human expression, in their book, initially published by the Harvard Business School Press, the Zanders see that, "All around us is vibrancy and energy. The universe is sparking with generative power. But how do we tap into the source—where can we find an electric socket for vitality? Do we have to pump up the energy on our own to carry out the day, or can we catch the current of another wellspring beyond ourselves? Suppose for a moment that vital, expressive energy flows everywhere, that it is the medium for that existence of life, and that any block to participating in that vitality lies within ourselves."[45]

## HARMONICS, VIBRANCY, ABUNDANCE

We saw in Chapter 1 that people describe their experience of greater health in the five primary relationships using terms related to harmony, vibrancy, and abundance. It turns out that these experiential terms that people use, relate directly to the light-energy world of physics. Taking liberty with the terms, we can use discoveries in physics to describe a potential-wave-particle (read: possibility-motion-matter) theory of human agreements.

Waves transfer energy from one point in space-time to another. A wave, in its entirety, vibrates at a fundamental frequency. This wave is made up of overtones that vibrate at higher frequencies. A harmonic is an integer multiple of the fundamental frequency, meaning that it has, for example, two or three times the frequency. The overtones and fundamental form a harmonic series. In music, the harmonic provides the sound, the characteristic tone you

---

44  This quote is from (B. Russell, 1969, pp. 139-140).
45  This description of the experience of possibility provides yet another example of how people describe their experience of life in terms of vibrancy, energy, and light (Zander & Zander, 2002, p. 113).

recognize.[46] We can connect this to our experience in Chapter 1, from the examples of when people derive greater wellbeing when the different voices and relationships interact in a harmonic way.

In physics, waves are vibrations. "Higher frequencies must imply short wavelength (since short strings vibrate faster) and...a shorter wavelength corresponds to a higher-energy particle."[47] Thus, greater vibrancy corresponds to higher energy. In chapter 1, we described vibrancy as the energy experienced in the primary relationships.

Now, for one last leap, Einstein showed conceptually, and rigorous research supported experimentally, that energy and matter are two different forms of the same thing: matter is stored energy, and energy is liberated matter. $E=mc^2$. Related by the speed of light multiplied by itself (a very large number!), this equation shows that there is an immense amount of energy in all material things. Sometimes people see this energy, usually very little is seen. This becomes a question of how—how to see more of the extraordinary energy resident in the thing. For all practical purposes, this very large amount of energy potential is abundant. In chapter 1, we described the outer circle of harmonic vibrancy as one where we experienced the abundance of energy available.

Thus, we see that harmony, vibrancy, and abundance are actually technical terms describing the harmonic interaction of relationships, the vibrant energy experienced, and the abundant energy available. I leave you with the question of why humans use light-energy terms to qualify their experience of greater wellbeing.

✳ ✳ ✳ ✳ ✳ ✳

## THREE LEVELS OF PERCEIVED REALITY AND THREE CIRCLES OF HARMONIC VIBRANCY

By this point, I hope you are beginning to see how your perceptions of reality affect your experiences of more or less abundance and vibrancy. I like to refer to these different perspectives as "levels of perceived reality" to reference this connection to low, medium and high harmonic vibrancy as well as to the different qualities of experience they entail: the grounded sensation of matter; the airy, flowing sensibility of motion; and the transcendent aspect of light.

---

46    For the quantum wave-particle description of music, see (Cox & Forshaw, 2011, p. 95).
47    Quote describes findings based on de Broglie's research (Cox & Forshaw, 2011, p. 105).

The table in Figure 9, which we will refer to as the "Levels of Reality Map," suggests how these distinctions appear in our experiences of the five primary relationships.

## The 3 Levels of Perceived Reality Table

| HV Relationships<br><br>(Circles) · Five Primary<br>Levels of · Relationships<br>Perceived Reality · (axis) | Self | Other | Group | Nature | Spirit |
|---|---|---|---|---|---|
| Possibility<br><br>Potential<br>(Light)<br><br>=a+b+c | Envisioning my highest potential | Envisioning your highest potential | Envisioning our highest potential | Envisioning infinite resources | Envisioning infinite creativity |
| Development<br><br>Motion<br>(Verb)<br><br>=a+b | Developing my capacities & relationships | Supporting your development | Contributing to our development | Developing resources | Encouraging the flow of creativity |
| Things<br><br>Matter<br>(Noun)<br><br>=a | Staying grounded in what I can do | Staying grounded in what you can do | Staying grounded in what we can do | Staying grounded in what natural resources we have | Staying grounded in the inspiration that has been given to us |

*Figure 9: Three Levels of Perceived Reality for the Five Primary Relationships*

Looking up and down each of the columns representing the five relationships in this table, we can begin to see how all three core aspects of reality are always present but not necessarily accessible, depending on our perception. At the level of things, we are dealing only with what exists now: the outcomes that have already occurred, the existing relationships, the capacities and resources we currently have, and the established ideas. We assume this is all there is to reality, and we base our agreements on that assumption. After giving a talk on this, a senior consultant wanted to make sure that I understood the importance of the things level and getting things done. "I feel responsible for the dozens of consultants in my group. We have lots of mouths to feed at home. Sometimes you have to focus on what you have in the short term. In those moments, we need to agree to do what we can with what we have now. That's what pays the bills. I would be irresponsible to act otherwise." There is a satisfying concreteness to this perception of reality but also scarcity, because the vision and energy needed to bring new things into being are lacking.

At the level of development, we are working with what exists *and* we assume that those outcomes, capacities, relationships, resources, and ideas can be enhanced, expanded, improved. We engage actively in pursuing positive change, shaping our agreements in support of that. Motion puts matter in movement as we focus on making some change that will make the things we have, tangible and intangible, more effective and valuable.

I recently met Julia at our local bank. An experience we had with her stood out, because of the unusually high level of attention she gave to our request. It was not my typical experience in that bank. As we worked through a series of forms, I inquired about her approach to customer service. She told me about how important she thought customer service was, and how she was always seeking to improve it. She shared, "In this branch office, we agree to spend some of our time and attention during the day on the experience of our customers; what we can learn, improving our services, and trying again." I asked if there was support for doing all of this extra work. She shook her head, "It doesn't take much time and we get better outcomes, but it does take attention and agreeing to value that attention. It seems to work well for us."

Light accelerates the motion that moves the matter. From this perspective, we assume that reality includes infinite possibility, and our agreements reflect that assumption. We give ourselves permission to scan the universe of possible relationships, resources, capacities, and creative ideas to sense which ones represent our highest potential. Then we have this sense to guide us in determining which specific possibilities we want to work toward in the motion realm in order to realize specific outcomes in the realm of matter.

A colleague of mine described recently how she and her partners only took on work that they were passionate about, in which they could see huge potential for growth. She said, "The excitement is in seeing the possibilities together and then seeing how to manifest those possibilities. We do this together, and we find that it makes our work more valuable to us and to our customers."

Integrating the three levels of perceived reality with the five primary relationships in this way allows us to get more specific about what creates the three circles of harmonic vibrancy. In Chapter 1 we saw that the inner circle is dominated by experiences of scarcity. Now we see that this scarcity derives from the fact that, in this experience, we can only access the things level of reality.

In our experience of the middle circle of harmonic vibrancy, the circle of occasional abundance, we can access both the development level and the things level. In the outer circle, where we experience abundance in all five relationships, we can access all three levels of perceived reality. Figure 10

The 3 Circle Graphic ➡ The Levels of Perceived Reality Table

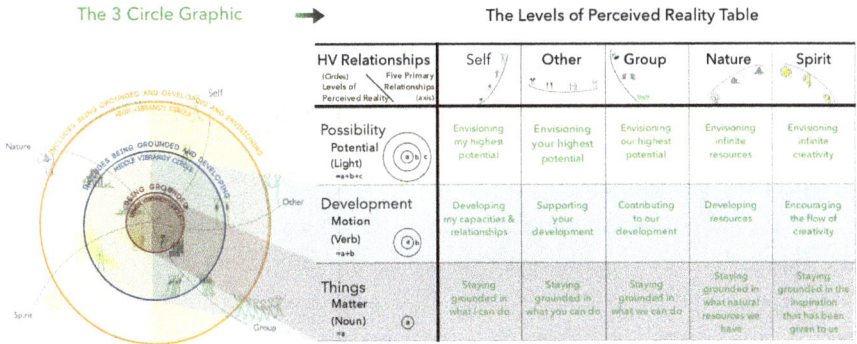

| HV Relationships (Circles) Levels of Perceived Reality | Five Primary Relationships (axis) | Self | Other | Group | Nature | Spirit |
|---|---|---|---|---|---|---|
| Possibility Potential (Light) =a+b+c | | Envisioning my highest potential | Envisioning your highest potential | Envisioning our highest potential | Envisioning infinite resources | Envisioning infinite creativity |
| Development Motion (Verb) =a+b | | Developing my capacities & relationships | Supporting your development | Contributing to our development | Developing resources | Encouraging the flow of creativity |
| Things Matter (Noun) =a | | Staying grounded in what I can do | Staying grounded in what you can do | Staying grounded in what we can do | Staying grounded in what natural resources we have | Staying grounded in the inspiration that has been given to us |

*Figure 10: Levels of Perceived Reality Accessible in 3 Circles of Harmonic Vibrancy*

captures this graphically, showing the available levels of perceived reality for each circle of harmonic vibrancy.

In each type of experience depicted in the Three Circles of Harmonic Vibrancy, people work with different processes, tools, and capacities because they are working with different perceptions of reality.

## THREE PATHWAYS

All of this leads us to a critical insight: the level of harmonic vibrancy and abundance available to you depends completely on how you work with the levels of perceived reality and relationships. To get a sense of how this works, think of the table in Figure 9 as a complete map of reality—all five fundamental relationships and all three levels of perceived reality. What different routes could you take across this terrain in your quest for harmonic vibrancy? Since harmonic vibrancy, by definition, means being on the same level across all five relationships, we know the path cannot be random or diagonal; it must be either horizontal or vertical. And in fact, as I have explored this question in my conversations, I have found that people tend to take one of three pathways. I have named them "on-the-level," "enlightened matter," and "grounded potential." Each path starts with a particular stance toward perceived reality and ends up in a completely different place relative to harmonic vibrancy.

## THE ON-THE-LEVEL PATH

On the on-the-level path, people simply stay at the level they start at. Their stance toward reality goes something like, "It's all about possibility," or "It's all about development," or "It's all about things." They dismiss alternative perspectives as irrelevant.

For example, a senior partner in a European consultancy focused on the matter-level-only path says, "It is all, and only, about what is actually here. Unlike the dreamers who talk endlessly about possibilities, and unlike the process people who keep us in endless meetings, we are realists, dealing with actual outcomes we can see right now. We focus on what is concrete, on outcomes we can count on."

A volunteer in our local "transition town" participative effort described the motion-level-only path, enthusiastically suggesting, "It is all about process. Without development nothing lives. It is in the dynamics of development that we can see all complexity. Dreaming of possibilities all day long is abstract, blue-sky thinking for academics. Working with the mundane of what is already here is for the tactical. We focus on what is real—process." One of the fathers of the total quality movement, W. Edwards Deming, described this worldview, "If you can't describe what you are doing as a process, you don't know what you're doing." The psychologist Carl Rogers said it another way, "The good life is a process, not a state of being. It is a direction not a destination." It is all about the journey, not the destination.

An excited teacher, joining the visioning group for the school, told me about the light-level-only path, "From possibility we can envision anything, seeing all of the great potential around us. This envisioning brings the best out of everyone. It is all about the vision. The rest is just about putting the vision into play. We leave that to the tactical folks." Carl Sandburg, the poet, captured this spirit, "I am an idealist. I don't know where I'm going, but I'm on my way."

Some groups you know place greater emphasis on things (matter), development (motion), or possibility (light) . They almost suggest that "reality" is really just at that level, and the other groups are missing the point. "Things" people see themselves as grounded, while the others are into that frou-frou stuff. "Development" people see themselves as in the flow, neither as crass as things-only types nor as flaky as infinite-possibility types. "Possibility" people see themselves as always living into their highest potential, riding the waves of the universe, while viewing all the others as less enlightened.

Most people have told me that they find some aspects of being in groups that operate in these on-the-level mindsets great and other aspects quite frustrating. Far more important for our quest for abundance and harmonic vibrancy, however, is the fact that working predominantly with just one level of perceived reality is a pathway that leads to scarcity, regardless of where it starts. If I just dream about possibility, nothing happens, and I starve. If I only work on development, I have no clear purpose for what I am developing, and I achieve no meaningful outcomes. If I just live in the material world, I do not mature, and when the world changes, I am caught by surprise.

In observing many low and high harmonic vibrancy groups, I have found that, to avoid a collapse into scarcity, people must work with all three levels simultaneously. This is the approach of the other two pathways. Each moves vertically on the map but from different perspectives, one top-down and the other bottom-up. This difference in starting point leads to quite different outcomes.

## THE ENLIGHTENED-MATTER PATH

Of the two pathways I have seen working with all three levels, one starts from the perspective that matter is the basis of reality. Thus, being healthy means more things. More things lead to greater well-being, the end desire of the good life. But things can run out. To be smart on this pathway, therefore, is to pay attention to the development of the capacities required to acquire more things. At the same time, wise matter management sees that one needs to look into the potential one can develop for generating more things, because the things that currently exist will eventually go away. The enlightened matter path thus means working with the motion that generates more matter and the light that nurtures and guides motion, all in service of matter.

That was very abstract. A work example might shine some light on this perspective. A few years ago, I worked with a Japanese journalist. She writes articles for her local newspaper. This is her "thing," what is real. When we met, she had just talked with her boss about further developing her skills at writing. She and her boss agreed that she would take some journalistic-writing classes. Over time, with practice, she would get better at her craft. She has brought the motion-development level of reality to her matter-thing reality. She then began to wonder whether she had the potential within her to take her writing to a whole new level. With her mentor, she explored her potential for being a book writer and found that she believed that that possibility was within her. Sure enough it was. She was able to write a book-length, journalistic piece covering a topic that impassioned her. Shifting into the light-possibility perception of reality showed her a possibility for further development that she had not seen before. The light-possibility perspective expanded the motion-development perspective, which led her to success at the matter-things level of perceived reality—all in service of the original thing. It all helped her do her job better. The scarcity in this perspective comes from the initial focus, on the thing-matter level of the task at hand. Her exploration was about her potential to develop her capacity to do the writing job better—the focus is on the job. The process started with the job, and asked if she was capable of doing the job better. Seeking to improve on the scarcity of the thing at hand still starts from scarcity, trying to lessen the grip of scarcity—trying to reduce scarcity—is not the same as accepting infinite abundance.

The enlightened-matter path certainly seems to be more productive and generative than the matter-only path. The consultancy where my friend works—heavily focused on financial outcomes—sees the need to develop its client relationships to ensure future income. A Guatemalan father told me about his son, who was already on the national soccer team. He told me about the team's coach, who spent lots of time on individual player capacity-development, clear that improving skills would lead to continued success on the field. Cooperation among team members at a global NGO I worked with certainly enhanced their capacity to deliver high-quality projects. In all these examples, I find that agreements formed on this path can achieve the middle circle of occasional abundance, but I have not found any of these examples that have achieved the outer circle of high harmonic vibrancy and abundance. Why? By starting from the matter-things perspective, an individual or group is starting with an assumption of scarcity, limiting the harmonic vibrancy they can experience. I will show this later in the book.

## THE GROUNDED-POTENTIAL PATH

The second path through all three levels of perceived reality starts at the light-possibility level. Starting at this level means starting with an assumption of infinite abundance. Light is the potential seen when envisioning possibilities. Motion-development starts the transformation of light energy into matter by shifting a particular possibility into a living probability. Thus, motion creates a special case of light as it filters out many possibilities to focus on realizing just one. In the same way, matter emerges as a special case of motion as time is filtered out to make a particular thing appear right here, right now. Thus, the grounded potential path involves choosing what to manifest from infinite possibility and then deciding when to stop development to bring forth a specific thing at a given space and time. This is the path that grounds the light, bringing it into motion-matter form.[48]

Let's return to the work example I described above with the Japanese writer I met. On the grounded-potential path she would start by asking a very different question. Instead of starting with, "Can I do the job better?" she would ask, "Who am I?" By pursuing this question, she finds she can uncover her deeper passion, her greater gifts. Maybe she sees that she has powerful stories to tell and wants to be a novelist. Seemingly, she has arrived at the same point as she did on the enlightened matter path—she is going to write a book. But her path is quite different. Once she chooses to be a novelist, she looks at the capacities she needs to develop over time, figuring out what to develop now and what to develop later. In this she is working at the motion-development level of perceived reality. She then looks at what she can do now, to have the experience of one outcome, knowing that in a while she will have different outcomes. This is the matter-thing level reality she chooses to manifest out of the motion-development of her light potential.

These are abundance-infused choices. In both cases, she is writing a book. On the enlightened-matter path, she arrived there as part of her job—a scarcity-minimizing search to improve the things level. On the grounded potential path, she lived into her passion—an abundance-maximizing exploration of the choices she could make. The first tried to expand from scarcity. The second brought abundance to life. This is a very different result, with completely different energy available to sustain it.

"Our universe is alive with sparks. We have at our fingertips an infinite capacity to light a spark of possibility. Passion, rather than fear, is the igniting force. Abundance, rather than scarcity, is the context...it is about playing together as partners in a field of light."[49]

## WHY THE PATH MATTERS

Each of the three paths started with different questions, followed different routes, and ended in very different outcomes. This is why the path matters. As the poet Ogden Nash said, in the book with the same title, "You can't get there

---

48    The very influential philosopher Alfred North Whitehead referred in Process and Reality (1929) to this becoming as the "creative advance into novelty" (Whitehead, 1978, p. 28).

49    In their practice of enrollment, which she uses in her therapy practice and he uses with his orchestra, the Zanders add practical steps to this quote: "Imagine that people are an invitation for enrollment. Stand ready to participate, willing to be moved and inspired. Offer that which lights you up. Have no doubt that others are eager to catch the spark" (Zander & Zander, 2002, p. 126).

from here."[50] If the destination is healthier outcomes and the journey is living the experience, then the path to living all three levels of perceived reality in all five primary relationships matters.

## SUMMARY: TWO PRINCIPLES FOR PERCEIVING THE REALITY OF ABUNDANCE

As we continued the exploration of what has emerged in my many conversations about the experiences of abundance-based agreements, we saw that embedded in the five relationships we described in Chapter 1, people described their experience of three levels of perceived reality (light, motion, and matter), when they show up, and when they do not. We described the experience of seeing the potential, the light, in the five relationships, calling this reality possibility. In this level, we saw infinite abundance in the visible future. We also described that along with this vision of possibility, we experienced being able to see the future results of that possibility: how it would show up. We called these outcomes that we could see in the future here-now "things" or matter. Finally, we also described the process we could see for moving from the possibility to the outcome. We called this motion, where we develop capacities and relationships, a path of development. Thus, we described the experience of three levels of reality: the potential we could see, the resulting outcomes, and the path for getting there over time.

We also described three pathways people take through these three levels of perceived reality. Some choose the "on-the-level" path, staying on one level. They tend to find emptiness in not manifesting anything. Possibility for the sake of possibility alone is as unfulfilling as development for development's sake or outcomes purely for the sake of outcomes. These are all examples of scarcity in many forms, as nothing of abundance manifested. Others we found started from possibility, seeing the future, the results they would obtain, and a path for getting there. On the "grounded potential" path, they started with infinite abundance in possibility and chose how to manifest it. Still others we found started from the reality of matter, of outcomes, and tried to add the development of capacities to manifest more things, invoking the possibilities of greater development. They found they were often able to expand their initial scarcity, but never to find abundance, as they started the "enlightened matter" path from scarcity.

From this exploration, we find two principles for perceiving the reality

---

50    For a book of Ogden Nash's poems, titled *You Can't Get There from Here*, see (Nash, 1953).

of abundance. First, it takes all three levels. We have two data points for this principle: what we have observed in the field and logic. In the field, through our survey, stories from many other observers, and our own visits, we find that in groups that experience abundance, all three levels are perceived as real. In groups experiencing scarcity, only one or two levels are present. Logically, this also makes sense. We experience scarcity in the things we have; some have them and others do not. We experience abundance in the possibilities we see; they are inexhaustibly everywhere. So, for abundance we start with possibility. To experience the outcomes, the things, they need to be developed over time. Thus, the three levels are all necessary to experience abundance.

The second principle is that the path matters. Since all three levels are necessary for abundance, staying on only one level of reality can only manifest scarcity. Likewise, starting with scarcity can only expand scarcity, not invite abundance. When moving from possibility to development to things, you start with the infinite abundance of potential and choose how and when it will come into being. This gives you choices all along the way. What possibilities are developed when, to produce what outcomes?

Within this experience of five relationships and three levels of perceived reality, we have the elements we need to see the agreements we want to choose, which leads us to the next topic, agreements.

# CHAPTER 3

# AGREEMENTS—CHOOSING YOUR EXPERIENCE

So far we have looked at the experiences of scarcity and abundance in your life, and it has been clear that you know the difference between these two experiences and that you prefer the one that is more abundant. We have also touched briefly on the role that agreements play in determining your experience. Now we want to focus our attention more fully on those agreements—how to see them clearly and how to see the choices you can make to influence them.

Perhaps you have noticed that in your more vibrant relationships, you experienced greater freedom to be yourself and to create the quality of relationship you want to have with others. This freedom to relate to yourself and others as fully and as vibrantly as you want—not as you assume you must—is a key part of the human experience of abundance. This is what learning to work with agreements is all about: gaining the freedom to choose your experiences so that more of your life is spent in abundance rather than scarcity.

## WHAT IS AN AGREEMENT?

If you experience some part of your day in scarcity, then you have agreed to play the game that is designed to give you that experience. Underlying all your experiences you will find what we might think of as "rules of the game"— guidelines that tell you and others how to act in various situations. I call these rules "agreements" for two reasons:

- First, all rules *are* agreements that some people, somewhere, at some time, and for some reason have made about how to interact with each other in a particular situation. In playing by these rules, you have agreed to them, whether or not you are aware of it.

- Second, I have found that naming these guidelines "agreements" is empowering. As long as you view the guidelines as "rules," you rarely think about changing them, but once you see that they are agreements, you begin to see the possibility of choice. You can choose what you agree with and what rules you are willing to play by, and in many cases you can play a role in shifting agreements to produce greater vibrancy and abundance.

The word agreement comes from the old French *agrément*, which means pleasing. It is defined as an arrangement between two or more persons as to a course of action; a mutual understanding; a covenant; concord; harmony. In other words, it is a social arrangement that people enter into willingly because they have had a hand in shaping it and it pleases them. The rules of the game do not seem like an agreement when we feel we have not had a say in creating them and, even more so, when we believe we have no choice but to follow them. The first step to empowerment is to see the choice in the agreement. You cannot see the choice if you cannot see the agreement in which the choice resides.

## RECOGNIZING AGREEMENTS—EXPERIENCE AND STRUCTURE

To see the agreements in your life, start with your experience. In Chapters 1 and 2 we explored the quality of your experiences in five fundamental relationships. As social arrangements, agreements are an integral part of these relationships. You know you are dealing with agreements when you experience yourself in one of these relationships. The quality of your experience—the feeling of scarcity or abundance it evokes—is an indication of how well or poorly the agreement is working for you.

Next, to see your options for choice in the agreement, look for the structure that supports it. Like the infrastructure in a building, this structure determines what substances (e.g., water, electricity, air, fuel, waste) flow in what direction for specific purposes (e.g., for washing, lighting, cooling, heating, cleaning). Unlike the built infrastructure, the structure supporting human agreements can be more readily changed. This structure of agreements has two parts: content and process. The content of an agreement consists of the rules that govern how you and others behave in the relationship, and the process is how those rules are established. In the house infrastructure example, the content is that clean water flows into the house and wastewater flows out. The process is the design and construction of the infrastructure, deciding what goes where. Sometimes the process by which the agreement is made is obvious, but often it is not, so we often participate in agreements without being aware of it.

Starting with an easy example, let us decide where we want to eat lunch today. We happen to be sitting in the middle of Madrid. There are options everywhere, and we both like to eat many different kinds of food. We can agree to go somewhere to eat seafood or Moroccan or tapas or Italian or Chinese or fast food. We find that we both like tapas and I know a café with great outdoor seating, which appeals to you. We are good to go! It is easy to see the agreement in this example because the relationship is direct—just you and me. The content is also obvious: (1) we want to eat (2) something interesting like tapas (3) in a nice, sunny place (4) together, (5) soon. The process for deciding is transparent, and we can both easily influence the decision. We both saw the five elements of content, we both suggested options, and we found an option that satisfied both of us. All of these things make it easy to recognize this as an agreement and add up to a positive experience of our relationship.

Keeping to the theme of eating, let's look at some agreements that are a little less obvious. Something we all do frequently is buy food. In doing so we agree to a certain price. In many cultures, the process for reaching this agreement is obvious: you shop in an open-air market and negotiate directly with the seller to determine a price for the fruit you want. Perhaps you convince her to give it to you for a little bit less because it is slightly overripe. Or you agree to buy a larger quantity and get a lower price per piece. Or you are willing to pay what she asks because you judge that her fruit is better than what the others are offering.

In contrast, there are many cultures in which you only buy food at a grocery store or supermarket. The price of the fruit is fixed, and the process of agreement is obscure. You do not know who sets the price, and there is no negotiation. You can reject this agreement. For example, you may decide not to buy fruit because it is too expensive, or you may go to another supermarket where the price might be lower. You might even organize or join a food co-op that allows buyers to have greater influence on the prices they pay by eliminating the supermarket as middleman. But if you buy the fruit in the supermarket, you implicitly accept the agreement.

In both these examples, the content of the agreement is the same: the desire for the fruit; the existence of fruit in conditions I will accept; and the price at which the exchange of money for fruit is made. Beyond that, there are

significant differences in the relationships involved and in the process part of
the agreement's structure. In the open-air market, the buyer and seller interact
directly as individuals, whereas in the supermarket the buyer is an individual
dealing with an anonymous group, the collective entity that owns and manages
the supermarket. In the open-air market, the process for establishing the price
is fairly close to what we followed in deciding on a restaurant for lunch: both
parties can influence the content and, by definition, accept it because it pleases
them. In the supermarket, the process is one-sided and not transparent. The
choice presented to the buyer is simply "take it or leave it."

These differences affect how easy or hard it is to recognize that we
are participating in an agreement. They also affect how we experience
the agreements. For example, you may find the one-to-one relationship of
bargaining for your fruit in an open-air market exhilarating and a source of
satisfying connection to another human being. And you may feel empowered
by having a say in setting the price. Someone else might be quite uncomfortable
and intimidated by that kind of interaction and prefer to pay exactly what the
vendor asks or avoid the market altogether. Some people feel oppressed by
the anonymity of large supermarket chains and their power to set prices for
necessities, you may not. The point is, when you experience scarcity, seeing the
agreements you are in is the first step toward seeing your choices for shifting
that experience.

## SOME AGREEMENTS ARE EASIER TO SEE, SOME ARE HARDER TO SEE

In general, I find that the agreements that have a structure similar to
the supermarket exchange are the ones that are the most difficult to see as
agreements. They are also the ones that tend to produce experiences of
scarcity. We often find these circumstances when dealing with larger groups of
people, like a company, a town or city, a national government, or even global
society. In most companies, I am hired to do a job, with nobody asking me
whether I want the company to do something else or to do it another way. No
agreement there, just compliance if I want a paycheck. In the town I live in,
the government has established rules and laws for what I have to do, like pay
local taxes, pay for recycling and check books out of the library. When I drive
around town or across the country, I drive under specified speed limits. When
I travel, no matter what country I am in, I am not allowed to take more than
three ounces of liquid in a bottle through airport security.

While I might agree with the rules at all of these different levels, I was not part of setting them and the people who did set them are unknown to me. No one asked me if I agreed to the rules or what would need to shift so that I could agree. In short, they do not obviously seem like agreements, and they do not contribute to the vibrancy in my life.

Other circumstances, in which it seems easier to see agreements, are those in which the relationships are personal and direct. The process of agreement tends to be transparent, and our opportunities for influencing the content of the agreement are greater. These are the situations when we are making agreements with ourselves, with other individuals or with small groups of people. For example, I might agree with myself that I want to eat a certain kind of diet, exercise daily and treat my friends more nicely. My proposed course of action is the content of this agreement, and the structure is as transparent and as open to my influence as possible.

Similarly, in small groups such as a family or a small unit at work, it can be relatively easy to have a process of agreement that is direct and transparent. In these settings, there are endless situations requiring agreements: about what we will do and how we will interact over time to do it; and about how we talk to each other and how we will treat each other. Some families and teams will even agree about how to agree: will we ask one person to develop the content for us? Will we try to reach consensus? How long will we spend on the decision? In the best cases, agreements in these small group settings adhere closely to their definition as mutual arrangements as to a course of action, and that mutuality makes them a source of experiences of vibrancy and abundance. The capacity to make agreements in this way is an attribute of healthy families and high-functioning teams.

To be sure, there are often power differences between partners, between parents and children, and within work groups, and power can be exercised in ways that push the agreement process towards rule setting. Relationships can collapse when some members of the group break the agreement. I can get frustrated and angry with myself if I break my agreements on healthy habits. There are many possible scenarios for dysfunction to arise. Nevertheless, compared to dealing with large, anonymous groups, it is far easier in these relatively intimate situations to recognize that we are dealing with agreements: easier to experience the relationship; easier to see the structure of the agreement; and easier to influence or change it.

Another common type of agreement is one that we deal with regularly yet often fail to recognize as an agreement: custom. Custom is an understanding, often unspoken, about how we will act in a certain situation. Some customs have emerged organically from shared experience, for example, in some cultures, waiting in lines for access to goods or services on a "first come-first served" basis. Others were perhaps established by agreement long ago, but the process of agreement is long forgotten while the content remains as "just the way things are done around here." This is the situation in many organizational cultures, for example, regarding how work gets done or how people communicate with each other.

Working with this kind of agreement can be confusing. For example, when someone cuts in front of me in a line, there are no clear-cut guidelines for how I should respond. If the way things are done around here is making it difficult for me to do my work or communicate effectively in my organization, there may be no apparent way for me to change things. Yet, in these situations, recognizing that in following a custom we are adhering to an agreement, is perhaps the only way to initiate a new agreement process to evaluate and possibly change those parts of the custom that are not working for us.

## CUES FOR SEEING AGREEMENTS MORE CLEARLY

As someone who has studied agreements extensively and, like everyone else, participated in agreements my whole life, I have come to realize that agreements are hard to see:

- When we are unaware that we are in an agreement
- When we do not see the judgments about values and facts that inform the structure of the agreement
- When we do not see how the different perspectives of the people participating in the agreement influence each other

My understanding of these three dimensions of seeing agreements draws on three fields of study—social psychology, decision science, and systems theory. Each of these, in its own way, offers essential insight into the problem of how to recognize the nature of our agreements and to determine our choices within them. These insights have enabled me to appreciate the role of agreements in human relationships and to understand how to work with them more effectively.

### SOCIAL PSYCHOLOGY

In the field of social psychology, the research of Ellen Langer showed me that the greatest obstacle to seeing the agreements we are enmeshed in is the mindlessness with which we go about living our lives most of the time.[51] In contrast, when we are mindful, we are paying attention and open to new information and to new ways of seeing things. We are no longer on autopilot and, most important, we can begin to see possibilities for changing our behavior and the qualities of our experience.

Many people assume mindfulness can only be the fruit of deep meditation and years of practice. Yet Langer and the researchers in her lab have shown through hundreds of experiments how easy it is to increase people's mindfulness with simple instructions, such as asking them to notice different perspectives or take in new information. I have applied Langer's approach to mindfulness in my own life and my work with others, as I will describe in later sections of this book. I have found it to be a simple yet reliable process for bringing the power of attention to the experiences we are having and thereby unlocking awareness of the agreements that are shaping that experience.

## DECISION SCIENCES

My work with the decision sciences is what enabled me to appreciate the challenges we face in fully grasping the content of the agreements we are party to. An interdisciplinary field, the decision sciences emerged in the middle of the 20th century.[52] It brings a great deal of accumulated wisdom to bear on the question of how people make decisions, with the aim of helping them make better decisions. The decision sciences do this by integrating the knowledge base and research techniques of diverse fields.

For example, psychologists and sociologists look at how people actually make decisions, either individually or in groups. To do this, sociologists may study the cultures of groups and the decision-making processes that evolve within them, while psychologists devise experiments to discover what decision rules individual people use and the biases that influence their thinking. Economists, on the other hand, study how people *should* make decisions; developing rational rules and mathematical models that optimize the outcomes for a given set of values. Engineers in this field also develop highly analytic processes for determining the best way to make decisions, for example, by

---

51    Through hundreds of experiments, Ellen Langer and her colleagues have demonstrated the general level of mindlessness, the ease with which it can be substituted with mindfulness, and the impact this mindlessness has on one's experience of agreements (E. Langer & Piper, 1987; E. J. Langer, 1989).

52    For a thorough overview of the many perspectives within the decision sciences, see (Kleindorfer, Kunreuther, & Schoemaker, 1993).

creating decision trees that incorporate different decision options under different risk assumptions. A great deal of understanding has emerged from such efforts to pursue common questions and learn from each other's findings.

The most important thing that decision theory taught me about agreements is the critical role of values in shaping their content. Two leading decision scientists, Herbert Simon and Ralph Keeney, showed that all decisions, including those that create agreements, contain judgments about values and about facts. These are the two fundamental elements of the content of an agreement. People's values reside in the desired future they envision as the outcome of the agreement. The facts of the agreement are simply how it will work.[53] Most people fail to separate these two elements and to look for the underlying values. Instead, they focus on what is said and on trying to determine if statements are true or false. As a result, people tend to make incorrect judgments about the values in an agreement, both their own values and those of others. The decision theorist knows that everyone has these incorrect judgments and that it is important to draw them out so that a more accurate reading of values can emerge and groups can begin to see where they can be in alignment. What to the untrained eye might look like conflicting opinions about what to do, to the decision theorist are simply different perspectives on what is important. From this viewpoint, an agreement can be much more achievable.[54]

## SYSTEMS THEORY

From systems theory, I learned how difficult it is for most people to see the interrelated dynamics of agreements and their consequences for future agreements. Systems theory was developed in the middle of the 20th century, bringing together insights into systems that were emerging in fields as diverse as biology, cybernetics, electrical engineering, information systems, and psychology. One of the founders of systems theory, Ludwig von Bertalanffy noticed that the observations of systems in these different fields of inquiry were, separately, pointing to common characteristics of systems: the relationships among a set of individual elements, which define the set; the dynamics in that set of relationships; and the feedback systems these relationship dynamics

---

53    Among many decision theorists who have worked with value judgments in decision making, I recommend starting with the work of Herbert Simon (Simon, 1997) and Ralph Kenney (Keeney, 1992).  Herbert Simon was awarded the 1978 Nobel Prize in Economics for his work in decision-making.

54    For descriptions of value and factual judgments and how to work with them, see (Hammond, 1996).

created. Once he pointed this out and named the emerging insights "Systems Theory," the new field coalesced and developed rapidly.

As the field advanced, researchers such as John Sterman at MIT showed that even people trained to think in complex forms struggle with understanding the dynamics of systems. We should not be surprised, therefore, that we find it difficult to see the systemic aspects of our agreements. For example, one reason people find it difficult to identify how to influence a system of agreements towards their desired ends is that the behavior of social systems is often counterintuitive.[55] Sterman's mentor, Jay Forrester, showed that this is due to the recursive nature of agreements—what I decide today often influences my ability or inclination to make that same decision in the future. These system dynamics form networks of interrelated feedback loops of agreements, which rapidly become far too complex for human beings to process accurately. To counter this difficulty, Forrester and colleagues designed "systems thinking" tools that make it easier to see the patterns in this complexity.

As many of the stories in this book will illustrate, when I work with groups, I often use systems thinking tools to help them see their agreements more clearly. Basically, systems thinking involves paying attention to the whole of something. It does this by focusing more on the relationships among the parts than on the parts themselves. This focus is especially useful in helping people to see how the problems they are facing are often the unintended consequences of past decisions and actions. These decisions were rational responses to conditions at the time, yet did not take into account the cause-and-effect aspect of relationships within the system. This perspective often provides the key to seeing the choices available to shift agreements that are not working.

## SEEING THE CHOICE TO BE MADE

In both the agreements that are easier to see and those that are harder to see, awareness that they are all agreements helps us see the choice in the content and process of the agreement. There is always a choice. Once you see that, then you can choose how you agree to the content and process in the agreement. You can choose to accept the agreement as it is or to initiate a shift

---

55    Sterman provides both experimental data about the difficulty of understanding dynamic complexity (Sterman, 1989a, 1989b, 1994; Sterman & Booth Sweeney, 2002) and an encyclopedic overview of the field of system dynamics (Sterman, 2000). Forrester summarized many of his deep insights into the difficulty of understanding the system dynamics of agreements in (Forrester, 1971).

in the agreement. I suggest that you *experience* a shift in either case.

When you choose to remain in an agreement as it already is, you are entering it consciously, much more aware of the limitations and opportunities available within the agreement. This is a very different experience from staying with an existing agreement unconscious of the possibilities within it. Alternatively, when you choose to work towards a new agreement, you experience both that shift in awareness and a shift in what is possible in the new agreements. In both cases, you enter differently, and what is possible is different. A few examples of shifted agreements will make it easier to see these two cases and how to make the shift.

## A PERSONAL SHIFT

Various times a day, every day, people in my home eat. In eating they dirty dishes, which need to be cleaned. Few volunteers seem to show up for the task of cleaning the dirty dishes. Since it bothered me least of the regular tasks at hand in the home, I usually took it up, though often begrudgingly. This was my experience of dishwashing, and it was primarily a negative one until the day I realized it was part of an agreement. Then I experienced choices—a choice in how I viewed the content of the agreement and also in how I could enter the agreement (the process).

Focused unconsciously on the things-matter level of reality—the stack of dirty dishes that needed to go away—I had mindlessly suffered through the low vibrancy of work done unwillingly. My family had also suffered, experiencing my negativity. Not only was I often grumpy about doing the dishes, I got annoyed at the kids for not doing the dishes, or for saying they would do them and then putting it off so the dishes were not done when I wanted them done, or even for eating and making the dishes dirty in the first place! My judgment about my family's values was that they were not valuing my doing the work of washing the dishes or the clean kitchen I had produced.

When I looked at this experience more mindfully, however, I saw that there was a larger, on-going process that the whole family joined in: preparing food, eating it, and cleaning up for the next time. This was an agreement we made, an agreement I had entered unconsciously and with a scarcity-based view of the dirty dishes. When I became mindful of the content of the agreement, I realized that I enjoyed the food preparation and nourishment parts, especially when we entered them with joy and creativity. My awareness allowed me to see the larger experience and the parts of it that I valued more than dishwashing. I could see that my children also enjoyed our meals and my wife, in particular, wanted to create something beautiful as well as healthy when she cooked. I also noticed that it was easier to enter this process with joy and creativity when we started with a clean workplace, including work surfaces, cooking tools and dishes.

In short, I began to have a sense of the system and the values at play within it. Seeing this I then saw a potential shift in my approach. From seeing myself as washing dirty dishes, I experienced a shift to seeing my role as something similar to preparing the canvas for the next creative work of art. This shift made it a joy for me to wash the dishes, as I was clearing the creative space of the kitchen for the next great cooking and eating experience. I began to anticipate this desirable experience while cleaning. These were my choices. I could choose to continue the experience of begrudgingly washing the dishes and feeling resentful of others, or of excitedly preparing a clean canvas. I could choose to see the content of the activity as dirty dishes or as not-yet prepared canvas.

The process of this shift was easy to make—no one in my family opposed my cleaning the dishes or having a clean kitchen to work in. On the contrary, as often happens, those closest to me enabled me to see my experience clearly and identify possibilities within it. Their reactions and mine helped me experience the scarcity in the earlier agreements, and they helped me choose a new agreement. As a result, I was able to shift from the things-matter level of the dirty dishes, to a development-motion-level focus on creating the conditions for a future process of food preparation, and a possibility-light-level focus on maximizing the potential in the next meal. While a relatively simple agreement, one I made primarily with myself, it is one that influenced many hours of my week and my mood during those hours.

In this example, I experienced the inner circle (of the 3-circle diagram in Figure 7) of scarcity in the five relationships. I applied mindfulness to this experience and was able to see the structure of the system and the underlying values in the agreement (the content) and how to shift it (the process). And while I engaged in the agreement with others, I had the autonomy to make the shift, while those who benefitted readily agreed. The next three examples of shifts in agreements add the complexity of a group of people working together—in a government agency, a large company, and a small company. With these examples, I address a question I often get, "Does Ecosynomics only apply to me as an individual? Does shifting agreements also work for a group, an organization, a community, or a nation?" The short answer is, yes: so far it seems that these principles apply at all levels. The stories in this and later chapters will show how.

## A TEAM SHIFT

Some years ago, I was asked to work with a high-level group within a large agency of the government of the United States. The senior executive who hired me asked me to help her group see how to reach the high standard of performance it had set for itself. The group had formed just 18 months earlier with a mission to establish a new service area to support other government departments working in the field. The need for this support was urgent, so there was intense pressure on the group to get up and running quickly without sacrificing the quality of the service they provided. From the moment of start-up, they had raced to fulfill a demanding workload with an ethos of "do your best, fast!" For the first 15 months, they had met the challenge. The group had grown quickly to over 150 people and, in terms of meeting the needs of its customers, had exceeded the high expectations set for it. Over the past three months, however, it had started to miss milestones, drop balls, and lose key personnel.

The team I worked with included a dozen of the senior leaders of this group. They were feeling stuck in the experience that something was no longer working. No matter how hard they had pushed, the experience had worsened. They were clear that this was not the experience they wanted.

To increase awareness of the agreements and to begin a discussion of the underlying values, we started by talking to each of the team members individually about the purpose of the group and his or her role in it. We were not surprised to find twelve different versions of why the group's work was valuable and what value each individual was contributing. Our feedback to the team showed this diversity of perspectives. It was not difficult for them to see that, at the highest level, they were in alignment on the group's purpose—to serve their country by helping others more effectively fulfill critical assignments in the field. When they got back to this sense of agreement on the underlying value, they could also get back to the specifics of the content of their agreement, namely, their original understanding of what was essential for each member of the leadership team and each sub-unit of the larger group to contribute.

In essence, the leadership team began to see that the group had fallen into an uncooperative mode of working, even though everyone knew that cooperation was essential for success. Everyone in the group had been selected because they were both highly skilled and high achievers. This was appropriate to an important project with challenging goals and a tight schedule. Yet, with all the pressure to produce results quickly, the group had unconsciously adopted a perspective on these capacities that was stuck at the things-matter level. They focused exclusively on utilizing the capacities at hand to deal with the demands on hand. The leadership team saw that this focus had led to an ethos of hand-offs: I will do the best with my hands, and then hand it off to you to do with yours. This was the usual way of working, and they had reverted to it without thinking or talking about it. It had worked for a while, but eventually the group was unable to meet the increasing demands placed on it.

When the group leaders saw how they had implicitly entered the agreement to operate in the traditional way, without considering the potential negative consequences, they realized that they had choices. They could choose to proceed with greater mindfulness, to be more aware of the values guiding individuals and groups within the system, and to pay attention to how group interactions were evolving as their work proceeded. This realization enabled them to enter a new agreement. This involved explicitly deciding to bring more of a development-motion perspective into their approach to managing the group's collective capacities. They agreed that the way each individual and sub-unit understood its particular role in the initiative would expand to include accountability for the success of the whole and not just its own part. They also agreed to treat each problem that arose—in a relationship or in a handoff that was not working—as a systemic issue, to be shared with and addressed by the whole group, because everyone was ultimately responsible for success.

This shift was fairly easy for the leadership team to make, partly because it was still relatively new and still in the mentality of start-up mode. They were motivated to change because they were living through the negative consequences of the scarcity-based, things-matter level agreements they had accepted. It was not difficult to engage the group as a whole in the shift because everyone wanted to perform at a higher level, and their customers wanted the better service they were trying to provide. Months later they told me that whenever they experienced a potential blockage in their agreements, inevitably someone would ask, "What would the agreement guy do?" They said this reminder helped them be more mindful of the systemic structure of their agreements, connect to the underlying values, and identify the choices available to them.

This story shows that a small group within a large agency can apply the same process as I did in seeing the agreements in washing dishes. In this case, the leader hired me to help her group see the content and process of the old agreements and choose new agreements. I used a common consultant's approach of interviewing people individually, then providing feedback to the group as a whole so they could see the system and values more clearly.

Whether you use an objective outsider or engage the questions yourself, the same process applies:

- Apply mindfulness to an experience of scarcity
- Determine the structure of the system—this is the content of the agreement
- Determine the values that inform the content of the agreement
- See where different choices are available to shift the agreement

## A LARGE COMPANY SHIFT

Often after hearing the personal story or the team story, someone will say, "Sure it works for an individual and a small group, but not for a large company." Here is an example of the same process in a large company. In the late 1990's, I worked with the engine-assembly team in a large capital equipment manufacturing company.[56] They were in a bind. For many years, their industry had been in decline, with fewer and fewer requests for their engines. Then within just a few months everything seemed to turn around and they experienced a massive growth in orders. While increased demand was a good thing—after all it represented growth of the business and more income—they had found they were not able to produce engines fast enough to meet it. This was a very bad thing, because there were significant penalties for failing to deliver the promised engines on time. The company's customers were unhappy, and the increased sales were not producing an increase in profits. Corporate executives did not like this experience of scarcity.

The company asked me to help answer the question of why this global industry leader was in the embarrassing position of not being able to meet the increase in orders for a key product. My team and I set out to understand the systemic relationships that determined how things got done in the company, as well as the values underlying key agreements. Because it was a big, old company, this involved talking to quite a few people and taking a long-term view. Yet, as it turned out, the dynamics of the system creating the company's problem were relatively simple. As we talked to people in different parts of the organization, the story emerged pretty clearly.

Since its founding in the late 19th century, the company's intense focus on efficiency had led it to push for greater and greater specialization, to the point that the organization was now divided into multiple stand-alone businesses. This meant that Sales and Assembly were each separately responsible for

---

56　The value and systems mapping of this capital equipment manufacturing case is detailed in (Ritchie-Dunham & Rabbino, 2001).

producing a profit, i.e. for creating revenue that exceeded costs. In lean times, like the previous decade, this had helped the company squeak out every possible efficiency. But when the economy improved and orders increased, it had had the unintended consequence of creating a systemic barrier to growth—lack of cooperation between Sales and Assembly. Since Assembly had been able to keep up with the orders Sales generated, neither unit had seen the need to take on the cost of an investment in the human resources and information systems needed to maintain an interface between them. They were both operating according to the same values: keep costs to a minimum to maximize efficiency and grow the bottom line, but as a result, the sales business was selling engines under delivery conditions that the assembly business could not meet.

When my colleagues and I brought this pattern to the attention of senior leadership as a systemic issue, the response was startling. The head of Sales immediately acknowledged his contribution to the company's problem. "The way we operate among the businesses today is an agreement we made in the past. The company pays me to sell, so I do. I know that I am making life more difficult for you in the assembly business, but that is not my responsibility. I am paid to sell. That is our agreement. We could shift the agreement, so that I sell only under conditions that you can deliver, while working with you to increase what you can deliver. But it would require investments in both of our businesses. That would be a new agreement." In the process of forming a new agreement, it became clear that the previous agreement had been founded on a things-matter perspective, which had produced an overwhelming concern with scarcity of resources, expressed in the drive for efficiency, and a static view of the capacities of each group. From this perspective, it had been impossible for company executives to see how to fix their problem. The new agreement involved a shift toward opening more to the potential for greater abundance (i.e., growth) and more of a development-motion level focus on the relationships among the different business areas, this included investing in capacities to create more interaction and monitor how outcomes changed over time.

Clearly, the greater size and (often) longer history of a large company can increase the difficulty of seeing agreements and their consequences. This is especially true in the current environment, in which so many large companies are operating with the high degree of functional specialization of the manufacturer in this example. In many cases, this is made even more extreme by the outsourcing of functions to different regions of the world. The scope of the task of mapping the system and its underlying values, showing how they are determining undesired outcomes and supporting the conversations necessary to work with this information will therefore likely require the assistance of someone who is trained to do this kind of work. Yet many teams of consultants and facilitators have the necessary skills, and the basic process I have outlined for seeing and shifting agreements remains the same even in this more complicated situation.

## A SMALL COMPANY SHIFT: A SPECIAL CASE

The third example of a group working with agreements comes from THORLO, a sock manufacturer based in Statesville, North Carolina, USA. I will be sharing a number of stories about THORLO in this book. This company is important to me because it presents a special case of work with Ecosynomics principles, a case in which people are explicitly using the concepts and tools, and trying to operate consistently in the outer circle of harmonic vibrancy.

When I was first invited to work with THORLO, in the summer of 2004, I thought my contribution would be as a systems-thinking expert. I saw quickly that, from a business-outcomes perspective, the company was very successful—reliably profitable, with loyal consumers, happy employees, and sustainable success in their industry niche. In Ecosynomics terminology, it was clearly excellent at delivering things-matter level outcomes. Strong structures and processes for functioning at the development-motion level supported this performance, such as deep trust in relationships throughout the company, dedication to continuous improvement and mastery at all levels, cooperation across all departments, and transparency in information sharing company-wide. It seemed THORLO would be the perfect place for my strategic systems-thinking expertise.

As I met more and more people in the company, however, I realized that these folks were also operating at the possibility-light level. No matter where I went in the company, I continuously heard stories about experiences I would describe as higher levels of harmonic vibrancy. For example, creative possibility was supported at all levels and in all areas of the business, such as when a couple of consumer service representatives teamed up with research and development to respond to a consumer request for a special sock for a child who had lost most of his foot.

These kinds of experiences had attracted employees and customers to THORLO and kept them loyally attached over many years. They were definitely about much more than a job or a sock, but what exactly was the company's leadership doing to create these experiences? To THORLO's CEO, Jim Throneburg, it seemed that whatever they were doing was largely unconscious. It soon appeared that my role would be to support them in seeing and understanding their competencies more fully so they could ensure these competencies would be sustained and further developed by succeeding generations of company leaders. Nine years later, I am still participating in that developmental work. I have become part of the leadership team at THORLO, and my colleagues there have become my partners in developing Ecosynomics from the ideas and practices I brought with me in 2004 into the specific framework and tools presented in this book. The company has been and continues to be my most valuable learning laboratory.

The example of working with agreements that I will share here is especially significant because it involves agreements around performance evaluation and compensation. This is an area that virtually every work organization struggles with. For most people, I am sure; the idea that a compensation review could be a high-vibrancy experience seems unthinkable. That was how the leadership team at THORLO viewed it until recently.

A few years ago, I began to work with members of the human resources group. This group felt great about relationships within the company on most dimensions. Going back many decades, the people who worked at THORLO felt it was like their family, a very healthy place for them to show up every day. The experiences around compensation review did not fit this pattern, however. It was the one area of interaction where hierarchy remained strong. This was a tough nut to crack with very little helpful advice available from the human resources field outside of the company. Yet, it was a nut everyone wanted to crack, as it was out of alignment with the rest of the culture and daily experience at THORLO.

These negative experiences of the compensation review process became more intense as the company moved through a large-scale change process aimed at making generative, collaborative conversations standard practice at all levels of the organization (described in Chapter 10). The leadership team was, quite explicitly, examining the agreements in place around conversations and looking for opportunities to create different agreements that would bring greater vibrancy into their daily interactions. When members of the human resources team brought the compensation review problem into this process, everyone saw the possibility of making a shift in this area.

When they looked at it from the perspective of their ongoing work with Ecosynomics, THORLO leaders saw that the compensation review was a scarcity-based interaction that assumed that employees care only about how much they are to be paid, as if that were the only value they derived from working in the company. Similarly, in compensation conversations, the company framed its relationship to employees strictly at the things-matter level, focusing on an individual's job, the tasks involved in the job, and that individual's current capacities for doing the job. All of this was at odds with the day-to-day reality of relationships at THORLO. What the leadership team then saw was that the agreements around compensation had evolved to meet changing legal criteria that were part of best practice within the human resources field. In other words, the values underlying those agreements were purely legal and contractual, not at all reflective of the decades-old emphasis on sustainable relationships that prevailed at THORLO.

To bring in more abundance to the agreement, the leadership team determined it could change the compensation review from a strictly things-matter level, compensation-for-task, conversation toward a "role growth compensation" conversation including more of the development-motion level perspective.[57] This conversation with each employee focused on the growth she saw in herself, the growth she wanted to see, the value she perceived from that growth and from participation in the community, and how compensation fit into that bigger picture. The leaders reported great relief in this shift, as everyone enjoyed the role growth compensation conversation, which fit much better in the culture.

Let us see some examples of how this works. Each conversation begins with the reviewer and reviewee together restating her own values, reflecting on the reviewee's performance in her role over the past year, and describing comments from her colleagues in different departments about her role and growth. In one case, this led to an inquiry about what she most valued in her role, whether she saw another or deeper role for herself, and what she thought would create more value in her experience. At the conclusion, both agreed that she was on track, strengthening her current level of mastery, and that she would receive some specific training and a pay increase.

In another case, an engineer had been asked earlier in the year to take on a different and much more expansive leadership role. Though reluctant to take this on, he had agreed to do so for the health of the company. The role growth compensation conversation therefore focused on clarifying the new area of responsibilities he had taken on, and the outcome was that, based on this clarification, THORLO's HR group would do market research to determine a fair-market salary for his new, expanded position. Other conversations have led to reviewees identifying new opportunities for themselves, usually within THORLO, occasionally outside. Of course, not all conversations lead

---

57    The Journal of Accountancy interviewed THORLO president Richard Oliver about the role growth compensation conversation (Amato, 2013).

to advancement and higher pay. In a case in which it was clear to all that the reviewee had repeatedly not met the expectations he had set for himself with his team and team leaders, everyone agreed he was not trying to improve, and he left the company.

In every case, however, the role growth compensation conversation is fundamentally about the experience the employee is having in the process of making his or her unique contribution within the company. Is he experiencing growth in that role? Does her performance and growth meet the agreements she has made? What can be done to support further growth? Does his current role continue to be the biggest contribution he can make to the company? With these kinds of conversations ongoing, THORLO's leadership team could begin to feel it had brought its compensation review process in line with the standards it had established in other aspects of the company's culture.

## CONCLUSION

Quite simply, agreements guide human interactions at all levels. In these examples, from an individual washing dishes, a small group, a small company, to a large company, or a large agency, you can see how people experience scarcity in relationships, see the choice, and make a different choice of agreements. Sometimes it is necessary to have the help of outsiders with skills in analyzing systems and facilitating conversations. But in many cases you and your colleagues or family members can shift agreements by becoming more mindful of the quality of your experiences, exploring the system that is operating and the values underlying it, and seeing where opportunities exist to make positive changes. In the chapters to follow, we will continue to expand our view of how agreements shape our experiences on a daily basis and build the toolkit for working with them to bring more abundance and harmonic vibrancy into our lives.

**PART II**

# ECOSYNOMICS AND ECONOMICS: LENSES FOR SEEING AGREEMENTS

# CHAPTER 4

# ECONOMICS AND THE PARADOX OF SCARCITY

*Abstraction, difficult as it is, is the source of practical power.*[58]

It can be difficult to see the agreements in all of your interactions. A simple, robust structure can make this easier. It needs to be simple, so that you can apply it intuitively in every relationship and circumstance. It needs to be robust, so that you know you are considering the most important and relevant elements every time. For this I will first need to abstract some key elements from all agreements. With these few elements, you will be able to see the agreements more clearly and how to choose them. This is practical power.

In Part I, we looked in depth at the basic principles of Ecosynomics. I showed you how these principles derive from life experiences that we all have and that they simply express the knowledge we have gained from those experiences about what makes a vibrant, abundant life. I also pointed out that when we experience scarcity and low vibrancy it is because, often without being aware of it, we have agreed to the relationships that produce these states. This is good news! It means that, once we have seen how our current agreements produce scarcity, we can begin to figure out how to move out of them and toward different agreements. We can choose agreements that will transform our relationships and allow us to attain the high quality of life experience we sometimes have and want more of.

In Part II, I want to show you how the Ecosynomics perspective—plus some key concepts from economics—can help you see how to do this. In this

58    Quote from (B. Russell, 1969, p. 144).

chapter, I will focus on the way economic thinking pervades our agreements, from those that shape the minutiae of our daily lives to those that determine the political-economic systems of nation states. In Chapter 5, I will introduce you to a framework for seeing current agreements more clearly and—more important—seeing opportunities to shift them toward greater abundance and harmonic vibrancy. In the final chapter of this section, Chapter 6, I will show how this framework becomes a powerful tool for seeing agreements—the Agreement Map. The Agreement Map enables us to perceive, through analysis of concrete actions, the nature of the agreements underlying and guiding those actions. This is the first step toward seeing where we have choices that can lead us toward more satisfying agreements.

## AN ECOSYNOMICS PERSPECTIVE ON ECONOMICS

Human beings in the 21st century may argue over which economic system—which specific rules of the game—we prefer to live under. Yet the reality is that political economics, broadly defined, sets *all* the rules. It is the pervasive body of thought today. Because it is so pervasive and has been for centuries, we tend to take economists' assumptions about reality as just the way things are, not something that can be challenged or changed, except in the details. Our first step will be to examine those assumptions.

Of all the social sciences, economics—or political economy, as this subject was originally called—is the most pervasive in its influence on the agreements that shape our lives. For example, governments rely heavily on the expert opinions of economists for policymaking in basic areas like taxation, spending and the rules that govern business activity. Economists also guide the activities of the central banks that manage national currencies and the regulation of national and international banking systems. Economic theories and research shape the way business executives think about fundamental issues such as markets, competition and business strategy. Rules, policies and decisions based on political economic principles determine the price you pay for a banana or a can of beans at the local grocery store or a meal at your favorite restaurant, the interest rate on your car loan, the quarterly earnings growth expected of your company, the value of the currency in your wallet, the conditions in the employment contract you sign at work, why some have money and others do not, how ownership of land and buildings is determined, and where a nation invests its money, whether in education, agriculture, infrastructure, or defense.

At a more general level, different economic theories provide the foundation for competing visions of government's proper role in society.

When we see labels like "capitalist," "socialist" and "communist" used in contests between political parties or in discussions of international affairs, or in our history books, we are being invited to make distinctions among political ideologies. But the differences among them are rooted in economics. In short, the influence of economics is all around us, shaping our lives for better and worse. Ecosynomics encourages us to question how this influence affects the abundance we are experiencing.

As we consider this question, it can be helpful to remember that economics is a field of study just like sociology, social psychology, political science and history. Each of these fields focuses on understanding a particular aspect of human society. In the case of economics, the focus is on material wellbeing and how the actions of individuals, organizations and governments contribute to securing it. It is also helpful to recognize that economic thinking has evolved within the context of the larger evolution of human society. In other words, it has a history. Understanding that history, at least in broad strokes, can offer valuable perspective.

## THE EMERGENCE OF ECONOMICS IN HISTORICAL CONTEXT

Economics as we know it originated as the product of a particular region and its particular history. Writings from ancient Babylonia, India and China, as well as the Hebrew Bible, the work of Greek philosophers and religious texts of the medieval era all addressed many issues that we would consider to be questions of economics. They are important precursors to economics. However, the formal discipline of economic study did not emerge in any of those times or places. It arose instead in Western Europe in response to the momentous changes in European society that occurred roughly from the 16th century through the 19th century. During this period, the feudalism of the medieval era gradually gave way to the rise of a market economy and the emergence of capitalism, industrialization, and the beginnings of a modern political and social order.[59]

The powerful forces shaping and unleashed by these changes inevitably affected how the people who were thinking about economic issues approached their topic. In the feudal era, there were markets, where goods such as food, spices, cloth, livestock and slaves were bought and sold, but there were no markets for labor, land or capital. Labor was the lifetime obligation of slaves

---

59    The overview presented in this section of the rise of capitalism and emergence of economics as a field is based on Alessandro Roncaglia (Roncaglia, 2006, pp. 18-23) and Robert L. Heilbroner and William Milberg (Heilbroner & Milberg, 2002, pp. 36-58).

or serfs to their owners or feudal lords. Land was territory to be conquered or ruled over, and wealth was the reward that came to those who conquered or ruled. By the 17th century, however, the discovery and colonization of America and the establishment of trade routes around the horn of Africa had created a merchant class whose wealth was not tied to land or objects but was money that could be used to launch new enterprises and build greater wealth, as well as to buy goods and services. The flood of new wealth and new enterprise unleashed by this "merchant capitalism" brought economic opportunity as well as painful dislocation for the individuals who lived through the period.

For example, in England, where the process moved faster than in other parts of Europe, thousands of peasants were displaced from land their families had farmed for generations so that the lords who owned the estates could enclose their fields and raise sheep for the emerging wool market. Land became a privately owned asset to be developed for the benefit of the owner. Rural people forced from their homes to look for employment in cities and towns were now free to work for any employer who would pay them. They and their work became "labor." Monetary wealth became capital, which could be invested in, say, expanding artisanal production to meet the demands of a growing urban population. In this way, the so-called factors of production—land, labor and capital—emerged in their modern form and became a central preoccupation of economic thinking.

More fundamentally, these changes transformed a system of stable economic relationships based on a tradition of top-down control into one that was dynamic and impersonal, with individual economic freedom at its core. The discipline of economics, as it began to take shape in the 17th century, reflected this fundamental change. In the words of historian Alessandro Roncaglia, "the philosophers of antiquity and theologians of the Middle Ages considered it their task . . . to provide advice on morally acceptable behavior in the field of economic relations." In contrast, Roncaglia says, political economists thinking about society in the context of emerging capitalism focused their attention on the "scientific issue" of how multitudes of actions by self-interested individuals could create an effectively functioning economy that would provide for society's material needs.[60]

This very basic history of the emergence of economics helps to explain the nature of its influence on the agreements we find ourselves working with in so many areas of our lives. The formative preoccupation of economics with the dynamics of a market economy gave the discipline—from an Ecosynomics

---

60    All quotes in this paragraph from (Roncaglia, 2006, p. 19).

perspective—an overly narrow focus on the self-interested individual as the key actor in creating the material wellbeing of society. We see this in its purest form in the seminal work of Adam Smith, perhaps the most well known work of economics: *The Wealth of Nations*, published in 1776. Smith showed how competition in a free market economy serves to channel, as if by an "invisible hand," the self-serving actions of individuals into positive economic outcomes for society as a whole. As we shall see later in this chapter, there have been challenges to this narrow focus on the individual. Yet Smith's exaltation of the individual was the basis of so-called classical economics and, especially in the United States, remains alive and influential today in neoclassical or "neoliberal" economics.

A second defining aspect of economics rooted in the history of its evolution is its central concern with material welfare, which means that it confines itself to the things-matter level of perceived reality. This, we have seen in previous chapters, is the realm of the concrete, the here-and-now. And it is the realm of scarcity. Now, working effectively with the concrete is important, and economics has given us an abundance of valuable knowledge about how to do this. Yet the idea of scarcity has taken on a life of its own within the discipline, to the point where it has become a fundamental assumption that scarcity dominates every aspect of life, not just material resources. From an Ecosynomics perspective, this is a big problem for our agreements. Another brief historical journey will help us see how this came about.

## HISTORY OF THE ASSUMPTION OF SCARCITY

In classical economics, the central issue to be addressed, the "economic problem," was to figure out what conditions were necessary to sustain an effectively functioning market economy. The focus of economic analysis was on the production of material goods and the mechanisms by which those goods are distributed within society. The value of the goods, and therefore the price, classical economists saw as primarily a function of the difficulty of production. The idea of price as a function of supply and demand, in which the scarcity of products relative to consumers' desire for those products is the determining factor, had always been part of economic thinking. But it was not a mainstream theory for the first century or so, when classical economics predominated the field.[61]

---

61    The historical overview in this and the next paragraph is based on (Roncaglia, 2006, pp. 278-285).

This changed in the 1870s, when economists in Austria, France and England published treatises that conceived of the economic problem as the task of determining the optimal utilization of scarce resources relative to the demands of economic actors. This formulation became the new mainstream view in economic thinking so abruptly, that the shift has been called a "revolution" within the field. In this new view, value is a subjective judgment by consumers about the utility of a given product, and price is an indicator of the scarcity of the product relative to consumers' demand for it. Theoretically, optimal utilization could exist as a state of equilibrium between demand and supply. Based on this assumption, the quest for an understanding of how an economic system could achieve this desirable state became primarily a matter of data analysis. This helped to make the new economics seem more of a science, as opposed to classical economics, in which the study of how social relations and government policies affect economic outcomes had been the main concern.

The discipline of economics continued to evolve in various respects after this dramatic change in focus. Yet the idea that its overriding focus is the allocation of scarce resources has remained central. In fact, the assumption of scarcity has become all encompassing in the worldview of mainstream economics. We can see this by comparing the perspectives of two influential economists writing about fifty years apart: Alfred Marshall and Lionel Robbins.

Marshall was one of the leading figures in the revolution within the discipline. In the view of many people, he was the founder of so-called neoclassical economics, the basis for the mainstream of the discipline today. He helped develop a rigorous framework to explain how to make optimal decisions in the context of scarcity: for example, by offering a seminal depiction of how price can be based on the intersection of trends in demand and supply. So, he clearly saw scarcity as the central concern of economics. But he also saw—correctly, from an Ecosynomics perspective—that economics concerned itself with only part of human experience.

"Political Economy or Economics is a study of mankind in the ordinary business of life," Marshall wrote in *Principles of Economics* (1890). "It examines that part of individual and social action which is most closely connected with the attainment and with the use of the material requisites of wellbeing."[62] Marshall then defined two types of *non-material* requisites of wellbeing, those aspects that economics does not address. The first class, he said, "consists of [a person's] own qualities and faculties for action and enjoyment; such for instance as business ability, professional skill or the faculty for deriving recreation from

---

62    See (Marshall, 1890, pp. Bk I, Ch 1, 1).

reading or music." The second class of non-material goods he defined as "beneficial" relations with other people, either in business or personal life. Economics is the "Science of Wealth," Marshall wrote. "All wealth consists of desirable things . . . but not all desirable things are reckoned as wealth. The affection of friends, for instance, is an important element of wellbeing, but it is not reckoned as wealth, except by a poetic license."[63]

Lionel Robbins, a professor of economics at the University of London writing in 1945, rejected this carefully delimited characterization of economics and offered what is now a universally accepted definition of the discipline: "Economics is a science which studies human behavior as a relationship between ends and scarce means which have alternative uses." Marshall's conception, said Robbins, "the conception we have rejected . . . marks off certain kinds of human behaviour, behaviour directed to the procuring of material welfare, and designates these as the subject-matter of Economics." In contrast, "The conception we have adopted . . . does not attempt to pick out certain *kinds* of behaviour, but focuses attention on a particular *aspect* of behaviour, the form imposed by the influence of scarcity. It follows from this, therefore, that insofar as it presents this aspect, any kind of human behaviour falls within the scope of economic generalizations."[64] From this perspective, Robbins and those mainstream economists who followed him came to see scarcity everywhere:

> The time at our disposal is limited. There are only twenty-four hours in the day. We have to choose between the different uses to which they may be put. The services, which others put at our disposal, are limited. The material means of achieving ends are limited. We have been turned out of Paradise. We have neither eternal life nor unlimited means of gratification. Everywhere we turn, if we choose one thing we must relinquish others which, in different circumstances, we would wish not to have relinquished. Scarcity of means to satisfy ends of varying importance is an almost ubiquitous condition of human behavior.[65]

---

63   See (Marshall, 1890, pp. 36, 39).
64   See (L. Robbins, 1945, pp. 16-17).
65   See (L. Robbins, 1945, p. 15).

## AN ECOSYNOMICS PERSPECTIVE ON SCARCITY

Why devote so much attention to this history of the idea of scarcity in economics? Because the founders of modern economics pointed us towards a powerful science of choice, choice in the arena of the material world, where we must deal with scarcity. This is the arena Ecosynomics proposes is the things-matter level of perceived reality, but it is not the totality of what is real. Rather, it captures a moment in the ebb and flow of resources at the development-motion level when motion stops and something concrete appears. While economics has taught us much about how to operate effectively at the things-matter level, we have come to apply its lessons to ALL cases. As a result, the assumption of scarcity pervades most human agreements today, especially the ones most affecting our experiences of life.

Ecosynomics, on the other hand, suggests that scarcity, as defined by many leading economists, is just one particular way of looking at the world. For example, many people point to the regions of the world that are experiencing a severe lack of access to water and suggest that the scarcity of water could lead to a third world war some time in the future. People need water to survive, and since there is only so much water available, they see it as scarce. Ecosynomics offers a different take on this issue: is there really not enough water on the planet? Two-thirds of Earth is covered in water, much more than we can consume. The vast water in the ocean is salty and therefore not drinkable. Yet we have plenty of technology used every day to desalinate water, lots of it. Is the problem then that we cannot get clean water to people cheaply? While I have not traveled the entire world, I have seen and am assured by other travelers that they have seen soft drinks in the most remote villages in Latin America, Asia, and Africa. If PepsiCo can get a can of soda to these villages and make a profit, then maybe we can get water there too.

This brief thought exercise suggests, in very simplified terms, that maybe we have a water scarcity problem because getting potable water to people in remote areas is not important to the people who could make it happen, just like they have done with other products. Maybe it is the dominant pattern of focusing narrowly on individual self-interest and accepting uncritically the assumption of scarcity that creates the limits to what is possible. If we start from abundance and stay in relationship in all five dimensions, maybe we could find a way to create abundance of water. In other words, the scarcity of water might just be a matter of perspective, perspective based on the fundamental assumption of scarcity.

Ecosynomics offers an alternative way of seeing reality, in which scarcity is again relegated to a limited sphere and the five relationships together provide the foundation for agreements. Ecosynomics does not reject or seek to replace economics, however. It builds on what economists have established. In particular, it incorporates as a basis for understanding agreements, four questions that are fundamental to economics. These questions concern what people see in their environment that can contribute to human wellbeing. Let's look at them next, then I will use them to illuminate differences and similarities among political-economic systems.

## FOUR QUESTIONS ECONOMISTS ASK

The four core questions of economics are: how much of the necessary factors of production are available (resources); who will decide how to use them (resource allocation mechanism); what criteria shall we use for allocation decisions (value); and how shall we interact with each other to get what we need (organization)? When economists bring these questions together it is usually to tell the basic story depicted in Figure 11, below: resources are inputs to the production process; management organizes activities to convert these resources into the outputs a consumer values; and the allocation mechanism determines how this all happens. This story is at the heart of economics because, as Paul Samuelson states in his classic textbook, it encompasses three fundamental economic problems that society must address: "(1) *what* outputs to produce, and in what quantity; (2) *how* to produce them—that is, by what techniques should inputs be combined to produce the desired outputs; and (3) *for whom* the outputs should be produced and distributed."[66]

Notice that Figure 11 presents this economic story as a linear flow. First resources come in, then people organize to transform them into something that, finally, others value. This is the most common way of showing these relationships—one, then another, then another. Gregory Mankiw, the author of another leading economics textbook, tells the story as a circular process, as follows: "households sell the use of their labor, land, and capital to the firms in the markets for the factors of production. The firms then use these factors to produce goods and services, which in turn are sold to households in the markets for goods and services." In both depictions, we see a process with distinct phases, and at each stage, there is a handoff—from resource owners to the organization and from the organization to the consumer, or household.[67]

---

66  See (Samuelson & Nordhaus, 1995, p. 8).
67  See (Mankiw, 2008, p. 22).

RESOURCES              ORGANIZATION              VALUE

*Business Strategy* - Resource-based view of the firm

*Business Strategy* - Organizing structure

*Business Strategy* - Value proposition

**INPUTS**          **TRANSFORM**          **OUTPUTS**

*Economics* - Factors of production

*Economics* - Production set of principals and agents

*Economics* - Income

*Business Strategy* - Stakeholder, principal-agent          *Economics* - Allocation mechanisms

**ORGANIZING PROCESS**

ALLOCATION MECHANISM

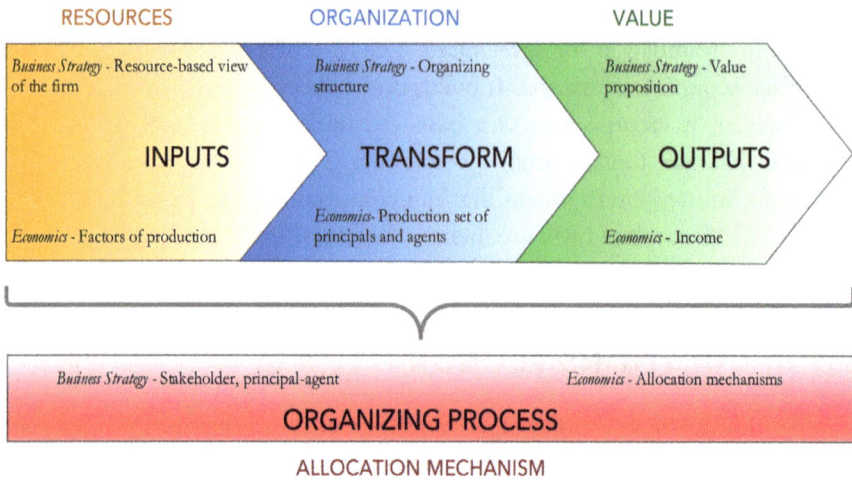

*Figure 11: Key Economic Theories*

This framework of distinct phases greatly simplifies a number of complexities and has allowed economists to delve deeply into and develop a comprehensive understanding of each of the four questions. At the same time, it led to dividing them up into distinct theoretical issues within either economics or the related field of business strategy, as indicated in Figure 11. While some theorists recognize the interdependence of the four questions and some practitioners in business organizations work with complex models that deal with these interdependencies, the more common usage of these four building blocks separates them into distinct disciplines. Similarly, common practice builds off of resource theories or allocation mechanism theories or organization theories or value theories, but rarely off all four together. We will look at each of the four questions separately in this chapter, and I will point out some of the ways in which economists' thinking on these questions affect your day-to-day experiences. In the next chapter, however, I will bring the questions together within the Ecosynomics framework, so that we can begin to see how their interdependencies affect agreements.

## RESOURCES

When considering the first basic economic question (How much resource is there?), the economists think about the factors of production—land, labor and capital. These are the basic building blocks of the economy. In economics, land includes anything that comes from the land, such as water, oil, minerals, forests, and natural gas. These natural resources are the raw materials for the production process. Labor is the effort people contribute to the production of goods and services. Capital is any man-made resource that makes it possible to assemble the other resources needed to produce goods and services, such as money or machines. In general, land receives its income in rents, labor in wages and capital in interest. Over the years, economists have expanded the definition of the factors of production to include intangible resources, such as intellectual property, goodwill, reputation and social capital (social relationships that have economic value).[68]

Your access to these basic economic inputs, either in their raw form or in the finished form of products and services you consume, directly influences your material wellbeing. Whether or not you are aware of it, economics-based principles determine how much is available and who has what rights to access what is available. For example, there might be fruit-full trees on your walk to the library. The fruit could satisfy your hunger, but if the trees are rooted on the land someone else owns, it is not available for you, no matter how hungry you are. This is the economic concept of ownership, and it underlies basic agreements about what resources are, who owns them and who has access to them. Ownership, as defined economically, is the exclusive right to use something, which implies scarcity. Once you own it, you have the right to determine how it is used, and others do not, which is enforced by law.

Another influential economics-based concept is price. Price is the moment of agreement between producers and consumers when goods or services are exchanged. Starting from an assumption of scarcity, economics sees this exchange as occurring in the context of competition for scarce goods, and this sets the foundation for the scarcity in your daily experience. You wake up on a bed you bought in a house that the bank probably owns. You acquired the bed in an exchange with a manufacturer or retail intermediary at a price set by a mix of the company's costs, expected profits, and supply-demand-based, competitive-market conditions. The same is true of the toothbrush and toothpaste you use to clean your teeth, the clothes you put on and the food you eat for breakfast. For the privilege of having a mortgage so you can eventually own your home, you pay the bank the principal (the price of the home) plus interest (the price of the mortgage). You can afford the bed, clothes and food, as well as the mortgage, because you earn income from a job. That is to say, you exchange your scarce labor for an employer's scarce money at a competitive "price," your wage.

68    See (Mankiw, 2008; Samuelson & Nordhaus, 1995).

In all of these transactions, you are trying to minimize what you must give up in order to get what you want, and the other party is doing the same. The relationship is colored by these competing goals and so cannot be one of fluidity, sharing and a sense of abundance. Since we are nearly always in that space, it is hard to get out of scarcity mode when we deal with our friends and families. Without being aware of it, we carry this sense of scarcity—not just of money, but also of time, energy and other nonmaterial resources—into all of our relationships. In this mode, we tend to ignore the motion and light levels of perceived reality and apply only a matter-level model of exchange. It can be quite a challenge to remain positive, to be as generous as we want to be and to value the contributions people make to the quality of our lives outside the framework of demand and supply. This is how the assumption of scarcity carries over from the innumerable price-based interactions we engage in each day into those parts of our lives where it is irrelevant.

Now, ownership and price have proven to be highly effective mechanisms for mobilizing resources and resource allocation in a market economy, and market economies have produced a high level of material wellbeing for hundreds of millions of people who participate in them. This is a good thing. From an Ecosynomics perspective, however, it has come with a downside: the pervasiveness of scarcity thinking and resulting experience of scarcity in our daily lives. This is what we want to learn to shift.

## RESOURCE ALLOCATION MECHANISM

Once we see what resources are available—the first question—we want to know who will decide how to allocate them across many possible uses. "Who decides?" is a fundamental question for society and has a direct influence on your daily life. This is because the answer to this question, expressed in the so-called resource allocation mechanism, defines the political-economic system you live in. In other words, it sets the rules of the game at the national level.

Allocation mechanism theory suggests optimal designs for allocating scarce resources within a given political economy, in the most efficient way—the most value for the least cost. Comparative economics looks at the resource allocation mechanisms that characterize different systems. Economists in this field have defined a continuum. On one end of the spectrum is the most individualistic system, in which resource allocation (theoretically) occurs wholly through the choices of individuals and the rules support individuals deciding with other individuals, as in the decision-making that happens within free markets. On the other end is a system that (theoretically) is wholly directed by the government.[69] For much of the 20th century, the Cold War between systems that seemed to represent these two extremes—the "free-market economy" on the one hand and the "command economy" on the other—dominated and divided the world. So far in the 21st century, the idea of a continuum is much more relevant.

Ecosynomics offers a different perspective on the question of who decides. Later in this chapter, I will show you how differences in resource allocation mechanisms and the political-economic systems they produce can also be understood in terms of the five relationships, to self, other, group, nature and spirit. In the process, we will see another way in which the assumption of scarcity in economics contributes to the experiences of scarcity we have in our daily lives.

## VALUE

The third core economic question has to do with the criteria used to allocate resources. Economists think of this question in terms of value—the value of specific goods and services determines their prices, and prices guide the economic decisions that determine how resources will be used to produce goods and services. Value theory in economics delves into how this process works.

Economists' thinking about value has shaped how most people think about what things are worth. Their understanding of value makes it easier for you to go to the market and exchange money for goods, to go to an employer and exchange work capacities for wages, to go to the bank and exchange future interest payments for loans today. In Ecosynomics terms, this branch of economic theory has developed ways of specifying what value is generated from existing resources at the things-matter level. This contribution has helped to create the improvements in material wellbeing experienced globally over the past two centuries.

At the same time, as noted above, a shift in thinking about value was at the heart of the 19th-century revolution in economics that enshrined the assumption of scarcity. Where classical economists considered value to be intrinsic to the good or service, derived from the inputs to production, the view in mainstream economics today is that value is a subjective criterion primarily influenced by scarcity. At least since the 13th century, however, economic thinkers have found

---

69   The "resource allocation mechanism" is used in comparative economics to distinguish different types of economy (Barkley Rosser & Rosser, 2004, p. 6). For Samuelson's distinction of the two extremes, see (Samuelson & Nordhaus, 1995, p. 6).

it useful to divide subjective criteria of value into three broad categories. One of these is *virtuositas*, the ability to satisfy human needs. Another is *complacibitas*, a personal preference. And finally, there is *raritas*, the scarcity of the good. These three can be considered separately because what drives them is different: I need to eat to live. I prefer brown bread to white bread. I will pay more for the brown bread I want if there is not much of it available.[70]

From the Ecosynomics perspective, we can see that it is important to work mindfully with all three of these categories of value. *Raritas* is important, but it deals only with the things-matter level of perceived reality. *Complacibitas*, personal preference, is also important and limited in scope, in that it deals exclusively with the primary relationship to self. *Virtuositas* addresses the broader question of what satisfies human needs and so can be seen as dealing with all five primary relationships at all three levels of perceived reality. Ecosynomics invites us to consider value from a broader perspective that includes all three forms.

Scarcity-based economic thinking about value influences our lives in various ways. For example, while many people think that grade school teachers play an important role in their children's lives, these teachers tend to be paid relatively low wages. The same is true for most caregivers, who are not paid or paid relatively poorly. The wages for teachers and the lack of wages for caregivers is determined by the supply and demand for replaceable units of resource, a scarcity-based view that values only the things-level outcomes and not the development and potential levels of value realized by teachers and caregivers—how many kids were taught how many hours of what subjects and how many hours of care were given. The economic value system is focused entirely on the things-matter level, where teaching young children and caring for the sick and elderly are "unproductive" activities. In a negotiation that is confined to pay for hours worked, these workers don't have much leverage.

Another example of scarcity-based thinking in economics that affects our daily lives places primary value on outcomes, giving much less value to learning at the developmental level of reality or to potential-realization at the possibility level. This value system shows up as the job contract based on a job description—you are paid to do the job, period. The contract specifies what outcomes meet the expectation; nothing about learning and the potential of the individual.

One other major example of scarcity-based thinking in economics is the focus on short time horizons. As the primary emphasis is on the things level,

---

70    Economic historian Alessandro Roncaglia describes Olivi's use of these three values (Roncaglia, 2006, p. 40).

most attention is given to what is in the immediate foreseeable future. This leads to a focus on immediate impacts of decisions, along with the costs and benefits of those impacts. This thinking ignores longer-term impacts, calling them "externalities," as they are economically external to the responsibility of the economic decision maker. Externalities today include pollution, and the management of common goods, such as air, forests, and water. This is how, as a society, we can have such conflicts between what we think is important and what we value in scarcity-based, economic terms.[71]

## ORGANIZATION

The fourth core question in economics looks at the organization of human activities to transform resource inputs into outputs people value. In economic thought, the heart of this question, rooted in the assumption of scarcity, is how to find the most efficient way to make the resource transformation happen. As in other areas, economic thinking about organization has contributed greatly to material wellbeing, even as it has introduced scarcity into other dimensions of life.

In fact, outside of the family most of our experiences with organization are influenced by the economic principles devised in Western Europe and the United States in the process of rapid industrialization in the late 19th and early 20th centuries. New manufacturing technology developed in that era, for example in the automobile industry, provided opportunities to produce more and more products at lower and lower costs through economies of scale. To take advantage of these opportunities, business owners needed to organize large numbers of workers as efficiently as possible, and two principles became central to the solution they devised: hierarchy and division of labor. These organizational devices made it possible for companies to closely control the activities of their employees, and for the employees to become increasingly proficient at executing specific tasks or operating specialized machinery at faster and faster rates of production.

The fact that, in industrialized societies today, many millions of people have access to a vast array of manufactured products at affordable prices is testimony to the effectiveness of the organizations operating along these lines, as well as to continuing advances in technology.

At the same time, however, the fact that hierarchy and the command-and-control style of management it encourages became the model for virtually

---

71    Author Riane Eisler documents the importance to many cultures of the "caring econo-my," and how it is critically undervalued in most cultures (Eisler, 2007).

all work organizations has made scarcity—of autonomy, of initiative, of relationship, of deep trust and commitment, of creativity, of responsibility—a common experience of the people who work in them. Similarly, the principle of division of labor lives on in all sorts of organizations in the form of specialization, dividing up the group's work into smaller and smaller chunks.

The basic economic idea here is that every task has a learning curve— you get better at doing something the more practice you have. The more individuals specialize, the more time they dedicate to moving up their own specific learning curves and the more efficient they get at their individual tasks. While this might allow individuals to experience some of the development level of reality, as they learn and build capacities, deeper learning and capacity development require relationships with others and the group's support for the development of that unique contribution. However, where things-matter-level efficiency is the overriding organizational goal, specialization can lead to scarcity in the relationships to the other and the group, limiting the level of vibrancy experienced. This is the more common experience.

Essentially, economists saw that every transaction has costs —the costs involved in informing oneself about the transaction, in taking the time to reach an agreement, and in making the effort to ensure that people stick to the agreement. The economic question is whether the benefits outweigh the costs. A particularly powerful framework in this arena—transaction cost economics— looks at the benefits and costs of every interaction in order to determine how to structure that interaction in a way that maximizes the net benefit. This kind of thinking about human interactions has had, and continues to have, a huge influence on the agreements by which most work organizations operate and the day-to-day experiences of the people they employ.

For example, there have been many innovations in the field of organizational science suggesting ways to increase collaboration, communication and teamwork. Transaction cost analysis might show that the costs of being in these kinds of relationships—the time involved in paying attention to each other and supporting each other—outweigh the benefits. Or it might not, and the experiment in collaboration might therefore be deemed a failure. While this transaction-cost approach has brought greater clarity to the efficiency of different forms of organizing, the benefits in human energy and creativity derived from greater vibrancy in the five relationships are not typically part of the calculation.[72]

---

72   Chester Barnard paved the way in the early 1900s with his description of why people come together to interact in the first place in a co-operative organization (Barnard, 1968). Coase and Williamson added a framework for assessing the benefits and costs of the transac-

Starting in the 1980s, great efforts in supply chain optimization and total quality began to open organizational thinking and practice into the motion-development level, integrating cooperative efforts across a set of previously isolated disciplines, in a continuous learning and improvement process focused on shared objectives. While these efforts have added great resiliency to many organizations, enabling them to survive turbulent times; their continued focus on the efficient transformation of scarce resources keeps them locked into the predominance of the things-based organizational task. This focus on the task versus on the human being restricts the amount of abundance available in the experience and outcomes, as I will show later.

## SEEING DIFFERENT WORLDS THROUGH THE FOUR ECONOMIC QUESTIONS

For nearly forty-five years, the Cold War polarized the world into two hostile camps. On one side, the United States with its friends and allies promoted and defended its ideal of a free-market economy and democratic political system; on the other, the Soviet Union with its friends and allies promoted and defended its ideal of a centrally managed economy and communist political system. This conflict between political-economic systems cost thousands of lives and trillions of dollars. With this episode in our collective history, there can be little doubt that people care greatly and disagree passionately about the agreements that set the terms of political and economic life in the nation states where we live.

Ecosynomics offers a fresh perspective on these political-economic differences. From this perspective, it may be possible to find greater understanding and perhaps even collaboration in shifting agreements to make all systems better at providing the abundance and harmonic vibrancy we humans want in our lives. The four basic economic questions will help me show you some important similarities and differences in the major systems.

### COMPARING POLITICAL-ECONOMIC SYSTEMS

Let's start with the most basic similarities: an exclusive focus on the things-matter level of perceived reality and preoccupation with the scarcity that exists in that realm. I have already described how these characteristics became

---

tions in human interactions in models of competition and cooperation with "transaction cost economics" (Coase, 1973; Williamson, 1981).

central to the mainstream of economics as it emerged along with capitalism in Western Europe and continued to evolve between the 17th and 20th centuries. The alternative systems that arose out of critiques of capitalism, primarily socialism and communism, challenged many of its basic principles but not the assumption that all resources are scarce. They therefore also share the tendency of scarcity thinking to see the world in terms of either/or dichotomies and trade-offs. As a result, all of these political-economic systems are organized around the principle that one, and only one, of the five relationships (to self, other, group, nature and spirit) should be privileged in guiding resource allocation.

The key difference among political-economic systems is thus the resource allocation mechanism. As described above, as a response to rule by the monarchy, the free-market capitalism of classical and neoclassical economics saw the self-interest of individuals as the centerpiece and guiding mechanism of the economy. Either as a corrective or as an alternative to unfettered individualism, other systems start from the premise that a different relationship should be primary in resource allocation. Significantly, from an Ecosynomics perspective, no existing political-economic system proposes a mechanism of resource allocation based on all five relationships together. This choice simply cannot be envisioned from the viewpoint of the things-matter level, where all these systems are stuck.

Yet much has been learned from the cumulative experience of billions of people who have lived under these different systems and from the analysis and insights of economists who have studied that experience. All of this will be relevant and useful when we humans get to the point of framing political-ecosynomic agreements that honor all five relationships simultaneously. As a first step, we need to stop thinking of competing political-economic systems as hostile or evil. To move in that direction, I propose that we explore how their differences can be understood in terms of privileging different relationships.

## THE ECONOMICS OF RELATIONSHIP TO SELF

I will conduct this exploration through a little thought experiment, beginning with the relationship to self. What would be my starting point for thinking about economic agreements if my relationship to myself were all that mattered to me? First of all, I would believe that I would experience greater wellbeing, health and success by experiencing more of my relationship to the self, more of my capacities, growth and potential. I would see my personal freedom as a key source of vibrancy in my life. After all, I am the only one who can know all of my truths, hence the only one who can make the best choices for me.

Approaching the resource question of "how much," I observe that some individuals seem to have certain things and some do not. I believe it is up to me to determine what I need and what I should do to get it. Thus, it is no surprise that when I look at the resource allocation question of "who decides," I think I should decide and act for myself and everyone else should do the same. When I then ask the value question of "what criteria," I go back to my desire to enhance my own capacities, development, and potential in order to maximize my happiness and wellbeing. Similarly, when I think about how economic relationships should be organized, I think about how I can interact in ways that benefit my own wellbeing. Since I assume that everyone else is thinking and doing the same thing, I believe that the health of the group is the aggregate wellbeing of all self-interested individuals. An elder statesman I talked to captured this perspective succinctly: "Look. It all starts with the individual. If you don't take up your own work and responsibility for your own actions, then nothing else matters."

It is not difficult to recognize the underpinnings of mainstream capitalist economics in these self-oriented responses to the four questions. Of course, there has been a great deal of criticism of free-market capitalism from many directions. Much of this criticism focuses on the effectiveness of unfettered individualism as a mechanism for allocating resources and keeping the economy running smoothly, to the benefit of society at large. Karl Marx, the most influential critic, argued in *Das Kapital* (1867) that, far from being a smooth-running mechanism, free-market capitalism has an inherent tendency to produce crises—both periodic economic crises and a more fundamental social crisis based on increasing inequity and conflict between the owners of capital and the rest of society. The criticism of inequitable outcomes became the basis for a number of alternative political-economic systems, which I will examine below. At the same time, the reality of recurring crises of capitalism—in particular the Great Depression of the 1930s and the so-called Great Recession, precipitated by the financial crisis of 2007-2008—has led even mainstream neo-liberal economists to accept the idea that unfettered individualism will not reliably produce acceptable outcomes for society.

## MAJOR ALTERNATIVES TO SELF—THE ECONOMICS OF OTHER AND GROUP

Focusing my attention again on my thought experiment, now I am completely engaged in my experience of the relationship to other individuals. This is the only relationship that I will pay attention to on this particular path. Again, the intention is to see what economic agreements might look like with this primary focus.

When on the path of the relationship to the other, I see that some people have certain things and some do not. People do not all have the same amount of the resources that seem to be scarce, and since I am most concerned about staying in a positive relationship to other individuals, I am concerned that the situation seems unfair. Therefore, to the second question of "who decides how resources should be allocated," I respond that everyone should have a say about what is fair. To the third question of "what criteria," I suggest that on this path the allocation of scarce resources should be balanced in a way that produces a sense of fairness. Recently, a school board member stated this principle to me clearly: "Look. If it doesn't feel fair to everyone involved, they will not participate. And, without their participation, we can never achieve our goals for the community." To the fourth question of how to organize economic activities, I answer that if everyone is treated equally, then all will do well, and the group will be healthier. I see this path as moving me toward an experience of greater vibrancy through greater equality.

These responses to the four basic economic questions express a logic that focuses on the utility of the greatest happiness for the greatest number, as described by the British philosopher Jeremy Bentham in 1776.[73] It also captures a central critique of free-market capitalism, leveled by Karl Marx and many others—the tendency toward greater and greater inequality of outcomes between the owners of capital and the laboring class. This critique and the underlying logic of the relationship to other is the basis for socialist political-economic systems. A priority in these systems is that people are perceived to have equal status under the rule of law, the purpose of which is to ensure felt-fair access of all to scarce resources.[74]

---

73   For Bentham's work, see (Bentham, 1988).

74   Socialist economics starts from scarcity, as described by a member of the socialist Fabian Society, G.D.H. Cole writes in 1950, ""The subject matter of socialist Economics is the good life as effected by the entire process of production and consumption of goods and services which are either naturally scarce or created only by the expenditure of human effort and ingenuity (Cole, 2011, p. vii)." The "rule of law" means that the government is held accountable, laws are clear and fair, law enactment and enforcement is fair and efficient, and fair and

The Marxist critique of capitalism also pointed to the path of the relationship to the group, the next excursion in my imaginative exercise. I take this path because I believe that my best chance for a healthy, vibrant life lies in being part of a healthy group. If my group is weak, I am weak. A manager I was visiting in Ecuador expressed this mindset when she reminded her team, "When the group does well, we all do well. When the group suffers, we all suffer. My ability to pay you is based on our success as a group."

From this perspective, when I take up the first economic question, "how much," I observe that some groups do better than others in gaining access to scarce resources. My focus is therefore on helping my group get as much as possible. To the second question of how to allocate resources, I respond that all group members must decide together how to allocate resources in the name of the group. The criteria for resource allocation decisions—the third question—must be that they enhance the health of the group as a whole. By the same token, the organization of economic activities needs to direct the work of individuals to secure the wellbeing of all. This is how I would answer the fourth question from an exclusive focus on the relationship to group. These responses to the four questions live in collectivist economics and communist political-economic systems.

With the end of the Cold War in 1991, the lines between the major forms of political-economic system have blurred. The global economy that has emerged operates on the free-market capitalist model, and virtually all nations have adopted that model to some extent. Yet nowhere does free-market capitalism mean complete individualism. From nation to nation, in varying degrees, government regulations and economic policies and the rule of law assert the principles of relationship to other and group within a mixed political-economic system. Yet the critique of neo-classical (aka neoliberal) economics is as strong as ever, and it now comes from some additional directions.

## FURTHER CRITIQUES—THE ECONOMICS OF NATURE AND SPIRIT

I will continue my thought experiment by exploring the perspectives informing these critiques. When I see my path to vibrancy as dependent primarily on my relationship to nature, I see it is essential that the abundance of the natural world that enriches me—the sunshine, clear air, the forests, lakes, rivers, mountains, and oceans—be sustained. Starting from an assumption of

---

competent adjudicators provide access to justice (Agrast, Botero, & Ponce, 2010).

scarcity, when I consider the question of "how much," I feel fearful that these precious resources are finite. I see that each member of an ecological system competes for enough of the available scarce resources to be able to survive. Those individuals or groups that survive and flourish tend to be the ones who are best prepared to succeed in the ecosystem, as well as those who are most resilient to changes in the ecosystem. I accept this natural competition as the appropriate allocation mechanism ("who decides"), because, to my mind, it is the ecosystem as a whole that is most important. What I do not find acceptable is how the consumer orientation of the market economy has led to overconsumption of natural resources, which threatens that ecosystem. To me the purpose of economic activity ("by what criteria") is to maintain a dynamic balance among all the parts of the system. The organizing principle for economic action should therefore be to optimize fitness and resilience for the system as a whole, as well as its parts. Best-selling author Daniel Goleman captures this organizing principle in his concept of "ecological intelligence": "From the Arctic Circle to the Sahara Desert, native peoples everywhere have survived only by understanding and exquisitely attuning themselves to the natural systems that surround them.[75]

This is the realm of "nature" economics. As the basis for economic systems, it can be found today only in some tribal economies and in eco-friendly communities. However, as a critique of the globalized, consumer-oriented market economy, it has various forms of expression. For example, ecological economics conceives of the economy as a subsystem of the global ecosystem and focuses upon developing strategies for preserving "natural capital."[76] Environmental economics is a separate field of study focused on "the economic effects of national or local environmental policies around the world, that is, cost-benefit analysis of efforts to deal with issues such as air pollution, water quality and global warming."[77]

Finally, in my thought experiment, I want to imagine what it is like to seek an experience of greater vibrancy in my life by following the path of the relationship to spirit. On this path, I am motivated primarily by my desire to be connected to a higher power, the source of creativity. How would I then answer the four economic questions? Assuming scarcity of material resources, I accept the reality I see that some people have more than others. I do this

---

75    In Ecological Intelligence, best-selling author Daniel Goleman invokes this logic (Goleman, 2010, p. 42).

76    For van den Bergh, see (van den Bergh, 2001).

77    This quote can be found on-line at (http://www.nber.org/programs/eee/ee_oldworkinggroup_directory/ee.html).

because I answer the question "who decides" from the belief that a higher power is the ultimate resource allocator, and I see the criteria for allocating resources as emphasizing transcendence, moving beyond the material world to get closer to spirit, the creative source. From this perspective, I value spiritual resources more than material ones: economic success is positive only up to a point; and it comes with a responsibility to act charitably toward those who are less successful. To the fourth question, I respond that these principles should be embodied in the organization of economic activities. This view is expressed in the Islamic economic principle of *Adalah*, or justice, which asserts that concern for the welfare of others and cooperation are the proper basis for economic organization.[78]

Of course, people have lived for many centuries within systems of economic agreements based on the relationship to spirit, for example, in Buddhist and Islamic communities, which today include nearly two billion members.[79] However, in the post-Cold War era, believers in this path have offered it as a middle ground between free-market capitalism and "command socialism" or communism. "Of all the modern economic theories, the economic system of Marxism is founded on moral principles, while capitalism is concerned only with gain and profitability," the Dalai Lama has said. "The failure of the regime in the former Soviet Union was, for me, not the failure of Marxism but the failure of totalitarianism. For this reason I still think of myself as half-Marxist, half-Buddhist."[80] Comparative economists J. Barkley Rosser and Marina Rosser document the emergence in recent decades of what they call the "new traditional economy," based on a spirit-oriented critique of major economic systems. They show that within Islam, Confucianism, Buddhism and Christianity there are movements of varying size and strength advocating this new traditional economic model. This, they point out, is not a model that envisions turning back the clock and doing away with the global economy. Rather it seeks to establish a version of free market capitalism infused with and

---

78   See (Rosser & Rosser, 2003, p. 100).

79   For an overview of Buddhist schools of economics, which expand over much of the Buddha Dhamma, see (His Holiness The Dalai Lama, 1999; Schumacher, 1973, Ch. 4). For a national productivity index based on Buddhist economics, see the Gross National Happiness Index in Bhutan (http://www.grossnationalhappiness.com). For an overview of Islamic economics, as expressed in the Shari'as, see the work by Muhammad Umer Chapra, Senior Research Advisor at Islamic Development Bank (Umer Chapra, 2000). Comparative economists Rosser and Rosser also provide an overview of Islamic Economics (Rosser & Rosser, 2003, pp. 100-108). The numbers of followers of Buddhism and Islam are conservative estimates from (The World Factbook 2011, 2011).

80   For the Dalai Lama's reflections, see (His Holiness The Dalai Lama, 1996, p. 110).

moderated by spiritual values.[81]

## CONCLUSION—THE PARADOX OF SCARCITY

In this chapter I have tried to open up a somewhat different perspective on a couple of very large and well-studied topics—the role of economics in society and the distinguishing characteristics of alternative political-economic systems. I have suggested how these systems are not intrinsically hostile to each other but are all seeking the same goal, just along different pathways. At the same time, I have suggested that it is because *all* economic systems start from the assumption of scarce resources, and because economics is so pervasive an influence on our agreements, that scarcity is such a common aspect of our daily experiences, without our consciously choosing or even being aware of it. This brings us face to face with the economic paradox.

People everywhere want to experience the outer circle of abundance, harmony and vibrancy, and most of us do experience it sometimes. As I described in Chapters 1 and 2, when we examine what we feel like at those times, we see that the essence of the experience of the outer circle is a high level of vibrancy in all five relationships at the same time. Yet the schools of economic thought that are so pervasive in shaping the agreements that determine our experience insist that one relationship must be primary. In practice, they may accept a hybrid, but additional relationships added in are still just added in; they do not weigh in equally. Thus the paradox: we are pursuing an experience of harmonic vibrancy and abundance in a context dominated by thinking that denies the possibility of its essential characteristic.

I call this the paradox of scarcity because it is only from a place of scarcity, the inner circle, that it seems possible to experience a higher level of vibrancy in any one of the five primary relationships, independent of the others. From the experience of abundance, the outer circle, this mindset seems odd. It is like expecting to get the experience of ice cream from a substance that is not cold or not sweet or not creamy.

Scarcity exists at the things-matter level, but is not all pervasive. The assumption of scarcity in economics limits us unnecessarily to seeking abundance on the enlightened-matter path. This is how the market system, which economics arose to explain, could have greatly improved material wellbeing for millions and produced great affluence for some while still leaving

---

81    For the comparative economics description of new traditional economies, see (Rosser & Rosser, 2003, p. Ch 4).

most of us stuck in an experience of scarcity much of the time. Ecosynomics enables us to distinguish "affluence," the accumulation of material wealth with a mindset of scarcity, from "abundance," the sense that there is enough and that what we need will be there when we need it. It suggests the existence of a different route to abundance, the grounded-potential path. This is what we will explore in the remainder of this book.

CHAPTER 5

# THE PARADOX RESOLVED: TAKING ECONOMICS BEYOND SCARCITY

In the previous chapter, I delved into the fundamental assumption of scarcity that has shaped the field of economics and, through it, much of our daily experience. Fundamental assumptions are the deep foundation for all agreements. Like the foundation of a building, these assumptions are often not visible. Yet the viability of the building depends on the stability and strength of this foundation. When it is a solid foundation, we do not even think about it. When the foundation is cracked, however, there are major consequences.

I contend that the foundation of the agreements we are now living with is cracked. Although it served humanity well in the last great strides we collectively made, it can no longer support the edifice we have constructed on top of it. We need to rebuild the foundation on different assumptions in order to meet the needs of people going forward. While we usually leave such questions of fundamental assumptions to philosophers, theologians, and academics, we can no longer do this. To live more abundantly, we need to change how we work together and exchange value. To work differently together, we need to change the group's agreements. To change the agreements, we need to be able to work at the foundational level.

Of course, it is easy to say and exciting to think that we can start from an assumption of abundance and pursue the grounded-potential path to achieve it, but what does that look like in practice? How is it possible, really, to resolve the economic paradox? How can you choose agreements in five primary relationships at three levels of perceived reality? How can you even begin the work of changing the agreements already in place?

I suggest working with a framework based on the four big questions of economics. As I have tried to show, these basic questions and the economic thought derived from them thoroughly pervade the agreements we currently live with, so we need to meet them head-on. By continuing to work with them, we can also hope to build on all that has been learned so far in the study of economics.

## FOUR QUESTIONS, MANY FIELDS OF STUDY

To use the economic questions in the way I propose, we need to bring together streams of thought that have been flowing quite separately for a long time. Economists know these streams as resources, allocation mechanism, value and organization. As I indicated in Chapter 4 (Figure 11), these are currently completely different fields of inquiry, each with its own research agenda, pursued in different departments of academic institutions by different researchers using different methods and different criteria for validating what they find in their experiments, as well as different language to describe the phenomena they observe. In economics textbooks, these findings are presented in separate chapters, chapters that are not integrated.

A brief tour will give you a sense of this separation. For example, resource economics is mainly the preserve of accountants and engineers, who focus on minimizing the costs of the resources that are inputs to the economic system. They pursue questions like whether to make or buy the resources and how to identify those resources that define a group's core competences; that is, what they are especially good at doing. Historians and political scientists tend to concern themselves with comparative economics. They study the history and politics related to different allocation mechanisms, disentangling the impacts of interwoven economic and political factors on the higher goal of the system, such as individual freedom or equality.

Financiers and mathematicians, pursuing the value question in financial and monetary economics, attempt to define the equilibrium point of supply and demand that determines the price of exchange. Economic philosophers also explore the value question in a quest to determine the criteria for human wellbeing, focusing on growth and maximizing the value generated.

In organization economics, we find specialists in industrial organization, labor and business. For these fields, the goal is to find optimal organizational forms, as well as incentives for the individuals working within these forms, to maximize organizational efficiency, effectiveness and innovation while minimizing risk.

Everyone working within these different aspects of economics knows, in theory, that the pieces are part of a system. As in many systems, however, they do not have the system map to show how the pieces are related. Most often, the textbooks provide a linear model such as the one in Figure 11 in Chapter 4, which might depict the flow of money in an economy or provide the basis for a value-chain analysis of how a firm delivers a particular product or service to market. Beyond this, the relationships that actually define the system are de-emphasized to the point that people forget they are there. When you delve deeper into the issues each discipline is pursuing, it is even more difficult to see how the pieces are part of a larger whole.

For example, as a student of economics, I learned all about contracting theory, but had no idea it could be viewed as a subset of theories of pricing, supply-and-demand and, ultimately, value. I had also studied organizational theories about performance reviews, organizational forms such as non-profits, for-profits, and governmental agencies, and group practices such as competition, cooperation, co-opetition, and collaboration. I did not see that they all fit together within the organization question of how the primary relationships interact. And, I never saw that the way the factors of production—land, labor, and capital—are defined greatly influences who receives most of the value generated.

## HOW THE STATE OF ECONOMICS AFFECTS THE AGREEMENTS IN OUR DAILY LIFE

What I offered in the previous section was a brief, very high-level overview of the current state of economics, emphasizing the fact that separate disciplines have formed around each of the four big questions, each discipline with a sophisticated line of inquiry and highly specialized methods and language. This separation and specialization has added greatly to the understanding of the issues embedded in the four questions, and it has made it very difficult to see any connections among the four areas of inquiry. These developments have a profound effect on our ability to see the choice in the agreements we are living with and leave us with chronic systemic inefficiencies and inconsistencies in what we are learning.

I will start with the choice. We do not usually see choice in the areas of resources, resource allocation, value and organization, because we do not see that we are dealing with questions. We think we are dealing with disciplines, or perhaps with discrete steps in a linear process of production. So, we do not see that within the initial questions of each of the four areas there is a choice—both in the content of what we see and how we apply it. For example, the basic resource question is how much is there of land, labor and capital? Yet we can also ask, how much is there right now? We can ask, what if we bring in more and consume less—how much could there be? In other words, does our question about resources include only the things level, or also the development and possibility levels?

We exercise choice in the content of what we see by choosing to look at different levels. Having done this, we can then choose what to do with that content. If I only see the things-level, seeing only how much I currently have, I only think about how much I have and whether it is enough. When I see the things and development levels, I can think about the net effect of the inflows and outflows of the resources I need. If I need more next week, then I need to get more than I use this week to increase how much I have, by next week.

In regard to the allocation mechanism, we can ask who says that one relationship is better than another? What are the assumptions implicit in choosing one over another? Would one work better than another in a different situation? What mechanisms do people actually use? We find that people often use a different allocation mechanism than they think they do.

Likewise, dealing with the value question, we can ask, what is important in the first place? Is it the same for everyone? Are we assigning value to what we actually care about? Who determines who gets what part of the value generated? Is it always the same? If so, does it need to be always the same?

Finally, around organization there can be questions such as why we decided to come together in the first place? What is the common purpose we share? How do we interact with each other? Competitively, cooperatively, collaboratively? What kind of structure and process best supports how we want to interact?

Each of these questions suggests there is a choice, which we normally ignore or assume as a given structure: one set of resources someone owns; one best political-economic system that should apply everywhere; one set of values; one way to organize. As we have seen, this view reflects a scarcity-based assumption. Reality can be much richer, more interesting and full of possibility. In later chapters, I will describe some of the ways that people who see this possibility are figuring out how to make different choices and create different agreements.

Our ability to see choices in our agreements is also diminished by the barriers to learning created by the separation of economic fields. What I mean by "systemic inefficiencies and inconsistencies" is that we are not applying what we learn in one area to another, because we see them as separate areas or, at best, linked in a linear process. For example, innovations within the field of system dynamics led to seeing interrelated sets of resources with related inflows and outflows, which cause the resources available to change over time at varying rates. These innovations brought a development-motion level of awareness to resources. With both development and things levels of awareness, people are now able to see how to influence the amount of a resource available today and into the future. One could imagine that this insight of resource dynamics applied to value systems might lead to innovations in determining value—not just the value that is there right now, as reflected in price, but also the value of what may be developing, for example, through learning. Yet, people working on pricing mechanisms, value systems and organizational forms have not taken up the innovations around questions of resources.

Similarly, in the field of organization design, there have been significant advances in understanding and mapping multi-stakeholder value systems, the networks of people who share a common interest, or stake, in a particular area or issue. This kind of mapping, such as the systems mapping process I highlight in the Vermont learning lab in Chapter 12, enables people to see how to interact with others who have similar and competing interests in a way that allows all stakeholders to gain. Imagine a monetary system informed by this kind of mapping exercise, in which all participants perceived more value (got wealthier) because they participated. The design of national monetary systems has not gained from this innovation, although there are a number of examples of local and regional complementary currencies that build on the concept of multi-stakeholder value systems. I will describe this phenomenon in Chapter 7.

In short, the total system that these four areas of economic study work with is not functioning as well as it could be, if there was learning going on across the disciplines. It is difficult for economists, much more so for ordinary people like us, to see the choices in these seemingly disparate, often complicated sub-systems. We find it even more difficult to learn from one area and apply it to another. This situation creates incongruence among the four areas and thus a sub-optimization of the whole system, which must over time; also weaken each area, as well.

# ECONOMIC QUESTIONS AS LENSES ON OUR EXPERIENCE

Ecosynomics addresses this problem of the separateness of the core streams of economic thought in two steps. The first step is to recognize the fundamental question at the heart of each one: how much (resources); who decides (allocation); by what criteria (value); how shall we interact (organization)? The second step is to re-envision these four questions as four lenses on a single, overarching question: how much abundance and harmonic vibrancy are we experiencing?

Figure 12 below depicts this use of the four economic questions as lenses. Notice that the left-hand face of the block is the Levels of Reality Map you encountered in Chapter 2, Figure 9. It is a two-dimensional representation of the experience we are all living: the five fundamental relationships with the three levels of perceived reality we have access to at any time. On the right-hand face of the block are the four main lines of economic inquiry—resources, allocation, value and organization. Now part of a single inquiry, they are integrated into the five relationships and three levels of perceived reality to create an expanded set of questions, presented in a more readable format in Figure 13.

To reiterate the key point made in Chapter 2: the level of harmonic vibrancy and abundance available to you depends completely on how you work with the levels of perceived reality and the five primary relationships. In other words, it depends on your agreements. Historically, economic thinking has contributed to our agreements becoming stuck at the things-matter level, the level of scarcity. However, in Figure 13 we can see that it is relatively easy to adapt the Fundamental questions that economics poses to an Ecosynomics inquiry, once the assumption of scarcity is relaxed. Now we can bring economic thinking to bear on the task of seeing and reshaping the agreements that determine our lived experience. The small blocks behind the Reality Map in Figure 12 represent these agreements.

By liberating the four economic questions from the constraint of the scarcity mentality, we can mobilize the analytical power in those questions to help us see our agreements and reshape them to produce more of the experiences we want. This is how we can find our way to the grounded-potential path. And this is how we can resolve the economic paradox.

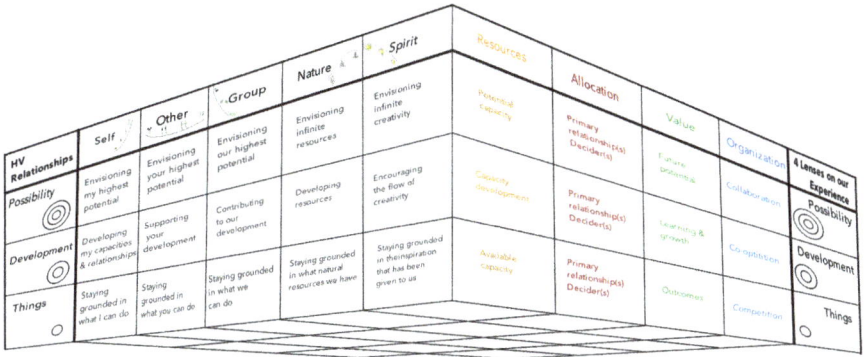

*Figure 12: Expanded Levels of Reality Map*

The overarching question that the four ecosynomic lenses address:
*How much harmonic vibrancy and abundance are we experiencing?*

| 4 Lenses on our experience | Resources ◯ How Much? | Allocation ◯ Who decides? | Value ◯ By what criteria? | Organization ◯ How shall we interact? |
|---|---|---|---|---|
| **Possibility** Potential (Light) | Potential Capacity — What is our potential capacity? ✕ | Which Relationship(s) decide our potential? ✕ | Future Potential — What is our most desired future? ✕ | Collaboration — How shall we interact to collaborate? ✕ |
| **Development** Motion (Verb) | Capacity Development — What capacities are we developing? ✕ | Which Relationship(s) decide how we develop our resources? ✕ | Learning & Growth — Where do we most want to learn and grow? ✕ | Co-opetition — How shall we interact to cooperate competitively? ✕ |
| **Things** Matter (Noun) | Available Capacity — What is our available capacity? ✕ | Which Relationship(s) decide how we allocate our resources? ✕ | Outcomes — What outcomes do we value most? ✕ | Competition — How shall we interact to compete? ✕ |

✕ = Each block speaks to all five relationships

*Figure 13: Expanded Levels of Reality Map, Right-hand Face*

## HARNESSING THE POWER OF ECONOMIC INQUIRY

The great thing about refocusing economic inquiry on our agreements is that behind each of the four big questions is a whole series of related questions. It is by following these lines of questions that we can begin to see the agreements currently buried deep in the economic systems we have today and even the unconscious assumptions that inform them. When we apply them to our immediate situations, these questions can also lead us, sometimes in seemingly obvious steps, to see choices in our agreements we never imagined could be possible. This second application will be our work with the Agreements Map, which I will introduce in the next chapter. First, I will give you a brief overview of some important lines of questions that will help us in that work. Within the core resources question of "how much?" lie three sub-questions business economists have begun to ask in the past fifty years. In asking the questions this way, they have begun to intuit the three levels of perceived reality. The first sub-question—how much resource is there right now?—is a current-capacity question focused on the things-matter level. The second sub-question directs our attention to the development-motion level—how does the amount of resource change as the result of inflows and outflows over time? The third important sub-question is—what are potential resources? This looks through the "how much" lens at the possibility-light level of the resources. We are fortunate that these lines of inquiry and all the knowledge that has flowed from them are already out there in economics.

In the area of resource allocation, three related sub-questions are embedded in the question of "who decides?" which is the focus of the field of comparative economics. The three sub-questions are—what is the motivating objective of the political-economic system? What relationship best meets that objective? And what process does the system use to make decisions in that relationship? The inquiry on these questions, some of it scholarly and some ideological, has produced strong characterizations (in some cases, caricatures) of the main systems (capitalism, socialism, communism, eco-economics, and traditional economics). In the past few decades, the picture has become more complex and interesting. In an Ecosynomics inquiry, these questions hold the potential for producing great understanding of the systems we are part of, large and small.

Three important sub-questions related to the value question of "what criteria?" have been pursued in many forms by economic thinkers over the centuries. The first of these is, what is valued? In the economics of exchange, this question opened up a large area of exploration around how to decide what something is worth at the point of exchange, both to the person who has it initially and to the one who wants it. Herein lies all of pricing theory, including supply and demand curves, which apply to commodity exchanges like your purchase of an ice cream cone as well as the labor exchange of your hour for a wage. The second question focuses on the mode of exchange: how will the value be exchanged between the two parties? This little question encompasses the whole field of barter and monetary systems and the search for the most efficient way to exchange the value we have agreed on. The third value sub-question narrows in on distribution: who gets what part of the value generated in the exchange? This goes to the deeper question of who gets most of the value generated, for example, in the rents paid to landowners, the wages paid to labor, or the profits paid to capital-owners. The distribution question also addresses the issue of which goods and services we consider publicly owned, to be paid for collectively, and which ones should be privately owned, paid for individually.

Finally, the three important sub-questions supporting the inquiry into "how we want to interact?" help us see our organizational agreements more clearly. The first question asks why we come together. This opens the whole area of why people cooperate in the first place, as captured in group charters, vision and mission statements, or sometimes cost-benefit analyses. The second question looks at how people agree to interact. It takes us into the realm of competitive, cooperative, and collaborative models in the field of organizational development. The third question focuses on what organizational form best supports how the group agrees to interact. Should it be a corporation, a partnership, a network or something else? What are the incentives people will need to participate in desired ways within that structure?

## INQUIRING INTO OUR AGREEMENTS

As with any significant change we undertake to make in our lives, moving toward agreements that will produce greater harmonic vibrancy and abundance requires a clear-eyed assessment of our current situation and the agreements underlying it. For many reasons, which I have discussed at length, these agreements and the opportunities for changing them can be difficult to perceive. However, in the Expanded Ecosynomics Levels of Reality Map (Figure 12) we have the framework for a systematic inquiry into these agreements using the powerful questions economics has provided.

## The Agreements Evidence Map (Template)

| The Agreements of our experience | Resources How Much? | Allocation Who decides? | Value By what criteria? | Organization How shall we interact? |
|---|---|---|---|---|
| Possibility Potential (Light) =a+b+c | Potential Capacity What is your potential capacity? | Primary Relationship(s) to decide our potential | Future Potential What is our most desired future? | Collaboration How shall we interact to collaborate? |
| Development Motion (Verb) =a+b | Capacity Development What capacities are we developing? | Which Relationship(s) to decide how we develop our resources | Learning and Growth Where do we most want to learn and grow? | Co-opetition How shall we interact to cooperate competitively? |
| Things Matter (Noun) =a | Available Capacity What is your available capacity? | Primary Relationship(s) to decide how we allocate our resources | Outcomes What outcomes do we value most? | Competition How shall we interact to compete? |

*Figure 14: The Agreements Map*

The Agreements Map (Figure 14) is a tool for recording the information gathered for recording the information gathered in this inquiry. It is simply the right hand face of the large block in the Expanded Ecosynomics Levels of Reality Map. You will notice, however, that the questions (Figure 13) are streamlined into category headings. This will make it easier to work with as you begin to fill in (i.e., "map") your data across the twelve areas of the Agreements Map. Now, let us move on to see how this actually works.

# CHAPTER 6

# THE AGREEMENTS EVIDENCE MAP— SEEING AGREEMENTS THROUGH THE LENSES OF ECOSYNOMICS

The purpose of the Agreements Evidence Map, which I will shorten to the "Agreements Map," is to enable you to see your agreements as they show up in the practices, structures and processes you experience in your life. The four economic questions lead you to identify patterns that signify the underlying agreements shaping lived reality. Locating this information on the terrain of the Agreements Map will allow you to assess these patterns relative to the five relationships and three levels of perceived reality and to determine which ones you want to strengthen and which you want to have less of. In other words, your completed Agreements Map will support your moving to a higher level of abundance in resources, a higher vibrancy in the value you experience, and a higher harmonic in the organization of human interactions.

In this chapter, I am going to take you through the steps of creating and interpreting Agreements Maps.[82] First, I will describe the process for gathering the information on which the Agreements Map will be based. Then I will delve into the details of creating the content of the map derived from that information. In addition to mapping the data on how agreements show up, you will be using color-coding to capture the strength of the patterns that emerge. This represents an adaptation of the idea of the "choropleth map," a map that

---

82    Mike Puleo, a board member at the Institute for Strategic Clarity and director at Deloitte, co-developed the Agreements Map with me as a tool for assessing the costs of scarcity. For more on the "agreements map" tool, and specifically how it was used with the costs of scarcity map, see (Ritchie-Dunham, Puleo, & Throneburg, 2012).

is color-coded based on some statistical property of the data in the map.[83] The color-coding will allow you to make your assessments and comparisons more readily. Finally, I will suggest how to go about determining what the content signifies and the various ways you can learn from Agreements Maps. Now, let's look at how you can go about constructing an Agreements Map for your own group.

## CREATING AN AGREEMENTS MAP

The Agreements Map captures your agreements by applying the four lenses to the five primary relationships at the three levels of perceived reality, all in one color-coded graphic. Yikes! As you approach the task of creating an Agreements Map, it may help to remember that this complicated and impersonal-looking table is just another way of drawing the 3-circle diagram that emerged from our reflections on personal experience. It is just not possible to write down all of our observations on the 3-circle diagram, so we need to work with the table instead. In the translation process, we do not want to forget that the Agreements Map is really the application of the four lenses to your own experience.

### BUILDING THE MAP—PROCESS

To build the Agreements Evidence Map, you need to populate it with data—evidence of the agreements that exist in the set of relationships you are examining. As in any exercise of this nature, it is extremely important to build the Agreements Map on credible evidence. The process involves identifying reliable sources of information, gathering and mapping the evidence, and then validating the map. I am going to describe how I do this when I am acting as an outside consultant to the group. Different groups can come up with different approaches, of course. The important thing is to find some way to ensure objectivity and reliability, so that group members will be willing to accept and work with the completed Agreements Map.

#### Sources

To address the issue of reliability, I try to get multiple sources for the evidence. Typically, I focus on interviewing individuals who have a deep

---

83    The first known use of the term "choropleth map" is attributed to the geographer John Kirtland Wright (Wright, 1938, pp. 1-18).

understanding of how the group functions, usually based on years of experience in the group. I complement these individuals' observations with my own observations of the group in action. I also look for documentary evidence of the group's processes and outcomes, both from its internal reports and from documents created outside the group. These three sources, as a starting point, let me triangulate different pieces of information to validate what I am seeing or hearing.

For example, if an interviewee in a service organization tells me emphatically that the group focuses on healthy relationships with its customers, I would expect to see documented processes, organizational structures, information systems, and customer feedback that supported that assertion. In a family setting, if Dad says the kids come first, then I might look for evidence of how much time he spends with them. The intention with the triangulation of data is to differentiate people's actual agreements from the "aspirational" agreements—that is, the agreements they would like to have.

People are very good at talking about what they think they should do or what they would like to do. Sometimes this varies significantly from what they actually do. The gap will show up in an Agreements Map inquiry. On the other hand, it can turn out that the practice is even stronger than people in the group suspected, and this becomes apparent when you can document that not only do they say something is important, they are actually really good at seeing it, valuing it, and organizing for it. This is how I have identified many of the leading edge, high-vibrancy practices I have found in high vibrancy groups.

### Validating the Agreements Map

Working with the different sources of information, I validate what I am learning along the way as much as possible. When someone tells me about an agreement, my inquiry starts to focus on determining whether the agreement actually exists and whether it is actually in use. How prevalent is the practice based on this agreement? Would most folks say they were aware of it or is it known only within a small group? Does it show up all of the time, some of the time, rarely or never? As you gather evidence on these distinctions, you are building up your case for the picture you will be drawing with the completed Agreements Map.

When you are unsure whether the evidence you find is valid, whether it be in the form of written data, interviews, or your own observations, I suggest you write down the evidence with a question mark next to it, and ask about it. The people who are living with the agreements will be able to help you determine whether the evidence is valid or not. For example, in a toy company I worked with there was one individual who told me about a collaborative practice that he said was very common in the group. Nobody else mentioned it. I could have taken this to mean that he was expressing wishful thinking. Instead I documented that he had said it, and that nobody else had. When I shared this with the group, they all acknowledged that he was right. I asked why nobody else had mentioned it, and they told me that it was so common in their agreements that they did not even think about it. Fortunately I had documented and not discounted it, as it turned out to be a very innovative practice that they had developed, one that I would have missed had I dismissed it.

I want to emphasize here the importance of keeping an open mind during this inquiry. There are no right or wrong answers; just the data you are finding. The intention is to be accurate, not to push an agenda such as showing how strong the group is, or finding its weak spots or trying to move it in a particular direction. Without this impartiality, you will not be able to see clearly what agreements actually live within the group or what agreements need to shift to a higher level. False data that does not represent what is actually happening can, at the very least, cloud your understanding of what is actually happening and the possibility that is available in the emerging agreements. In the worst-case scenario, false evidence might make a group believe it is at a higher level than it actually is and lead it to take on new agreements that are too far beyond its capacity.

Once you have populated the Agreements Map with evidence from interviews, observations, and printed materials, you can validate it with the group. When I can, I try to validate the map with individual interviews first. Then I talk with the group as a whole and possibly with external sources, such as other people who live near them, someone who works with them, or someone who knows of them in the industry. I have found that starting with individual validation interviews gives each person a chance to give me their input—their stories—without the political charge of competing with other voices and opinions.

I also like to have a group validation conversation, because I find that the diversity in the group offers perspectives the individuals cannot have on their own. These conversations can be highly collaborative and creative, especially if each participant has already contributed through an individual validation interview. If all goes well, the Agreements Map will not only be accurate and accepted as credible by the group, it will provide a solid foundation for moving toward agreements that will lead to higher vibrancy and abundance for everyone involved.

## BUILDING THE MAP—CONTENT

To create the content of an Agreements Map, I work systematically through the four lenses looking across the five relationships at each of the three levels of perceived reality. Keep in mind that the Agreements Map is a two-dimensional snapshot of this three-dimensional way of looking at your experience. (See the three-dimensional view in Chapter 5, Figure 12.) Its purpose is to synthesize the data in a way that allows you to see the existing agreements through all four lenses at the same time so that you can understand why you are getting the outcomes and experiences that you are. It will also highlight the possible agreements available in the relationships.

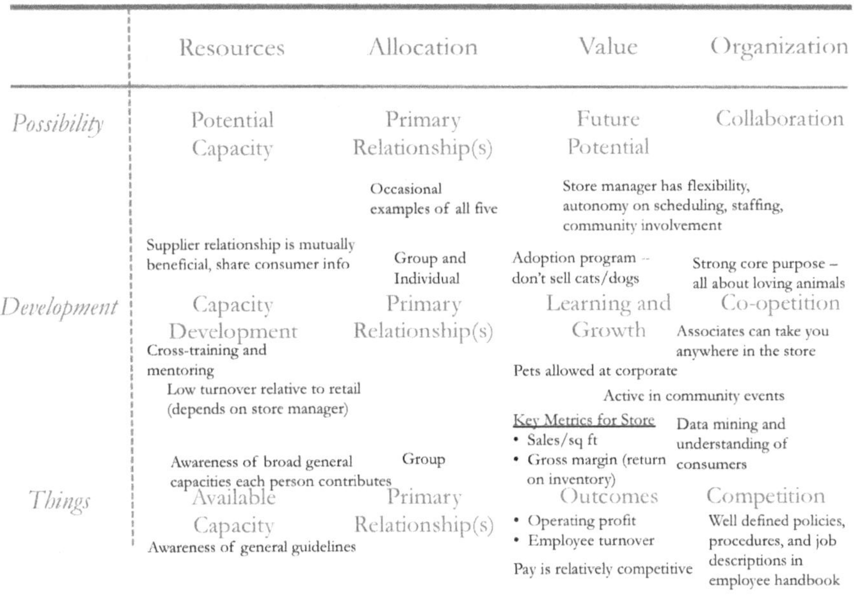

|  | Resources | Allocation | Value | Organization |
|---|---|---|---|---|
| *Possibility* | Potential Capacity | Primary Relationship(s) | Future Potential | Collaboration |
| *Development* | Supplier relationship is mutually beneficial, share consumer info — Capacity Development — Cross-training and mentoring — Low turnover relative to retail (depends on store manager) | Occasional examples of all five — Group and Individual — Primary Relationship(s) | Store manager has flexibility, autonomy on scheduling, staffing, community involvement — Adoption program – don't sell cats/dogs — Learning and Growth — Pets allowed at corporate — Active in community events | Strong core purpose – all about loving animals — Co-opetition — Associates can take you anywhere in the store |
| *Things* | Awareness of broad general capacities each person contributes — Available Capacity — Awareness of general guidelines | Group — Primary Relationship(s) | Key Metrics for Store • Sales/sq ft • Gross margin (return on inventory) — Outcomes • Operating profit • Employee turnover — Pay is relatively competitive | Data mining and understanding of consumers — Competition — Well defined policies, procedures, and job descriptions in employee handbook |

*Figure 15: Example Agreements Map of a Pet Store Chain*

As I walk through the construction of an Agreements Map, I will use as an example a completed map from a chain of pet stores my colleagues and I worked with some years ago (Figure 15). The chain of stores was interested in identifying those practices in different stores that led to stronger outcomes, and a better experience for the consumer and for the employee. This exercise showed the practices as agreements, highlighting those agreements that were common to all stores in the chain, and which were specific to higher performing stores. While the Agreements Map was used for a large company in this case, it can be applied the same way for both small groups or large; whether businesses, communities, government agencies, nonprofits or families. Basically it can be used in any situation to record the evidence of agreements seen when looking through the four lenses at any experience.

### Available capacity

When I ask the resource question at the things-matter level, the inquiry is all about what capacities are available now. There are two parts to the question: first, what is the awareness of available capacity; and second, to what extent is the capacity being applied. I ask these questions of each of the five primary relationships.

Starting with the relationship to self, if there is awareness, I would expect that when I ask an individual about the specific capacities she brings to the job, she could tell me. To see if those capacities were being applied, I would look for a degree of corroboration of her self-perception in some form of job description or performance evaluations. For example, when asked, an associate in the pet store knew what capacities were required to do his job: knowledge about specific breeds of dogs and cats, including what they eat; skill in asking questions so he could see what the pet owner wanted to get at the store; and very importantly, he needed to be good with animals. As a matter of fact, many associates told me that part of their job interview process included cleaning out an animal cage, with an animal in it, to test how well they dealt with animals, and how animals responded to them. This seemed to me to be strong evidence that the pet store employees were aware of their individual capacities.

Now, what does it mean that this individual awareness of capacities is part of the agreements in the relationship to self at the things level? What I am looking for is whether or not there is an agreement that this individual self-awareness is important. I often find that people in the groups I work with are completely unaware of basic capacities that are available to them—the knowledge and skills that individual group members have. When I point out these capacities, the group members readily acknowledge how important they are. When I ask why they do not pay attention to them or support them, these same people look at me with a shocked face: "We have never even talked about it. It seems obvious when you point it out, but it's just not part of our conversation." I suggest that this pattern reflects an agreement—the opposite of the agreement in the pet stores—that paying attention to individual capacities is not a priority for the success of the group.

Continuing with the mapping in the relationship to the other, I look for some form of awareness and acknowledgement of the capacities that other individuals bring. Can people in one area tell me what capacities individuals in other areas have? In the pet stores, for example, they said they all knew who had particular knowledge about cats or pet grooming. I then look for evidence that this awareness exists in practice and is supported. In some groups, this support might be a directory of special capacities. In the pet stores, it was a resource person who knew who to call for specific needs: "John, I have a 2-year old Labrador that seems to have a fussy intestine. Who should I ask about organic food?"

To explore the relationship to the group, I look for the level of awareness of the unique contribution each individual's capacities make to the group. That is, in addition to knowing their own capacities and what other individuals can do, do people know how these individual capacities contribute to the group? I ask them about this to ascertain awareness, and I also ask about and observe how awareness shows up in actual practices. For example, in the pet store, do they think about the different capacities needed in helping someone through the whole cat adoption process? When helping someone adopt a cat, do they bring in the colleague who knows most about cat adoptions and is best at making the moment when the customer meets the cat comfortable? Do they then bring in the person who knows most about cat products, like food, toys, scratch pads, and litter boxes? Or do they not even think about all of these parts of the process or who knows most about these parts?

Since the relationship to nature at the things-matter level is all about the concrete, I would look for awareness of available resources that is focused on outcomes. Sticking with the cat adoption example; are people clear about what cats are available, what the customer wants to leave with, and all of the possible accessories the store could sell the new cat owner? If this awareness exists and is put into practice, I would expect to see some protocol or check sheet for the process of taking customers through cat acquisition. Likewise, in the relationship to spirit, the source of creativity, I would look for written-down protocols that everyone knows to follow—the rules that have been handed down.

Now, to summarize what I described above, so that I can record it in the Agreements Map, I found ample evidence of both awareness and application of available capacities in the pet store chain. The employees were aware of their own capacities, those of others, how they each contributed specific, unique capacities to the group, what the expected outcomes were for the customer, and the protocols to follow. The practices supporting their awareness at the things level were very clear, efficient, and effective. This is what I recorded in the Available Capacity cell of the Agreements Map.

So, what would you expect to see in your group if indeed people were aware of available capacities and applying them effectively in each of the five primary relationships? Do the individuals know what capacities they have? In the family, do my kids know they can sing, draw, wash dishes and clean up their rooms? Do group members or family members acknowledge each other's capacities? While my daughter might be a great songwriter and knows it, do I know it? At the kids' school, do the different parents know what each family is able to contribute uniquely to the school community? For example, when it comes to school events, do we know which ones are better at planning, or at making things, or at motivating others to participate? At the town hall, do we have procedures written down to explain how to go about, say, getting a hunting license; or does every resident have to figure this out for himself each and every time?

The tricky part of dealing with this section of the Agreements Map is to maintain the focus on resources—the "how much?" question. This is not a value question about the criteria for allocating resources. For example, if the resource is money, deal only with how much money is available, not with who gets to keep what part of that money. Nor is it an organization question of how the relationships should interact, for example should they compete with each other, each providing their own capacities. That would be an organization question. Here we are only focused on the level of awareness and application of knowing what capacities are available in each of the five primary relationships right now.

### Capacity development

To continue the inquiry through the resources lens at the development-motion level, I add the dimension of time. Now my questions are the following: is there awareness of how resources develop over time; and how frequently is this awareness applied? This is the development level of perceived reality of the five primary relationships, as seen through the first lens of resources.

Here are the kinds of questions you can ask to look at each of the primary relationships through this lens: do our agreements include an awareness of how we are individually developing our capacities over time? Do we support each other in the development of these capacities? Are we learning and developing as a group? Do we focus on improving our processes to achieve better outcomes over time? Do we, as a matter of daily practice, look for creativity to enter into our work? You should also look for evidence of thinking and practices reflecting sensitivity to change over time. For example, do people actually spend time during the day thinking about what they know and what they are learning? Are there moments or spaces for this kind of reflection and inquiry? Is there a way that people keep track of what is being learned?

In the pet stores represented in our sample Agreements Map, everyone was expected to learn about the different areas through cross training in how the different departments worked. There was also quite a bit of mentoring, with people who knew more about a specific area, such as grooming, supporting others as they learned about that area. We found evidence for healthy appreciation of the development level of capacity in some stores in their low turnover of employees, meaning that people stayed in the job much longer than normal, especially in relation to other retail stores. When we inquired into this in the lower turnover stores, the associates shared how much they liked their work, their colleagues, and being able to work with the animals. We found this was truer in some stores than others. I also noted that the store's management worked closely with suppliers in a mutually beneficial manner, sharing customer information, so that the supplier could recommend products that better served the specific needs of each store's customer base.

All of this information went into the Agreements Map as an indication that there was awareness of capacity development and application of that awareness. In other settings, we might find practices that track the inflows and outflows of a resource—like tracking the changes in the level of the water in our local lake, as a function of what is flowing in and out over time. Later we will see alternative exchange systems that track the amount of currency people have flowing in and out of their accounts as the result of the activities that they engage in with each other. Some networks track the development of relationships among different members of the network, to see where influence is shifting to over time. The point is to look at change over time in the development of capacities and relationships.

In this section, you are concerned to see how aware you are of the capacities you need, both now and in the future. What do you need to do, over time, to develop those capacities, to meet in those ever-changing needs for resources? Be careful, though. This section only includes the awareness of capacity development, not the cooperative processes you may have for developing these capacities and relationships. That comes later, when you are working with the organization lens.

### Potential capacity

Finally, I want to apply the resources lens to the possibility-light level. The inquiry here revolves around one key issue: does the group look for potential capacities in each of the five relationships, potential that it can sense but that has not shown up yet? To determine whether this is the case, I look for evidence that people are actively inviting in the possibility for new resources to emerge. This often shows up as a consistent expectation by all involved, that creativity is everywhere, all of the time, in all of the relationships, and it is just a matter of being open to and looking for it.

In the case of the pet store chain, you can see by the open space in this cell of the Agreements Map that I did not find evidence of awareness at this level. In examples we will see later in the book, at this level we look for evidence of people acknowledging each other's emerging potential. What possibilities do I see right now in myself? In you? Do we make time in our daily lives to reflect on what we see emerging? Do we make time to share it? Do we record it in journals, so that we can see what we are enacting of that potential?

Discerning awareness at the possibility-light level can be tricky sometimes because you have to be alert to the difference between talk and practice. In many groups, people feel they should be talking about possibilities for development. One organization I worked with had the motto, "Our people and their potential is the most critical resource we have" boldly written on the wall in its headquarters lobby. But my inquiry discovered that this was not the reality. As soon as profits began to decrease, this company laid off fifteen percent of its more experienced staff, because they were more expensive. Remember, it is what actually happens that we want to capture in the Agreements Map. Consistency is also important. Are people continuously exploring the possibilities, or does this attitude only show up sporadically?

Finally, it helps to be aware that there are many groups where possibility is the *only* reality that shows up in the resources lens. This is tricky because it looks like people are exploring possibility, but they are only looking at possibility. They are not choosing to develop a particular possibility and bring it into being at the concrete level. Functioning at the possibility level of reality requires functioning at the development and things levels as well. Groups that only live in possibilities, never choosing, developing and manifesting any of those possibilities, have actually converted the "art of possibility" into a thing. For them, seeing the possibility is the outcome, the only outcome.

I capture this "possibility-only" awareness on the Agreements map at the things level of available capacity, an example of the on-the-level only thinking I described in Chapter 2. For example, for one group I wrote on the things level of resources: "many conversations about possibilities—no outcomes." Noting this on the map at the things level highlighted the gap between their talk and what they were actually doing. This is important so that groups do not think they are working at a higher level of harmonic vibrancy than they are.

### Primary relationship(s)

We now shift to the second lens, the question of who decides how to allocate the resources. Chapter 4 showed how economic thinking that sees scarcity through the resources lens creates the tendency to see one of the five relationships as primary. Hence, most systems of agreement place one relationship above all others, with the assumption that the others will also be met. This is as true in organizations, communities, and families as it is in political-economic systems. The goal in developing the content of this section of the Agreements Map is to determine which relationship predominates in guiding decision-making about how resources will be used.

As a starting point, I use the basic characteristics of the five types of political-economic system presented in Chapter 4 as guidelines for what the primacy of different relationships looks like. Is the emphasis on freedom and self-determination of individuals? Is equity the all-important consideration? Is the prevailing mindset that the wellbeing of the group as a whole comes before all else and ensures the wellbeing of all? Is resource allocation guided by a systemic view that emphasizes maintaining a dynamic balance among the parts of the system? Or does the organization privilege creativity over all other considerations?

Here I look for the practices people have around how decisions are made about resource allocation. Who is included in the decision—just one person, a couple of people, many or everyone? Also, what is the overriding concern in decision making? Is it every individual for himself or herself? When the decisions are in the hands of two people, are those two representing their personal needs or the needs of the family or team of which they are a part? Does there seem to be one relationship that is primary or are there indications of multiple forms of decision making? For example, does the father decide for the whole family or the founder for the whole company? Or does the group engage many people in its decision processes? Or is there evidence for all five relationships engaged in resource decisions: individuals deciding for themselves; pairs of individuals working with each other to achieve a sense of felt-fair equity; and the group deciding on the basis of the health of the whole, in a way that works with the choosing of possibilities to develop towards specific outcomes and invokes the full creativity available to the group?

Often I find that groups hold different relationships primary at different levels of perceived reality. In the pet store chain, for example, I determined that the allocation of resources at the things-matter level definitely focused primarily on the health of the group. However, when the things-matter level outcomes—such as having the capacities needed in the store to respond on a given day to the needs of customers and their pets—were healthy, at above average levels, the company also gave employees the freedom to focus on their own development and engagement. This is why the pet store Agreements Map indicates awareness of both group and individual relationships at the development level. When we look through this lens at the possibility level, we see occasional examples of all five primary relationships at the same time, like a store where the manager and associates worked together very collaboratively; exploring many creative ideas for ways to engage the community, to improve the store's processes, and to develop the potential the associates and manager brought to the group, both individually and as a group.

I find that what I see through the allocation lens is often the expression of a deeply held philosophy within the group, not just what the leadership is saying but also what the community is living. In the pet store chain, this cornerstone philosophy might be stated as, "We care about animals and how our customers raise them." In a friend's family, the philosophy is one of full participation by all family members in decision-making about resources. They enact this philosophy in their daily practices.

The tricky spot in this section of the Agreements Map is to tease out the allocation mechanism actually being used, not just the one people say they use. For example, the leaders of many companies talk publicly with great passion about the importance of individual freedom as part of their advocacy for free-market policies. In reality, many of them only mean freedom for the company as an entity, in the marketplace of companies—in essence freedom for the owner. They do not believe in or practice freedom for the individual within the company. Rather they see that individual as an employee, contributing through very specific tasks to the good of the group. Within many of these companies, you will find that they actually make most agreements based on the health of the group—the company—and not the individuals within the company. In these cases, I record on the Agreements Map what the companies are actually doing, prioritizing the health of the group in its actual practices of resource allocation decisions, rather than what the leader is saying about personal freedom. Similarly, in some networks I have worked with, there is much verbiage about fairness among the network members in relation to resource allocation, when in practice individuals are expected to fend for themselves. Here again, I highlight the individual-oriented practices in resource allocation and I do not emphasize the words about fairness.

### Value—outcomes

Next, we will look through the third lens, Value, to explore what guides the allocation of resources in the group. Applying this lens first at the things-matter level, I expect to find thinking about value that is focused on concrete outcomes. This is a transactional mindset: what are we getting for what we put in? When looking through the value lens at the things level, my inquiry focuses on determining what is the value, if any, placed on the existing capacities of the individual, the other, the group, the outcomes, and the creative offer of the group? I look to see if everyone is aware of this value, in each relationship, and if they practice it continuously.

My notations in the Agreements Map in this section record the specific processes and structures the group uses to track the value it is producing with its resources. I look to see whether the group has outcome metrics focused on efficiency, and how much resource they used to achieve what outcomes. I observe whether the incentives for the group and for individuals are clearly aligned with their outcomes. For example, the pet store chain gathered information on store-by-store operation including; the volume of sales revenues per square foot of storefront, the financial return on the investment in inventory in the store, net operating profit, and the rate of employee turnover. It was also paying competitive wages relative to other businesses of its type. In this case, I determined that the organization was rewarding its employees based largely on the specific capacities they brought, with a heavy focus on financial and operational outcomes.

### Value—learning and growth

To see if groups are thinking about value at the development-motion level, I try to discover whether they see value in the building of capacities and relationships over time in the five relationships. Do they value and support individual growth and development? Do individuals support learning and growth in others? Is there awareness of how the development of individuals contributes to the group as a whole, and what is the group's capacity to support those contributions? Do people see the value of process, of the journey and learning along the way? And, finally, do they see the value in moments of creativity springing forth from individuals?

On the Agreements Map in this section, I want to capture structures and processes that show how prevalent these experiences of value are and how much the group values the development of relationships. In the pet store, I saw people talking about the value they get from training across the different areas of the store and the importance they placed on the quality of their relationships with customers, customers' pets and the other employees in the store. Depending on the store manager, some pet store employees had quite a bit of autonomy, for example, to schedule and hire the staff they wanted or to engage their local communities in creative ways, such as pet adoption or pet appreciation events.

Another example of the value the company placed on relationships revolved around the animals. Associates who valued their relationships with the clients' pets also tended to value the relationship with their own pets. The corporation showed respect for these relationships through its policy of allowing employees' pets at the corporate office, just as it allowed customers to bring their pets into the stores. The high value the company gave to relationships with animals also led it to stop selling cats and dogs, and to develop an in-store adoption program that partners with local shelters to rescue orphaned animals instead, encouraging its customers to see themselves as saving the life of a pet.

Awareness of capacity development shows up in other form in different groups, for example, in the merit badges awarded to scouts. These awards acknowledge their development and lead to their stepping into greater responsibilities. Similarly, in certain religious groups, the development of the ability to read the core book is marked with a celebration of the attainment of a higher level of development. I also find various kinds of evidence of the development of relationships over time. In a network, for example, I look for signs that the network is becoming stronger because of the relationships that are developing among its members.

### Value—potential

At the possibility-light level, I inquire into whether the group places importance on its members' living into their full potential in the five relationships. Do the practices, systems and culture support looking for the best in each individual? Do individuals support each other in that exploration? Does the group as a whole value the search for its own highest possibilities and invite what each member might contribute to achieving them? What value is placed on the process of seeing new possibilities and working with them? To what extent does the group value creativity in all of its forms?

To capture the results of this inquiry on the Agreements Map, I need to record those structures and processes that express the nature and degree of how the group values possibility. In the case of the pet store chain, I noted the fact that the store manager has flexibility to make decisions in a number of key areas—scheduling, staffing and community involvement. This is an example of valuing the store manager's ability to see potential in her employees, to run the store in a way that enables it to meet emerging consumer needs and to identify and reach out to potential new markets.

### Competition

The organization lens focuses on how people interact to achieve what they value. At the things level, this fourth lens highlights the group's ability to utilize its available resources in a way that maximizes desirable outcomes relative to what it values. I want to see, quite simply, whether or not the group is organized in a way that enables it to deliver on its purpose: whether it can produce results. As evidence of this, I look for well-defined procedures, policies, structures and job descriptions that can support people in performing effectively and efficiently, across all five primary relationships. In the pet store chain, I found all of this in the employee handbook.

A friend described the competitive logic of the experience of his kid's football team, as seen through the lens of organization. The focus is very much on the specific skills each kid brings, with some kids being stars and others being supporters of the stars. While they train all season, the training is focused on strengthening the existing capacities. This is different than a developmental approach, which would look to learn about the evolving capacities of each kid—here the focus is on being more efficient, stronger, and more able to do the task at hand with the kid's given capacities. In this case, I would capture the careful assessment of each kid's capacities and results (speed, dexterity, strength, endurance). I would also note the fixation on record keeping of all of these stats, the clear and precise ranking of kids by results, and the focus on those who make the best contribution, the stars, using the coach's play book of best offense moves. These are all indicators of an organizational focus on the things-outcomes level of scarce resources put to optimal use to obtain a scarce outcome, winning. There is, after all, only one team who scores the most points.

### Co-opetition

At the development-motion level, the organization lens sheds light on how a group is organized to build capacities and relationships. The label for this area of the Agreements Map, "co-opetition," is shorthand for cooperative competition, which is what I look for at this level of perceived reality.[84] The word competition comes from the Latin root for striving—striving to be better than others. The trick in this section of the Agreements Map is to distinguish whether the group you are looking at is not-competitive, only-competitive, or also-competitive. The distinction among these three is significant. Not-competitive means that the group cannot compete successfully. Only-competitive means that competition is the principal drive of the organization—striving to be better than others is its main focus. Also-competitive means that the group is organized for a purpose other than competition, *and* it is also very competitive. This is what co-opetition typically looks like.

In the pet store chain, I found evidence of functioning at the level of co-opetition in the company's processes for developing its associates' understanding of, and belief in, its core purpose—which is all about loving animals. Everyone pays attention to how associates work with the animals, and they talk about this in meetings. The company encourages taking extra time with customers to make sure that the needs of their pets are met; the opposite of trying to get people out of the store quickly with as much merchandise as possible. The stores' organizational practices reflect the corporate attitude that building the customer relationship is critical to its mission as well as to its success as a business. This attitude is also clearly visible in how the associates engage with pet owners and their pets as they enter the store and the quality of care they give the animals.

I have found that many groups who look through the organization lens at their experience and see co-opetition are much more efficient than the only-competitive groups they meet. On my son's soccer team, for example, the kids have all worked together in many activities related to art, sports and academics, because teaching students how to work cooperatively is a priority at his school. As a result, the team members know each other very well and cooperate effectively and efficiently. They compete against many teams that seem to be focused on only competition, as evidenced by the fact that they have a couple of star players who are always aggressively doing the work of the rest of the team. My son's team usually beats such opponents. The point is that also-competitive groups that are very efficient cooperators or collaborators,

---

84    We borrow the term co-opetition from (Brandenburger & Nalebuff, 1998).

are able to play the game as well as or better than the only-competitive, and usually without the negative costs of the exclusive focus on competition.

In groups that are successful at co-opetition, I expect to see people working together to achieve the shared goal of performing effectively and achieving success, with some degree of focus on learning and growing together. In the relationship to self, I look for whether individuals are motivated toward personal growth and working with others. Are there processes to support individuals' knowing what others can contribute, not just with their current capabilities, but also with the new capabilities they are in the process of developing? Does the group focus on teamwork and readily form new teams as projects require them? All of these things are indicators of co-opetition. In the pet stores, I saw evidence of this level of functioning in the fact that every associate is expected to be able to take the customer anywhere in the store. This means they must know about all parts of the store and be able to determine what services a customer needs, beyond their immediate area of responsibility. They must also be aware of the overall needs of their customers and the customers' pets and be able to think of ways to meet them. All of this requires a great deal of capacity development and teamwork.

### Collaboration

The final section of the Agreements Map looks through the fourth lens of organizing interactions at the possibility-light level. To see if a group is operating at this level, I look for collaboration. By collaboration I mean that people are working together toward a shared purpose that transcends operational effectiveness. Everyone is participating and contributing creatively to imagine future possibilities in all five relationships on a continuous basis.

I also look for patterns, processes and structures that support collaboration. Is there a flow of mutual support among group members at meetings, in interactions between meetings and in all forms of communication? Is everyone aware of the core purposes and how their local tasks align (or not) with those purposes? Do people continuously seek clarity around this alignment? Do the group's communication and information systems and processes of interaction enable its members to identify moments of creativity and know how to capitalize on those moments?

There was no evidence of this level of organizing in the pet store chain. However, I have seen it frequently in high vibrancy groups. One such group is THORLO, the high-tech sock company I introduced in Chapter 3. Many of THORLO's possibility-light-level organizational practices came into existence to support what the company calls "integrated collaborative conversations." These conversations are designed to keep different parts of the organization in constant interaction and create a continuous flow of information, all focused on THORLO's clearly articulated purpose—to ensure the foot health of its loyal customers. One of the processes supporting the integrity of these conversations is "surfacing surprises." It is part of the agenda every time the "conversation" gets together, often weekly, to see what new, big, or different things are happening. It represents an effort to avoid gaps in communication that might create future problems.

For example, there might be this exchange: "It surprised me today when you placed an order without asking me." "I did that in response to a special case that required a quick turnaround." "Okay, what can we learn from this surprise about how to do quick-turnaround orders without keeping me in the dark?" This is an example of the kind of evidence I have found at THORLO, which shows me that the group is actively collaborating based on a sense of shared purpose. Everyone knows that this purpose requires each person's unique contributions. All must be aligned on who is doing what when, but they must also be responsive to moments of creativity throughout the system. This is what I mean by effective collaboration.

## BUILDING THE MAP—COLOR CODING

With the content of the Agreements Map in place, I can delve into the nature of the agreements in the group in some detail. At the same time, however, I want to be able to tell with a quick look how much the agreements support the group's functioning within a specific combination of relationship, level and lens. How aware are people in the group of available capacity, or learning and growth, or collaboration; and how consistently do they apply that awareness? This is where color-coding comes in. It shows me at a glance the patterns across all sections of the map.

I create the color codes by rating the strength of awareness and application in resources, value and organization, using a scale of 1 to 10. A score of 1 means that folks are almost never aware of, say, potential capacity in the group, and there is little to no evidence of its being applied. By implication, it is not part of their agreements. On the other end of the scale, a 10 means that they are almost always aware of it and almost always apply that awareness. It is an integral part of the agreements.

I use the color green for the high end of the scale, yellow for the middle, red for the low end and white to show no awareness or application. In other words, for green, most people are aware of the element—capacity development, outcomes, competition—and they apply that awareness most of the time. Yellow shows that some people are aware of it some of the time and apply it some of the time. Red means that most people are not aware of the element and rarely if ever apply it; that is, little to no awareness and very infrequent application. White means that there is no evidence that it happens at all.

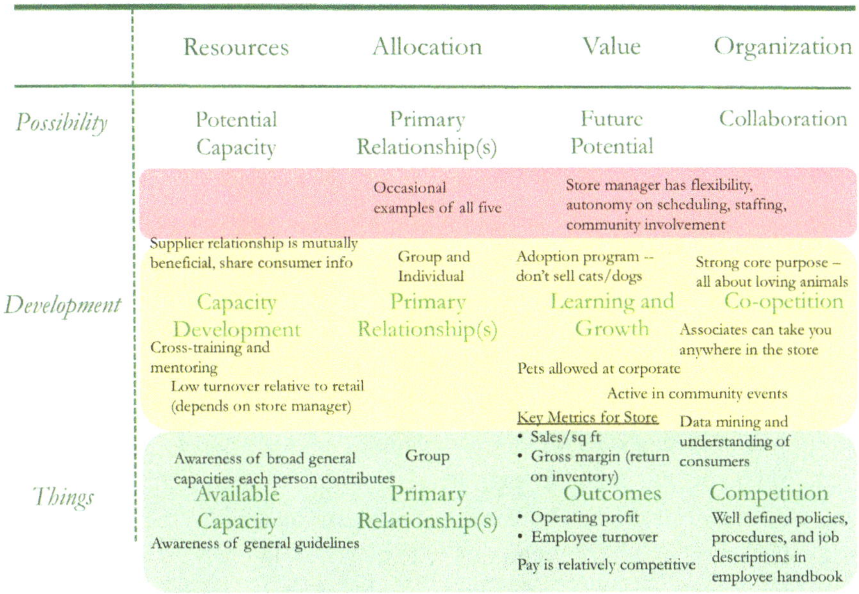

|  | Resources | Allocation | Value | Organization |
|---|---|---|---|---|
| *Possibility* | Potential Capacity | Primary Relationship(s) | Future Potential | Collaboration |
|  |  | Occasional examples of all five | Store manager has flexibility, autonomy on scheduling, staffing, community involvement |  |
| *Development* | Supplier relationship is mutually beneficial, share consumer info **Capacity Development** Cross-training and mentoring Low turnover relative to retail (depends on store manager) | Group and Individual **Primary Relationship(s)** | Adoption program -- don't sell cats/dogs **Learning and Growth** Pets allowed at corporate Active in community events Key Metrics for Store • Sales/sq ft • Gross margin (return on inventory) • Operating profit • Employee turnover Pay is relatively competitive | Strong core purpose – all about loving animals **Co-opetition** Associates can take you anywhere in the store Data mining and understanding of consumers |
| *Things* | Awareness of broad general capacities each person contributes **Available Capacity** Awareness of general guidelines | Group **Primary Relationship(s)** | **Outcomes** | **Competition** Well defined policies, procedures, and job descriptions in employee handbook |

*Figure 16: Color-coded Pet Store Chain Agreements Map*

Another way of thinking about the colors is that green means go, all systems are good; yellow means watch out, as some systems are working and some are not; red means to stop and notice as this is rare; and white means it does not exist in the agreements. You can also think of it as red is where the newest opportunities are for growth, yellow is where there is growth beginning to happen that could be nurtured, and green is where the success needs to be maintained, while supporting new growth. White shows completely new territory for the group.

Figure 16, above, shows the color-coded version of the pet store chain's Agreements Map. You will notice that the color-coding forms bands across the different levels of perceived reality. This is true of all Agreements Maps, although not all Agreements Maps have four different colored bands like this example. It is a basic principle of Ecosynomics that the level at which an individual or group is functioning applies across all five relationships, as part of an integrated experience of reality. Now we are also integrating the different perspectives on that experience provided by the lenses. Bringing those perspectives together with the color-coding gives greater meaning to the data in the Agreements Map.

### At the things-matter level

A green band at the things-matter level is an indication that the group has a strong foundation for its operations. This is what we see in the pet store example. In the resources area, there is a conscious awareness of the capacities available right now and the outcomes achievable with those capacities. Green in the value section at this level indicates a healthy clarity about the value of the capacities that exist in the group and of the outcomes those resources can produce. Similarly, green in the organization section shows a group that has structured its interactions to deliver those outcomes. All of these positive conditions existed in the pet store chain and are captured in the Agreements Map.

A yellow or red band at the things-matter level would suggest that a group was operating on a weaker foundation (yellow) or no foundation at all (red). Yellow in the available capacity section could mean that the group is only slightly aware of the core capacities it has or it lacks the practices to acknowledge them. I have found this state of yellow in many groups that have only some awareness of the capacities available to them internally. When I ask what can Fred or Susan do to contribute to this group and only a couple of people can tell me some of the capacities they bring, even though I know those capacities are critical to the group's functioning, I see yellow. Think about your kids' ability to describe what Mom or Dad contributes on a daily or weekly basis to the family.

Yellow in the value section signifies that the group struggles with valuing the available resources, and others only occasionally acknowledge that value too. At a school I have worked with, the faculty seems mostly oblivious to the great love and deep capacities that the parent body has and could contribute to solving fundamental problems the school has, such as fundraising and community outreach. Through the organization lens at the things-matter level, yellow means that the group struggles with consistency in delivering results that others value.

Red at the things level shows a very weak or completely lacking awareness of the available capacity in the five primary relationships. A group in this situation usually has little self-awareness and poor communication about what the group needs, what it can do as a group and what the various members of the group can contribute. People in such groups often tell me that they do not even know what they bring to the group or if they are necessary for its success. Red means that the group places little value on the resources it gets and, as a result, barely gets by. The group's organizing rarely results in specific, measurable outcomes.

White at the things level means there is no evidence of any awareness of resources. They are not valued and there are no organizational practices in place to help the group perform effectively. In essence, there are no agreements in place. I have never seen a group that has a solid white band at the things level, but I have found evidence of things-level agreements that indicate a rather primitive level of things awareness. In these cases, the green, yellow and red bands only cover the lower part of the things level, while the upper part of the band is white. We will see a couple of examples of this pattern in subsequent chapters. It is an indication that the agreements are focused on how many resources are available right now and the transactional value of those limited resources. Organizational practices are focused purely on obtaining that transactional value from the limited resources.

### At the development-motion level

At the development-motion level, the color-coding signifies the degree of conscious awareness and application of practices around developing capacities and relationships. Green at this level means that people are aware of how much they are developing capacities and relationships (the resource lens), and that people value this conscious and continuous development (the value lens). Green shows the tendency to use multiple primary relationships in decision-making (the allocation mechanism lens). It also indicates clear processes for cooperating in the service of a shared purpose (the organization lens), and those processes typically reward individuals for both their efforts toward self-development and the outcomes they deliver, individually and as a group. Basically, green at this level means that anyone and everyone in the group could describe the experience of developing capacities and relationships, as this experience is central to the group.

A yellow band across the development-motion level shows that the expressions of development I just described, as seen through the four lenses, are not completely conscious or consistent. While there is evidence that people do see the development level and work with it, this behavior is sporadic. This is the situation captured in the pet store Agreements Map, indicating a group that operates occasionally but not consistently at this level. There were many examples of capacity development in the stores; however, these efforts were mostly focused on getting better at the job of delivering outcomes. I consider this a low-level of resource awareness at the development level. For an intermediate to high (i.e., green) code here, I would look for the focus to be instead on capacity development as an end in itself across all five primary relationships. Since there was ample evidence of low-level capacity development in the pet store, and sporadic examples of high-level capacity development, I colored this section yellow in the Agreements Map. Similarly, across the band, yellow signifies sporadic awareness of the value of learning and growth and only occasional efforts to work cooperatively and organize to learn from experience and develop further capacities.

Color coding the development level of the Agreements Map red means that this experience is rarely to never evident, happening only by mistake if it does. Red means that few people if any see development as an important resource: development is not valued in the group. The group rarely cooperates and is not organized to learn and develop capacities over time. White at the development level means that there is no evidence of any awareness or practice around development. A group like this, with no practices at the development level, is at risk of not having the basic resources it needs to survive, even over the short term. Such a group tends to have high turnover of personnel, because people come into the group for purely transactional purposes, and there is no conscious development within the group.

### At the possibility-light level

The band across the possibility-light level highlights the degree of awareness of the emerging future in the group and the extent to which the group is thinking creatively about how to shape its agreements to fit with that emerging future. The red color of the lower portion of this band in the pet store chain Agreements Map signifies that there was some evidence that some of the store managers work with emerging possibilities and that, in some practices in some stores, there was evidence of all five primary relationships being used to allocate resources. However, these patterns were far from common in the stores. I use red here to show that it is possible, just very infrequent. The fact that the upper part of this section is colored in white shows that I found no evidence of working with the deeper potential and creativity inherent within the five primary relationships.

Basically, red in this section shows very little awareness of possibility as a resource available to the group, typically coupled with little to no valuing of potential and no organizational processes set up to support working with potential in the five primary relationships. Red at this level indicates low awareness of the potential resident within group members. Most groups I have identified as experiencing red at this level struggle to bring the best out of their people. Individual group members might aspire to engage more of themselves in the work but do not know how. Development-level practices alone do not enable them to achieve the higher potential they sense in themselves; this requires a collective vision of what may be available at the possibility level.

In contrast, green at this level indicates that the group is constantly asking the questions about what the emerging possibilities may be and what capacities it might develop in the future. It also signifies serious investment in sustainability in all five relationships, with great clarity about what is most valuable in each relationship and continuous monitoring to ensure that the group is meeting that value expectation. Finally, green across this band portrays a group that is effectively organized to work collaboratively toward seeing and taking advantage of future possibilities. A group like this is actively working to engage the full potential of its people in the five primary relationships. While this does not ensure the group's sustainability, it greatly increases the chances for it, especially compared to groups for which this section is colored yellow, red, or white.

Yellow, on the other hand, says that some people in the group are aware of potential capacity and future possibilities and/or the group as a whole occasionally becomes aware, perhaps because of a sudden realization that things are not going well. This is a reactive posture. It also may be that a group works off and on with possibility, maybe on a cyclical basis or due to the awareness and efforts of certain individuals or small pockets of people. Some people place a high value on future potential and that can sometimes move the whole group. I use yellow when a group is experimenting with possibilities and organizing itself collaboratively in small pockets, by accident or out of a sense of necessity rather than a perception of value. Yellow in this section shows that the group has some awareness of the potential in the five primary relationships and is working towards engaging it. There is promise here, and evidence for the group that it is possible.

# INTERPRETING THE AGREEMENTS MAP—SEEING AGREEMENTS AND CHOICES

With the content filled in and the color-coding complete, an Agreements Map provides two powerful views of the group—a high-level overview with broad bands of color and a ground-level view with a lot of concrete details. The broad overview offers a quick, forceful impression of the state of the group, based on its current agreements. The view from the ground level, on the other hand, includes the kind of information needed to analyze the agreements and perhaps see how to change them and move the group in a positive direction.

## HIGH-LEVEL OVERVIEW

In the high-level overview, you can see at a glance what the group is paying attention to and what levels of perceived reality are informing its operations. Lots of red looks very different from lots of green, obviously, and different colors suggest very different situations in the group. Just this simple observation can give you a good sense of what the agreements in the group are enabling it to do and, by inference, what is possible.

For example, the Agreements Map can give you a quick read on a group's resilience, its ability to sustain itself when it faces uncertainty. The more red there is on the map, the more scarcity the group is likely to be experiencing in terms of lower efficiency, higher costs of operation and fewer desirable outcomes. This is a recipe for low resilience or failure. Green all over the map does not necessarily mean continued high resilience and sustainable success, but it is a much stronger place to start. At the same time, you can often see what is possible by the yellow areas. When at least some people are aware of resources, value and organization at the development or possibility level, there is a greater likelihood that the group as a whole can step into that awareness and lift its functioning to a higher level.

The intention is not to value green over yellow or red or white or higher levels over lower ones. The purpose of the Agreements Map is simply to highlight where the group is. There is nothing wrong with focusing primarily on the things level. Better to know that is the case than be misled by what I call "brochure-talk" about what the group values, what it is paying attention to and what it can achieve. This brochure-talk, what one says as opposed to what one does, can be dangerous when people begin to believe in it and it raises their expectations above the reality they are living. By providing a clear picture of the current reality the Agreements Map can help to uncover opportunities for moving with intention toward new agreements.

The high-level view provided by the Agreements Map also makes it easy to compare groups or see how one group is changing over time. This can facilitate the process of changing agreements, for example by identifying groups that are living with agreements at the level you want to be at—where your group's map is red or yellow, their maps are green. You can then look more closely and see what practices you may want to adopt. You can also create before and after Agreements Maps. By seeing where you were before and where you are now, you have a picture of how the group functions under different agreements. This picture can help you determine what shifted with the change in agreements and how the shifts affected the experience you are having.

### Patterns of color

The color pattern of the pet store example is a common one in groups I have met. These groups are successful in delivering results, that is, they achieve things on a regular basis, whether it is getting the kids to school every morning or delivering quality products and services to their customers or communities. The people in these groups are also aware that continued success means that they have to develop capacities and relationships. They know they must learn to get better at what they do and keep learning as circumstances in their environment change. As the kids get older, what used to work to motivate them no longer does; new techniques are needed. When a competing shop or restaurant in a neighboring town provides more attractive goods or higher-quality service, the group needs to improve its own performance by learning about new techniques and practices.

Of course, different patterns are quite possible, and you will see some of in later chapters. Many companies and communities I have encountered or read about have Agreements Maps that are mostly white, with the green, yellow and red bands confined to the things-matter level. As I mentioned above, these things-only groups focus only on transactional outcomes in the present moment. I have also seen a few instances of Agreements Maps that are mostly green. We will look at one such case in the next chapter. This pattern shows groups that are consciously working with all three levels of perceived reality in all five primary relationships. They are also often achieving results most people would believe are impossible, simply because they are attempting to engage the whole human being.

Another significant pattern I have seen in Agreements Maps is small bands of yellow and red above a larger band of green. The green band might cover only part of the things level, or it might cover things, development and part of the possibility level. At whatever level, the thin yellow and red bands cover only part of a level of perceived reality. Based on what I have seen so far, I interpret this pattern as signifying a fairly consistent set of agreements throughout the group, colored green, with small pockets of people occasionally attempting practices at the next level, colored yellow or red. These small bands of yellow and red may also indicate that the practices at the next level of harmonic vibrancy are different enough from those that are commonly agreed to that the group finds it difficult to see, much less appreciate, those practices and their importance. I will discuss this pattern further in the next section and subsequent chapters.

## GROUND-LEVEL VIEW

The ground-level view focuses on the specific practices, processes and structures showing up in the group as an expression of existing agreements. By mapping them onto the levels of perceived reality, the Agreements Map exercise enables the group to see and discuss in detail its current experience relative to the experience group members want to be having. The group can then begin to see the need to change the underlying agreements in order to move to a higher level of harmonic vibrancy, as well as identify opportunities for doing so.

One of the best ways I know to clarify what a group needs and wants to change is to assess the "costs of scarcity" in areas of the Agreements Map where it is not functioning strongly. What are the costs of not living into the benefit of abundance in experiencing the middle and outer circles of harmonic vibrancy? Seeing these costs clearly can be a strong motivator to change. It highlights the undesirable effects of scarcity and, by implication, the benefits of abundance in a particular area. Specifying the costs of scarcity makes it clear what structures and processes need to be changed if the group desires to shift to a higher level of harmonic vibrancy.[85]

Figure 17, below, suggests costs of scarcity in the different areas of the Agreements Map. My colleague Mike Puleo and I developed this example of the costs of scarcity with business organizations in mind. We identified common examples of costs we had found in groups where they did not include one of the levels of perceived reality in their agreements. For example, what

---

85    For deeper exploration of the "costs of scarcity" framework and its application to more cases, see (Ritchie-Dunham, Puleo, & Throneburg, 2012).

are the costs of not including possibility in the agreements? Of not including development and possibility in the agreements? We also identified a measurable indicator—a proxy—for each cost. For example, a proxy for the quality of the work environment might be the rate of employee turnover. Proxies make it possible to calculate the costs of what is missing.

So far it seems that the costs of scarcity we identified initially are applicable in various settings, not just in businesses, but also in communities, groups of friends and families. For example, when looking through the resources lens at the possibility level, one of the costs of scarcity is the high probability of obsolescence. When people do not pay attention to the possibilities they can see in each of the five primary relationships, they run the risk of missing something new that turns out to be important. Instead, they depend on what has already been developed, and when the environment changes—when consumers move from landline phones to cell phones, or when kids evolve from babies into teenagers—what used to work does not work anymore. It has become obsolete. Looking for ways to measure this risk of obsolescence within a business, Mike and I saw that some companies were tracking the percentage of their revenues coming from products developed within the previous three years. The higher this percentage, they reasoned, the lower the risk of their products becoming obsolete.

While the percentage of revenues might not be applicable as a proxy in the situation with the kids, clearly, something like it might. For example, to see the potential my kids experience in our family, I might look at what percentage of my thoughts about them come from ideas they have shared in the past six months. This would indicate how much I engage them in what they can see in themselves now, as compared with what we could see in them when they were much younger. Do I still think of my 18-year old as I did when she was five, or have I updated my understanding of her potential? Now, let us look at the costs of scarcity more generally.

## The Costs of Scarcity

| What are the Costs of Scarcity? | Resources ⃝ <br> How Much? | Allocation ⃝ <br> Who decides? | Value ⃝ <br> By what criteria? | Organization ⃝ <br> How shall we interact? |
|---|---|---|---|---|
| **Possibility** <br><br> Potential (Light) | [Proxies: % rev from new product in last 3 years] <br><br> **Potential Capacity** <br> - Lack of new opportunities <br> - Higher probability of obsolescence <br> - Unintended consequences | | [Proxies: %of one's potential contributed to group, % bonded loyal stakeholders, price premium brand value] <br><br> **Future Potential** <br> - Lack of inviting best contribution | [Proxies: % top performing employees in niche, % highest margins prod/serv in niche, ranking in innovativeness] <br><br> **Collaboration** <br> - Lack of high potential people/ relationships <br> - Lack of inspiring innovation <br> - Lack of credibility as expert |
| **Development** <br><br> Motion (Verb) | [Proxies: costs of over-production, over-processing, % defects-rework, inventory turns] <br><br> **Capacity Development** <br> - Lack of necessary resources <br> - Lost opportunities (compromise) <br> - Expensive resources | Which Primary Relationship(s) | [Proxies: % of customer needs met] <br><br> **Learning & Growth** <br> - Lack of belonging | [Proxies: employee turnover rate] <br><br> **Co-opetition** <br> - Lack of cooperation (redundancy) <br> - Lack of healthy work environment (high turnover, stress) |
| **Things** <br><br> Matter (Noun) | [Proxies: mistakes in resources] <br><br> **Available Capacity** <br> - Not enough self-funding <br> - Resource turnover <br> - Low productivity of assets, human resources, funding | | [Proxies: cost of capital, profit margin] <br><br> **Outcomes** <br> - Interest rate of money | [Proxies: cycle time, % of one-time customers] <br><br> **Competition** <br> - Lost intellectual capital <br> - Lost social capital |

*Figure 17: The Costs of Scarcity*

### *SCARCITY AT THE POSSIBILITY-LIGHT LEVEL*

We need possibility in our lives. When we ignore possibility, we experience lower harmonic vibrancy. The costs of not explicitly including possibility are the real costs of what never showed up, in the resources we never had, the best contributions that never appeared, and the collaborative creativity that was not in the room.[86]

Looking through the resources lens, the costs of scarcity start with the new opportunities that we never saw (see Figure 17). The strategic resource we could have seen remained invisible; the potential abundance in an existing resource went unrecognized. This is the gift that was knocking on the door that was never answered. We have to stick with the existing resources and old opportunities. A related cost is the obsolescence of the existing resources. A reputation built on past success eventually erodes, as does the training in old technologies that are no longer used.

---

86    The benefits of collaboration and abundance are also described in Tribal Leadership (Logan, King, & Fischer-Wright, 2008, p. 31).

Through the value lens of "what criteria?" we can see the high cost of scarcity in not inviting in the best contributions group members could make. The people are already there. You have already engaged them. For the lack of the ability to work at the possibility-light level, their best gifts, which were already available, were never engaged. A proxy for the existence or non-existence of this possibility-level value is the percentage of an individual's potential he or she experiences within and contributes to the group. Another proxy might be the value of the group's reputation or brand—a measure of certainty in future potential.

The organizational costs of scarcity at this level come from the lack of the kind of talented people who thrive in and expect to work in environments that invite their creative contributions. Without these very creative, high-potential people, another cost comes into play: the inability to attract other people who want to engage with them. These might be friends who will make an effort to join groups that are really fun, adventurous or humorous. In a business or professional setting, they might be clients who are willing to pay a premium to access talented, creative people, whether they be actors, comedians, musicians, thought-leaders, consultants, teachers, architects or the great waiters in a restaurant. Lack of collaboration can also lead to a lack of the creative solutions that enable a group to take leadership in its field, relegating it to the position of follower. Proxies for the possibility-level of organization might be the percentage of people in the group considered to be the best at what they do. Another proxy might be how well known the group is for consistent innovation.

### SCARCITY AT THE DEVELOPMENT-MOTION LEVEL

Motion and emergence are our lifeblood. When we ignore them, we experience very low harmonic vibrancy. Scarcity at this level shows up as ossification. The costs of not explicitly maintaining awareness of development are the real costs of underutilized resources and inefficiency in the system, as well as the opportunity cost of not having the resources we need when we need them. Scarcity at this level also means that we are not further developing across the five primary relationships. We are looking at them solely in terms of existing capacities rather than with awareness of what we are learning in each relationship over time. When we do not develop these relationships, we also do not develop the understanding and trust that are vital to healthy relationships. Hence scarcity at this level also shows up as weak or unhealthy relationships.

In the area of resources, the most basic cost of not functioning at the development-motion level is the inability to see how to accumulate and maintain the required resources. When we are not aware of the net effect of the inflows and outflows, resources seem to erode all of a sudden. If we pay attention to the dynamic nature of resources, we can avoid such unpleasant surprises. On the other hand, attempting to respond to unexpected opportunities through sudden acquisition of resources is expensive. This is the cost of not having foreseen the need for the resources and how to accumulate them.

A proxy for these scarcity costs in the area of human resources is the percentage of defects in products made or process errors. A group that is learning over time improves its ability to do repetitive activities well, becoming more efficient and creating fewer defects or errors. Another proxy is the rate of turnover in inventory. Here the idea is that the more finely tuned we are to the development process, the more efficiently we use the materials at hand and the faster we use them up. Another way to think of this is that, when our awareness at the development level is low, we tend to be afraid that we might run out of resources, so we tend to have too much on hand or use it up and find it difficult to replenish. Either way, more awareness at the development level will usually be reflected in a higher, more consistent turnover rate in resources. Another common proxy here is the cost of making the mistake of underestimating the capacities required at any given time, which leads to overpaying for expediting acquisition of the required resources. This proxy also indicates the lack of awareness of how much resource is present.

Looking through the value lens, the development-motion level focuses on the importance given to learning and growth as one experiences the flow of creativity in the five relationships. When the group is low in awareness here, the deficit shows up in group members having a sense of not belonging and often leads to diminished contributions and, ultimately, high turnover. A proxy for the level of scarcity or abundance in this area might be the percentage of times the group meets an agreed-upon expectation of an outcome at a specific time. For instance, we promised to deliver every customer's order of skis within seven working days; for what percentage of orders did we accomplish that in the last six months? Meeting someone's expectations requires a process for developing a strong enough relationship to know what those expectations are, as well as an attempt to meet them.

When a group is not functioning at the development-motion level in the arena of organization, it is missing out on the key benefits of cooperation and alliances—the development of individuals and relationships.[87] Lack of

87    Recent research has found that the intelligence of the cooperative group predicts group

cooperation also usually leads to severe duplication of resources, a direct cost of scarcity at this level. Lack of appreciation of relationships leads over time to poor working environments, high employee turnover and difficulty in attracting better employees, suppliers and customers. The rate of turnover in these key relationships is a good proxy for the level of scarcity or abundance in this area.

### SCARCITY AT THE THINGS-MATTER LEVEL

We are matter. We eat food, wear clothes, and drive cars. When we ignore matter, we experience deep scarcity. There just is not enough of what is needed to keep moving forward.

Not understanding the things-matter level of resources inevitably means that there are never enough of them. Poorly worked land becomes infertile. Poorly supported labor renders little and quits. Poorly understood capital rarely shows up, and only in small amounts. People are always begging for more, and this has a high cost for the group. A proxy for this cost of scarcity looks at the mistakes made in estimating the amount of resource needed. What were the costs in not having the necessary resources? We were not able to produce food on the infertile land. We produced very little because we were constantly having to train new staff. We did not have enough money to do the programs we wanted to do.

In value, lack of awareness at this level leads to poor use of money and a high cost of money, usually reflected in higher interest rates. The cost of capital—interest paid on bank loans and other credit—is a useful proxy for this poor use of money. At this level, not valuing the basic capacities in the five primary relationships leads to a gross underutilization and under-engagement of the capacities that are available to the group.

Seen through the organization lens, a lack of things-level understanding leads to poor contracts, which lead to the loss of individuals, their talents, and their relationships. This direct loss of intellectual and social capital makes it difficult for any group to function well. A proxy for scarcity or abundance at the things level of organization, in this case, might be the percentage of one-time customers. Without even a basic level of organization at the things level, the group lacks any capacity for efficiency. In these groups, people feel like they

---

performance across a wide variety of metrics. This collective intelligence is most correlated with the average social sensibility of group members and equality in the distribution of conversational turn taking, and not the average or maximum intelligence of individuals (Woolley, Chabris, Pentland, Hashmi, & Malone, 2010). This depicts the middle of the three circles of harmonic vibrancy.

are wasting their time, as the group is unable to produce much of anything. This lack of engagement leads to a high turnover of people, leading to the loss of what the people learned while in the group and the relationships they developed while in the group.

## USING THE AGREEMENTS MAP

In my work as a strategy advisor to companies, communities, government agencies and networks, I have found the Agreements Map to be an invaluable tool. Before I had this tool, I often struggled to figure out which strategic framework to apply in a particular situation. Was the key issue the cost-benefit equation? Was it all about market systems—neoliberal versus egalitarian? Did the situation call for developing an intentional learning community or just becoming more efficient in delivering agreed-upon outcomes? Did the group need to engage people in a creative, participatory design process or focus on optimizing the existing agreements? Was it about resources, value or organization theories? It was often unclear.

Now, with the Agreements Map, which incorporates all of these dimensions at a high level, I can see the patterns of agreements along all of the dimensions at once. It is now clear, from the color-coding of the Agreements Map, at which levels of perceived reality a group is functioning strongly, where it is developing new capacities, and where it is not yet developing. Knowing that a group is consciously working at a particular level lets me know what types of strategic work the group is ready to take on. If it is strong at the things level only, for example, I proceed with caution in raising development-level questions. Likewise, if it is strong at the things and development levels, then I assume folks are able to work with processes that might strengthen those levels and begin to explore possibility-level efforts.

The integration of the four lenses into one map helps me see the essential interrelatedness of what might seem to be disparate processes. For example, in the past I have been in the situation of trying to help a group think about its resources at the development level, using resource-systems modeling techniques, like the ones I will highlight in the learning labs in Part 4 of the book. The group had contracted for my work independently of the values work being done by another consultant and also independently of the organizational learning practices emerging within the company. These days I would not agree to such an arrangement. Now that I can see how the resources, allocation mechanism, value and organization lenses highlight different questions about the same experience, I know these different types of work cannot effectively be done in isolation of each other.

Furthermore, because the Agreements Map gives me a quick sense of how a group's agreements incorporate the five primary relationships at the three levels of perceived reality, as seen through the four lenses, I have a powerful diagnostic tool to help groups determine what work they need to do. I can now point out the full set of agreements they are working with, as seen from all of these perspectives. The map also highlights those areas that might be quite challenging for the group to take on right away. If there is no evidence of practices or agreements at the level of perceived reality above where they are currently functioning, then the practices at that next level will probably be very different from what they are used to. For example, it takes time to create the high-trust environment required for collaboration at the possibility level, trust which is likely to be absent in a group focused solely on competition-based organizational practices at the things level. This does not mean that the group could not eventually get there, rather that these new practices at the possibility and development levels are very different from the things-only level practices and require time and dedication to bring them into the group's agreements and culture.

With this initial framing and example of the Agreements Map, I hope you begin to see how a quick assessment can highlight what the group's agreements are able to embrace—the primary relationships and levels of perceived reality included, as seen through the four lenses—and therefore what is immediately available to the group and what practices it might be able to adopt in time. Once you get used to working with Agreements Maps, you will find there are various ways you can use it as a diagnostic tool. When you determine which of the five relationships and three levels of perceived reality your agreements encompass, you also see which ones they do *not* include. This shows you where you can focus attention in order to start functioning at a higher level of perceived reality and start experiencing higher levels of abundance and harmonic vibrancy. Calculating the costs of scarcity will help provide the motivation and direction for change.

It can also be helpful to look at your agreements over time. For example, you can reconstruct what they looked like before you made some changes and what they look like now. How do the shifts in agreements relate to shifts in your experience? Or you can establish where you are right now, your current status, and assess the impact of changes you make going forward. Finally, you can learn a great deal by comparing your agreements to those of another group. If that group is experiencing more or less harmony, vibrancy and abundance than yours, its agreements might be different. The Agreements Map will help you see where those difference lie.

In the rest of this book, I will use the Agreements Map and the concept of costs of scarcity to illuminate a variety of examples of how groups are innovating to achieve greater harmonic vibrancy and to bring greater abundance into their experience. I will also show you how to use these tools to support positive change in your own groups.

# PART III

# MOVING TO GREATER HARMONIC VIBRANCY

# CHAPTER 7

# WHAT PEOPLE ARE EXPERIENCING; WHAT PEOPLE ARE DOING

So far in this book, I have laid out some basic principles of Ecosynomics, as follows: it is possible to experience harmonic vibrancy and abundance, as we know from the times we have done so. This desirable experience, by definition, involves all five relationships (to self, other, group, nature and spirit) and all three levels of perceived reality (things-matter, development-motion and possibility-light). The actual experiences we have in different situations are the results of the agreements we are party to. This means that we have it in our power to change our experience for the better by changing our agreements.

I have also shared my analysis of the role the discipline of economics has played in shaping the agreements that govern many, if not most, aspects of life in modern society. Economic thinking embraces only the things-matter level, where scarcity is the norm. Yet it has evolved to see scarcity everywhere. Its pervasiveness as a foundation for human agreements means that scarcity and low vibrancy really are the "normal" experience for most people most of the time.

On the other hand, economic inquiry into four key aspects of human activity—resources, resource allocation, value and organization—has created a wealth of knowledge and insight about how things work at the things-matter level. Ecosynomics builds on this foundation of understanding. With the agreements map, Ecosynomics also carries the inquiry to the higher levels of perceived reality. It does so by using the core questions at the heart of the four main lines of economic study as lenses on human experience at all three levels and in all five relationships. The perspective gained through this rich analysis enables us to sense the underlying agreements shaping our experience and, potentially, the opportunities we may have to change them for the better.

Now, in Part 3, it is time to consider what this kind of change looks like and how you can go about creating it for yourself. These are questions I have been pursuing for many years. In the next chapter, I will lay out a four-step process for moving toward greater harmonic vibrancy. This process has grown out of my hands-on experience working with individuals and groups to bring about more of the experiences they want. To prepare the way for that, I will present in this chapter some broader findings I have made through two main avenues of exploration: asking people what they are experiencing and looking at what they are doing.

## ASKING WHAT PEOPLE ARE EXPERIENCING

First, I will share some striking survey results showing that many groups of all types are already experiencing the outer circle of harmonic vibrancy. This is important information. Knowing that others have succeeded in bringing greater vibrancy and abundance into their lives offers assurance that it is possible.

In 2010, I gathered a team of people interested in exploring how the Ecosynomics framework applies to the real-life experiences people are having in different sorts of groups. We created a survey, which asks dozens of questions about experiences in each of the five relationships. A little bit later, we added a non-verbal version of the survey by using the stick figures I introduced you to in Chapter 1 to depict low, medium or high vibrancy in each of the relationships. This graphic survey avoids language barriers and takes only a minute or so to complete. You can take the survey yourself, in either form, at the website http://ecosynomicssurvey.net.

As of October 1, 2013, 1,600 people from 789 different groups in 89 countries have taken the Harmonic Vibrancy survey. The respondents are about equally divided between men and women (53 to 47 percent). The groups they are reporting on include mostly work groups (64 percent); some civic, church and sports groups (25 percent); and a smaller number of families (11 percent). About half of the groups (48 percent) include between 10 and 100 people. Just under a third (31 percent) are smaller than that; 12 percent have between 100 and 1000 people; and 9 percent have over 1000. The responses so far have mostly come from people we have invited to take the survey, whether as members of a specific network, a classroom assignment, or as members of a group we were visiting. About 10% of the responses have come from people who found the survey on the web.

The two graphs in Figure 18, below, provide a strong visual image of the results we are seeing in these surveys. The figures in the graphs are three-dimensional cubes (it would be nice to graph data for all relationships at once, but a five-dimensional graph is not technically possible.) Each dot represents the response of one survey taker and is located within its cube according to how that individual rated the vibrancy of his or her experience in three of the relationships. In the left-hand cube, the relationships are self, other and group. In the right-hand cube, they are self, nature and spirit. The rating scale for each relationship is from 1 (low vibrancy) to 5 (high vibrancy).

## Surveyed Responses to Primary Relationships
### (1,600 surveys)

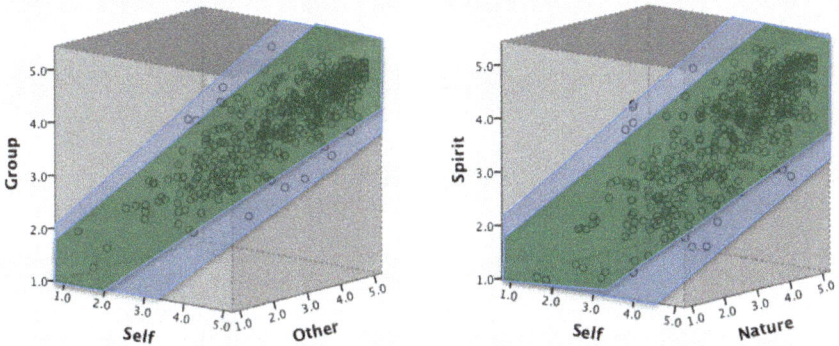

*Figure 18: Harmonic Vibrancy Survey Data*

Each cube has 1,600 dots. In both cubes, the dots form a clearly defined band running from the lower left-hand corner, where there are low vibrancy scores on all three relationships, to the upper right-hand corner, where the scores indicate high vibrancy in all three relationships. This pattern means that there is a strong correlation between the levels of vibrancy experienced in these relationships. In other words, a low level of vibrancy in the relationship to self comes with correspondingly low levels in relationships to other, group, nature and spirit. High vibrancy in one relationship means high vibrancy in all. There are no instances of someone experiencing a high level of harmonic vibrancy in the relationship to self and low vibrancy in relationship to other, group, nature, or spirit. They all come together at the same level.

In Figure 19, I have superimposed one of these cubes on the now-familiar image of the 3-Circles of Harmonic Vibrancy. This allows you to see clearly how the pattern in the survey data confirms the experiences of low, medium, and high levels of vibrancy that so many people have described in my conversations. We can also take heart from the fact that so many dots cluster at the high end of the continuum in each graph. This tells us that it is quite possible for groups to function in the outer circle of harmonic vibrancy and abundance. The challenge now is to understand how they are doing this and to enable more people to enjoy this positive experience.

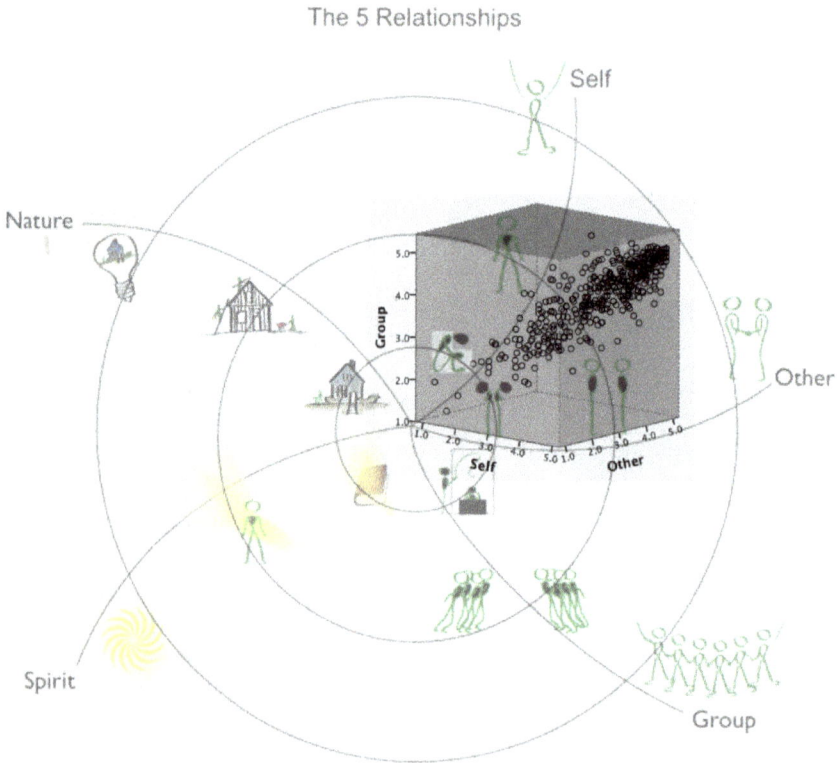

*Figure 19: Comparison of Survey Data to 3-Circles of Harmonic Vibrancy*

## SEEING WHAT PEOPLE ARE DOING

One way I have approached the question of what groups are doing to move to higher levels of harmonic vibrancy is to use the Agreements Map to analyze a number of well-documented innovations using the Ecosynomics framework. These examples seem, superficially, to be quite unrelated. Through the perspective of Ecosynomics, however, we can see that all of these innovations involve moving from operating only at the things-matter level to functioning at a higher level. The Agreements Map makes it possible to see similarities and patterns that suggest what is actually involved in this kind of a move. In other words, we can begin to recognize a move to a higher level of harmonic vibrancy and abundance when we see one.

While most people see and experience scarcity as the norm in many aspects of their lives, there are plenty of examples of people breaking through to create abundance for themselves. For example, a school in El Salvador has tripled the percentage of young girls entering and staying in primary school. A community health center in Texas maintains top-hospital-level services for an increasingly uninsured population, when all other centers are cutting even basic services. A textile mill in North Carolina pays living wages to its high-craftsmanship shop workers in an industry that has outsourced its low margin commodity products to low skilled workers in Asia. A small town in New York has created the equivalent of hundreds of jobs by circulating millions of dollars of trade with its own local currency. A private currency system in Japan has replaced a large percentage of expensive, hospital-based elderly care not covered by the national insurance plan, with a more effective system based on people exchanging "caring relationship" credits.

I have met many of the people involved in these activities, and I have seen how they are redefining what is possible through innovations in human agreements. In science, cases such as this are called "positive deviants."[88] They are deviant because their behavior differs from the norm, and their deviant behavior leads to positive outcomes. These outliers are important to researchers in that they suggest how those whose behavior is "normal" might change to get better outcomes for themselves. That is how I want to use these cases and similar ones I will discuss in this chapter.

As I started to gain a better understanding of the innovations I was personally acquainted with, and as I gained greater clarity about the principles of Ecosynomics, I realized that thousands of groups around the world are making similar abundance-creating breakthroughs. This led me to explore a wider range of reported innovations, such as Asset-based Community Development and the cooperative movement, from an Ecosynomics perspective. I recognized that the groups involved in these activities had shifted from operating solely

---

88    This term and the significance of positive deviance became well known through the publication of the work of researchers at Tufts University (Pascale, Sternin, & Sternin, 2010).

at the things-matter level to functioning effectively at both the development-motion *and* things-matter level. They seem to have made different kinds of agreements and created abundance for themselves by doing so. Similarly, I could identify groups working at the possibility-light level and see the positive results of that. The Ecosynomics perspective makes these innovations recognizable as moves toward abundance with some common elements, which may help people replicate them in other areas.

A couple of caveats about these examples: First, since they are not formal Ecosynomics experiments, I cannot tell you that I know the innovators have explicitly embraced the fundamental assumptions of abundance. Nor can I say for certain that they have stepped into the outer circle of harmonic vibrancy in the five primary relationships. Future Ecosynomics research may address these questions. However, because the outcomes they are achieving and the processes and structures they are using are well documented, I can show you with the Agreements Map how they are working at different levels to create greater abundance.

Second, I have not been exhaustive in searching out existing innovations. I am sure there are many being documented in fields I do not even know about. However, if I have rather easily found a handful of innovations involving thousands of groups, I believe it is safe to say there must be many thousands more out there beyond what I will share with you here. The move toward greater vibrancy and abundance is not, in other words, the isolated experience of a few lucky people; rather it is a broad-based phenomenon from which many are benefiting.

## INNOVATIONS AT THE THINGS-MATTER AND DEVELOPMENT-MOTION LEVELS

A huge shift in the abundance experienced in groups can come from working with structures and processes on multiple levels. Remember that, at the things-matter level, one only thinks about what one has. At this level, groups perceive that they either have resources or they do not, and this perspective makes the resources seem scarce. The groups then organize their interactions only around working with those scarce resources. They find value in having the resources and exchanging them for other resources they also value. However, there are "costs of scarcity" associated with operating only at the things-matter level, as we saw in Chapter 6.

For example, because they are not thinking about the development of resources, organization and value over time, groups often have experiences such as having to pay higher prices for last-minute purchases, not being prepared to take advantage of new opportunities, having lots of redundant processes, or having high rates of burnout and turnover among group members who feel underappreciated. This is all that is available when the things-matter perspective is all there is.

In contrast, at the development-motion level, people approach resources, organizing and value in a very different ways. They think about *both* how much resource they have *and* how they can grow or enhance that resource over time. In organizing their interactions, groups holding this perspective think about how group members can build their capacities and strengthen their relationships over time. They also think about the value the development of those capacities and relationships will have, both for those within the group and for those who interact with it. The "costs of scarcity" experienced when groups operate only at the matter-things level do not occur at the resource-development level, because the benefits of abundance created through resource development have been included. We can see this dynamic clearly in the innovations I will now describe.

## FIRMS OF ENDEARMENT

The first innovation I want to present is documented in the 2007 book *Firms of Endearment.*[89] It involves large, for-profit corporations choosing to define business success in terms of "humanistic performance" as well as financial performance. The authors of this study selected thirty companies that met their criteria for a high level of positive relationships with employees, customers, investors, partners and society—their defining characteristic of humanistic performance. A "great" group, they said, is "one that makes the world a better place because it exists, not simply a company that outperforms the market by a certain percentage over a certain period of time."[90]

The *Firms of Endearment* authors organize the descriptors of great groups by stakeholders:

- *Employees.* A happy and productive work environment motivates, values, and rewards employees.
- *Customers.* Honoring the legal and unspoken emotional contract with the consumer strengthens the relationship.

---

89    For more on the Firms of Endearment study, see (Sisodia, Wolfe, & Seth, 2007).

90    For a complete description of the companies selected, see (Sisodia et al., 2007).

- *Investors.* Investors value the financial and emotional relationship with the group.
- *Partners.* A mutually beneficial, symbiotic relationship with business partners brings synergies to both.
- *Society.* Communities appreciate the group's values and outcomes, welcoming them where they operate. Creating value with government leverages the strengths of both.

To render these findings in Ecosynomics terms, I placed the relationship descriptors on an Agreements Map (Figure 20, below). A glance at this map shows groups that are functioning fully at the development-motion to things-matter levels.[91] This is where everything on the heat map is in green, the areas of a high index of success.

This use of the Agreements Map extends the way I used it in chapter 6. Here I am mapping characteristics that someone else has found to be common in a subset of groups, in this case, companies meeting the *Firms of Endearment* criteria. For example, the authors write that these companies "demonstrate their commitment to the local community in highly tangible ways." This is evidence to me that they develop and deliver outcomes, which are visible through the resources lens. That these companies "honor the legal and unspoken emotional contract with the customer" provide evidence that they see themselves as bound in a contractual relationship and pay attention to it. The existence of the contract and the relationships show functioning at both the things-matter and development-motion levels, as seen through the resources lens.

The *Firms of Endearment* authors also documented a tendency in these firms to have decentralized decision-making processes. I take this as evidence of developmental-level practices, as seen through the resource allocation question of "who decides?" Through the value lens, I found a number of indicators of things-level health—frontline staff paid above average wages in their category, and in general, highly motivated employees who feel valued and well rewarded. Signs of development-level health showing up in the value lens were the development and maintenance of financial and emotional relationships with investors and the incorporation of the government as a partner in value creation. Through the organization lens, the study identifies things-level health of a happy, productive work environment, which moves into development-level health with the evidence of a symbiotic and mutually beneficial relationship with business partners. These nine characteristics found

---

91   The descriptions in Figure 21 and Figure 22 are directly from the book Firms of Endearment (Sisodia et al., 2007, p. 21).

in the *Firms of Endearment* study provide ample evidence for organizational health at the things and development levels. This is what the green band on Figure 20 means.

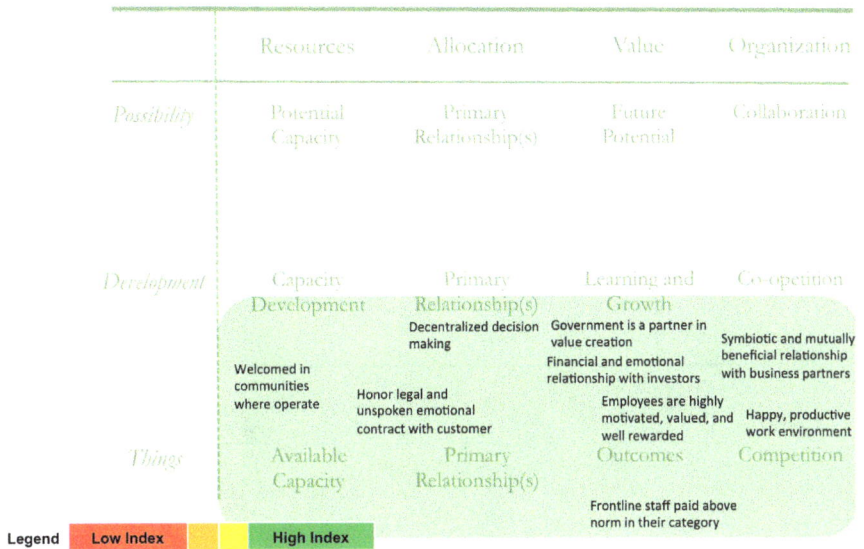

|  | Resources | Allocation | Value | Organization |
|---|---|---|---|---|
| *Possibility* | Potential Capacity | Primary Relationship(s) | Future Potential | Collaboration |
| *Development* | Capacity Development | Primary Relationship(s) | Learning and Growth | Co-opetition |
|  | Welcomed in communities where operate | Decentralized decision making / Honor legal and unspoken emotional contract with customer | Government is a partner in value creation / Financial and emotional relationship with investors / Employees are highly motivated, valued, and well rewarded | Symbiotic and mutually beneficial relationship with business partners / Happy, productive work environment |
| *Things* | Available Capacity | Primary Relationship(s) | Outcomes / Frontline staff paid above norm in their category | Competition |

Legend   Low Index        High Index

*Figure 20: Firms of Endearment Agreements Map*

As you may remember from Chapter 2 (Figure 10), the pattern we see in the Firms of Endearment Agreements map correlates with the experience of living in the inner-to-middle circle of harmonic vibrancy. The authors of the study also seem to recognize this higher level of experience when they write of the "both-and" definition of success in these companies. By this they mean that the companies define success both in terms of financial performance and in terms of humanistic performance, i.e., meeting the needs of multiple stakeholders. Figure 21, below, renders their observation in Ecosynomics terms. In my experience, all of the groups innovating at the development-motion/things-matter levels share this characteristic "both-and" definition of success.

The study also shows that the *Firms of Endearment* companies are extremely effective, producing greater, more sustainable financial success than comparable companies. In Chapter 6, I suggested that groups working consciously at both the development and things levels tend to be more competitive than those just working at the things level, if for no other reason than that they do not have the same development-level costs of scarcity. The *Firms of Endearment* study supports this observation. The authors discovered that these companies working at the motion and matter levels equaled the three-year financial performance of the companies in the classic study, *Good to Great* (2001).[92] However, they exceeded the performance of the *Good to Great* companies by a ratio of 1.7 to 1 over five years and by a ratio of 3.1-to-1 over ten years.[93] None of the eleven companies in the *Good to Great* study met the criteria set for *Firms of Endearment*. The two studies defined success at different levels. The *Firms of Endearment* were selected for proven success at both motion and matter levels, while the *Good to Great* companies were selected for success at the matter-outcomes level only.[94]

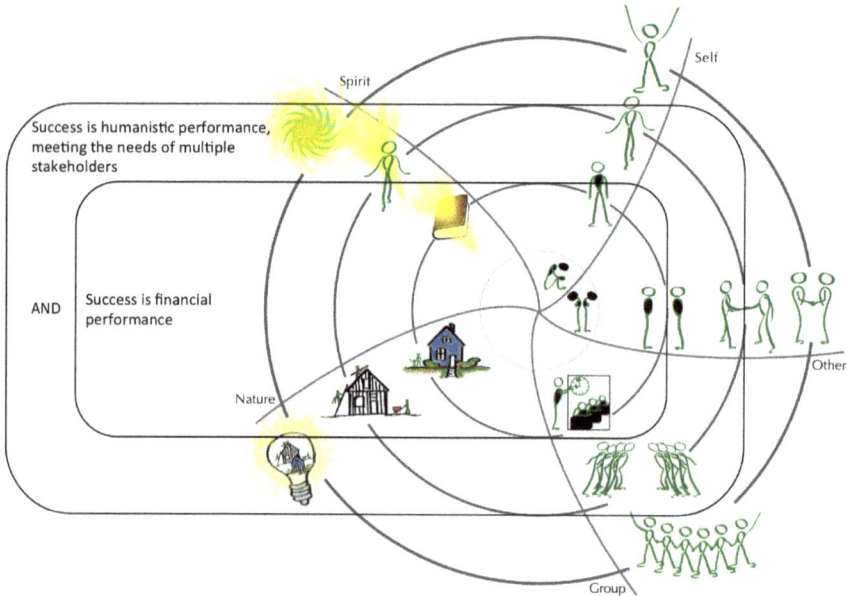

*Figure 21: Definitions of Success for Firms of Endearment*

Before anyone begins to judge the companies in either of these studies, however, let us be clear that we do not know what practices the companies

---

92   For the Good to Great study, see (Collins, 2001).

93   These data from the authors' study are provided in (Sisodia et al., 2007, p. 17).

94   I shared the Firms of Endearment criteria above. The Good to Great study filtered for "fifteen-year cumulative stock returns at or below the general stock market, punctuated by a transition point, then cumulative returns at least three times the market over the next fifteen years" (Collins, 2001, p. 6). Far from being a critique of the Good to Great study, I merely point out that the two studies describe different groups, which they identified through different filters.

actually have. They might be working at a higher level than depicted in the studies. All we know is what the authors saw through the lenses they used. Significantly though, other well known surveys find similar matter-and-motion results. One of these is the "Great Places to Work" survey highlighted annually in *Fortune* magazine. "Great Places" assesses trust in management (an indicator of relationship to the group), pride in the job (an indicator of relationship to self) and camaraderie with other employees (an indicator of relationship to the other). These are all matter-and-motion level characteristics. As with the *Firms of Endearment* study, matter-and-motion level groups outperform matter-level-only groups in the "Great Places" study. Its "100 Best" companies outperformed the S&P 500, a barometer of stock market performance, by two-fold between 1998 and 2009.[95]

## ASSET-BASED COMMUNITY DEVELOPMENT

A couple of years ago, I was sitting on the front porch of a friend's house, telling him what I was learning about Ecosynomics. He told me how his church was using a process called asset-based community development (ABCD). He said it sounded like the principles I was uncovering were similar to those on which this process was based, so I looked it up. ABCD is the name two Northwestern University professors, John Kretzmann and John McKnight, gave to community-building work they described in their 1993 "guidebook," *Building Communities from the Inside Out*.[96] Since then, the approach has been adopted widely. At ABCD global conferences in 2007 and 2009 representatives from two-dozen countries presented their stories of ABCD-based citizen initiatives in communities ranging from remote rural areas and towns to large urban metropolises.[97]

Most traditional approaches to urban issues focus on the community's deficiencies and its needs.[98] A recent United Nations report described this

---

95    For more detail on the "Great Places to Work" survey and the financial performance of the 100 Best, see (Burchell & Robin, 2011; Edmans, 2011). Similar studies include the "Great Workplace Award" from the global polling company Gallup and the "Dream Company" study from business professors Goffee and Jones (Goffee & Jones, 2013; Harter, Schmidt, Agrawal, & Plowman, 2013).

96    For the guidebook, see (Kretzmann & McKnight, 1993). For more on ABCD, visit John McKnight and Jody Kretzmann at The Asset-Based Community Development Institute (abcdinstitute.org), which is located at the School of Education and Social Policy at Northwestern University.

97    See research by Cormac Russell of the ABCD Institute in (C. Russell, 2009, p. 7).

98    For discussion of this shift and how it applied to development efforts in Nepal, see (Khadka, 2012). In a recent book he co-authored, William Bratton, former chief of the

approach as follows: "need-based government policies typically focus on what communities lack as opposed to what they have. For decades, governments—both in developed and developing countries—have used a 'standard deficits calculations approach' . . . to quantify community needs (such as an x number of housing units to be built, or a certain amount of retail space, schools, parks, public spaces, etc.). Urban planners, for example, calculate housing deficit as the difference between the necessary number of dwelling units and the number of units produced."[99] "Contrasting the typical need-based "deficit model," the UN report continues, "an asset-based approach does not seek to quantify needs. Instead, it aims to encourage an attitude favorable to change and capacity building by cutting across professional boundaries. Some consider this to be a community-design process, based on which 'the environment works better if people affected by its changes are actively involved in its creation and management instead of being treated as passive consumers.' This asset-based approach seeks to identify, and capitalize on, the tangible and intangible assets available to a community, rather than [focusing] on what it lacks."[100]

With ABCD, moreover, the definition of community assets is broad. It includes the usual physical resources, buildings and other infrastructure, financial resources and so forth. It also takes into account intangible assets. These might be the specific capacities of people in the community or relational assets, such as the connections among community members, and between them and people and institutions outside the community. Once the community gets clear about the full range of resources it has to work with, ABCD looks at how the existing relationships can support new agreements regarding how these assets might be developed over time.

To create the Agreements Maps in Figure 22, below, I used descriptors from the work of Kretzmann and McNight. The maps clearly show very different levels of functioning. The "needs-based" map depicts an approach in which the focus is wholly on the things level. Communities taking this approach see their resources only in terms of needs and deficiencies in the neighborhoods. They delegate decision making to top-down planners, who allocate resources based on the single criterion of meeting those needs. The planners design

---

LAPD and commissioner of the Boston and New York City Police Departments, gives a similar assessment of traditional deficiency-based approaches and emerging asset-based approaches (Bratton & Tumin, 2012).

99    This is from the United Nations report on "Asset-based Approaches to Community Development" (Arefi, 2008, p. 1). The report cites examples from MIT's Professor of Urban Anthropology Lisa Peattie's examples of the "standard deficits calculations approach" (Peattie, 1983, p. 229).

100    See (Arefi, 2008, p. 9).

development activities based on "solutions" to the "problem" of unmet needs and deficiencies. All of this activity is centered on the lower things levels of concrete outcomes.

In contrast, the ABCD Agreements Map shows an approach that starts from an assumption of abundance of resources in the community. I noted on that map that these resources typically include the actual things the community has, in terms of physical infrastructure and spaces, as well as its intangible resources such as people's skills. I also noted that ABCD draws as much as possible on the tangible and intangible resources of the public, private and non-profit institutions within the community. The ABCD approach also counts relationships as a valuable resource, a practice I mapped at the development-motion level. I even saw ABCD stretching into the possibility level with its emphasis on seeing the potential in the community's existing economic resources and local places.

"Needs-based" approach to urban issues          Asset-based community development

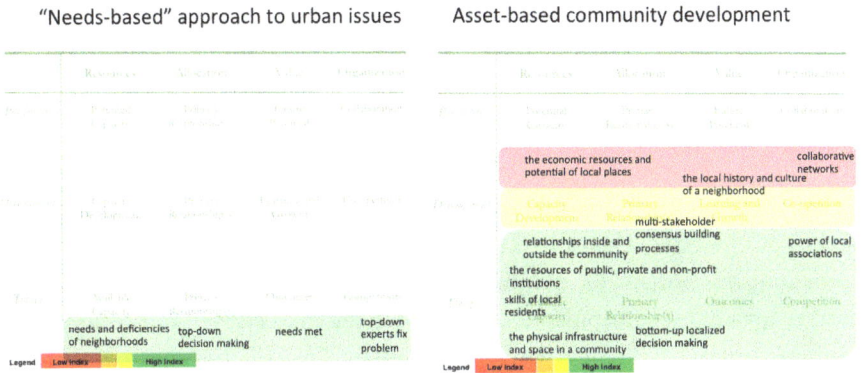

*Figure 22: Agreements Maps of Needs-based Approaches to Urban Issues and ABCD*

Through the resource allocation lens, I also saw strong contrasts with the needs-based approach to development. ABCD answers the "who decides?" question with bottom-up, localized decision making on specific issues, which takes place within a larger, community-wide, multi-stakeholder process of consensus building. I mapped the local, outcomes-focused process at the things level and the larger-scale, consensus-building process at the development level. Seeing the development potential in the community's own local history and culture is a core value in this approach, and organizing in collaborative networks that capitalize on the power of local associations is a core strategy. Thus, through both the value and organization lenses, I see ABCD moving into functioning at the possibility-light level. I color-coded the map to highlight these patterns: a strong focus on the things and development levels shows up in the broad green band, while the narrower yellow and red bands capture forays into developing resources and seeing potential. While the map for needs-based development indicates its things-level approach with a narrow green band at that level.

The research of Kretzmann and McKnight, and now many others, has provided a wealth of examples of how community assets, broadly defined, can be the building blocks of sustainable urban and rural community revitalization efforts. For instance, in Minneapolis, Minnesota (USA), a Latino immigrant community joined forces using the ABCD approach to develop a traditional marketplace, Mercado Central, in an inner-city neighborhood. This development used the community's capacities to create its own economic engine for change in a way that reflects its Latino traditions.[101]

The Mercado story starts with Isaiah, a coalition of churches in the Minneapolis area committed to mobilizing congregations to social action. Isaiah's community-organizing efforts identified the community's talent and energy around the related issues of building a more unified church community and addressing the economic and cultural needs of the immigrant population in different parts of the city. Once people in the different congregations came together, they realized they already had the land, experience, leadership and community relationships needed to create something to address all of their issues at one time. This was the Mercado Central. Within ten years from the launch of this project, the community raised and spent $2.4 million to purchase and renovate three dilapidated buildings for the marketplace and secured over $277,000 in loans to new Latino businesses. Overall, forty-four businesses either started up or expanded in the local community, providing seventy new jobs employing mostly local people. In the first year of the Mercado Central's operation, it contributed over $80,000 in sales taxes to the city and state.

Thus, instead of asking the city to meet its needs, the Latino community of Minneapolis built on its own assets, created its own abundance and ultimately, contributed from its abundance to the broader community. The initiative gave people greater freedom to provide for themselves. It also reduced their costs of scarcity, by decreasing their dependency on externally provided resources while increasing their cooperative efforts within the community and with associations outside of the community. With Mercado Central, the community was able to meet its immediate economic needs, such as employment and

---

101   The Mercado Central case of ABCD is described in (Sheehan, 2003). Visit Mercado Central at (mercadocentral.net).

building renovation, and build a sustainable capacity to provide for those needs in the future by developing its own leaders and community relationships. This example nicely illustrates an innovation that involves a step toward the development-motion level, while including the just-what-exists things-matter level.

From an Ecosynomics perspective, it is not surprising that communities around the world are embracing the ABCD approach. In fact, it is part of a broad pattern of recognition of a core principle of Ecosynomics—that focusing only on the things-matter level perpetuates the scarcity that exists there. At both the national and international levels, since the 1990s, there has been a shift of emphasis from providing food and other necessities to poor individuals and communities toward helping those communities and individuals develop "sustainable livelihoods." This shift has involved a growing awareness that focusing solely on current "needs" at the things-matter level causes people and groups to enter agreements that generate dependency on others to provide for those needs. The most detrimental agreement is a cultural acceptance of the idea "I am poor," lacking in all capacities and potential. This is completely different from the thought, "In this moment, I do not have enough money or food."[102]

Through new approaches, like ABCD, the underdeveloped communities are collectively identifying and enhancing the agreements, relationships and capacities that enable them to create the assets they want to satisfy their needs on their own. This gives them greater sovereignty over how they develop the assets they want, and it contributes to building community along the way. All of which leads to the experience of a fuller and freer life for community members. This is the essence of the move from a matter-level only to a matter-motion level mode of operation.

---

102    For a global view of this dependency, see (Easterly, 2006). For "livelihood" approaches, about people's ability to access and put to productive use their social, human, physical, financial and natural capital or assets, see Livelihood Connect (http://www.eldis.org/go/livelihoods/). The British Department for International Development shifted to a sustainable livelihoods approach in the late 1990's in its funding, see (http://www.eldis.org/vfile/upload/1/document/0902/DOC7388.pdf). CARE, the global humanitarian organization, uses a "unifying framework" to address the underlying causes of poverty, building the community's own assets. For a description of the unifying framework and a critique of dependency-based approaches, see (http://pqdl.care.org/CuttingEdge/Mapping%20CARE%27s%20Unifying%20Framework.pdf). For the welfare dependency indicators of the United States Department of Health and Human Services, see (http://aspe.hhs.gov/_/office_specific/topic2.cfm?sub_topic_id=137&sub_subtopic_name=Welfare%20Data&sub_id=481&tpc_topic_name=Welfare,%20Work,%20and%20Self-Sufficiency).

## TOWN MEETINGS

Having grown up in the southern parts of the United States and spent most of my early adulthood in Spain and Mexico, I was shocked when I moved to New England in 2002 and experienced its form of local government. I was used to living in places where few people knew who their elected officials were, much less became involved in the process of decision-making. When I went to my first annual town meeting in Wilton, New Hampshire, almost everyone I knew in town was there. Everyone had a copy of the booklet with all of the budget proposals that had been prepared by the town's elected "selectmen," plus specific project proposals that had been put forth by some of the citizens.[103] Most people were well informed, and everyone had an opportunity to speak up and ask whatever questions they wanted. And speak up they did. I was amazed that such a large proportion of the town's residents showed up for and engaged in the process. At the end of the day, it was the citizens who voted on each point, not the selectmen.

Town Meeting, as this process is called, is both a moment-in-time and an institution. As a moment-in-time, it is when town's eligible voters gather to appropriate money to run the town and to vote on salaries for the elected officials, as well as on any changes to the town's local statutes or by-laws. As an institution, Town Meeting is the legislative body for the towns.[104] This form of local government has been practiced in New England since the start of English settlements in the 1600s and is still alive in over 3,000 towns in seven states.[105]

Yet, when I started thinking about it and investigating the topic of local government more broadly, I realized it might also be seen as part of a much larger, more recent pattern of innovation. This is the movement toward citizen engagement and participatory budgeting, which started in Porto Alegre, Brazil, in 1989 and has since spread to over 140 municipalities in Brazil and over 1,500 cities across the world.[106] The core idea in this movement is that an increase in

---

103    You can see the minutes of this town meeting, as an example, at (http://www.ci.wilton.nh.us/Town%20Meeting%20Minutes/).

104    The Massachusetts Secretary of State provides a citizen's guide to town meeting, which you can find at (http://www.sec.state.ma.us/cis/cistwn/twnidx.htm).

105    The town meeting is the predominant form of local government practiced in the US region of New England since the 1600s and is still practiced in 169 towns in Connecticut, 432 in Maine, 297 in Massachusetts, 1,785 in Minnesota, 221 towns in New Hampshire, 31 in Rhode Island, and 237 in Vermont (see the National Association of Towns and Townships http://www.natat.org/ and http://en.wikipedia.org/wiki/Town_meeting). For a description of town meeting in the USA and Switzerland, from the late 1890s, see (Sullivan, 1892).

106    For data on the birth and growth of the participatory budgeting process in Brazil, see

the frequency, extent and diversity of citizen engagement in local government leads to an increase in the quality and positive impact of the decisions made by local governments, community organizations and public agencies.[107] This is a significant innovation compared to the predominant model of expert-driven town or city management, in which few, if any, citizens engage in the process and none can feel that they truly share responsibility for the outcomes local government produces.

In the Agreements Maps below in Figure 23, I have tried to capture the essence of differences between these two models of local government in Ecosynomics terms. In the traditional model, town management is the responsibility of elected politicians, who run organizations of town employees. Their focus is strictly on outcomes. The objective is to maintain the town's health, as assessed through its basic infrastructure of common resources, such as education, water, fire, police, and transportation, while staying within the established budget if possible. These town managers rely on expert opinions to guide decision-making, or perhaps a public referendum for particularly large, novel or controversial issues. I have mapped these aspects of the traditional model at the bottom of the things-matter level. In a few more vibrant communities, the town leadership begins to open to the community through open meeting consultations with citizens. I have placed this on the map to suggest that it is a foray in the direction of functioning at the development-motion level.

The spirit and practice of local government in communities using the town meeting or other form of participatory governance looks quite different. In these communities the citizens themselves decide on the budget and make up most of the committees that manage how it is spent. The outcome of maintaining the health of the basic infrastructure is still a central goal. However, the town meeting is also guided by three key operating principles, which I see as development-level, and even possibility-level, practices. First, there is the principle of citizen participation; not just in budgeting and management, but also in the development of the town's vision for itself and how it will use the

the World Bank report "Participatory Budgeting In Brazil" and Professor Sampler's (Bhatnagar, Rathore, Moreno Torres, & Kanungo, 2003; Wampler, 2009). For data on the use of "participatory budgeting globally, see (participatorybudgeting.org) and (http://web.worldbank.org/wbsite/external/topics/extsocialdevelopment/extpceng/0,,contentmdk:20509380~pagepk:148956~pipk:216618~thesitepk:410306,00.html).

107     For resources on community engagement, visit (http://civiccommons.org/engagement-commons). For more on participatory budgeting, see the United Nations Habitat (http://www.unhabitat.org/documents/faqqPP.pdf). For a partial global map of participatory budgeting processes, see (http://tiny.cc/pbmapping).

tangible and intangible resources it values. Second, there is the principle of transparency and stewardship of the public process; meaning that the citizens take responsibility for the transparency of the information and the process in which decisions are made and results assessed. Finally, there is the principle of shared responsibility for public resources. In other words, the town meeting form of local government depends upon citizens having a clear sense that "this is our town."

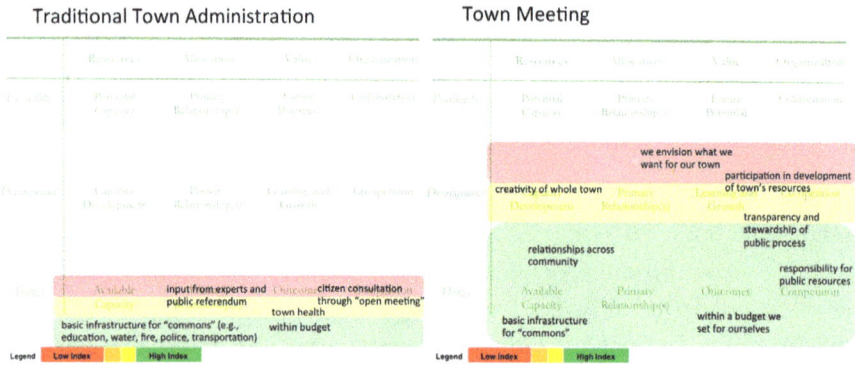

*Figure 23: Agreements Maps of Traditional Town Administration and Town Meeting*

My color-coding of the Agreements Map for traditional town administration, with green covering only the lower part of the things level, conveys the fact that this model focuses mostly at that level, on very specific results. Some towns operating traditionally are inspired to engage their citizens a little, occasionally, while remaining focused on the desired outcomes. This is what the yellow and red bands at the higher reaches of the things level conveys. In contrast, I have color-coded the map of the town meeting model with a broad green band covering all of the things-matter level and the lower part of the development-motion level, transitioning to yellow in the upper part of the development level. This pattern is meant to convey the fact that, while outcomes are important, the town also gives lots of time and attention to the clear assessment of the resources they have, to the value they assign to those resources, and to their maintenance over time. Citizens share responsibility for stewarding those resources for the benefit of the whole town and for including as many citizens in the process as want to be involved. Some towns venture even farther into the realm of possibility by collaboratively envisioning the future they want to choose.[108]

---

108    For examples of communities engaging collaboratively to envision the future they

## COOPERATIVES

Cooperatives are everywhere. The name of these organizations defines their purpose: to enable people to achieve cooperatively something they could not achieve on their own.[109] In many cases, the specific purpose of the cooperative is to provide greater purchasing power to consumers willing to act together. Cooperatives have been formed to buy and sell a wide variety of products and services, such as farm supplies, biofuels, groceries, and arts and crafts. Many cooperatives provide social services, such as healthcare, childcare, housing, transport, and education. They also operate in financial services in the form of credit unions, farm credit bureaus, mutual insurance companies, and cooperative finance programs. Many utilities, such as rural electric, telephone, and water companies, just to name a few, are organized as cooperatives.

The two Agreements Maps below (Figure 24) present my analysis of the innovation of the cooperative movement from an Ecosynomics viewpoint. Cooperatives offer consumers an alternative to the predominant pattern of individualism in market systems. The most obvious benefit of this innovation to cooperative members comes at the things-matter level in the lower prices for goods and services that can be negotiated by a large group buying collectively. A large group of people purchasing something in a transaction has much more power in the transaction with a large supplier than an individual can have, simply because of the higher volume of demand. I capture this in the Agreements Map at the things level of how exchanges are organized. With no cooperation an individual faces a large supplier on his own; whereas a cooperative represents a group that has more leverage in bargaining with that supplier.

Significantly, cooperatives also add the power of the development-motion level of relationships to the individual's experience of the things-matter level purchasing transaction. This increase in purchasing power through aggregation of individuals has a double impact. The cooperative brings a development-motion level to the relationships among individuals, inviting them to act *both* individually *and* as a group and to enjoy the benefits of both positions. The individuals act together through shared ownership and increased demand and

---

choose to steward together, see the "Heart & Soul Handbook" at (http://www.orton.org/resources/heart_soul_handbook).

109    The cooperative movement has grown so large globally that the UN has joined the movement. The United Nations defines a cooperative as an independent, voluntary group of people who come together to satisfy their shared economic, social, and cultural needs and aspirations. They typically do this through a jointly owned and democratically controlled enterprise. (http://www.un.org/News/Press/docs/2009/dev2784.doc.htm).

on their own through individual choice. In coming together and developing relationships around a shared purpose, this individual and group impact increases the choices and power of individuals. Shared ownership brings the individual into the decision making process about what the cooperative does. A community begins to form. Within the cooperative, individuals have greater bargaining power; increasing the choices they can make for themselves individually.

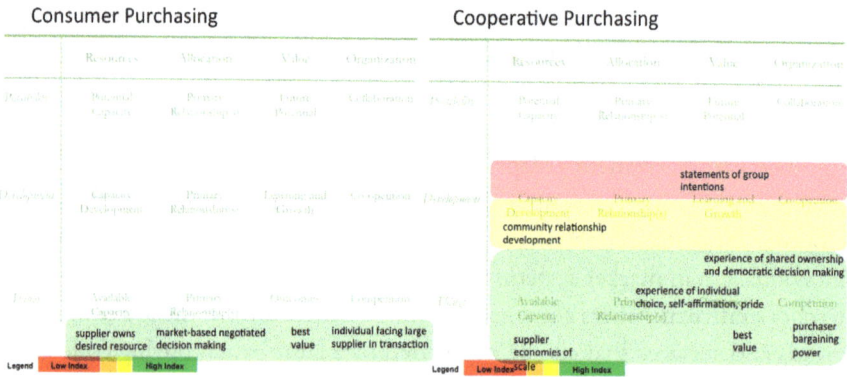

*Figure 24: Agreements Maps of Consumer Purchasing and Cooperative Purchasing*

This innovation shifts the thinking from the idea that one has power *either* as an individual *or* as a group to the realization that one can have power *both* as an individual *and* as a group. This is, of course, a key aspect of the Ecosynomics perspective. We know that we experience higher levels of harmonic vibrancy when all five primary relationships are healthy. When we focus on either the individual or the group, we tend to sacrifice the other one; but when we focus on both the individual and the group, we tend to strengthen both. The cooperative innovation suggests one way of achieving this simultaneous strengthening of the experience of the relationship to the self and to the group. In addition to the economic power I just described, social power comes through democratic participation and community-relationship development.

In a study of Latin American cooperatives, Professor Albert O. Hirschman, an economist at the Institute for Advanced Study, described the social impact of cooperatives in this way, "For many groups, the fact of joining forces, be it even for a modest purpose, such as setting up a cooperative consumer store, has a great deal of symbolic value. It is an act of self-affirmation that fills people with pride and may even be felt as a beginning of liberation, particularly by long-suffering and long-oppressed groups."

One historian suggests that some weavers started the first cooperative in Scotland in 1769. Since then it has become a worldwide phenomenon. The United Nations named 2012 the International Year of Cooperatives. At that time, the International Co-operative Alliance had 240 member organizations in 90 countries, representing 800 million individuals. In Europe, there were 58,000 cooperatives with 13.8 million members. In the USA, 14 federations represent 40,000 cooperatives with 75 million individual members. Americans hold 350 million memberships in cooperatives. Just these American cooperatives alone have over $3 trillion in assets, bring in nearly $654 billion in revenue, and provide two million jobs with $75 billion in wages and benefits paid. The scale and scope of this movement demonstrates powerfully that shifts toward greater vibrancy and abundance need not be just for the lucky few.[110]

## COMPLEMENTARY CURRENCIES

A few years ago, I was talking with a friend about the beauty of the paper currency in some countries. He showed me a BerkShare. At first I thought it was play money. He assured me it was real and told me about the community in the western part of Massachusetts that had created the BerkShare to serve as a complementary currency. In the moment, this sounded like a great innovation. In all of the economics classes I had taken, and after years as a business professor, I had never heard of complementary currencies. How many could there be—two or three? I then discovered the writings of Bernard Lietaer. He had identified two complementary currencies existing in 1984, observed their growth to 200 in 1990, and has now documented over 4,800 in existence today![111]

110    The first cooperative was the Fenwick Weavers Society (thefenwickweavers.coop), see (Fairbairn, 1994). The United Nations data on global memberships in cooperatives (un.org/News/Press/docs/2009/dev2784.doc.htm). On American cooperatives, the National Cooperative Business Association conducted research with the University of Wisconsin Center for Cooperatives, which was funded by the US Department of Agriculture to assess the economic impact of cooperatives, see (http://www.ncba.coop/ncba/about-co-ops/research-economic-impact).

111    For the story of BerkShares, visit (berkshares.org) or see (Barry, 2007). Bernard Lietaer has documented the development of complementary currencies, which you can follow at (lietaer.com) or read in (B. A. Lietaer, 2001). For the number of complementary currencies, visit the Complementary Currency database (http://www.complementarycurrency.org/ccDatabase/les_public.html) or see (B. Lietaer, 2003). Bernard Lietaer estimates there are over 5,000 community currency systems in operation, as of 2009, as cited in (Gelleri, 2009). Another estimate in 2006 was 4,000 (Wheatley, 2006).

These are called complementary currencies or alternative currencies, because people use them to complement, not replace, their national currency. To see the innovation in complementary currencies, I will start by describing the currencies we all know—national currencies. Most countries have their own currency, the money people can use to buy stuff in that country. For example, Japan has the yen and Mexico has the peso. With approximately 195 countries in the world, there are about 180 "national" currencies, allowing for some shared currencies like the euro and the dollar.[112] I call these "fiat currencies" because national governments decree the value they place on the paper bills that constitute their currency. The paper the currency is printed on has no value of its own. Rather it symbolizes, in a form that is easily held, counted and exchanged, something else that does have value. Governments and banks carefully control who gets to print it and how much there is in circulation. In other words, this money is designed to be scarce.[113]

The Agreements Maps in Figure 25, below, compare fiat currency and complementary currency from an Ecosynomics perspective. Economists describe three functions of money: it is a medium of exchange, it is a unit of measurement for accounting purposes, and it is a repository of value.[114] These three functions described the things-matter levels attributes of what is seen in the fiat currency systems through the lenses of resources, organization, and value, which I have captured in the Agreements Map.

The motion-level innovation of complementary currencies speaks directly to the nature of agreements people make around the value questions explored in Chapters 4 and 5. These questions are: what is the value of an exchange, what is the mode of the exchange, and who participates in the distribution of value in the exchange? Complementary currencies shift the things-matter level assumption of scarcity into a development-motion level assumption of abundance by changing the agreements that back up the currency. When looking through the value lens in Chapter 5, I showed how the three value questions look quite different at the light, motion, and matter levels. The three questions address the value, mode, and distribution of exchange. The motion-

---

112   I say that the number of countries in the world is approximate, because it depends on who is counting, and the criteria they use, which are mostly political. The CIA's World Fact-book counts 195 countries (The World Factbook 2011, 2011). There are 193 member states in the United Nations (http://www.un.org/en/members/growth.shtml). One source for the number of active currencies in the world is (The World Factbook 2011, 2011).

113   For more on the dynamics of money, see (Ritchie-Dunham, 2009a).

114   For standard, economic descriptions of the functions of money, see (Greenwald, 1983, p. 300; Mankiw, 2008, pp. 642-643). For economic and anthropologic perspectives on the historical development of money, see (Ferguson, 2008; Galbraith, 1975; Graeber, 2011; Needleman, 1991).

level expands the "what is of value?" question to include both the things we pay for and the things we do not usually pay for in our experience of day-to-day life and in our own development. Examples include our time taking care of family and volunteering at the local soup kitchen[115]. The motion-level also expands the "mode of exchange" question to include a broader definition of how we might exchange it, bringing into question matter-level concepts such as interest rates (e.g., positive, neutral, negative) and what is being exchanged (e.g., paper, time, bartered things and services).

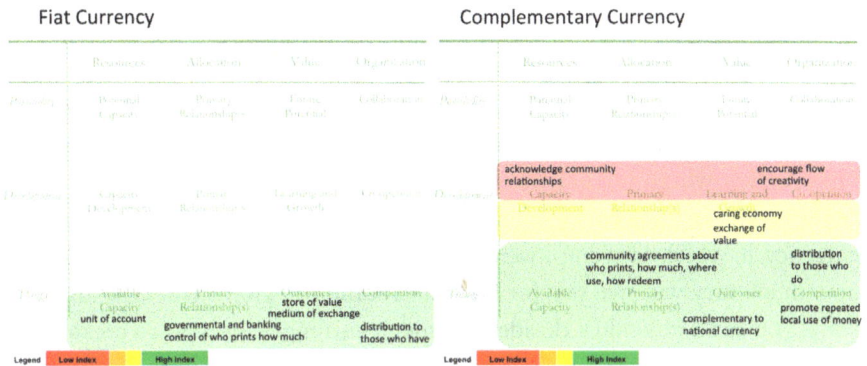

*Figure 25: Agreements Maps of Fiat Currencies and Complementary Currencies*

The distribution question at the motion level suggests that the person experiences value at both the development and outcomes levels. One way this is done is by keeping the currency moving locally. Economists use the "velocity of money" to determine how much a currency is exchanged in a given period of time within a given geography. Simply defined, the amount of value exchanged equals the amount of money times the velocity of money. I captured this in the Agreements Map as "promoting the repeated local use of money." This means that when $100 comes into a community, it is available for increasing the total value exchanged in the community. National currencies promote money coming into the community, say via wages and then being spent at a large store, which usually takes the money right back out of the community. It was exchanged once for a total value to the community of $100. A very different approach uses complementary currencies, such as the BerkShare to local use. A consumer buys $1 of BerkShares at the bank for

115    Riane Eisler, Lynne Twist, and colleagues have written extensively about the "caring economy" and new models for incorporating it into what is counted in the economy (Eisler, 2007; Twist, 2003).

90 cents of USA national currency. This BerkShare can only be redeemed at the bank by local businesses. This design promotes that same $100 to be used a dozen times locally before it comes back to the bank and leaves the community. This would be $1,200 of total value exchanged from that original $100. This greatly increases the local output.

The creators of each complementary currency decide which of these motion-and-matter-level features it designs into its complementary currency.[116] Again, the main point to make with the Agreements Map is to highlight the explicit differences in the two systems, so that people can be aware of the choices they are making in the agreements they enter. In the case of time banks, a complementary currency now in communities across the globe, people create their own "currency" by giving hours of their own time to an activity that someone else wants and receiving credit they can use to obtain services they need. For example, I can give a day of management consulting to a local business, knowing I can get two weeks of daycare for my child with the credit I create. This is different from having to work under a contract for a national currency, in which case employers tend to have the upper hand in determining how much they will give you for how much time you give them. With the time bank, you as an individual decide how much currency you want to create.

In complementary currencies, cooperatives, town meetings, ABCD and *Firms of Endearment* we see very different types of groups; operating in different arenas and in different parts of the world, making agreements that bring greater abundance into their lives. Without the Ecosynomics framework, it would be difficult to discern a pattern in these apparently disparate developments. Yet there is clearly a common pattern of shifting from a things-matter perspective to embrace the more dynamic perspective of development-motion. Having recognized this, we are now in a position to bring together lessons from these different experiences to shed light on how to bring about such shifts in other areas.

Now I want to share examples of innovations that generate even greater abundance by taking on the perspective of possibility-light, to function at all three levels of perceived reality simultaneously.

## INNOVATIONS AT ALL LEVELS

To the motion-matter level innovations we just saw, the possibility-light level adds an additional dimension of potentiality, opening up even greater

---

116   For recent descriptions of complementary currencies in use, see (Hallsmith & Lietaer, 2011; North, 2010).

choice, freedom and flexibility for responding to the conditions and demands life presents. To frame this in the negative, if one is stuck in a things-matter perspective, or even a development-motion perspective, the options for how one responds to challenges will be limited. The innovations I will now share illustrate how some groups manage to hold all three perspectives together and what they are able to accomplish by operating at all three levels as part of their work.

Groups that operate at all three levels take a distinctive approach when addressing the four basic economic questions. They think first about what they would like to achieve. Then they consider what resources would support them in achieving that objective and how to develop those resources over time in order to have what they need when they need it. In organizing human interaction, these groups look for, recognize and invite in the potential they see in the people they work with and in their relationships. They choose the capacities and relationships they want to develop over time and, with these developing resources, are able to be at their best at any given moment. Finally, they think about value in terms of their vision of what can flow from the development of their capacities and relationships, and their vision embraces the benefits to be enjoyed, not only by group members, but also by all who interact with the group.

This grounded-potential path envisions abundance and takes the steps needed to bring it into reality. It also avoids the costs of scarcity experienced at the things-matter and development-motion levels that are not experienced when simultaneously engaging all three levels together. I will share some examples I have found.

## THORLO

In Chapter 3, I introduced you to THORLO, the small textile company in North Carolina (USA) that I have been working with for nearly a decade. I described its unusual "role growth compensation conversations" and, in Chapter 6, its practice of "surfacing surprises" as part of a larger process of "integrated collaborative conversations." Now I want to use the "definitions of success" graphic and the Agreements Map to look in a more general way at how THORLO works with all three levels of perceived reality.[117]

---

117    The data in this section comes from three diagnostics in which three outside observers from the Institute for Strategic Clarity, not the author, visited THORLO over a 2-year period. They interviewed individuals, observed group processes, applied the Institute's Harmonic Vibrancy survey to 12 teams including 151 employees, and read through company reports, which

By any measure of business success, THORLO is functioning effectively at the things-matter level. Its high-tech socks, designed to provide preventive foot care, are highly competitive in the marketplace and have been since their introduction in the 1970s. Over the past decade, THORLO has maintained a gross margin on branded products that is 14 percentage points higher than its branded competitors. Its gross margin on commodity products in the same period has been double that of the competition. Recently, THORLO was able to reduce its workforce by 15 percent and its inventory by 30 percent while maintaining production rates, delivery schedules and product quality. Thus the company has found a way to be sustainably innovative and profitable, despite the fact that it produces all of its products in the U.S. at its North Carolina mill, while most of its competitors have moved production to low-wage factories abroad. Using the framework and tools of Ecosynomics, we can uncover the sources of these impressive outcomes in THORLO's organizational culture and way of operating.

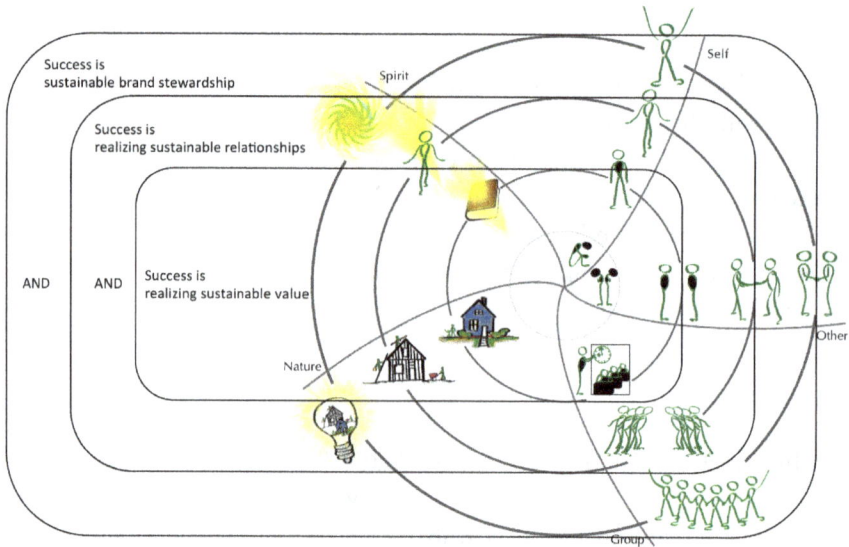

*Figure 26: Definitions of Success at THORLO*

First, let's look at how the company's definition of success shows its focus on all three levels of perceived reality (Figure 26). You can ask anyone at THORLO, from top leadership throughout the organization, what success looks like in their business and they will reply, "brand stewardship." This is the they documented in (Leaf and Hulbert 2009, Puleo and RD 2011).

term they use to convey the company's mission to provide its customers with the best foot health possible through THORLO brand socks. Everything they do is measured against this criterion. For example, every major decision within the company must pass the "more life" test: does the solution to this problem add more life to the consumer's experience and to the employee's experience? In looking for an answer to this question, the folks at THORLO are careful to consider all five relationships at all three levels of perceived reality.

A second way THORLO defines success is by its ability to create "sustainable relationships" with all of its stakeholders, by which it means its loyal customers, loyal employees, loyal suppliers and vendors, and loyal shareholders, in that order of priority. For customers, the company uses "product integrity" to assess the quality of the total consumer experience. For employees, it uses "cultural integrity." This is a composite measure that considers the things-matter question of what pay each employee is receiving, relative to the wages they would receive in similar positions in the region, together with the development-motion level issue of how that employee's professional development is progressing. THORLO assesses the sustainability of its relationships with suppliers and vendors with a metric it calls "business systems integrity." This is the percentage of the orders delivered by THORLO that meet all expectations. Finally for shareholders, it uses "capital integrity," which is determined by calculating the company's return on investment and the efficiency of its use of capital.

THORLO routinely uses these "four integrities" in decision-making, to ensure the quality and sustainability of its critical relationships. The cross-functional nature of some of the criteria, for example in the ability to deliver an order exactly as specified, means that it takes a cross-company group or conversation to make sure that the standard is being met. This happens through the Integrated Collaborative Conversations (ICC) structure-process noted on the Agreements Map below (Figure 27). The sustainable relationships definition of success encompasses the level of development of capacities and relationships as well as the things-matter level of outcomes.

Finally, THORLO also defines its success at the things-matter level, as creating "sustainable value" for those same stakeholders. In this domain, it uses traditional financial indicators to track its success, for example, return on invested capital, the percentage of profits available for future investments, and the percentage of revenues from premium-priced products. This definition of success includes the outcomes level for the five primary relationships.

The Agreements Map in Figure 27, below, offers a more detailed examination of the practices that show THORLO functioning at the things, development and possibility levels of perceived reality. In previous examples, I shared the evidence by lens, starting with what I saw through the resource lens at the different levels, then the allocation, value, and organization lenses. For the THORLO case, I will organize the information by level of perceived reality. At the things-matter level of perceived reality, the level of outcomes, I look through the resource lens and see a strong, widespread awareness of the capacities available in the company. This is evidenced by clear written descriptions and established measurement systems for jobs, processes and financial indicators.

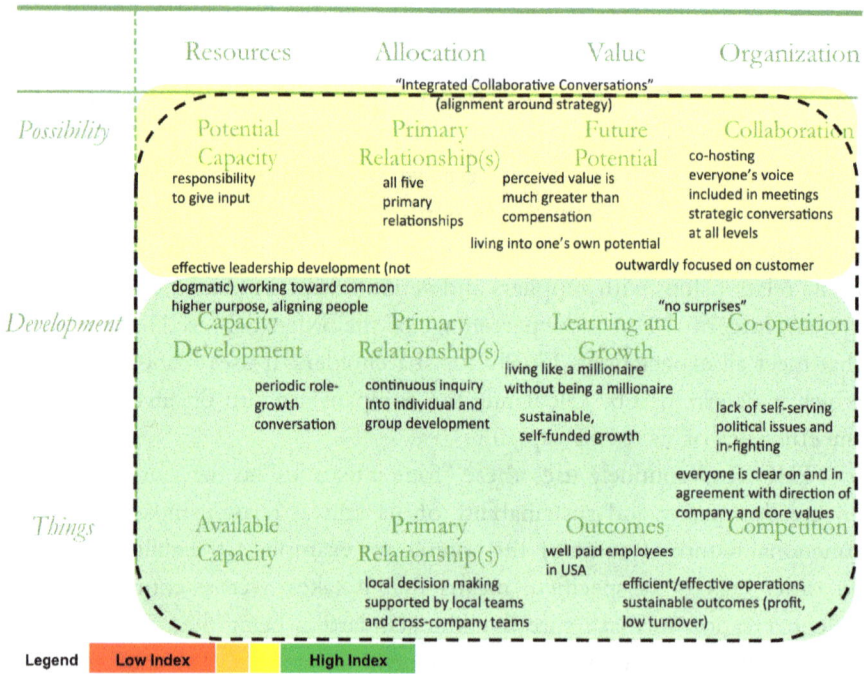

*Figure 27: THORLO Agreements Map*

Through the allocation lens at the things-matter level, I see well-documented evidence of structures and processes to support local group and individual decision-making. For example, people throughout the organization are always actively engaged in multi-functional, cross-company teams, in which conversation is explicitly focused on tending to all five primary relationships. I also see at this level that THORLO concretely expresses the value it places on the capacities and experience people bring to work each day through above-average pay. This is rare in an industry that has sent most jobs to low-wage countries. Finally, through the organization lens, I find processes designed for high efficiency and effectiveness, including industry-leading quality-control practices. I also see a long record of low employee turnover and high profitability, both of which run counter to the textile industry standard.

At the development level, through the resource lens I see various ways in which THORLO is paying attention to its people's development. These include clear definition of the developmental steps in each area, for example, from novice to master craftsman. These definitions acknowledge an employee's investment in the mastery of a profession, which is further supported by periodic role-growth conversations with every employee. Through the allocation lens at the development level, I find processes like the role-growth conversation that invite employees into continuous inquiry about their own development and that of the groups they are part of. My notation in the value column of the map at this level captures the added value THORLO personnel experience in an environment so supportive of developing capacities and relationships. As one employee it, "I live like a millionaire, without the responsibilities of a millionaire. I get to do what I love to do with people I love and enjoy, and I get paid well for it!" The company's focus on sustainable, self-funded, growth is further evidence through the value lens of its effective functioning at the development level. Through the organization lens, we see processes that keep everyone informed about, clear on, and in agreement with the company's core values and direction.

One of the outside observers who gathered data for THORLO's Assessment Map was surprised to find such a strong procedural focus on development. "While a lot of companies talk about it," he wrote, "I have never seen such a lack of self-serving political issues. Everyone is focused on shared goals and contributions. There is no in-fighting."

At the possibility-light level, I found evidence of uncommon practices made common. For example, the company has a practice it calls "100 percent responsibility." This means that anyone who sees potential in another person or possibilities for new developments is responsible for speaking up and giving his input. This is a possibility-level practice seen through the resource lens. Through the allocation lens, I see decision processes supporting possibility in the five primary relationships. Through the value lens, I see possibility-level functioning in the fact that most people at THORLO will tell you that the opportunity to work with others exploring and manifesting possibilities is more valuable to them than their monetary compensation. Through the organization lens, one sees many processes and structures supporting intentional work with potential. For example, each cross-company team has an assigned co-host whose role it is to ensure that potential is acknowledged and worked with, and that the voice of everyone in the meeting can be heard. THORLO's organizational structure also integrates the constant flow of information and decision-making through the three levels of reality, so that strategic conversations take place at all levels throughout the company.

Looking at the color-coding of the THORLO Agreements Map, we see the pattern of a healthy organization. The band of green extends from the things-matter level all the way into the lower half of the possibility-light level, signifying that most people, most of the time, are aware and functioning effectively at those levels. The yellow band indicates that some people, some of the time, are aware and functioning at the possibility-light level.

To summarize, this map tells a story of high efficiency and effective policies that reflect healthy functioning at the things-matter level, the level of outcomes. We also see healthy expressions at the development-motion level, reflecting a liquid conversation across areas about the flows of strategic resources. This figure also shows quite a few strategic processes at the possibility-light level, explicitly exploring possibility in the short and long term throughout the organization. All of this is interwoven very clearly in a process-structure that THORLO calls the integrated collaborative conversation, working the continuous chain of transitions from light to motion to matter to motion to light.

Together the pictures in Figure 26 and Figure 27 offer an Ecosynomics explanation of THORLO's seemingly extraordinary business outcomes. Starting with "more life" and an assumption of abundant potential in the five primary relationships, the people of THORLO have found, customized and invented structures and processes that support their agreements. Basically, those agreements are to see potential, choose how to develop it, and deliver high quality, profitable outcomes in most everything they do. While they will be the first to tell you they do not always practice what they know, they work hard at maintaining awareness of what they know. THORLO folks describe this way of being and working together as just a healthier, nicer, more efficient and effective way. It is a fundamental agreement. They look around and see potential and beauty, and they enjoy finding effective ways to engage that potential and bring it to the customer experience. In the words of one THORLO engineer, "We 'see' more life, and say, 'Yes.'"

## GLOBAL ACTION NETWORKS

My colleague Steve Waddell introduced me a few years ago to an emerging phenomenon, which he identified and named Global Action Networks (GANs).[118] These GANs are pursuing an alternative to traditional approaches to dealing with large-scale problems that exist across national boundaries and affect people both locally and globally. GANs arose because the traditional approaches were not working well on these issues, such as poverty, corruption, climate change, disease, and the disappearance of natural resources.

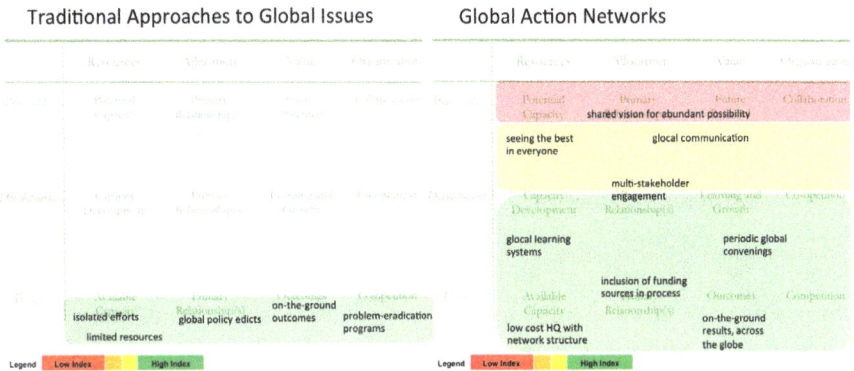

*Figure 28: Agreements Maps of Traditional Approaches to Global Issues and GANs*

The traditional approaches rely on national governments and inter-governmental organizations like the United Nations. This approach tends to isolate groups or sectors, driving them to act alone, competing with other agencies for the limited resources available for global concerns (see Figure 28). For example, there are countless instances of water projects around the world in which one humanitarian aid group provided a water pump in one village while another group provided training to maintain a pump in a different village. The placement of the pump and the training rarely coincided. Similarly, one group might be working on keeping girls in school, while another works on building schools for girls to go to, while yet another is providing funds for teachers, but all in different regions of the country. The shortcomings of these uncoordinated efforts are obvious to the people working on the projects at the local level. However, they are not in a position to influence an initiative in which the funding, planning and project timelines all come from an international

118    For great detail about the over eighty global action networks and what they are learning, see (Waddell, 2011).

agency that is typically unaware of the situation on the ground.[119]

I used these well-documented cases to create the Agreements Map on the left side of Figure 28. Through the resource lens we see the separate aid efforts competing for limited resources, with a strong focus on short-term delivery of the resources available in the moment. This is a classic things-level mode of operation. In most of these traditional aid organizations, resource allocation happens at the headquarters office, located in a developed country. From there, global policy edicts guide local implementation. Through the value lens, we see that this approach is focused on achieving the specific goals of each project. The organization of these efforts reflects the belief that the most efficient way to manage the limited resources of the international group is to mount problem-eradication programs. The steps of this approach are straightforward: identify a problem, engage experts to develop a solution, direct local actors to carry out the expert-designed plan, and the problem is resolved.

In contrast, the way GANs operate tends to bring people and organizations from the different sectors together to tackle big challenges at local and global levels simultaneously. To give you a sense of what a GAN looks like and how it works, let's look at the example of Transparency International (TI). TI came into being in 1993 with a mission to stop corruption and promote transparency, accountability and integrity at all levels and across all sectors of society. By 2010 it had a global headquarters staff of 138, based in Geneva, Switzerland, and an annual budget of a little more than 18 million Euros—a small amount to cover a worldwide fight against corruption. Outside of Geneva, TI consists of a network of more than ninety national chapters. Each chapter works in its own country to engage key people in government, civil society, business, and the media to promote transparency in elections, in public administration, in government procurement, and in business. The global network of chapters, along with their local partners, mounts advocacy campaigns to raise international awareness of the corruption problem and to put pressure on national governments to implement anti-corruption reforms.[120]

These efforts have made some significant inroads against the problem of corruption. For example, they have provided a common language for talking about corruption and a common standard for measuring it. TI has also made corruption the topic of a national-level conversation within many countries.

---

119   Two influential economists describe these traditional "planner knows better" approaches in (Easterly, 2006; Sachs, 2011).
120   The observations in this section come from my work over the past 10 years with leaders of dozens of GANS through my research in GAN-Net and iScale, a convening network of GANs (Ritchie-Dunham, 2009b).

For example, Transparency Ethiopia, in cooperation with the Ethiopian Federal Ethics and Anti-Corruption Commission, convened prominent reporters in a public roundtable discussion of the existing barriers to reporting on corruption. This group agreed to continue what started as a one-time discussion by coming together to support an on-going series of public anti-corruption discussions. Similarly, TI El Salvador partnered with two federal agencies to launch an initiative to enhance fiscal transparency by subjecting the country's budget process to more citizen access and input. In this way, TI has been able to make global changes, one nation at a time, with very limited resources but an effective strategy of collaboration.

TI's strategy is representative of how other GANs, such as the Global Partnership for the Prevention of Armed Conflict and the Global Water Partnership operate. The GANs do their work by focusing simultaneously on the three levels of perceived reality. The GAN keeps the topic of its global advocacy—its deep vision for the change that is possible—front and center, as an organizing principle. This is what we see through the value lens. This possibility-light level focus drives the work of the whole network. From within its possibility-light vision, the GAN chooses the highest-leverage, development-motion level processes to bring that possibility into development in local settings around the world.

Through the resource lens, we encounter another GAN principle: to see the best in everyone. Many GANs do a good job of documenting what different groups have to offer. This is a possibility-level approach to resources. Looking through the resource allocation lens, we find that GANs typically seek to engage all relevant voices at all levels of decision-making. Organizationally, they make this possible in part by maintaining a strong focus on "glocal" (global-local) network communication and learning systems. They do a lot of experimenting with ways to share across the globe what is being learned locally. One organizational innovation that particularly intrigues me is the GAN pattern of maintaining a very lean staff in headquarters. Often you will find a group of fewer than 20 people coordinating a networked organizational structure that spans the globe. At the same time, the GANs, show up strongly in local action, delivering clear outcomes for their funders. This is effective functioning at the things-matter level.

GANs provide a great example of what Ecosynomics is all about. No matter what global issue they are taking on, the founders of these GANs all seem to see the same thing when looking through the resource lens—they see abundance. They see this abundance at all three levels of reality—in the future that is possible, in the capacities and relationships to develop over time, and in the worldwide actions that people can take on to bring about that change.

Through the allocation lens, the GANs hold all five primary relationships to be necessary to work with the abundant possibilities they envision. In the self, they believe they need the best each individual can bring. In the other, they know that their work requires collaborative processes of mutuality among the different members and stakeholders engaged in the work. In the group, they see that each person and perspective needs to be clear in the contribution his or her work makes to the higher aspiration. In nature, they have to be able to take an audacious possibility, develop high-leverage capacities to achieve it, and deliver very real outcomes, all over the globe. In spirit, this audacious goal can only be achieved if all of the creativity available, everywhere and in everyone, is brought to the work. This means that they are clear that they cannot achieve what they want without the explicit inclusion of all five primary relationships from the beginning.

Thus, when they look through the value lens, they see the need to develop global-local, multi-sector, multi-stakeholder approaches for identifying the allocation criteria everyone holds in common, as well as the criteria unique to each stakeholder. This does not keep them from assessing on-the-ground results from their localized efforts around the world. Finally, through organization lens, the GANs have taken on the commitment to experiment with continuous learning systems that facilitate sharing globally what is being learned locally. This ongoing communication is interwoven with periodic global face-to-face meetings that are carefully designed to support all five primary relationships. GANs provide us a concrete example of what working in such a system can look like.

## CONCLUSION

In this chapter, I have used the Agreements Map to highlight the differences between various pairs of systems that seem to have similar goals but different approaches to achieving them. It can be difficult to see why the experience of one system seems so different from another: why traditional town administration is different from town meeting; why needs-based development is different from asset-based development; why traditional ways of addressing global issues are different from GANs. The Agreements Map helps to make the differences easier to see by capturing evidence of the underlying agreements in each system. These are the understandings that everyone knows about, uses and could describe, and they help to explain why living in the different systems can be so different at the experiential level.

This use of the Agreements Map demonstrates how the lenses derived from the four basic questions of economics can clarify our experiences of the five primary relationships at the three levels of perceived reality. The maps organize the evidence of what the experience in a particular system is like and allow comparison between that and the experience of a different system. We can ask ourselves, which experience do we prefer? Then we can start to uncover the agreements that support the preferred experience and begin to think about how we can shift our agreements in that direction. This is the topic of Chapter 8.

Before I move on to describing a process for making such a shift, however, I want to state clearly that I do *not* assume that one system is "better" than another because people are working with more levels of perceived reality—that is, more of the map is colored green. I believe that higher vibrancy agreements bring out more human potential and lead to greater development of that potential. I also believe that they incur lower costs of scarcity, as discussed in Chapter 6. That does not mean they are better. They are just different.

For example, the needs-based developmental approach has helped many people. One large recent example of this is the development of the United Nation's Millennium Development Goals. As one of the intellectual authors of the goals, economist Jeffrey Sachs made clear in his many speeches that this initiative addressed some very basic needs that had to be met, such as providing inexpensive bed nets to fight the mosquitoes causing malaria. It is a relatively easy solution to a huge problem that just needs to happen.[121]

One approach is not necessarily better than the other, and the agreements supporting them are very different. The point of this whole exercise is to enable ourselves to choose the experience we want by choosing the agreements that support that kind of experience. To choose the system we want, we need to be able to see and work with agreements. With that clarification, let's move on to looking at ways to do just that.

---

121    For many such "needs-based" arguments eloquently documented by Professor Jeffrey Sachs, see (Sachs, 2005).

# CHAPTER 8

# WHAT YOU CAN DO, THE HARMONIC VIBRANCY MOVE

In the last chapter, I shared the evidence I have gathered so far showing that many people are living experienc.es of abundance and harmonic vibrancy. I also described a number of significant innovations in quite disparate fields of activity, demonstrating that groups are finding ways to function effectively at *both* the things-matter level *and* the higher levels of perceived reality. The Ecosynomics framework allows us to recognize the basic commonality in those innovations and see patterns from which we can learn to innovate in other fields. The Agreements Map offers concrete details of what their higher-level functioning looks like, and on that basis, we can make inferences about the underlying agreements that make it possible.

Now it is time to consider how you can get to that kind of agreement in your own groups. The Agreements Map is a key part of a process that can lead you there. I call this process the Harmonic Vibrancy Move. I hope this name will help you keep in mind that the goal is high vibrancy and abundance, experienced in all five primary relationships simultaneously. Like the harmony achieved by voices or instruments coming together skillfully in a musical offering, effective functioning in all relationships across all three levels of perceived reality creates a sense of richness and vitality. This is harmonic vibrancy, the experience we all want to have as often as possible.

In Chapter 2, I described three common pathways people take across the five-relationship-three-level terrain in search of a better quality of life experiences. Followers of the on-the-level path are convinced that possibility or development or things is the only "real" and relevant realm of operation.

This path leads only to three separate versions of scarcity: unrealized dreams of what is possible; endless development without tangible results; or a finite amount of things with no prospects for renewal. The enlightened-matter path starts at the things-matter level and seeks to reach abundance by adding in activities at the levels of development-motion and possibility-light. This path leads to occasional experiences of abundance. It cannot take you all the way to the outer circle of harmonic vibrancy, however, because it is built on an assumption of scarcity. In contrast, on the grounded-potential path, one starts with abundance, chooses from infinite possibility what to develop, and then stops development when the time is right to bring forth a specific, desired outcome. This process is the basis for the Harmonic Vibrancy Move.

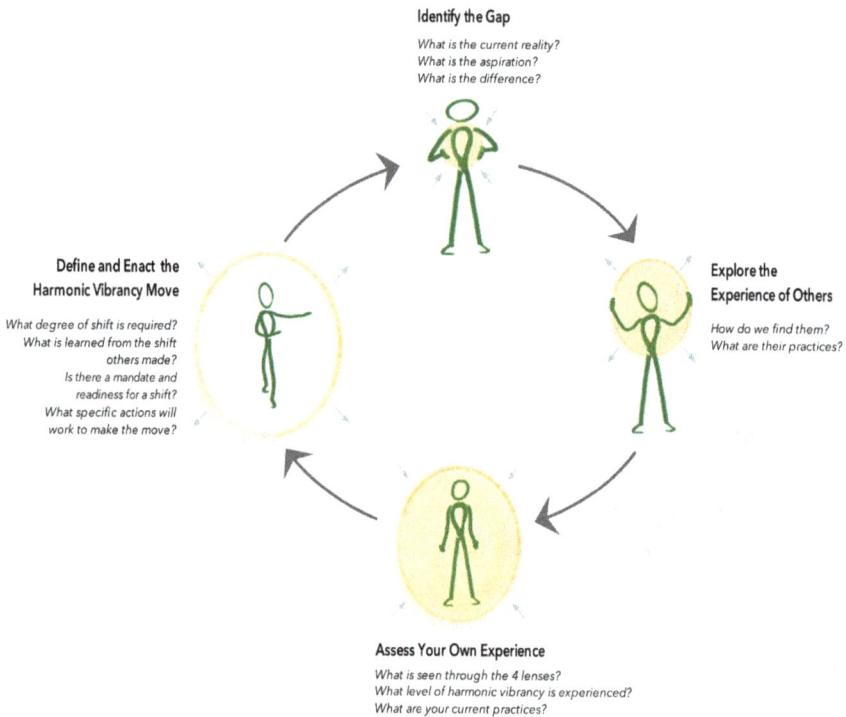

**Identify the Gap**
*What is the current reality?*
*What is the aspiration?*
*What is the difference?*

**Explore the Experience of Others**
*How do we find them?*
*What are their practices?*

**Define and Enact the Harmonic Vibrancy Move**
*What degree of shift is required?*
*What is learned from the shift others made?*
*Is there a mandate and readiness for a shift?*
*What specific actions will work to make the move?*

**Assess Your Own Experience**
*What is seen through the 4 lenses?*
*What level of harmonic vibrancy is experienced?*
*What are your current practices?*

*Figure 29: Harmonic Vibrancy Move Process*

## PROCESS OVERVIEW

Of course, each group must determine and then implement the specifics of its own Harmonic Vibrancy Move. What I offer here is a four-step process for proceeding along the grounded-potential path to get to those specifics (see Figure 29). The first step, Identify the Gap, is an awareness-raising exercise. It brings people into the Ecosynomics realm by inviting them to look into the quality of their experiences in the group, both their current experience and the experience they would like to be having. It is an opportunity for them, individually and collectively, to get in touch with their highest aspirations for what the group experience could be like. The second step, Explore the Experience of Others, opens up a more concrete consideration of what might be possible. It does this by extending the inquiry to take in the details of how other groups are living with the kind of experience your group desires—what does a higher level of harmonic vibrancy actually look like?

In the third step, Assess Your Own Experience, the group lays the groundwork for moving to the next level of experience and outcomes. The key tool for this step is the Agreements Map. With a detailed understanding of the group's current practices in all five relationships, as seen through the four economic lenses and mapped onto the three levels of perceived reality, the areas in need of development will be abundantly clear. This clarity provides a basis for seeing how the underlying agreements can shift and need to shift in order to move to a higher level of harmonic vibrancy. On this basis, the group can move to the fourth step, Define and Enact the Harmonic Vibrancy Move.

Figure 30 lays out the four steps in table form and suggests what each step involves, including some of the questions to be addressed. In principle, the steps are relatively simple and straightforward, yet many groups will need to have some assistance in following them. There are a wide variety of group practices and process tools that can support your group in moving through this process, as well as many consultants who can use those practices and tools to facilitate the kinds of analysis, reflection and conversation the process requires. I propose Ecosynomics and the Harmonic Vibrancy Move as general frameworks; they are not meant to be a branded, proprietary approach to individual or group transformation. Rather, they provide a broad, inclusive framework—a way of looking at and making sense of our experience—that can inform any change strategy and increase its chances of creating the results people want.[122]

In this chapter, I will explain each of the steps in more detail. In the following chapters, I will share the stories of some individuals and groups I have worked with and supported in using these steps to make a Harmonic

---

122　While I mention some of the practices in these pages, much more detail on the practices and examples of their application are available in these publications (Ritchie-Dunham, 2002, 2005, 2008a; Ritchie-Dunham & Puente, 2008; Ritchie-Dunham & Rabbino, 2001).

Vibrancy Move. I will describe some of the process tools I use and provide some practical tips from my experience. I hope that in the wide variety of examples you will find one that is suggestive of the kinds of issues you are facing.

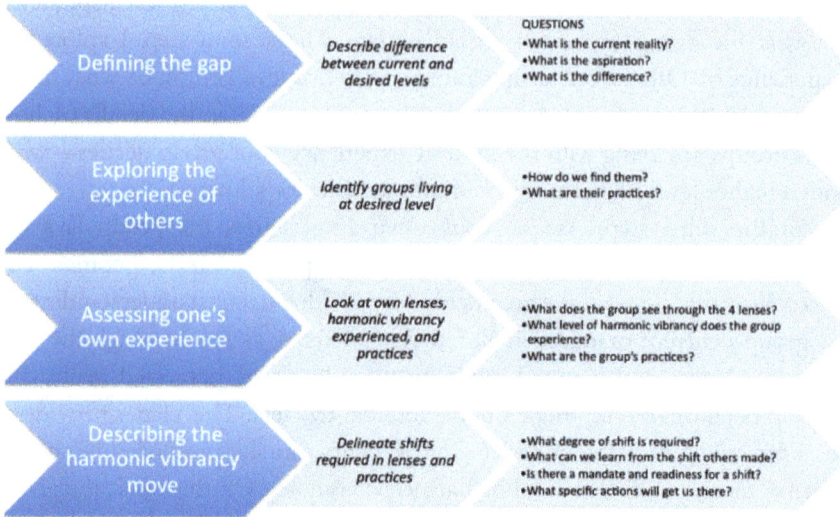

| | | QUESTIONS |
|---|---|---|
| **Defining the gap** | *Describe difference between current and desired levels* | • What is the current reality?<br>• What is the aspiration?<br>• What is the difference? |
| **Exploring the experience of others** | *Identify groups living at desired level* | • How do we find them?<br>• What are their practices? |
| **Assessing one's own experience** | *Look at own lenses, harmonic vibrancy experienced, and practices* | • What does the group see through the 4 lenses?<br>• What level of harmonic vibrancy does the group experience?<br>• What are the group's practices? |
| **Describing the harmonic vibrancy move** | *Delineate shifts required in lenses and practices* | • What degree of shift is required?<br>• What can we learn from the shift others made?<br>• Is there a mandate and readiness for a shift?<br>• What specific actions will get us there? |

*Figure 30: Four-step Harmonic Vibrancy Move Process*

## IDENTIFY THE GAP

To move to a higher level of harmonic vibrancy, the first step is to visualize the gap between the level of harmonic vibrancy you believe is available to you and the level you currently experience (see Figure 31).

Determining the desired level creates a clear goal by showing you where you want yourself or your group to end up. Then, seeing the gap between that goal and your current experience shows you just how much work you will need to do to get there. This is a common way of starting a change process, because, for most people, identifying this gap provides direction and also a strong motivation for change. In a Harmonic Vibrancy Move, however, there is a particular focus in this exercise on exploring current and desired states and defining the gap clearly in terms of the five relationships and the three levels of perceived reality.

## Identify the Gap

### What is the current reality?
### What is the aspiration?
### What is the difference?

*Figure 31: Identify the Gap between Current Reality and Aspiration*

## CURRENT LEVEL

Let us start with the current level of harmonic vibrancy you are experiencing. To determine this, you need to determine the quality of experience you are having in the five primary relationships. The 3 Circles of Harmonic Vibrancy diagram will help you to do this. Look at the three different levels of each of the five relationships in Figure 32 and circle the picture that best captures your current experience of that relationship in the group. For example, think about your experience of your self in the group. How much of you shows up? What does it feel like? If none of your true self shows up, then circle the sitting person who is crouched over in the inner circle. If you feel that you and your capacities are present and seen by others and you stand strong, then circle the upright figure in the middle circle. If, on the other hand, you feel that you bring and share your greatest gifts in this group, then circle the celebrating figure in the outer circle. When you have gone through this exercise with all five relationships, you will have described the vibrancy you experience with this group.

When I did this with a friend who works at a local school, she said, "Most of the time I feel insignificant. I do my job, get criticized and am rarely appreciated for everything I do for the kids. It is very draining." When she saw the graphic in Figure 32, she immediately pointed at the inner circle. "That's my life," she said, "and I don't want it to be."

In a different setting, a small group of executives in a training company I worked with saw themselves living just inside the middle circle of Harmonic Vibrancy. They had done the exercise with the 3 Circles diagram individually and compared their results. It emerged that they all felt proud of their professional capabilities and also felt acknowledged for their individual and team successes.

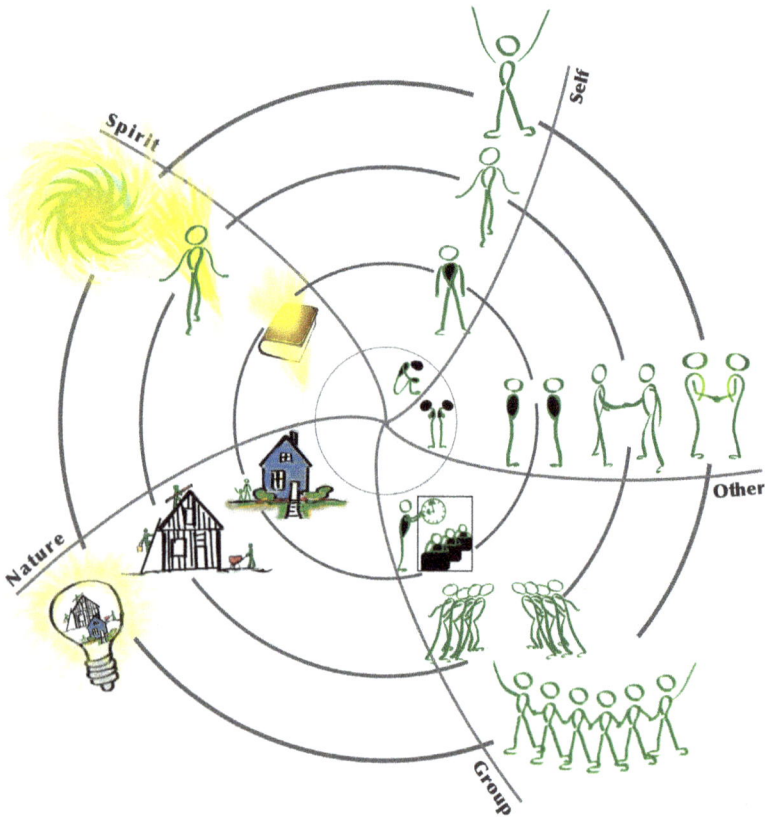

*Figure 32: Determining Current State in Five Relationships*

## DESIRED LEVEL

Once you have described your experience in all five relationships, ask yourself, "Is this the best the group can do?" If the answer is yes—your experience of the five relationships in this group is as good as it is possible to get—then there is nothing more to do except consider how you will sustain that experience. Many of the higher vibrancy groups I have worked with were happy with the level of vibrancy they were currently experiencing, but since their leader would soon be moving on to another group, they were not sure how to maintain the experience they were having. In this case, the desired future level is similar to the current, but the expectation is that the current level will fall quickly, and thus there is still a gap. If, on the other hand, the answer to this question is no, then you can explore what something better might look like.

Exploring what a better state might look like can take you in a couple of directions. In many cases, people realize that their experience is varied. Sometimes, or perhaps all the time in some situations, there are experiences of higher harmonic vibrancy in the group. On those occasions, things just seem to work better. More of me and more of you show up. We are better together. We see in each other the potential for creativity that we can develop and bring into action. But this only happens sometimes. At other times, or more of the time, less shows up. Because you know that the group is capable of performing at a higher level, at least some of the time, you might reflect that a higher level of harmonic vibrancy would be possible if the agreements shifted. For example, my friend who worked at the local school realized upon reflection that every now and then she experienced the middle to outer circle. This happened when she was in charge of a bigger project and was focused on doing something very creative with others for the kids and their parents. This gave her the sense that something better was possible.

Another direction this inquiry can take is to lead a group to imagine a positive change in outcomes and harmonic vibrancy even though it has never demonstrated the capacity to achieve this higher level. The small group of IT executives I described above developed this kind of aspiration. They saw that the improvements in performance they needed to make would require changing their agreements and shifting their culture toward the outer circle, a level of harmonic vibrancy they had never experienced. Yet they could envision that experience and wanted it. One of them summarized the group's thoughts as follows: "What we want is to experience the greater efficiencies and innovation possible in collaboration. We want to move to the outer circle with other teams in our company. We can be much better than we are."

## THE GAP

Now, having described the harmonic vibrancy you *currently* experience in a group and the level you *want* to experience, you have identified the gap between the two. This exercise often provides a positive motivation for change. My friend who worked in the school was very clear at this stage of our conversation. "I want to experience more of my life like those special times," she said. The executives were also clear that they had to try to make the shift they envisioned. Their current successes would not get them where they needed to go.

This first step, identifying the gap, is the most important step of the Harmonic Vibrancy Move. It sets the foundation, the future course, and the amount of energy that will be required for the move. You have now shifted from a question, "Is this the best we can do?" to a statement of the harmonic vibrancy you know is possible. From this vantage point, the next question is, "What does life look like at the 'desired' level?"

## EXPLORE THE EXPERIENCE OF OTHERS

The second step in a Harmonic Vibrancy Move is to explore what people do at the higher level of harmonic vibrancy you aspire to (see Figure 33). I have worked with dozens of groups trying to do this, and they all needed some kind of example to guide them toward what they were aiming for. Sometimes they could find this example in their own occasional experiences of higher-level harmonic vibrancy. More often, however, they needed to find another group or individual to demonstrate what that higher-level functioning looks like.

### FINDING A GROUP

The task of identifying an exemplary group or individual can seem daunting. How many people are even thinking about their experiences of harmonic vibrancy, much less in a position to provide guidance? You know there are groups functioning at higher levels, and the survey data I presented from over 1,600 groups confirm this. However, they may be in different lines of work or different parts of the world. How will you find them?

The answer is shockingly simple: just start asking the question. Ask yourself what you want to experience, and ask others if they have experienced that. Use the conversations I described in the early chapters of this book as a model. Just as I did, ask people if they have had the experience of greater vibrancy. They always answer "yes." Then ask them to describe what created that experience, what were they doing? People know that they have had the experience of higher vibrancy, and they can usually tell you a great deal about it. I found this out in my own research. By asking around, I began to find dozens of higher vibrancy groups. This is a very "soft" way of identifying higher vibrancy groups—not hard science. But it is effective.

**Explore the Experience of Others**

**How do we find them? What are their practices?**

*Figure 33: Exploring the Experience of Others*

For example, I asked this question of a group of parents having a hard time working together on a project at their kids' school. Their answer surprised them. They knew exactly where they experienced the higher level of relationship they wanted in their group—in their kids' classroom. Having either chaperoned a field trip or assisted the teacher in a main lesson, they had seen how the teacher and students interacted. The parents talked among themselves and with the class teacher to extract the practices they experienced in their kids' classroom. This led to them taking on those practices for themselves, remembering the experience they wanted.

In another case, I was working with the founders of a very successful toy store who aspired to outer-circle leadership. When I asked them what groups were living the experience they wanted, the leadership team immediately identified three groups in which they had experienced the types of processes and relationships that I had identified as characteristics of that higher-level functioning. When we looked more closely at those three groups, we saw that they all responded similarly to the four economic questions, and all had similar practices, even though they were situated in completely different industries in different countries.

In another instance, my colleagues and I were supporting a community group in the Coatán region of western Guatemala. This area is one of the poorest, most vulnerable regions in the Americas. The group aspired to move its community from the inner circle of scarcity and low harmonic vibrancy into the middle circle but had no way of knowing what that desired state might look like. My team was able to help them by finding many examples of communities in other parts of the world that were working in the middle-circle level, with processes that bridged the things and development levels. These examples included, for example, groups working in cooperatives or with complementary currencies or asset-based community development. All these innovations were potentially applicable in Coatán.

In all of these cases, I was the one asking the question of whether the group knew of another, higher-vibrancy group or had previous experience of higher vibrancy. But of course, groups are able to ask themselves this question, and usually someone will have an example or an experience of higher vibrancy. If this is not the case, however, then the group can look to the examples I highlight in this book and on the Institute for Strategic Clarity website, or simply scan the news. One group found me by doing just that. By searching on the Internet, they found my work under the terms "harmony," "vibrancy," and "better outcomes." Much is being shared these days about these higher levels of agreements.

## MAPPING THE GROUP'S PRACTICES

Once you find a group that is living at the level of harmonic vibrancy you desire, you will need to find out what its practices are like at that higher level. I have found that often someone has a direct relationship to the higher-vibrancy group, which is how it was identified as an example in the first place. It is usually through this kind of personal connection that the request to observe a group is made. Start by meeting with that person from the higher-vibrancy group and ask if you can visit and observe its practices, to better understand how it operates and what agreements it has in place to support its higher level of vibrancy. While not every group will be open to this kind of invitation, I find that most are. You are asking to understand their agreements and how those agreements support the level of vibrancy you aspire to. All groups I have approached in this way have said yes.

Once you meet the group, you can use the Agreements Map to guide your inquiry and record the information you find, as in the example in the last chapter. Look at what the higher-vibrancy group says it does, for example in its public documents, and observe in your visit what it actually does. You will see quickly whether and how its practices support the higher level of vibrancy the group experiences. The questions to ask in this exercise are the ones we asked in the last chapter when constructing the Agreements Evidence map.

## ASSESS YOUR OWN EXPERIENCE

So far in the Harmonic Vibrancy Move, in Step 1 you asked yourselves if you want more. In Step 2, you asked what "more" looked like. Next, Step 3 looks through the four lenses at your own experiences, agreements, and practices (see Figure 34).

### Assess Your Own Experience

What is seen through the 4 lenses?
What level of harmonic vibrancy is experienced?
What are your current practices?

*Figure 34: Assess Your Own Experience*

As in Step 2, the Agreements Map can support you in synthesizing the three questions in this step to get a clear picture of the agreements your group is currently using, the quality of the experiences it is having, and the practices it has in place to support those agreements and experiences. Using the Agreements Map to analyze another group can be challenging; applying it to one's own group can seem even more daunting. However, there are many processes available for running and validating a rigorous internal audit, which is essentially what this step is. Most important, when you do this, you need to be skeptical and make the effort to find multiple pieces of evidence to document your conclusions about the existing agreements.

Does the picture you describe when looking at your group's practices through the four lenses align with the level of harmonic vibrancy group members are actually experiencing? If so, you have some validation of both. If not, you need to explore a bit further. For example, the senior team of a large utility company assured me that they looked through the lenses and saw abundance, widespread awareness of all five relationships, and the harmonic vibrancy experienced. The results from the Harmonic Vibrancy Survey, administered to over one hundred employees, told quite a different story, however. It showed their experience to be halfway between the inner and middle circles of harmonic vibrancy—in other words, an experience of quite a bit of scarcity.

What caused this mismatch between the view of top management and the reality in the company? What might be happening? In fact, this is a common situation, in which a group thinks it is working with one set of assumptions but is really using quite a different set in practice. Some time ago, Harvard professor Chris Argyris named this pattern as the discrepancy between "espoused theory" and "theory in use."[123] You have experienced it if you have ever heard someone expound on some idea of how things work and thought to yourself, "That's nice, but what actually happens?" Somehow you knew that he was making up a story that did not jibe with reality. The espoused theory and the theory-in-use diverged.

In the case of the utility company, we re-examined the Agreements Map, pushing more deeply into what was actually happening, as opposed to what they wanted to see. Then we could uncover how the company was operating on the assumption that it needed to allocate scarce resources to maximize returns to investors for every quarterly report. All other relationships had been sacrificed to this group-level focus. The senior team could see that this picture more closely aligned with the company's Harmonic Vibrancy Survey results. This awareness provided a firmer foundation for undertaking a Harmonic Vibrancy Move.

The process was different for my friend in the local school. She had pointed to the inner circle of harmonic vibrancy as representative of her experience at work. The Agreements Map then enabled her to see, through the four lenses, that this experience derived from things-matter level agreements in all five primary relationships. Through the lens of "how much?" she saw that her

---

123   For Chris Argyris's description of two different theories of action, espoused theories and theories in use, see (Argyris, 1993, p. 65).

school was always scrounging and begging for resources. Through the lenses of "who decides?" and "by what criteria?" she recognized an overwhelming emphasis on group. In every situation, the "health" of the whole school was the overriding consideration. My friend could then see, through the fourth lens, that all activities were organized to serve this dominant value: "we decide what the school needs, what jobs need doing and who will do them. That's as far as we get."

The Agreements Map showed a predominantly scarcity-based set of agreements, which aligned with her experience of the inner circle of harmonic vibrancy, with only occasional experiences at the development-motion level. She saw that the agreements in place supported an experience that she did not want. In step 1 of the process, my friend had identified the experience of a higher level of vibrancy in those times when she was engaged in a special project, when people had permission to bring more of their creativity to the task. In step 2, she had delved more deeply into the conditions that made that experience possible and examined the practices followed by her higher-vibrancy project groups. Now, step 3 gave her a clear sense of the difference between the agreements she was living with most of the time and those that she had observed. This set her up for step 4.

## DEFINE AND ENACT A HARMONIC VIBRANCY MOVE

The fourth step in the Harmonic Vibrancy Move process involves developing and launching an action plan for the necessary shifts to close the gap between the current level of harmonic vibrancy and the level the group aspires to (see Figure 35).

An important part of this step is assessing your group's readiness for the move. The agreements you will need to support a higher level of harmonic vibrancy will likely be completely different from those currently supporting you at the lower level, because they will have to enable to you function at a higher level of perceived reality. As we saw in the Agreements Maps we examined, the practices in all areas—resources, allocation, value and organization—differ significantly from level to level. By implication, the underlying agreements will have to be different as well. Your group will need to be ready and willing to define and enter into those new agreements.

### Define and Enact the Harmonic Vibrancy Move

What degree of shift is required?

What is learned from the shift others made?

Is there a mandate and readiness for a shift?

What specific actions will work to make the move?

*Figure 35: Define and Enact a Harmonic Vibrancy Move*

A basic assumption of the Ecosynomics framework is that, whether we are aware of it or not, human beings live in a constant state of movement among the three levels of perceived reality. We live into the possibilities that we see as we develop new capacities and relationships and create outcomes. This perspective has implications for the Harmonic Vibrancy Move process, because it means that our groups too are always in a state of change. The group's implicit and explicit agreements around "who we are," "what we have," "what we value" and "how we interact" are constantly adapting to the changing world around it, as well as to the internal dynamics created by the actions of individual group members. Even when we think our group culture is very established and stable, it is constantly changing.

This means, on the one hand, that even if we just want to maintain what we do well with our current culture, we must work at it. On the other hand, it means that cultural change—changing our agreements—might not be as difficult as it looks. If, in fact, we are already living in a river of change, then changing agreements may be more a question of influencing the direction of the flow than having to start a new flow. When groups believe their culture is going to be hard to move, that they are stuck, I suggest that they are ignoring this constant change. We have a choice here. Instead of ignoring the change, we can give it our attention and bring intention into the process. Working with the four questions in this fourth step will help you do that.

The answers to the four questions will determine the contours of your action plan. The response to the first question specifies the scope of the change you need to make in your agreements and the supporting practices. Does the shift need to be small, moderate, or huge? Is it a shift of degree or a more basic shift in the kind of agreements you are working with? Your answers to the second question in this step—how have others made this shift?—will start the process of determining the actions you need to take to make your move. The third question invites you to look inward, individually and as a group. Your responses will tell you whether you are truly ready to make the shift successfully. The fourth question then points you toward the specific actions you will need to take to make the change. Answering this question brings you to the point of enacting the move. Let us now look at each question in a bit more detail, to see what you can do with it.

## THE SCOPE OF CHANGE

To answer the question, what is the scope of change required for a successful Harmonic Vibrancy Move? is to define the move in broad strokes. The analysis your group has done in the previous steps will enable you to do this. Basically, there are two possibilities for a Harmonic Vibrancy Move: it can move you higher within one level of perceived reality; or it can take you across levels. A move within a level can be large or small, but it is essentially a shift of degree. A move across levels is a more fundamental shift in how your group sees the world and functions within it.

### Moves within a level of perceived reality

A shift within a level seeks to move to a higher level of harmonic vibrancy within the same level of perceived reality. For example, a group working intentionally at the lower end of the development-motion level and functioning solidly at the things-matter level is likely to be experiencing itself between the inner and middle circles of harmonic vibrancy. This group might want to move more fully into the experience of the middle circle, supported by agreements at the development level of perceived reality. This would call for a Harmonic Vibrancy Move *within* that level. The group would still be working with the same kind of reality, but now at a different level of awareness and agreement.

A small within-level shift often means that the group's fundamental assumptions about the five relationships and the three levels of perceived reality remain the same. The shift is in the degree of awareness that informs its agreements and how it functions. For example, in the Mexican office of a global engineering firm, there was a low-end development-motion level awareness of the importance of learning, supported with a database of "lessons learned." In contemplating a Harmonic Vibrancy Move, the group recognized that it had created this database mostly for the purpose of "auditing"—determining whether or not learning was happening. This is a things-matter level focus on outcomes. When the group formulated a desire to move solidly into the experience of the middle circle of harmonic vibrancy, it saw that it needed to take on a greater awareness of the importance of learning. In addition to using the lessons learned for the audit, the engineers began to pay more attention to the content of the lessons learned and to bring the learning more directly into their daily work. This brought it more into their awareness, a relatively small shift of degree.

A large shift of degree within the same level of reality adds another dimension. In addition to a shift in awareness, it typically requires developing agreements to create different practices and structures. I saw this in a food company I worked with in the UK. The management team wanted to move the organization from living with the experience of being inside the second circle of harmonic vibrancy to being solidly outside the second circle, heading towards the third circle. From working through the second and third steps of the Harmonic Vibrancy Move process, the team realized this would involve a jump in how it was operating, from low to high within the development-motion level of perceived reality, with new agreements and awareness to match. For instance, the managers saw that, if they wanted to transform development and learning from occasional occurrences into a valued discipline practiced routinely throughout the organization, they needed to go from asking a question or two about learning at annual performance reviews to providing mentoring on an ongoing basis. A higher-level process such as mentoring could support changed behaviors and a shift in what people were paying attention to, both of which are required to create a higher-level experience.

### Moves across levels of perceived reality

As compared to a shift of "degree" within a level, a shift between levels of perceived reality is a shift of "kind." The agreements and processes at another level of perceived reality are very different in character. For example, valuing learning is very different from valuing outcomes. Learning takes place over time; it is what you "are doing." Outcomes are the events of specific moments in time; they are what you "did." To make a shift in orientation from one to the other, a group will need to deal explicitly with its fundamental assumptions about what people should be paying attention to, and why. This then provides the basis for moving into new agreements.

A between-levels shift also involves rethinking agreements in terms of the five relationships. At the things-matter level, it may be possible to produce acceptable outcomes while holding just one relationship as primary, as in my friend's situation, where the primacy of group was expressed in the overriding emphasis on "the good of the school." Yet all the evidence I have gathered, from my personal experience, my wide-ranging conversations, and my research, indicates that groups must honor and attend to multiple relationships in order to function sustainably at the development or possibility levels of perceived reality. This then is another area in which your group will need to address its underlying assumptions. If this is the kind of work your group needs to do, Step 4 is the place to consider how to go about it.

In many cases, the cultural transformation required can build on what is already available, perhaps subconsciously. In most of the Agreements Maps I have presented so far, there have been bands of yellow and/or red. These signify that there are partial or weak indications of agreements at higher levels of perceived reality than the one at which the group is primarily functioning. I interpret this to mean that, in most groups, there is some tendency toward higher-level agreements. It may exist below the level of collective consciousness, but it represents an emerging awareness of possible new agreements already alive within the community. When this is the case, the cultural transformation can focus on awakening what is already there, for example, by highlighting instances of higher-level functioning and learning how people have been able to do this within the group's culture. In Chapter 11, I will share the story of how this strategy worked at THORLO in the company's adoption of "integrated collaborative conversations." This was a significant move across levels, which the community was able to take up quickly by making explicit many assumptions about shared purpose and respect for the different voices that were already resident within the community.

The requirements of a cultural transformation are quite different when it entails taking up a completely new set of assumptions, never experienced before within the group. As we have explored throughout the book, there are various ways to broach the possibility and desire for this new experience, such as agreeing on the experience of harmonic vibrancy and outcomes we know we want and are not achieving, or maybe finding that there are indeed pockets of people within the group who have found a way to interact at the higher level of vibrancy.

This fourth step in the Harmonic Vibrancy Move process rests on the previous steps. The group has explored its desire for a new experience in Step 1, looked at what a higher-level experience looks like in Step 2, and compared that to its own experience in Step 3. It is essential to do those steps thoroughly to bring the group to the point of deciding what new agreements it needs in order to move to a higher level and that it indeed wants to invite in such agreements. Many group processes, such as the "Immunity to Change" approach developed by Robert Kegan and Lisa Lahey, are available to support you in uncovering and shifting existing agreements, including those that limit the group's ability to make changes.[124]

## HOW HAVE OTHERS MADE THE SHIFT?

This part of Step 4 repeats the exercise undertaken in Step 2 but now with a particular focus on the process of group transformation. Of course, each situation is unique in the specifics of what changes are called for, but the groups I have seen be most successful in shifting their agreements have learned from how others have done it. It is also a way to avoid the common trap of relying on experts to tell you what your group needs to change and how to go about it. The group needs to see the new agreements for itself and adapt them to its culture as it moves to a higher level of functioning. This task requires intention and attention—intention to experience a higher level of harmonic vibrancy and attention to the shifts in agreements and practices needed to obtain that. These cannot be outsourced.

To assess how prepared your group is to shift its agreements; I suggest you start by creating a clear understanding of the potential benefits. A good way to define these benefits is to work with the Costs of Scarcity analysis I shared in Chapter 6. Seeing the likely costs of *not* changing is a good way to clarify the reasons to change. It will provide a concrete and specific way to think and talk about it. How big a deal is this shift? How much do we stand to benefit from achieving it? Keeping these benefits in mind will help the group remain clear about its purpose and the potential rewards as it pushes forward with the work required to shift its agreements to those that support a higher level of harmonic vibrancy.

## SPECIFIC ACTIONS

I am a guy who loves acronyms, and for this final step in the Harmonic Vibrancy Move process, I like the acronym CLOSE. For me, it expresses the

---

124   See (Kegan & Lahey, 2009).

excitement of "getting close" to the manifestation of actual changes that will enable the group to experience greater harmonic vibrancy. CLOSE also stands for the five elements that I suggest are essential parts of this step: Customization; Lenses; the O Process; Structures; and Experience. Perhaps you will find this acronym helpful, as I do.

### Customization

It may seem obvious to many, but I think it cannot be repeated often enough that any new agreements your group takes up must be customized to the group's culture. This is a delicate and iterative process, as the culture itself will evolve as the group formulates new agreements. I emphasize this point, because there seems to be a strong tendency in organizations to look to experts for a transition template. The attitude is, "Just tell us what to do, and help us to do it quickly." In my experience, shifting a group's agreements does not have to be a long and painful process. But it cannot be done with a generic formula, or done too quickly, or left to others. After all, these are your group's agreements, and the group must fully own them.

### Lenses

It is important to continue using the four economic questions as lenses on your agreements as the group proceeds to defining and implementing an action plan. They are what will enable you to uncover the fundamental assumptions underlying the existing agreements you wish to change. By the same token, they will guide you in articulating a different set of assumptions to provide the basis for new agreements.

### The O Process

The way to achieve customization of agreements is, in the simplest terms, to engage the group fully in imagining a new, desirable reality and taking the steps needed to bring that reality into being. This requires a great deal of open and inclusive conversation, as well as a great deal of experimentation. No one can do this for you, but there are many consultants who can help by facilitating the dialogue and guiding the analysis that needs to take place within the group. There is also an array of process options for this dialogue.[125]

---

125    For information on dialogue processes, see the Resources Center on the website of the National Coalition for Dialogue and Deliberation (www.ncdd.org); and Pruitt and Thomas (2007).

My colleague Scott Spann and I developed one such process, the O Process, which I have since used with many groups, large and small. The O Process got its name because the image I use to describe it to people is a circle. There are six steps in the process, each one involving a good deal of conversation. The steps are meant to be taken sequentially. But the whole process is iterative, so the group will move through the steps—around the "O"—a number of times. Each time it does so, its capacity for collaborative decision-making and aligned action will grow.

I provide a fuller explanation, including an image, in a Tool Sidebar on the O Process in Chapter 11. Briefly, however, the six steps are as follows:

1. Create alignment around the group's shared higher purpose
2. Create shared awareness of the unique contribution each group member has to offer
3. Determine the specific possibilities each group member can see from his or her unique perspective
4. Develop a collective vision of a desired future reality (I call this a "shared probability")
5. Determine the commitment each group member can make to the effort to realize the shared probability
6. Create alignment around the specific actions needed to enact those commitments collaboratively

### Structures

The group needs to define the new structures derived from the Agreements Map. These structures are the agreements that support the higher level of harmonic vibrancy, as described in the Agreements Map. These agreements come in the form of formal and informal organizational structures, processes, and practices. These structures need to be aligned with the new fundamental assumptions seen through the four lenses.

### Experience

Experience comes last in the acronym, but it is usually where I start. Making sure that everyone in the group agrees on the experience of harmonic vibrancy they want provides the motivation to move from the current experience to the desired one. It establishes the firm foundation needed to move forward.

## CONCLUSION

Now we have come full circle to where we started in Chapter 1, with you becoming aware of the quality of your experience. You now have a way of thinking about "experience" that encompasses the five fundamental relationships and the three levels of perceived reality and gives particular meaning to the idea of harmonic vibrancy—the state you know you have experienced before and want to experience more consistently. With the help of some powerful concepts borrowed from economics, I have given you tools to analyze the structures and practices that shape your experience in particular groups. You can see through those structures and practices to the agreements on which they are based, as well as the fundamental assumptions underlying the agreements. All of this makes it possible to challenge the governing assumptions, particularly assumptions of scarcity, to create new agreements, and to shift your experience in the direction of greater harmonic vibrancy.

In a previous chapter, I shared evidence indicating that many people have made this kind of shift. The final chapters of the book offer a different kind of evidence: the stories of change processes I have witnessed and participated in directly. I call these episodes "learning laboratories," because it is through them that the Ecosynomics framework has emerged. They will provide some concrete examples of what the Harmonic Vibrancy Move looks like in different settings.

# PART IV

# LEARNING IN LABORATORIES

# CHAPTER 9

# INDIVIDUAL MOVES

Over the years, I have worked with many individuals as coach, mentor, teacher, advisor and facilitator of group processes. I have learned from this experience that people are often motivated to undertake a Harmonic Vibrancy Move when they have seen, or more often felt firsthand, the experience of higher vibrancy. They want to bring it into their lives on a regular basis. Typically, however, they don't know what to change to experience higher vibrancy more of the time.

I discovered that I could support these individuals, because I could see what they wanted and could ask questions that helped them uncover a path to getting it for themselves. Most people, I found, already know what to do at the next level of harmonic vibrancy, at least to some degree. The problem is they cannot see the agreements required to sustain their functioning at that level. Yet through inquiry, experimentation and feedback from the five primary relationships, they are able to find a path to new agreements. Sometimes this has happened in a matter of months. In other cases, we have continued the process for many years, taking multiple steps along the way.

## SEEING ONE'S OWN LIGHT-MOTION-MATTER TRANSFORMATION

I met Marjan in 2003. She was part of a group participating in an "executive coaching" program some colleagues and I offered to a large government agency. We had been hired to support senior executives in their personal leadership development over a 6-month period. Tall, athletically thin and stylishly dressed,

Marjan looked the part of a senior executive who had worked her way up over 20-plus years in government service. Now she was leading a large, multi-agency project.

## IDENTIFYING THE GAP

Our first meeting took place in a nondescript cafeteria in the middle of a large government complex. I started our exploration together by asking Marjan what she needed to be able to do that she could not do. She answered that she wanted to increase her influence in the organization by being more effective and efficient at engaging her peers and superiors in meetings. I asked her to give me examples of what she meant and to share experiences she had with this. She said she had found that, while her ideas were well thought out and well presented, they were often dismissed or only partially taken up. She noticed that some of her peers were much more aware of what others were thinking and also more aware of the dynamics among the people in the room. It seemed to her that this awareness enabled them to shape the understanding of others. It was also clear to her that the senior executives who advanced to higher levels were very efficient at this shaping of understanding in groups. Indeed, it was expected of leaders in the top positions that they be able to influence more people and do it quickly.

It quickly became clear to me that Marjan was actually quite aware of what was going on in the room, both within herself and with others. She did not acknowledge that capacity for awareness, however. I asked her if there were situations in which she experienced herself operating in groups in the way she aspired to do at work. The examples she shared were from her volunteer coaching of young people, both in her church and at the local theater. We talked about why she could influence people effectively outside of work but not at work, and why she realized that she normally left those capacities "checked at the door." She had assumed that the work culture did not support the development and use of these "soft" capacities. Now she saw that she needed them. She had clearly delineated the gap between her current work experience of scarcity in relation to her capacities and leadership potential, and the experience of greater abundance she knew she could have if she were to bring her whole self, with all her capacities, into her workplace.

## EXPLORING THE EXPERIENCES OF OTHERS

To identify practices she could take up in order to experience this new level, I asked her to pay attention over the next couple of weeks to people who seemed to be doing what she wanted to be able to do. When we came back together, she had three examples. Two were other executives she worked with, and she was the third, in her coaching of some kids at church. "I actually know how to do what I want, most of the time. I just don't seem to be able to do it here." This was an important realization.

For the next few weeks, I gave her the assignment to observe what those people were doing, herself included. What she observed was a practice she named "self-moderation." This meant being watchful of what was going on with others and, equally important, what was going on internally. When Marjan herself did this, she invoked a "little Marjan," who sat on her shoulder and reflected impartially on what was happening within Marjan, within the others in the room and within the group dynamics. When she saw how she used this practice in her acting and in coaching young actors, she was able to recognize when others used it at work.

## ASSESSING HER OWN EXPERIENCE

Seeing that she knew how to do in other settings what she wanted to do in her work setting, we set out to understand the source of the discrepancy. Over the next few weeks, Marjan observed and documented what happened. This evidence-based approach supported our exploration of the dynamics inhibiting her practice and gave concreteness to what we were learning along the way. We found that, at work, Marjan saw herself as a really "smart head"—period. This emphasis on cognitive intelligence had been reinforced throughout her career. The culture of the organization promoted this with an attitude of "we are the smartest." Her bosses promoted people based on this criterion, and she guided her own groups with this focus. Unfortunately, this meant that she always tried to figure out, in her head, what was going to happen.

Recently, however, life had gotten too complex for that approach to be reliable. The capacity of self-moderation she had identified incorporated both the head and the heart. It meant not just figuring out what was going to happen but being attuned to the thoughts, emotions and energies people in the group were bringing to the situation. This insight clearly established the nature of the shift Marjan wanted to make as a step toward integrating her head and heart at work.

## DEFINING AND ENACTING THE MOVE

Our first step was to name the shifts she wanted to make in (1) the fundamental assumptions determining how she perceived herself at work, as viewed through the four lenses, and (2) what she did in practice. Marjan compared how she functioned inside and outside of work. She realized that outside of work she was operating at the possibility-light level, exploring her potential to work with both head and heart. She could choose to practice that capacity in various situations, to bring it more fully into being at the development-motion level. After awhile, she noticed a change in how her capacity manifested at the things-matter level. In her activities outside of work, where the environment supported her development and experimentation, she began to use her head-heart intelligence seamlessly, whenever she wanted. The kids welcomed her acting coaching in the local theater, and their performance improved. At church her contributions were so appreciated that she was asked to coach the head of the council of elders.

Being able to see and name this process as a light-motion-matter transformation gave Marjan the confidence that she could find a way to safely experiment with changes in how she functioned at work. Previously, she had unconsciously accepted the skills she was using in the local theater and in church without realizing she could also use them at work. Now she saw head-heart intelligence as a competency that could enable her to recognize possibilities and also see the pathways to manifest them. Recognizing each of the three levels of perceived reality and being able to work across them are critical skills for an individual who is taking up her own change process.

Marjan and I next planned a series of experiments. First, to gain confidence in her capacity for awareness, she worked on just noticing when she saw an opportunity to use her head-heart intelligence. She focused on situations when she was briefing other executives and tried to determine whether the communication required attention to conveying the idea, attention to the relationship, or attention to both at once. For example, in one instance, she saw that the other executive had understood the idea she was trying to convey but that the feeling of trust between them was low. This situation called for her to give more heart attention to the relational dimension in her communication. In another instance, when presenting to a higher up, she noticed that the level of trust was fine but the concept was troubling the executive. Here she needed to acknowledge the trust and focus on conveying the idea. These observations allowed her to broaden her understanding of interactions she had previously seen simply as cases of executives not aligning with her on the thoughts she was trying to convey, a head-space only awareness.

Next, Marjan worked on just consciously noting to herself what she was observing, without actually doing anything. Finally, once she had become more comfortable with her own insights, she began slowly to put them into practice. For example, she began to sense when to engage more with either the head or the heart, and she experimented with ways of doing that during briefings. At each step, we revisited what she had set out to learn, what she observed, what her observations taught her, and what this learning meant for the next step.

After four months, with coaching sessions every few weeks, Marjan began to see concrete results. She received feedback from her colleagues that her leadership skills had jumped "to a whole new level." She paid attention to the feedback she received in each of the five relationships: what she noticed in herself; her experiences with other individuals; how the group appreciated and welcomed her unique contributions; how she experienced the process of transforming possibilities into development into things; and the degree to which her creativity and that of others was available in the process. When she was asked to take on the direction of a much more challenging project, she knew she was ready to accept. Years later, Marjan told me that she had so deeply integrated her head-heart intelligence into her practice that it had become second nature.

This work with Marjan convinced me of the power of the light-motion-matter transformative process in relation to individual capacity development. This involves the ability to work with one's capacities at all three levels of perceived reality—as potential, as developing capabilities, and as skills manifesting concretely at the things level. And it involves moving from one level to another. The impact of this transformative process on one's experience of harmonic vibrancy is great. It is the surest pathway to experiencing fully one's creativity and one's unique contribution to the group. My experience with Marjan also reinforced my observation that people can usually see the next steps they need to take in a Harmonic Vibrancy Move. Sometimes they just need a helping hand—from a colleague, a mentor, or a coach—to recognize it.

## SPEAKING A HARMONIC

Donald and I started working together eight years ago when I became a consultant to a leadership team of which he was a part. The team was working on developing its ability to work together more collaboratively. Donald is a strong basketball player and a man who likes to call the shots. On first impression, it seemed to me that his contributions made the whole team better. He could see and give words to successes and challenges within the group's dynamics. By making those dynamics visible, he made them easier to work with. As my engagement with the team continued, I noticed that Donald was always one of the first to take on the more challenging, self-reflective parts of the work. He was also the first to pull me aside and explore the subtler implications of what we were discovering.

## IDENTIFYING THE GAP

A few years into that process, Donald asked me one day about "speaking a harmonic." We had been talking about the harmonic that emerges when the voices in a group come together in a particular way, and Donald had lit up. "I do that, from the other side," he told me. He explained how he was sometimes able to voice what the group was getting at collectively in such a way that each individual could still hear his or her own voice in what he was saying. To his understanding, this was "speaking a harmonic." The problem, he said, was that he did not know how he did it. Sometimes this capacity showed up and other times it did not. Could I help him learn how to do it when he wanted? This started us on a path of learning how a person could hear the distinct voices in the room and also know how to become the voice for the harmonic that emerges when these voices come together. If this sounds odd, consider that you actually experience this capacity quite frequently. Have you ever been completely captivated by a speaker or singer, and realized that everyone else was too? This person had the capacity to meet each and every one of you, all at the same time. In these instances, the performer is speaking-being in a way that allows many others to experience the performance in their own personal way, even though they are all hearing the same thing. In addition to this "speaking," Donald was also able to hear the harmony that resulted from the alignment of many unique contributions and then give voice to that harmony. This gave a double impact to his speaking: he made the harmony audible and enabled all the other team members to see how they were contributing to it. This is what we came to call "speaking the harmonic."

## \EXPLORING THE EXPERIENCE OF OTHERS

We started Donald's exploration by looking at examples of people in his life who spoke a harmonic. For example, he experienced how his pastor at church was able to offer a message during the sermon that was received in different ways by people he knew had very different approaches to the concepts he was presenting. Some heard morality; some heard stories; some heard guidelines for their own behavior; and some heard guidelines for what others should do. We also observed what happened when Donald spoke a harmonic himself. This exploration uncovered some interesting practices. It turned out that "speaking" the harmonic was as much about inquiry and listening as it was about synthesis and speaking. For example, Donald began to see that his pastor was listening for how his congregation, full of individuals he knew very well, was receiving the message in his sermon. He then adjusted how he was speaking and what he was sharing, as he noticed the individual and collective responses.

## ASSESSING HIS OWN EXPERIENCE

While clear that he often communicated in a harmonic way, Donald was not always conscious of when it was happening or what he was doing. He wanted this to be a conscious awareness and choice that he could use and improve. At this stage of the exploration, Donald was clear that he wanted to "speak the harmonic." He had the term clear. When we look at what others did, he and I differentiated specific practices around a "harmonic voice," which colleagues with musical training helped us describe: one's own voice; the voice of the other person(s); the emergent resultant from mixing the voices; the process of realizing the outcome; and the emergent creativity being played within all the voices. We recognized this as the five primary relationships (self, other, group, nature, and spirit).

When looking at Donald's own experience, we saw that he was quite experienced at speaking each of these. He could vocalize what his own voice was saying. He could give voice to the other person's perspective. He could name what was emerging as the group's voice. He could talk about the process that people were using to bring together the voices. He could also describe the emerging creativity. And, he saw that he was not able to do all of these at the same time. He decided then that developing further capacities, consciously, in each and in their combination would support the shift he wanted to make to being able to speak the harmonic.

## DEFINING AND ENACTING THE MOVE

To make the shift, Donald saw that he needed to deepen his awareness of, and work with, the five primary relationships. Our experimentation over the next couple of years worked with each of the five primary relationships in turn. The goal was to deepen Donald's understanding of them and their influence on his ability to speak the harmonic.

At the level of fundamental assumptions, this work required him to develop trust in the abundance that became available to each group member, and to the group as a whole through his acts of making visible what he valued in the group's work. It also required that he take up specific practices related to the five relationships. To do this, he worked intensively with exercises for each of the five relationships. We did these exercises initially with the entire leadership team, but Donald went further in learning how to incorporate them into his daily practices. For the relationship to self, we worked with autobiography and understanding action logics. For the relationship to the other, we learned the tools of inquiry and heart-to-heart feedback. To strengthen relationship to group, we developed skills in dialogue and action inquiry, and we learned how to create harmony from individual contributions and develop collective will. For the relationship to nature, we worked on developing greater conceptual and practical understanding of moving from possibility through development to action, using the O Process and Theory U. Finally, for the relationship to spirit, we worked with the concept of "strategy as conversation," an approach to decision-making that invites in the individual and collective creativity of the group. Donald used the O Process as a way of pulling all of these elements together. He gradually built his capacity to speak into the five different relationships, one at a time, and together.

What does "speaking into" the five relationships look like? When Donald talks with different parts of his organization, he is able to remind everyone of the shared purpose that unites them. He does this in language that speaks effectively to the individuals in the room. For example, he might remind the group of its collective purpose, to produce and sell products in a way that makes a tangible, positive impact on the lives of the company's customers. Donald states this intention in words that remind his listeners of their personal connection to their work, a connection that they all share. This is the voice of the "we-in-the-I." It gives each individual an experience of being part of the group.

After voicing the shared purpose, Donald shows how every individual present makes a unique contribution to the group by acknowledging each person in the room. He shows people why they are important to the conversation—the unique character and the value of their different perspectives to the work at hand. He might point out, for example, the ways in which marketing, sales, operations, production, customer service, and finance each contributes to the process of filling a customer's order and satisfying that customer's needs. As he does this, everyone experiences being seen, acknowledged and supported in what they bring to each other and to the group. He is supporting them in relating to self, other and group.

Next, Donald will ask each person to share whatever possibilities he or she can see for dealing with the specific issue at hand. He invites in the relationship to spirit by opening this space for their creativity. He then names both those possibilities seen individually and the possibility that seems to be emerging collectively. Donald reframes this shared vision of possibility as a "probability," based on the implied commitments people have made by contributing to its creation. Here, speaking into the relationship to nature, he makes explicit the feeling that the group now shares a reality it can collectively see and begin to manifest. As he speaks into all these relationships, everyone in the group feels seen and heard, as an individual contributor and as a "we." This is the experience of the middle-to-outer circle of harmonic vibrancy. This is speaking in a harmonic, where all of the individual voices can be heard and, in addition, there is an emergent voice of the "we" that also can be heard.

Once he came to understand this process of speaking into the five relationships, Donald was able to help his leadership team and other groups in his company work together much more effectively. For example, when charged with creating an online presence for the company, the team was able to see clearly how to adjust the way the different parts of the organization worked together to fit the online environment and went on to develop many new dimensions of the online business. Donald reflected later on how he experienced the shift in his awareness around speaking the harmonic. What had seemed before to be an innate gift that showed up sometimes, he now saw as a skill he could use consciously whenever he wanted. A couple of years later, he caught me after a meeting and said, "Now that I know how to speak the harmonic, I am interested in learning how to call it forth without any words. Interested in the journey?"

# FINDING HEALTHY AND VIBRANT LIVING

The previous two cases have come out of my work coaching others in their process of a Harmonic Vibrancy Move. Now I want to share the story of the coaching I have received over the years from my life partner, Leslie. This story involves identifying not just one gap but a series of gaps that have appeared over time as what seems to be most relevant in my life has shifted. My path toward harmonic vibrancy has looked more like a spiral than a straight line, as I have kept coming back to the same issues, just in different forms. It seems that once I learn the lessons at one level and integrate them into my living of life, I meet new experiences to challenge and invite me to continually advance what I am learning. I want to share this story because I believe this is the way it is for everyone: life requires many Harmonic Vibrancy Moves, and the people who can help us make those moves are often close at hand.

Leslie and I have been married for more than twenty years. We have lived in nine different cities and raised two children together. Over the years, she has taken on many roles: architect, general contractor, educator, gardener, hostess, knitter, colorist, designer, nutritionist, herbalist, home brewer, intrepid explorer, mother, friend, daughter and spouse. I tended to see these endeavors, like my own different roles and activities, as separate things—titles we had or stuff we were doing. At various times, as I struggled to deal with the scarcity that perspective created in my life, Leslie showed me how to find abundance by bringing them all together. She has named the unifying theme in her own diverse roles "Healthy and Vibrant Living," and this is what she has helped me achieve for myself. I now see that, in coaching me through my challenges, Leslie was following a long-term process of moving our family to higher levels of harmonic vibrancy.

## KNOWING STUFF

In my late twenties, I felt that there was something I needed to know that doctoral studies would give me. I thought if I could just fill my head with something different from what was already there, then I would be what I wanted to be—educated. This was the gap I identified in my "knowing stuff" Harmonic Vibrancy Move process. I knew from somewhere in my experience that much more was available to me.

With Leslie by my side, I began to explore the scholarly path toward what life looked like at my desired level of knowing stuff. I found that the people who were already functioning at that level were doing something quite different from what I had imagined. They were evolving. Yes, they were constantly learning, and they saw learning as a journey. It was not hard for me to grasp this idea intellectually, yet it has taken many years to live into it. The hard part for me was the daily practice, which required a somewhat painful reassessment of my current approach. In the beginning, I studied to know something; then I figured I knew it. I was done. Gradually I began to shift, from this view of learning as an event to an understanding of learning as a process—a process of noticing what was to be learned, experiencing the learning, integrating the new awareness, and then looking around for what more there was to learn.

Early on in the doctoral program, Leslie expressed the fear that my already-strong cognitive orientation was going to become even stronger. I would become "a PhD-head." She was pointing to my focus on learning for knowing and suggesting a possible shift to experiencing. That was the shift I needed to make.

Over the years, I have experienced this "knowing stuff" gap a few other times. In each instance I come back to what seems like the same gap, but at a different level of the learning spiral. I begin to see a new body of knowledge I need to have. This is the gap. Then I find people who are living with the knowledge I want to know and I try to understand their experience. I then begin to experiment with different practices to see which ones will support my Harmonic Vibrancy Move. I have found two leverage points in my life for this process. First, I ask people who have the capacities I seek to support my learning process in some way. This is how I embrace the second step of the Harmonic Vibrancy Move process, inviting in those who can give me the experience of the next higher level. Second, I have Leslie to always question and support what I am learning along the way.

## FOOD

I have always enjoyed food and have experienced many different cuisines in the different places I have lived. I never thought much about it. I needed it, it tasted good, and that is what is was about it. Then came Leslie. She saw that I was frequently sick, getting bronchitis twice a year. For many years, I had been taking strong medicines for severe allergies, and I had a constant low-grade sinus headache. I saw these as three separate things: tasty food, allergy medicine and headaches. They were just part of my life. Leslie could see, however, that they were related within the system of my body. She could see the gaps between how I was living and how I could live if I attended to this system. I was not clear about this, but I trusted Leslie completely.

She started by asking if we could have the goal of not needing the allergy medicine. This would be a big, positive shift in harmonic vibrancy for me, so why not? We identified a gap in regard to allergies, and I started my first trip around the food spiral. As we looked around for the practices of people at the higher level we wanted to experience, she slowly changed what I ate. Since Leslie is a great cook, the new dishes were always tasty, so they met my one criterion for putting food in my mouth. I began to notice differences—less congestion, less sinus drainage and less need for medication. I stopped taking the allergy medicine and also experienced a fundamental shift in my assumptions about the role of food in my life. The shift in assumptions supported the shift in behavior around what I ate, and this resulted in the desired shift of outcomes.

With success in this trip around the spiral, Leslie and I moved on to focus on the headaches gap. We refined our diet even more by focusing on locally grown food and "shopping the perimeter of the grocery store," i.e., avoiding processed foods. I started feeling better, and the headaches started to go away. Once I experienced life without the constant drowsiness caused by the allergy medicine and without my constant headache, I could see even more clearly how the fuel I put into my body influenced my body's functioning. It seems obvious to say it that way, but it was not a connection I had made. I was healthier, my body worked better, and I still enjoyed tasty food. The daily practice for me was easy. I was not dieting or restricting what I ate, but I could make a clear connection between what went into my system and the impact it had on my physical experience and how I felt. This made it easy for me to make different choices. Years down the road, I am much healthier physically at 47 than I was at 25. Now that I feel better, I exercise regularly. I think I am ready for another trip around the spiral of understanding my body's relationship to food.

## CHILDREN

I wanted kids. I did not know why, but somehow, based on my experience, I knew I wanted them. I grew up in a functional family, with good parents, two brothers, and hundreds of guests constantly streaming through our family home. So, it seemed obvious to me that it was my turn. Having a young family while in graduate school was not an easy situation to manage, however. I began to see parenting as a responsibility, a burden I had chosen, and this did not feel right. I could see that there was a more joyful way to be a father, but I could not see how to do it. This was the gap. Stepping across it would be a huge Harmonic Vibrancy Move for me.

Once the gap was identified, the teachers started showing up. Leslie showed me by her example how to appreciate the beauty in the moment with the kids. This was what life could look like. My kids made that easy; I was the one making it hard. That was the big shift in assumptions I needed to make. Examples of great fathers arrived. I saw what they did. Then I just had to figure out how to practice it in my own life. As I worked at it, I began to see that parenting with a sense of joy, rather than a sense of duty, was really just a choice. The hard part for me was seeing the choice and choosing in the moment. Gradually, though, I started to do this more frequently. Sure enough, when I did, I had a great time. My children and I created some great memories together.

As I started to make the connection more often between seeing the choice, making it and experiencing the outcome, joyful parenting became easier. I became more aware in my body of the toxicity caused by not making the choice. It began to hurt. I now had a new signal and deterrent, helping me increase my awareness of the choice and the outcomes. This was another trip around the father spiral. Now that my daughter has completed high school and my son is taller than I am, I suspect I am ready for the next round of this journey.

Knowing stuff, food and children: the way I experience these parts of my life has transformed right in front of my eyes. They have gone from being things I did not think much about, to areas of personal development, and finally to connections to the highest possibilities available. In essence, what I am learning is that healthy and vibrant living is a process for bringing in whatever one experiences as relevant to one's life in the most vibrant way possible. This is outer-circle living, functioning at all three levels of perceived reality as a daily practice in everything I do. From food to nutrition, from school to education, from parental duty to joyful connection—these shifts have given me a healthy physical vessel for moving through my life, a vital process for growing and creating, and a vibrant relational space for my family living. It is a good thing that I met my dance partner, that she said yes, and that for over two decades now she has showed me the path to a life well lived.

## LESSONS LEARNED

These three examples of individuals making moves to higher levels of harmonic vibrancy highlight a common experience I see in all of them and a common set of practices that supported the moves. The common experience is that that people generally know something about the level of harmonic vibrancy they aspire to. They can see the next level because they have already begun to have experiences of it and to develop some of the capacities for it. This means that the idea of moving to the next level is not purely fantasy and not impossible. Rather the potential for functioning at that level is already there, just not in a way that allows it to be accessed at will.

The Harmonic Vibrancy Move process helps people bring awareness to those occasional experiences of the higher level and then supports them in learning how to choose to have the experience when they want it. I have seen this in every case. From an Ecosynomics perspective this finding is significant. Most people believe they are stuck in the rules of the game that bring them scarcity. The Harmonic Vibrancy Move process shows them that there are no fixed rules, just agreements. People can choose to move to a better experience, and they already have most of the capacities needed for the journey.

I also learned that I could support each of these individual journeys with a set of simple, well-established practices: inquiry, experimentation, and feedback. Through inquiry, the people I have worked with—myself included—were able to see into aspects of our lives that we had perceived as invisible because we had never asked about them. Just ask—it is the easiest and the hardest thing to do, so it seems.

Through experimentation we learned what worked and what did not. We would have a hypothesis. Then we would try something and observe the results. We tried again with modifications based on those results. Over time, we learned. Each individual learned what worked for himself or herself, and in the process we learned a new way of experiencing. We changed in a way that worked for us.

The feedback we needed to see what we were learning and how best to adapt it for our specific needs came from all five of the primary relationships. We received feedback from our own behaviors, feelings, thoughts and awareness. Feedback also came from other individuals, who engaged with us in the course of our experimentation, who noticed the differences and shared their observations and insights. It came from the group in the form of responses to the contributions we made, or requests for our contributions, or the outcomes we were able to achieve as a group. Feedback from the relationship to nature came through the experience of consciously moving among the levels of reality and the abundance that showed up when we were able to work with all three levels. Finally, feedback came through the relationship to spirit when we were able to enjoy the vibrancy that comes with experiencing creativity in ourselves, in others and in the environment that surrounds us.

I have also learned what does not work. When the tools are not used, the move does not happen. That is, when we refuse to inquire and only want to talk, learning slows down to a trickle, at best. When we refuse to experiment and want someone to just tell us what to do, we fail to customize the new perspective or practice, and it never fits. When we neglect the feedback from the five primary relationships, the feedback seems to either get louder or go away. A Harmonic Vibrancy Move is a choice. It must be an agreement the individual makes with herself or himself. Only then will the determination and energy needed for change become available.

# CHAPTER 10

# MOVING A LEADERSHIP TEAM

In Chapter 9, I described experiences I have had in coaching others through personal change initiatives and in being coached myself in my own journey toward greater harmonic vibrancy. These experiences have been my "learning laboratory" for individual change. Through them I have developed much of my understanding about how the Harmonic Vibrancy Move process enables people to step up to a higher level of vibrancy and abundance. In this chapter and the following ones, I want to share some of my experiences working with larger groups and the learning I have gained from those experiences.

Most important, perhaps, I have learned that group transformation starts with the individual. By this I mean that each group member must be willing to look critically at his or her own needs, feelings, assumptions and behaviors, and then to address those assumptions and behaviors that may need to change in order for the group to change. By the same token, leadership teams must change their own internal agreements and group dynamics in order to lead change on a larger scale. Chapters 10 and 11 deal with this small-to-large-group process through the example of a corporate leadership team that changed itself and went on to initiate a company-wide transformation on the same principles. Chapter 12 describes how a small team took on the task of making changes at the societal level. Each of these chapters also illustrates in its own way lessons I have learned from these experiences about how to facilitate individual change leading to group change.

The stories I present in this chapter and Chapter 11 come from my most important learning laboratory – the North Carolina sock company, THORLO, Inc. (THORLO). As I described in Chapter 3, I have worked with THORLO for nine years, during which time this organization has partnered with me in developing the Ecosynomics concepts, language, tools and insights presented in this book. By 2009, when this chapter's story begins, I had been a member of THORLO's leadership team for four years, and we had cycled through the Harmonic Vibrancy Move process a number of times. In those previous iterations, we had developed agreements about what the company's leadership culture, structure and processes should look like and the language we would use to talk about them. We had formed a team that was ready and willing to take up leadership on those terms, and we had begun to develop practices we thought would enable the team to function consistently in the outer circle of harmonic vibrancy.

My role also evolved over those years. I had started with THORLO as an outside consultant and moved into facilitating the leadership team through the change processes envisioned by the CEO, Jim Throneburg. By 2008, I was no longer an outsider with inside access through the CEO. I had moved into my current role as an insider who brings outside perspective, based on my way of looking at the world and the fact that I am not a full-time employee of the company. I have made the commitment to show up at THORLO bi-monthly and to play a role equivalent to that of a chief culture officer, particularly within the leadership team. Throughout this evolution, the folks at THORLO have been learning partners in the development of Ecosynomics. The company also supports my work on Ecosynomics through grants it makes to the Institute for Strategic Clarity.

## STEPPING UP TO A HIGHER LEVEL OF RELATIONSHIP

In September 2008, Jim Throneburg (known as "JLT" within the company) had an experience that dramatically changed how he and the leadership team thought about organizational transformation at THORLO. He had been walking through the manufacturing facility when he noticed a problem. He walked over to the engineering room to see if folks there knew about the problem and were working on correcting it. They acknowledged that they knew about this problem and had done nothing about it. From his perspective as the owner of the business, as well as its CEO, JLT was shocked and infuriated by this situation. Rather than taking action, however, he resolved to reflect on it.

Over the next couple of days, he came to the realization that the behavior he observed in those engineers existed because he had allowed the same behavior in himself. He saw that, while he acted like an owner in many ways, he was selective in what he paid attention to. There were parts of the business that he just did not focus on. For example, he tended to leave the complexities of accounting to the finance department rather than truly "owning" its work and its results. From these reflections, JLT determined that, if he wanted THORLO employees to act more like owners, he needed to take on the responsibilities of ownership more fully himself.

JLT resolved that he would take up ownership for every aspect of THORLO's operations. As he began to put this intention into practice over the next few weeks, the change was quite noticeable. For example, in his next meeting with the finance department, JLT said he wanted to understand the details behind the numbers in the company's financial statements. In the past, he had only wanted to discuss the implications of what the financial statement showed, so this was a big shift in behavior. JLT assured the finance team that he was not acting out of lack of respect for its work. Rather, he had decided he could no longer simply delegate to others the responsibility for THORLO's financial management; he needed to fully understand the financial statement for himself. The head of finance then acknowledged that he, too, had delegated the details of the financial statement to his team. He realized that he could not explain them to JLT, and he needed to change that.

As he interacted with people in different parts of the company, JLT observed that his shift in behavior caused others to shift as well. When he took up greater responsibility for the whole, they felt inspired to do the same. Nowhere was this feeling stronger than in the leadership team. The name JLT gave to his concept of ownership of the whole was "brand stewardship." This evoked all that the THORLO brand represented—our relationships with our customers, employees and key partners, as well as the sole shareholder, JLT. Over the next few months, the leadership team committed itself to learning how to transform its leadership of the company into a consistent practice of "collective brand stewardship." We renamed the team "5/09," for the five who took up leadership of the whole company, as a group, in 2009. Then we embarked on a Harmonic Vibrancy Move process to figure out how we were going to enact the agreements necessary to realize our goal.

# THE HARMONIC VIBRANCY MOVE PROCESS

## IDENTIFYING THE GAP

The initial task in our Harmonic Vibrancy Move process was to distinguish between our current way of functioning as a team and the collective brand stewardship we aspired to. When we examined our shared experience, it was not difficult to identify what we all thought was the kind of team dynamic we were after. We brainstormed what collective brand stewardship looked like and agreed that, when we are doing it successfully, everyone is awake and paying attention as brand stewards; alignment within the team is effortless.

We knew what this looked like because we had experienced it in the aftermath of THORLO's "Black Friday," the day in the Fall of 2007 when the team had had to lay off many colleagues and friends. In this difficult situation, a deep sense of company-wide responsibility and ownership had infused the team's interactions. The general consensus within the 5/09, however, was that the experience had peaked in the two months following the crisis and then declined. On a regular basis, we had moments of collective brand stewardship but no consistent practice of it.

We also knew what the opposite of collective brand stewardship looked like. In this mode, we would come to team meetings as individuals, each person trying to do the best for his part of the whole and advocating for his own perspective. Each said, in effect, "Here is my story of what I see about this business issue. I want you to see and accept my interpretation as complete." We thought we were "owning it all," but we really owned just what we could each see individually. We agreed that, when we are operating in this mode, everyone is asleep and, in the five relationships, we are in a completely collapsed state. Alignment is difficult, if not impossible. This had been our norm before the post-Black Friday experience, and the way we were going it seemed likely we would be back there within a year.

We defined the gap as the distance between these two extremes. It was clear that we did not have the agreements and practices in place to support a higher, more consistent level of collective brand stewardship. To fulfill our charter as the 5/09, we had to achieve this higher level of functioning and maintain it over the long term. The sustainability of the company depended on it. We set the intention of closing the gap within a year.

## EXPLORING THE EXPERIENCE OF OTHERS

In this step of the Harmonic Vibrancy Move process, the 5/09 identified and agreed to take up two new practices to support it in realizing collective brand stewardship. These were "declarations" and "co-hosting relationships." The practice of declarations came from JLT's reading on personal and organizational transformation. It was also a practice he had taken up himself. For example, he had shared his intention to become a fully engaged owner of the company as a declaration—a public statement of his intention to act in a different way. The declaration also included a request that others support him in following through on his intention, both with patience in knowing that he was trying something new, and with persistence in reminding him of his declaration when he seemed to have forgotten it.

The team saw that this device could be a daily reminder of our determination to adopt new behaviors. By publicly declaring our commitment to collective brand stewardship, we could also declare our awareness that change in the company needed to start with change in the leadership team. We were clear that we needed to establish a high degree of consistency in practicing collective brand stewardship before we could expect this of others.

The practice of co-hosting relationships came from my experience in working with high performing, high vibrancy groups around the world. In these groups, I have observed many relational capacities and practices not usually present in groups experiencing the middle circle of harmonic vibrancy. I see these both in the individual group members and in the practices of the group as a whole. In particular, I find that in groups experiencing the outer circle of harmonic vibrancy, many of the individuals have developed capacities for self-reflection that enable them to see and work with their own potential at the possibility-light level, manage their own learning processes at the development-verb level, and make use of feedback on the outcomes they produce at the things-noun level. These individuals, in other words, are constantly working inwardly and outwardly on all three levels of reality. Typically, they have also developed the capacity to support others in a similar process. Group practices support this exploration and inquiry with continuous reflection and experimentation. They enable both individuals and group to engage actively with all five primary relationships at all three levels of perceived reality on a consistent basis.

For example, the practice of sharing one's own personal insights and reflective processes connects the individual to the group through the relationship to self. A consistent practice of mentoring others in the process of exploring their own potential keeps the relationship to other alive in a vital way. Another practice in high vibrancy groups involves regular, public acknowledgment of the specific contributions each individual is making to the group's purpose and activity. In this way, they maintain a strong positive relationship to group and also to spirit, by strengthening the group's awareness of the creativity available in its members. Finally, high vibrancy groups tend to have and use clear terminology to take note of the level of perceived reality the group is working with in the moment. For example, one group I observed referred to "possibility thinking" when it was engaged at the level of possibility-light, "learning" and "over time" when it was dealing with development-motion, and "here now" when it was pursuing outcomes at the things-matter level. Another group color-coded the levels, referring to the possibility level as "red-red" to indicate that people should not run to action with the content at the possibility level, "orange" for the development level, and "green" for the green light to act at the outcomes level.

I call this high vibrancy set of individual capacities and group practices "co-hosting" relationship. When I am "hosting" a party effectively, I do not try to manage all of the interactions happening in the party—who is talking to whom about what, or who is engaging in what activity. To do otherwise would make me a real busybody and drive most people crazy. Instead, as the host, I merely establish the conditions for interactions to take place and then try to remain mindful of how changes in the environment may be influencing them. More than this, I realize that the guests themselves do a great deal of the hosting in a successful party. When I "co-host," I am acknowledging the role each of the participants and the space play in hosting the party with me.[126]

It seemed to me, in observing high vibrancy groups, that the individuals with the capacities for engaging with the five primary relationships and three levels of perceived reality create the conditions for the group as a whole to do the same. Yet the group also participates in creating the right environment and establishing the practices for harmonic vibrancy. This is co-hosting relationship.

For the 5/09, co-hosting became the model of how we wanted to enact brand stewardship, first within our team and eventually across the entire THORLO organization. We began immediately to use the language of "co-hosting collective brand stewardship," meaning that we wanted to promote

---

126    In their book The Abundant Community, best-selling author Peter Block and North-western University Professor John McKnight describe a dynamic similar to co-hosting that they experience in high vibrancy communities, which they call "hospitality." They find that, "Hospitality is the signature of not only an abundant community, but a confident one. The extent of hospitality becomes a measure of the belief that people have in their community (McKnight & Block, 2010, p. 79)."

this new attitude and behavior within the company in a way that was fully engaged with the five relationships and three levels of perceived reality. We recognized that we needed to develop both individual capacities and group practices to make that possible, and the experiences that JLT and I brought in gave the group ideas about how to go about that. We could envision a set of agreements and practices for declaring a new behavior, holding ourselves to our declaration and co-hosting relationship, all of which we saw could support us in moving to the higher level experience we desired.

## ASSESSING OUR OWN EXPERIENCE

When the 5/09 reached the step of evaluating our current state relative to our desired state, JLT's personal experience once again provided a core framework and inspiration. As the son of the company's founder, its owner, and its CEO for more than forty years, he was deeply concerned about its sustainability after his retirement. The key to sustainability, he believed, was a leadership team that could run THORLO "as a living, self-evolving, self-organizing system." He envisioned "a community of leaders able to shift from an old, layered, hierarchical structure that was inwardly focused and rules- and regulation-based, toward a structure able to develop the responsiveness and flexibility increasingly required of a globally competitive entity." Three times before, JLT had tried unsuccessfully to develop such a team. Each time he had ended up feeling frustrated by the inability of the people he had brought into those previous teams to communicate openly and collaborate fully.

Then he had experienced a humbling insight. He realized that his own way of holding the vision of sustainability for the company was the major obstacle to its manifestation. This was the self-assessment he shared with the team: "Only when I finally 'showed up'—and by that, I mean being 100-percent personally responsible for my experience, getting beyond my own ego, being real, vulnerable, and acting as a collaborative equal in dialogue, not 'boss'—did others begin to appear who could work in the same spirit."

The other members of the 5/09 shared JLT's vision of sustainability. Having worked together for a couple of years, however, they also recognized that their willingness to work collaboratively had so far not been enough to realize that vision. As one team member expressed it:

"In hindsight, I can see we all wanted a non-hierarchical structure driven by a craftsman's attention to detail, an entrepreneurial spirit of all-inclusive ownership and a sustainable business model. We wanted an environment where everyone in the company worked for more than a paycheck, for something bigger than himself or herself. But we didn't yet have a way for our group to manifest this intention, other than just working hard."

Our self-assessment helped the team get a clearer picture of why we were "working hard" and not getting the results we wanted. When we compared our agreements and practices with those of the groups achieving what we desired, the main thing we saw was that we had the individual competencies we needed, we just did not practice them consistently. That is, we had experience with self-reflection; we knew how to recognize and support other individuals; we were comfortable acknowledging the unique contributions of each individual to the group; we knew how to engage in a creative process; and we could often see the creativity available to the group. Yet, we saw that we did not bring in those capacities on a consistent basis.

When we looked through the four lenses, we recognized that we knew what agreements we needed. In response to the resource question, we knew that we wanted to agree that the world was abundant, though we often seemed to assume scarcity. Looking through the allocation lens, we knew that we were more effective and efficient when we included more of the primary relationships in determining the use of our resources. Through the value lens, we agreed that we placed a high value on the differences in perspectives and life experiences that our colleagues bring to the table. Through the organization lens, we saw that we included more of the relationships and perspectives we valued when we inquired into each other's perspective and synthesized what we each saw.

We talked about how, in practice, when we started from an assumption of abundance, we tended to look for the unique perspective each of the others brought. From a place of abundance we took a stance of openness and curiosity about those differences: "You must see the world differently, given your completely different experience base and I want to know what your perspective looks like." More often, however, we started from a sense of scarcity and did not think to look for those differences in perspective, much less appreciate them. When we started from a sense of abundance and awareness of the rich differences in perspectives, we were able to see much richer solutions to the presenting problem of the moment. When we started from scarcity, missing those important nuances, we also missed many seemingly obvious solutions that were right under our noses but invisible to us. Sometimes we operated with abundance-based practices, but more frequently we collapsed out of them. Since we had experienced them, they were not completely foreign to us. Yet neither were they comfortably familiar and easy to apply.

When we assessed our experience of harmonic vibrancy, using the 3 Circles diagram, we confirmed that we usually inhabited the lower level between the inner and middle circles—not a place of great abundance. We saw that we agreed to this, however, even though it was not what we wanted. We recognized that while the organizational culture of THORLO strongly encourages cross-functional collaboration in service to the customer, our team practices tended toward separation in responsibility and communication, and a lack of ownership of the whole. The reality was that we each came to meetings of the 5/09 representing our own functional perspective and what we saw of the whole company from that perspective, whether in engineering, finance, information systems, marketing or culture. We agreed that we wanted something different: to be able to see the larger whole available to us when we could also see through each other's perspectives. This would require a different set of practices, which, in turn, would require a different set of agreements.

## DEFINING AND ENACTING THE MOVE

To make the desired shift, the 5/09 determined it would need to develop the capacity, individually and as a team, to co-host the five primary relationships on a routine, reliable basis. We made a declaration to change the group's behavior and to "be the change" we wanted to see in the company as a whole, before expecting it from others. We said we wanted to operate consistently from an assumption of abundance, to always invite in the highest potential in all of us, and to develop practices that would support the experience of the outer circle of harmonic vibrancy for everyone we worked with, as well as ourselves.

It became my assignment to design a series of capacity-building exercises for the team. We agreed that, for a couple of days every two months, we would work on learning to co-host two to three of the relationships. We followed this program for the next year and a half.

### Relationship to self

As part of the group's declaration to change, we each also made an individual declaration of intention to pursue self-awareness and growth. Our scan of high-vibrancy groups had shown us that their high level of functioning depends largely upon the group members' individual practices of self-reflection, which enable them to see clearly who they are, where they are in their life journeys, what their potential is, and how they are growing. I had participated in a few groups that used specific exercises for experiencing and developing these capacities in the relationship to the self. The 5/09 was starting with a pretty high level of trust in each other and in me. I thought this would allow us to dig deeply into the relationship to self.

The exercises we used come from the field of adult development, a broad-ranging inquiry into how individuals make sense of the world. This includes how they perceive and work with the strengths they have already developed, how they determine areas in which they could develop next, and how they interact with feedback from the external environment and the information it provides about what is happening there. We worked with action logics, autobiography and heart-to-heart feedback. The goal was to see the underlying patterns in our lives and thereby to understand why we had each taken up certain questions, how we had developed in pursuit of those questions and what questions remained to be addressed in the future.

### Understanding action logics

Action logics are the ways we make sense of our surroundings and ourselves. Operating largely unconsciously, they determine how we act and interact with others. Through rigorous research with thousands of cases, Susanne Cook-Greuter has described a developmental model of these action logics, with each developmental stage adding greater complexity and subtlety. For example, one stage is characterized by the Expert-Technician action logic. People operating from this logic have a well-established sense of individual identity, distinct from the groups of which they are a part. They have excellent problem-solving skills, are confident in what they believe to be true, have a strong sense of "right and wrong," and are often harshly critical of the opinions of others. The next stage, characterized by the Achiever action logic, builds on the Expert's self-awareness and capacity for logical thinking. In addition, the Achiever has an acute awareness of change over time and so is more focused on how he is developing, what his motivations are and who he really is. At the same time, he is more open to diverse people and opinions. Idealistic and action-oriented, the Achiever firmly believes in the power of knowledge and rational analysis to control nature, human nature and society. At another stage, the Individualist action logic places much less value on rational thought and scientific analysis and more on subjective "knowing." He cares less about achievement than self-knowledge. Far from merely tolerating differences in others, the Individualist goes out of his way to understand and embrace them.[127]

---

127    For stages of awareness, we used the developmental theory of Susanne Cook-Greuter (Cook-Greuter, 2002) as expressed by Bill Torbert (Torbert, 1994), and put into practice by Maureen Metcalf (Metcalf & Palmer, 2011). We did the MAP assessment with Dr. Susanne

The above are very simplified descriptions of three prevalent action logics. Cook-Greuter offers a detailed online survey to assess one's primary action logic. All the members of the 5/09 took this survey. Then we reflected individually and together on what the results showed us about how we each made sense of our actions in the world. We saw that we had a distribution of action logics that we used, with most of our sense making typically in one of them, and a leading edge in another. For example, while one team member looked at the world predominantly through the Achiever action logic, comfortable in expressing the creativity he brought to many situations, he was frequently experiencing the Individualist action logic, seeing the creativity available in others as well. For him, this leading edge of the Individualist action logic was intriguing, and he wanted to explore what practices would support him in this new arena. We then saw that one of our colleagues was firmly in the Individualist action logic, and that he might mentor the other to share practices he had developed.

### Autobiography

For the autobiography exercise, we each focused on major events in our lives that had influenced how we see ourselves, the paths we have taken, how we act as leaders, and our deeper aspirations. I asked each individual to reflect on these major events and patterns, for themselves, writing them down in a way that felt comfortable to them. Some wrote down bullet points, while a couple others wrote down prose. Some wrote them down in chronological order, while others focused on the patterns they saw. We then shared some of the major events in our stories and the patterns we saw in them.[128]

After sharing what we were each seeing on our own path, one of the group commented, "While I am the one who has lived my life, it was not that clear to me where I was in it. I now see the flow of my life, where I am in it, and I have a greater sense of where I am heading." Another described his path within the company: "I see that I have shifted in how I perceive myself within the community. I started with my identity as the first degreed engineer, and then I was the Director of R&D, then the Director of Technology, then responsible for all of manufacturing. Now I am just David, a brand steward for it all." Seeing each other's path more clearly made it easier to see where they were struggling with new challenges that were stretching them and how to support them.

---

Cook-Greuter, available at (cook-greuter.com). For the power of declarations, we looked to the experience of Jim Throneburg, a member of the group.

128    For biography, we were inspired by (O'Neil & O'Neil, 1990).

### Heart-to-heart feedback

We also started a series of "heart-to-heart" feedback sessions focused on our capacities as brand stewards. As defined in one of THORLO's core documents:

> "Heart to Heart" refers to the contextual framework in which one experiences their environment, moment-by-moment. When one is "listening from their heart," they experience their environment from this perspective. The "listening from your heart" perspective is where we "feel" totally connected to everything and everyone in our environment. From this perspective we are aware of ourselves as individuals, others as individuals, all the relationships within the system, and the system as a whole. A perspective that does not include all the aforementioned levels of awareness limits one's availability to "hear" and "see" themselves as the "creator" of their own environment. Therefore one can still maintain the perspective that the responsibility for what is happening "to" them is external to themselves.

Every two months we spent a half-day providing feedback to one team member. On his day for feedback, the individual completed a self-assessment, while the rest of the team evaluated him using the same assessment form. He then described what the assessment had helped him to see about his own brand stewardship behaviors. The rest of the team inquired into what he had shared and added their observations.[129]

Through this process, each team member determined what declaration he would make about the change in brand stewardship behavior he was going to personally take on. At the same time, other members of the team had the opportunity to offer to partner with him in support of those behaviors. For example, one person wanted to work on being more present as a co-host of the five relationships in meetings. He declared his intention to adopt the practice of preparing for this co-hosting before each meeting, by getting in touch with his own state of mind and calling to mind the gifts and contributions of others who would be in the meeting. Another member of the 5/09 volunteered to meet with him for a few minutes before meetings to support this preparation for co-hosting.

---

129   The 5/09 designed the heart-to-heart feedback protocol itself. It has now become part of the THORLO Employee and Leadership Handbook (Throneburg, 2011).

As we moved through these exercises and took up our new practices, we started to see ripple effects extending beyond the 5/09. One team member's co-workers noticed the difference in his behavior almost immediately and asked him what was causing it. When he told them, they wanted to learn the new practices as well. We also noticed what seems obvious in retrospect: until we asked the questions, "Who am I, where have I come from, and where am I going?" we did not see the answer. Only by asking those questions and sharing what we discovered with our colleagues did the path become clear and easier to take up.

## RELATIONSHIP TO OTHER, GROUP, NATURE, AND SPIRIT

### Other

We observed that in the groups experiencing higher levels of harmonic vibrancy, much attention was given to seeing and supporting the other. It was clear that the key assumption was one of the abundant potential in the other, and the key skills for this practice were based on inquiry. We determined that we had to improve our skills in seeing, listening to, and supporting the other.

One of the first inquiry practices we brought to the relationship to the other was simply listening. We agreed that, as we worked through the exercises, we would truly listen to each other, holding the question of whether we could see what the other was seeing. This practice entailed listening carefully, asking for clarification if necessary, and then restating what we had heard as a way of confirming that it agreed with what the speaker thought he was saying. This form of active listening was an important aspect of our heart-to-heart feedback sessions, as described above. Through it we found we could demonstrate that we had received what the self-assessor said and help him understand more fully how we experienced him through his behaviors.

In addition to more effective listening, we worked on strengthening inquiry skills with William Torbert's "four parts of speech," from the field of action inquiry.[130] These are framing, advocating, illustrating, and inquiring. We worked on differentiating and learning how to use the different parts of speech by telling stories in which we stated when we were using each one. For example: "This is a story about how I see the issues around the customer's experience with our new sock. I will frame it by describing how I see our

---

130    In action inquiry, we used the four parts of speech: framing, advocating, illustrating, and inquiring (Torbert, 1994).

shared intention in regard to customer experience, how I define the problem that we face with the new sock, and my understanding of where we agree or disagree on underlying assumptions. Here is how I think we need to address the problem. I am advocating for this solution and will illustrate why I think it will work with a customer's story about how this fix has worked in the past. Now I wish to inquire what clarifications you may need or what you see is missing from my story." While it seemed a little cumbersome at first to name each of the four parts of speech, we found it enhanced our own awareness of what we were saying and what we might be missing. For example, I might realize that I was only advocating a position, without framing or illustrating it and without inquiring into how others saw it. This practice also helped us to nuance whether we were actually inquiring, as we might say we were, when we were really advocating what we thought, using the language of a question. "Isn't it obvious that…?"

We framed all of this work on inquiry within an invitational practice of expecting and inviting in the greatness of the other, and a mindfulness practice of noticing new information, perspectives, and categories.[131] To develop the invitational practice, we started by agreeing on what we meant by the word "invitation," sharing examples of when we had experienced the best of ourselves being invited into a conversation or relationship. We then agreed to use the word in our communication with each other as a way of reminding ourselves that we wanted to be more invitational with each other. This is a direct practice of co-hosting the primary relationship to spirit by seeing the source of creativity as available everywhere all of the time. After trying this exercise, one of the 5/09 team members said: "It's amazing how easy it is to see the available potential and creativity in you when I remind myself that I want to invite that in, to 'be invitational.'"

### Group

In regard to co-hosting the relationship to the group, we observed that the high vibrancy groups were very clear on the uniqueness of the contributions each individual made to the group. We wanted to develop practices to strengthen our awareness of the diversity of distinct voices that make up the "we" in each group. We settled on a 3-step process for approaching each specific business

---

131   A colleague of ours had studied with William Watson Purkey, a founder of Invitational Theory and Invitational Education, a professor at the University of North Carolina at Greens-boro. The mindfulness practices came through my work with Ellen Langer in her Mindfulness Lab at Harvard University since 2004. She describes an array of "mindfulness" techniques in (E. J. Langer, 1989, 2009).

issue with mindfulness of that diversity. The three steps are: (1) reminding everyone about the "local" purpose of the group; (2) determining how that "local" purpose is connected to the shared, higher purpose of THORLO; and (3) asking what voices need to be part of the conversation about how we will address the specific business issue within the context of both local and shared purposes.

Through this seemingly simple practice, we found we could easily see that certain voices "obviously" needed to be in the room when a particular issue was discussed. For example, an order fulfillment issue was not simply a problem for the distribution function of the business, but an issue affected by decisions made throughout the company, from marketing and sales through production and then into distribution. Yet we had not typically thought to engage all of those voices in conversations about order fulfillment. After working with this practice of co-hosting the group, one member of the 5/09 shared this realization: "I now see more clearly the absolute necessity of each of your voices and what you can see, if we are ever to achieve our shared higher purpose through brand stewardship."

### Nature

To develop our capacities for co-hosting the relationship to nature, we started to practice consciously bringing the three levels of perceived reality into our awareness. We began by identifying situations in which we naturally integrated all three levels, such as the design process in the department of Research and Development. The design engineer in the 5/09 said, "I know the exact moment when we, as a group, see a possibility and it becomes a probability. At that moment, we begin to convert the potential we saw into a process of development, in which we can already begin to see the outcomes we will achieve over time. We do this often, as a matter of being creative, and yet we don't apply it in most of our committee meetings. We need to, as they all involve acts of creation!"

Based on this realization, we agreed to be explicit in our meetings over the next month about the three levels in our process. We would clarify when we were working in possibility, when we were beginning to develop the possibility we saw together, and when we were focusing on the specific outcomes from that development process. We found that the practice of naming the levels of perceived reality when we were working with them sensitized us to the different feel each level has when we are in it. This experience led us to design the THORLO development process, with "Thorlorized" language for when we were working in one of the levels of reality and when we were transitioning to another level.

### Spirit

Our approach to developing capacities for co-hosting the relationship to spirit was the simplest of all—reflection and observation. Through many hours of dialogue about our experiences, we realized that we knew, at some deeper level, that the potential for creativity exists in everyone, everywhere, all of the time. We saw the available creativity in moments when we expected it, such as in the design work for new ads or new products. Creativity also showed up when we somewhat expected it, such as in brainstorming sessions or when we were looking for creative ways of responding to problems. It also showed up, however, when we did not expect it, such as when we thought we were simply reporting out business results to another group. In all of these moments, we realized that the source of creativity was sitting right there. Sometimes we were open to seeing it, and many times we were not. We also realized that we achieved much better results and had much more fun, when the creativity came in, even where we did not expect it.

Between sessions, we agreed to observe what we did to collapse our awareness of this creativity and what we could do to reengage it. When we came back together as the 5/09, we shared examples of what we observed in our own daily practices, both potential-enhancing and potential-collapsing. Sometimes it involved simply recognizing the potential-collapsing experience. For some they experienced it in their gut, while for others it was more of a heart-related sensation. We also noticed that when we were in a meeting together, often one of us would notice the shift from potential-enhancing to potential-collapsing, and the mere calling it out allowed the group to see it and change course, back to the potential-enhancing dynamic. Through this exercise, we came up with some simple practices for reminding each other to see the potential always available to us. As these took hold, we began to see that we were indeed declaring that we were open to co-hosting creativity, in all of its forms.

# RESULTS AND LESSONS LEARNED

### Results

Thirty months after our initial declaration, the 5/09 team reviewed its experience of the Harmonic Vibrancy Move. We depicted the results by the vertical blue lines in the Behavior over Time graph in Figure 36, below.

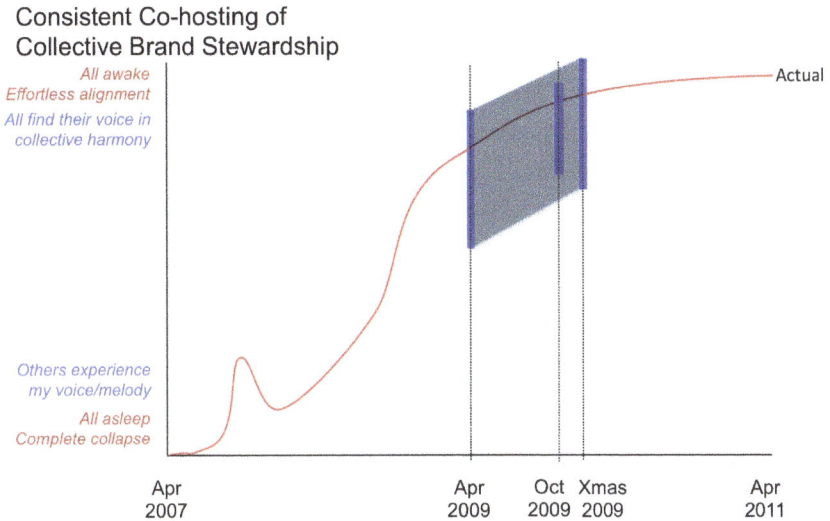

Note: Blue bars represent the distribution of assessments of the 5.

*Figure 36: Reassessing the 5/09 Experiences, April 2011*

As the graph indicates, the group felt we had fulfilled part of JLT's vision for a group of leaders able to be in deep dialogue as they work. We were working routinely in cross-functional teams, and regularly coaching and otherwise supporting each other in co-hosting relationships in those settings, by preparing together before the team meeting, being present during the meeting, and providing coaching feedback after the meeting. We were giving each other constant heart-to-heart feedback about our behaviors and what others perceived as the consequences of those behaviors within the larger organization. And, when we needed to, we were going back to the exercises and experiences we shared during the Harmonic Vibrancy Move process, to renew our understanding of and capacity for co-hosting.

In Ecosynomics terms, this team developed the capacity to continuously bring abundance into its daily work, from its tactical, day-to-day projects to its strategic, long-term inquiry. The harmonic interaction and the vibrancy they experienced, the abundance available to them, and the reduced costs of scarcity are the benefits they brought to THORLO. Most organizational leaders can only dream of such results.

### Lessons learned

The 5/09 had an experience of moving to a higher level of harmonic vibrancy that it now could help others have as well. Ecosynomics provided a framework for understanding the structures and processes they were working with. It also gave them the language for talking about this work in terms others within THORLO could understand. The members of the 5/09 realized that, through their own change process, they had developed the capacity to co-host a Harmonic Vibrancy Move process with other groups, both within and outside the company.

Through this process, I have confirmed for myself what others have told me, that group transformation starts with the individual. Each person has to take on the behaviors he or she needs to change before the group as a whole can change. I also learned the importance of building in practices to support these individual shifts, and the challenge of doing this at the same time that people are starting their individual change processes.

# CHAPTER 11

# MOVING A WHOLE COMPANY

As I shared in Chapters 9 and 10, one of the more important lessons I have learned is that group transformation starts with the individual. If individuals are not willing or able to change, change in the group as a whole is impossible. Chapter 10 described how a small, close-knit, corporate leadership team transformed itself both at the individual and group level and prepared to lead a company-wide change process based on the same principles. This chapter describes that larger initiative.

The question of how to effect change in large groups is an important one. Based on my experience, an essential ingredient is a leadership team that has already transformed itself sufficiently to "be the change" that it seeks to create in the larger group. This chapter details how this small-to-large-group process has been taking place at THORLO.[132]

## STEPPING UP TO "OWNING IT ALL"

The transformation that had occurred in THORLO's leadership team in 2009-2010 had revolved around the concept of ownership. First the company's owner-CEO, Jim Throneburg (JLT), had committed himself to take an owner's

---

[132]   To hear the heart and soul of THORLO's story, visit (http://www.thorlo.com/ws6/video_view.php?video_id=18). For case studies on THORLO's experience of applying the Ecosynomic principles, see (Leaf, Hulbert, & Throneburg, 2010; Ritchie-Dunham, Throneburg, & Puleo, 2010). Journalist Donna Fenn provides a different take on the THORLO story, looking at how they made something as "mundane" as a sock into an innovation with major impact (Fenn, 2005). In her recent book, Martina Navratilova says, "Thank you, Thor-Lo socks. I have not worn anything else on my feet since 1981" (Navratilova, 2006). Martina won 9 Wimbledon singles titles and 58 Grand Slam titles from 1975 to 1991.

interest in every aspect of the business. The changes this commitment brought about in his behavior inspired the leadership team, of which I am a part, to take up the same level of ownership responsibility, both as individuals and collectively as a team. The team named itself the 5/09 to signify the five who had taken on leadership of the whole company in 2009.

As the changes described in chapter 10 unfolded, the team became clearer about the distinctions between its experiences of different levels of harmonic vibrancy. We started to think of our experience of the outer circle of harmonic vibrancy as "owning it all, all of the time." Gradually, with a great deal of mutual feedback and support, we became more solidly grounded in our ability to operate at that level. It was in this period that two outside observers from the Institute for Strategic Clarity conducted an in-depth Ecosynomics assessment of THORLO's operations and produced the agreements map I presented in Chapter 7 (Figure 27), showing a high level of functioning, frequently engaging all five relationships at all three levels of perceived reality. In this sense, "owning it all" was also an expression of the company's mission statement of "realizing sustainable relationships."

Not surprisingly, people within the broader THORLO community took notice of the changes in how the members of the 5/09 were acting and the things we were saying about the changes. A conversation about ownership arose within the company and expanded over the course of 2010. Through this conversation, it became apparent that many people felt a sense of ownership for the whole community but were not able to operate consistently on that basis. People agreed they wanted to be responsible to and for the whole community. In their day-to-day practice, however, they most often focused only on their particular piece of the whole. One THORLO employee expressed it this way:

"I love this place, and have for over twenty years. This is my family. I care about the whole experience our consumer has with us, and yet I find that I usually only pay attention to being great at my part at the tail end of the process. While I might be happy for or get mad at other parts of the process when they are successful or fail, I now see that I do not act as if I owned the whole process. If I did, that love and attention would go into making sure the whole thing works for our consumer."

## THE HARMONIC VIBRANCY MOVE PROCESS

As people around the company had more and more of these conversations and experienced members of the 5/09 taking on responsibility for the whole, they began to express interest in learning how to do the same. The 5/09 responded by undertaking a new Harmonic Vibrancy Move. The challenge of this process was to engage the entire organization in a way that would encourage and support the individual-level transformation needed to create change in the group as a whole.

## IDENTIFYING THE GAP

To support the whole THORLO community in taking on a higher level of ownership, the 5/09 set out to determine the current status of owning it all throughout the community. As we searched for a way to assess this, we came back to how we had come to experience a direct correlation between owning it all and our level of harmonic vibrancy. When we experienced ownership for more of the whole, we also experienced broader and healthier relatedness to the self, other, group, nature, and spirit. Realizing this, the 5/09 decided we could use the harmonic vibrancy survey to assess the current state of both ownership and sustainable relationship throughout the community. This would give us a sense of the gap we needed to address.

In April 2011, the 5/09 asked seven different teams, representing one-fifth of the THORLO community, to take the harmonic vibrancy survey. Among other things, this survey allows people to rate their experiences of the five fundamental relationships on a scale of 1 to 5. The inner circle of harmonic vibrancy is 1.0, the middle circle is 3.0, and the outer circle is 5.0. In this instance, the average score for all the teams together was 3.6. In other words, the survey told us that most of the people in these groups were experiencing medium-to-high levels harmonic vibrancy.

Looking more closely, we found that there were really two clusters of team scores. Three of the groups clustered around the experience of the middle circle of harmonic vibrancy, averaging 3.2 in all five relationships. Four of the groups clustered halfway between the middle and outer circle, averaging 3.9. When we reviewed the results in the 5/09, these differences were illuminating, especially to those members of the leadership team who participated in groups in both clusters. Everyone agreed that, in the middle-circle cluster of teams, the primary focus was on process and outcomes, the motion and matter levels of perceived reality. In contrast, the outer-circle cluster of teams was focusing on process and outcomes and also consciously paying attention to manifesting potential and creativity. They were working with all three levels of perceived reality.

Additionally, members of teams in both clusters noted that in the lower-scoring group, their experience often felt heavy and energy depleting, while the higher-scoring group felt much lighter and energy enhancing. One of the team leaders reflected on this difference:

"We are the same leaders in a lower-cluster group and a higher-cluster group. We are the same people, and these are our groups. And, the experience in the two is completely different. Since they are both our groups, we can agree to something different, and I don't know why we haven't. But now I know that we can. We already know how to live the way of the second cluster—we're already doing it—and we just don't in the first-cluster group. We have to change that, now. And since we are the leaders, we can make the changes we need."

Next the 5/09 debriefed each team on its survey results. These conversations confirmed that most people in the community felt like they owned it all yet were often unclear about how to live into that ownership on a practical basis. Again, there were differences between the two clusters of teams. People within the teams that clustered at the middle circle of harmonic vibrancy said they wanted to act as if they owned it all but felt powerless to do so. In contrast, people in the teams at the outer circle said they often felt they had the greater capacity to experience owning it all. It became clear to the 5/09 that most people were uncertain about how to choose agreements that would enable them to enact their commitment to ownership. The gap we identified was between the intention to own it all and the enactment of that intention on a regular basis.

## EXPLORING THE EXPERIENCE OF OTHERS

The 5/09 was now at the point of needing to tap our personal experiences and those of others to define what life might look like for THORLO if we could close the gap. As before, JLT provided direction based on his deep reflection and wide reading. He was clear, for example, that moving the company to the next level of ownership experience meant that people throughout the organization would have to make a conscious choice to take on the ownership perspective. He saw that the 5/09 needed to support this by being specific and explicit about what we meant by owning it all. If this really was important to the company, JLT argued, it should be included in core documents, such as the Leadership and Employee Handbook. As the team continued to develop its plans for the Harmonic Vibrancy Move over the course of 2011, revising this handbook became an integral part of the process. The revised handbook played an important role as the Harmonic Vibrancy Move unfolded in 2012 and 2013.

Another significant contribution came from JLT's reading on complexity.[133] Taking on ownership of it all, he realized, was an individual practice but one that people would enact in community. That is, the decision and daily practice would require the awareness and initiative of the individual; and the individual would have to practice ownership as part of a group process. What would support this individual-group process on a continuous basis? Framing the question of what company-wide ownership would look like in these terms opened it to the insights provided in the literature about the nature of complex adaptive systems. These insights led us to see that a clear shared purpose and the systemic exchange of information would be essential to support the individual-group process of owning it all.

To this exploration of what the next level might look like, I brought my experiences with other groups moving to higher vibrancy agreements, a number of which I shared in Chapter 3. I also brought my training in collaborative decision-making and the O Process. The other members of the 5/09 brought their daily practice in bringing greater ownership to the community and how that practice was beginning to develop in others. Through our conversations about what we saw about the next level of experience, we clarified for ourselves that we wanted all THORLO employees to be able to make a conscious choice at the individual level to take on being an owner of it all. We also saw that they would need strong support, both within and across teams, in order to practice ownership on a continuous basis.

## ASSESSING OUR OWN EXPERIENCE

With this clarity about the next level of experience, the 5/09 turned to the task of looking at the current situation at THORLO. We decided to include a wide range of THORLO voices in this inquiry by introducing it into the company's ongoing, community-wide leadership conversations. The practice of leadership conversations had been in place for many years. Conceived as running parallel to the conversations by which the business ran, they were designed to give people an opportunity to talk about their experience of taking responsibility for running the business. The top-executive team was engaging in leadership conversations twice weekly; other groups of department heads

---

133    JLT attributes the greatest clarity in thinking on the core attributes of complex adaptive systems to his reading of the Austrian complexity theorist Erich Jantsch's The Self-organizing Universe (Jantsch, 1980).

and functional leaders were doing so monthly. There was also a group open to anyone in the company who was willing to engage actively in the conversation, which often involved reading and discussing an article on leadership. Usually about sixty people participated in this leadership conversation, which was personally hosted by JLT in small groups of fifteen to twenty.

The assessment of current reality thus engaged a wide swath of THORLO personnel, about a quarter of the whole company. Through the hosting of JLT and other members of the 5/09, the leadership conversations explored the assumptions and agreements supporting the existing patterns of behavior around ownership. They used the four lenses of resources, resource allocation, value, and organization to guide this exploration. As this leadership conversation evolved in the community over the course of 2011, people got clearer and clearer on the differences between what they wanted and what they were experiencing.

When the 5/09 and other groups addressed the resources question, "how much?," they found that, while most assumed abundance, in reality the practice was more based in scarcity. While they saw abundance in the infinite potential that seemed obvious in each other and what the company could bring to the foot health of the consumer, their daily practices focused on the scarcity of just doing their jobs and on eking out sales and delivering products in a competitive retail market.

Similarly, in exploring the resource allocation question, "who decides?," the conversations uncovered a discrepancy between the desire that decisions be made with all five primary relationships in mind and the reality that most were driven by an overriding focus on the group. The culture supported making decisions based on the needs of the individual in his self development, on the supporting of the other in their development, on the diversity of unique contributions to the group, on the development of possibilities that resulted in clear outcomes, and on the seeing of creativity and inviting that creativity into every moment. And sometimes it happened. And many times the conversation and the work focused on what the group needed from each individual in order to meet the needs of the group.

Through asking the value question, "by what criteria?," people saw that there was a strong culture of believing that all five primary relationships were guiding key decisions. Everyone agreed that part of what they loved about the THORLO community was the process of taking the time and space to explore the perspectives of the self, other, group, nature, and spirit. They gave time and space to this because everyone in the company valued it. Sometimes this happened when there was a product development challenge, such as a special sock for a young boy whose foot had been damaged in an accident at home. All five primary relationships were engaged in deciding how to allocate resources to produce that sock. In most cases, though, the rationale behind decisions was focused on outcomes and process. "How are we going to get this product out the door for that order in the most efficient, cost-effective way?"

Finally, through the organization lens and the question of "how do we interact?" the leadership conversations explored THORLO's commitment to ownership. Growing out of its long history of a strong community culture focused on the customer, there seemed to be a shared desire for individuals to own it all and for the group to support that ownership. However, with the exception of a couple of recent experiments with cross-functional teams dealing with specific issues, the company still tended to organize by parts, with each individual doing his or her own piece.

As the leadership conversations confronted these discrepancies, people began to realize they could decide to choose different agreements, designed to produce the experiences they wanted. They also realized that, through their conversations, they were all inviting that shift to happen. Having gone through the experience of previous Harmonic Vibrancy Moves, the 5/09 found it had confidence that it could guide the shifts in agreements needed for this current move.[134]

## DEFINING AND ENACTING THE HARMONIC VIBRANCY MOVE

The fourth step of THORLO's Harmonic Vibrancy Move process unfolded in two stages. The first stage, defining, took place concurrently with the process described above of assessing current experience in the context of the expanding leadership conversations. This occurred over the first three quarters of 2011. The second stage, enacting, began toward the end of that year, carried on through 2012 and 2013 and is still proceeding as I write. Dividing the story up into these two stages makes it easier to describe what happened, but in reality, they overlapped considerably. We began enacting the move in the process of defining it, and the process of definition has continued as we have moved forward with the enactment.

### Defining the move – rewriting the employee handbook

For the 5/09, getting our ideas down in writing in THORLO's *Leadership*

---

134    For documentation of earlier harmonic vibrancy moves at THORLO, see (Leaf & Hulbert, 2010; Ritchie-Dunham et al., 2010).

*and Employee Handbook* was essential. It was our way of following through on our commitment to being really clear on what we meant by owning it all. Only then, we felt, could THORLO employees consciously choose whether or not they wanted to join us in taking it on. In an important sense, the handbook was an invitation. One way we tried to frame it as such was to introduce it with personal statements of some of the 5/09-team members, in which they described how they had experienced the moves toward ownership we had already made. In this way, we invited and encouraged others to reflect on their own process of development, and to be open about what they were experiencing. The example below gives a sense of what these statements were like:

> My name is David Varsik and I have been employed at THORLO since 1995. My background is in mechanical engineering. I was the first degreed engineer hired by THORLO with the intent of ensuring the sustainability of our technology. Over the years, my responsibilities have grown to include Director of R & D, Director of Technology and most recently I have taken on responsibility for all of Manufacturing at THORLO.
>
> In the past, my approach to issues and opportunities was based in my engineering discipline and education. A few years ago I took on the mindset that I was responsible for what was, or was not showing up in my environment. This caused a change in the way I engaged with the people around me. I began to no longer provide input to them as an expert, but instead I engaged them in conversations about our higher purpose and about the "what and why" of what we were doing. The environment around me started to change, as best I can describe, from that of firefighting to fire prevention. I learned that the conversation was the key. As long as we were in conversation throughout the day about the "what and why," individual decisions became more effective and efficient, because the group stayed aligned and on purpose. Over time this conversation has become more informal and is now the group's normal mode of operation.
>
> This way of operating continues to pay dividends for THORLO. In the span of a little over a year, we were able to reduce our

operating inventory by 35%. We are continuing to reduce our inventory, while maintaining a better than 98.2% on-time-delivery percentage. Over this same period of time, we have reduced defects in knitting from 2.9% to 2.1%.

This conversation strategy has also affected and evolved my personal life as well. I discovered several years ago that my greatest gift to the people around me was the sharing of myself and my gifts. I gained the awareness that in many situations there were internal obstacles that I was holding onto that prevented me from being able to fully share my gifts. I quickly learned that the more I gave up, the richer and more meaningful were the gifts I had to offer. The more I gave, the more I received, and I began to not only see the gifts in others, but the harmony that can be achieved when people feel free to share their gifts. Creating this environment of freedom and harmony has both deepened and broadened my relationships.

JLT and I took the lead in drafting the revised handbook, bringing in language and practices from the complexity theory of Erich Jantsch, the integral theory of Ken Wilber and the development theories of Susanne Cook-Greuter and William Torbert.[135] However, the process of shaping these materials into agreements and practices for THORLO came about through company-wide interaction and experimentation. The first step involved developing a common domain of language, a Thorlorized way of describing the experiences we were aiming for with the Harmonic Vibrancy Move.

This started as members of the 5/09 tried to find a precise and understandable way to describe their experiences. After we worked out some new terms, the team played with them until everyone agreed they seemed to describe the experience well. Then 5/09 members began to "road test" the language with their other colleagues at THORLO. This testing helped show what made sense and what did not and often led to simpler language with added layers of meaning. The term "Brand Stewardship" emerged in this way, as did "O leadership" (for ownership-leadership) and integrated collaborative conversations (ICCs). The 5/09 saw this process of developing and testing new language in groups across the company as essential to both defining and

135    Exemplary teachers JLT found include complexity theorist Jantsch (Jantsch, 1980), integral theorist Wilber (Wilber, 2000), and developmental theorists Cook-Greuter (Cook-Greuter, 2002) and Torbert (Torbert, 1994).

enacting the Harmonic Vibrancy Move. It was a way of building the common understanding that would enable people to articulate and share the experiences they were having and seeking to have.

### Offering new agreements

We saw the revised handbook as another way of creating shared understanding of what this Harmonic Vibrancy Move was all about. This was especially true in regard to agreements. "The company aspires to shift its intent to a new set of 'Ecosynomic' agreements and axioms," the handbook states. "These agreements are understood and accepted as guides for all our interactions, and are as follows:

> I choose to accept, step into, and contribute from my creative self, my greatest gifts, as deeply as I can see them now (for the benefit of the Whole). I see how my awareness influences our relationships. I choose to accept and support you stepping into and contributing of the best you can be, as you request it of me. I see our collective as healthiest when you and I each contribute from our best. I choose to increase my awareness of how I, you, and we, together, benefit when we are in harmony as a whole collective. I choose to be in balance with nature's processes, for that which is visible and for that which is yet unseen. I give my commitment and will collaboratively to what I can see manifesting for the whole. I look for and support the 'spirit' of who THORLO is and what we serve through our Brand Stewardship. I acknowledge THORLO's spirit in whatever form it shows up today. It is these choices that lead to realizing the sustainable relationships that, in turn, realize the sustainable value for all bonded loyal stakeholders." [136]

The main assumption underlying these agreements is that all of the behavior they envision could emerge from integrated collaborative conversations. "Collaborative engagement, the handbook says, "starts with the premise of abundance and regenerates it in the awareness of all participants, making possible self-sustaining processes that are not visible from the competitive agreements formed around scarcity."

"Collaboration in the preservation and use of resources fuels the belief and knowledge of abundance, because it expands our ability to see ourselves

---

136   The quotations in this section are from (Throneburg, 2011), p. 30.

and other people as a Harmonic whole. In collaborative abundance, the system catalyzes and expands externally exchanged energy and generates its own energy to thrive. The knowledge of the possibility that there is 'enough,' enables the system to think creatively and enact solutions that can actually reverse negative trends. Agreements reached in an environment of perceived abundance are therefore self-sustaining."

The handbook distinguishes the worlds of abundance and scarcity by contrasting these proposed Ecosynomic-based agreements with the economics-based agreements they are replacing and the rules-based agreements of prior eras. "The 'economic' rules and basic assumptions represent what a great majority of us have been working under for most of our lives without ever knowing this consciously," says the handbook. "These have always been understood and accepted as the rules that guide our interactions and are as follows:

> I do my best (for compensation). I learn from practice, study, and reflection and put that in my work. You also need to do your best, bringing the skills and capacities you have developed. I contribute from what I know and can do. I support you in contributing what you know and can do. I minimize my impact on nature. I support the unique THORLO-ness of who we are. Our collective success depends on everyone contributing his or her part. Our success is a function of how well we perform. Our products have a minimal impact on nature, because of what we put into them and how long they last. We provide excellent products and services to our loyal consumers, for which they pay us well.

The "basic set of often unconscious assumptions" supporting economic agreements include the beliefs that resources are scarce and that individuals and groups within the company need to compete to get the resources they need to do "the job at hand." This mindset does not encourage collaboration, however, and so keeps people from realizing the abundance available in the group. Economic agreements, the handbook states, "lead inevitably to sub-optimization of community resources."

Nevertheless, economic agreements represent an advance beyond the "nomic" agreements by which many groups are living. "*Nomics* are agreements based on the rules set by the whim of someone else," the handbook states. "What might they look like in an earlier stage of THORLO's evolution? This question led us to the development of the following 'nomic' agreements:

I work hard and give from what I have, and in exchange for that I will be given what I need to do my work. Since we each need to do our part, I support you in working hard, and you need to give of your best, according to what you have been given. You need to meet your obligations. If we each take on a part, then there can be enough for all of us.

The rationale for describing all three kinds of agreements in the handbook was to emphasize the choice each THORLO employee was invited to make. Sticking with the existing, economic agreements was an acceptable choice. Yet everyone was invited to join the 5/09 in stepping into the Ecosynomic agreements.

"THORLO, Inc. is seeking a few special people who seek employment alternatives to their current employment that will allow them to learn continually and to grow personally and professionally long-term. People who want to work in a team environment where the experience is one of "creative family." People who love people, love life, and want to love their work again. People who are creative and love working with other creative, dedicated people. People who will grow and thrive in a community serving others in creative ways. People who will appreciate being an integral part of something bigger than themselves. People who want to be excited every day coming to work. People who want to share their thoughts and opinions, and know they will be heard."

### Linking the new agreements to Brand Stewardship and ICC's

Choosing Ecosynomic agreements was at the heart of the Harmonic Vibrancy Move. However, the handbook emphasizes, its purpose was to serve Brand Stewardship, and the way it would be enacted was through the "integrated collaborative conversation" (ICC). Brand Stewardship, the handbook states, is THORLO's 'North Star.'

[It] acknowledges that our bonded loyal consumers 'own' the Company and that our single filter by which we make our business decisions is anchored in the question, 'What is in the best long-term foot health interest of our bonded loyal consumers?' After the primary context of the bonded loyal consumer, the filter becomes the bonded loyal employees, the bonded loyal stakeholders, and finally the bonded loyal shareholders."

The handbook describes the ICC as "a dialogue among people who seek emergent, creative opportunities to harness previously untapped potential, both as individuals and as a group, to serve as Brand Stewards." The ICC is both a structure and a process.[137] It is the main support of the collaborative engagement envisioned in the Ecosynomics agreements, as well as "the primary strategy of the Company." Implementing ICCs across the THORLO community was therefore the foundational shift the company needed to make.

### ENACTING THE MOVE – RESTRUCTURING INTO ICC'S

As the 5/09 entered the fourth quarter of 2011, ready to enact the Harmonic Vibrancy Move it had laid out in the revised *Leadership and Employee Handbook*, it changed its name. It was now the Culture ICC or CULICC (pronounced as a spelling out of the letters, C-U-L I-C-C). The team chose this name to reflect its belief that THORLO's culture was the context for THORLO's business, not the other way around. A successful business would be the manifestation of a healthy culture, and therefore the focus of the company's top management needed to be nurturing that culture.

The name change also signaled the importance that ICCs were to have within THORLO going forward. The CULICC had been working intensively on its own practice of collaborative conversation and had begun to develop a model of the ICC based on the O Process (described in the sidebar below). We determined four essential characteristics of an effective ICC:

1.  A facilitator to guide the process and a co-host to ensure that the other three characteristics are in place.
2.  Clarity of purpose: the shared deeper purpose of the group; the local or specific purpose of the conversation; and how the two are connected. When it seems like the conversation might be off purpose, the role of the co-host is to ask those in the conversation whether they are on purpose or not and how so. If they decide they are not, the group will put the subject of their conversation in the "parking lot," to be connected to another conversation.
3.  The requisite diversity in the room to address the local purpose and clarity about the specific reason why each of the voices is present. The co-host makes sure these conditions are present and the people are open to listening for the different voices.
4.  100-percent participation in exploring what can be seen in the realm of possibility from all the perspectives in the room. The co-host and facilitator make sure that all voices participate. When a possibility is shared and "becomes real," they see that it is named and that is it

---

137    David Bohm suggested a structure-process continuum, where a "structure" is both the static aspect of a process and the basis for future movement and development of the process (Bohm, 1992).

has become a probability the group collectively recognizes. They work together to help people see how the new probability relates to each of the voices in the room and to confirm their commitment to enact the shared probability, as expressed in action items.

By early 2012, the CULICC was satisfied with its understanding of this process and announced the restructuring of all the major groups, teams and processes in the company as a series of nested ICCs. Going forward, THORLO's strategy would live in a network of continuous and interweaving conversations, in which all three levels of perceived reality would constantly be present, to be transformed with input from everyone engaged in the work. The people who had been leaders of the teams and groups, for the most part, took on the role of facilitator in the ICCs. People who had already been part of the co-hosting leadership conversation (mostly members of the CULICC) became the co-hosts.

The existing practice of leadership conversations helped prepare THORLO employees for this transition. In addition, at the beginning of 2012, JLT began meeting with small groups to discuss the concepts, language and agreements in the new *Leadership and Employee Handbook*. Over the course of 2012-2013 every employee participated in one of these conversations. The feedback to the CULICC was that this process gave them language to think and speak more openly about their experiences with the company.

We also heard that people felt the personal stories of transformation that members of the CULICC had shared in the handbook gave them permission to talk more openly about their experiences. For some time, a central thread of the leadership conversations taking place around the company had been about the need for individuals to take responsibility for their own development and how their actions affected others. This was related to owning it all and also to the new Ecosynomics agreements in the sense that self-responsibility is needed to support responsibility to the other, to the group, to nature and to spirit. Starting in 2012, the company invested heavily in supporting employees in their personal development through continuing leadership conversations. The CULICC also led a series of workshops, inspired by positive psychology, to help individuals become more aware of the capacities they already had to function effectively in relationships.

Over the course of 2012-2013, every THORLO employee became engaged in the strategy process through the ICCs. The mindset at all levels has shifted from "we are having a conversation about strategy" to "the conversation is the strategy." Information is flowing continuously among nested ICCs that include both cross-organizational processes and range across time horizons, potentially touching on new business development (a long-term horizon), organizational optimization (a medium-term horizon), and implementation (a short-term horizon) in a single conversation. Depending on the ICC, this conversation occurs on a weekly or monthly cycle, creating a continuous flow of information through all levels of the company.

## EARLY RESULTS

Over the past two years, the cultural shift that has occurred in THORLO as the result of this Harmonic Vibrancy Move has affected all of the company's employees in some way. Eventually all have been engaged in the process through collaborative leadership and the ICCs. The language we developed for the handbook now permeates how they talk about everything. While our Thorlorized terms will mean little to someone from a different culture, this language has made our agreements explicit and part of THORLO's everyday dialogue. When I visit the company these days, I hear a lot of O Process language. People talk about supporting each other in being their higher selves or bringing out more of their contributions, about seeing possibilities and converting them to probabilities, and about the diversity in the room. I also hear lots of use of the word "agreements" and the concept of choosing agreements, as well as frequent references to the three levels of perceived reality.

Many employees have made their own personal leadership declaration, committing to developing their own potential co-creatively within the community. The role and growth conversations described in Chapter 3 support them in making this move. These came about within the context of THORLO's cultural shift. As people began to notice inconsistency between the established practice around performance and compensation reviews and the far more supportive ethos of the ICCs, the old approach had to give way.

Within the community, the greater clarity and higher levels of commitment have helped people function more effectively, because they have greater awareness and understanding of what they are doing and take more responsibility for how they are acting. These changes, within the context of the structure-process of nested ICCs have produced some significant business results.

## EFFICIENCY

At first, THORLO folks have told me, it felt like they were in endless conversations, moving from one ICC to the next. Soon, however, they noticed two things. First, much of the information flow and decision making was happening more seamlessly because of the nested flow of the ICCs, from more strategic to more tactical, from the front end through to the back end of the business, on a continuous basis. Second, in the informal, between-ICC conversations, people were much better informed and focused on doing meaningful work that is on-purpose and aligned. Decisions bring everyone together, in appropriate contexts (ICCs) to deal with dimensions of issues specific to an ICC and then those feed into other issues in other ICCs, on a fluid, continuous basis.

As a result, there have been far fewer "surprises," unwelcome events that used to disrupt the whole system because nobody was expecting them. Potential problems now surface in the conversation and get dealt with early on. In Ecosynomics terms, THORLO has reduced its costs of scarcity, experiencing far fewer of the inefficiencies that result from not operating at the higher levels of harmonic vibrancy.

## EFFECTIVENESS

The implementation of ICCs has helped everyone have greater clarity on what to do and greater success in doing it. The co-hosting role has worked to ensure that each conversation stays focused on its local ICC purpose and that everyone remains clear about how that relates to the shared higher purpose. That connection is part of the conversation most of the time. Now THORLO folks ask each other, in most conversations, to get clear individually and as a group about why they are doing what they are doing. While this now occurs in about ¾ of the conversations, it continues to be a learning process. In the cases where the ICC is not yet as effective, the difference is felt. The co-hosts are using that experience of the felt difference as an opportunity to see what still needs to be understood about their agreements, in order to shift those less effective ICCs, hoping to achieve a higher percentage of ICCs experiencing higher states of harmonic vibrancy and outcomes. For the co-hosts, this is a process of shifting the unconscious to the conscious, so that it can be seen, let go, and another agreement chosen.

In addition, there is conversation at the CULICC level on a daily basis about the shifts being experienced in direction and alignment of the nested sets of ICCs. When something new emerges, such as the response to a request for a new product or service, it is possible to adjust quickly, both within a specific ICC and across ICCs, to align the local purposes with the shared higher purpose.

## INNOVATION

The co-hosting function in the ICCs also ensures that each group has the requisite diversity of voices in the room and that everyone is aware of the unique contributions each person is expected to make. This discipline has everyone in the circle looking for creativity in each other, inquiring into insights and inviting them in. It seems they are now almost addicted to this inquiry and to the exhilaration they experience when creativity shows up, which it does on a regular basis. In addition, because of the continuous overlapping flow of information, anything learned in one ICC immediately flows to the others. For example, a process innovation that proves valuable in one group, such as "presencing the consumer at the beginning of the ICC" or seeking out "anything that has surprised someone since the last meeting" quickly spreads to other groups.

## RESILIENCY

A key aspect of resiliency is the ability to respond to changes that emerge in the business context. Because of the deep trust in each other and the experience that any issue that comes up will be dealt with purposefully, quickly and transparently, the interweaving of the ICCs now makes it relatively easy for THORLO to respond as a unified whole when shifts occur in its environment. For example, when there was no snow in the winter of 2012, all the ICCs were able to work together to respond quickly to this big, unexpected challenge, which affected every aspect of the business. No snow meant no ski-related products moving off the shelves in stores, when a lot had already been manufactured and was being shipped. The different ICCs were able to respond together, rapidly responding to the short-term needs of the retail customers.

## INFLUENCE IN THE SUPPLY CHAIN

THORLO's ability to influence its suppliers and biggest customers has increased exponentially since the start of its cultural change. Recently, the company has negotiated agreements for co-management of inventory with a number of giant customers, in a mutual risk-taking model. This model means that THORLO takes on much of the risk in the retail-consumer relationship with the big-box store. It has to be very flexible in response to the stores' needs for particular styles, volume of product or in-store displays. Most of THORLO's competitors are in the commodity business of selling large volumes at low profit margins. They do not have the internal processes or flexibility to respond quickly to this type of retail risk, so they cannot make a mutual risk-taking kind of commitment. THORLO can, and the ICC is critical to its being able to do so.

## LESSONS LEARNED

In this company-wide learning lab, I was able to work directly with the four lenses and incorporate the concepts and language of Ecosynomics transparently into the Harmonic Vibrancy Move process. I saw how these perspectives, ideas and terminology, when Thorlorized, enabled the company to move into the outer circle of harmonic vibrancy. In the process, I realized that the main contribution of Ecosynomics was to provide a framework that helped the folks at THORLO become more conscious and effective in doing what they were already doing. As I have said before, many people are making moves toward greater vibrancy and abundance. The Ecosynomics perspective helps us see how these efforts are similar and different, and how we can learn from all of them.

THORLO is a small, privately owned company. Yet I am finding similar kinds of re-structuring happening in large groups within publicly traded corporations, such as a global bank I work with in Mexico. It seems that more and more there are "conscious capitalism" types of movements afoot, promoting learning, development, and awareness as strategic to the business. I also see lots of groups working with the idea of "conversation" as the strategic move.[138]

JLT is an unusual business leader. Yet more and more business owners are investing for sustainability, fairness, and resiliency. Over the past decade, many of the companies singled out for being both successful and great places to work have started from a premise that it is important to create higher vibrancy relationships with their customers, their employees, and their supply chain, as well as their investors. Their questions seem to focus on where to invest in the

---

138    See, for example, a recent *Harvard Business Review* article on "Leadership Is a Conversation as Leadership" (Groysberg & Slind, 2012).

organization to create these better relationships. Indeed, that is the million-dollar question today. The THORLO story and the Ecosynomics framework offer some answers for that.

* * *SIDEBAR* * *

# THE O PROCESS

Over the years, colleagues have taught me much about good processes for building collaboration.[139] I have distilled these processes into an overarching process with six elements, which I draw out in Figure 37. After enough people began to call it the "O Process," because of its shape, the name stuck. The O Process supports two forms of alignment that I have found critical to deep collaboration. The first alignment is within six areas, and the second alignment is across them. I find that most high performing groups have strength in both alignments, that most mediocre and weak groups have little of either, and that people working independent of each other have none of either.

### Deepest shared purpose

I first seek to find and make transparent the alignment that exists in the deeper purpose that everyone involved finds important. Whether it is the health of children in a school community, a feeling of patriotism among citizens of a country or Brand Stewardship in THORLO, something brings the stakeholders of a specific interest together. When people see they are aligned around this deeper purpose, they can also define a common goal, even though they came into the process seemingly at odds with each other.[140]

---

139    This framework evolved out of my many years of working with Scott Spann (Spann, 2008; Spann & Ritchie-Dunham, 2008).

140    The broad category of process and content tools for aligning around shared purpose describe the hidden purpose and shared values that are already present. For a broad overview and integration of specific processes for forming and working with shared objectives and values, see (Hammond, 1996; Keeney, 1992). Recent case studies highlight the benefits of shared purpose, as reflected in the "extraordinary economic and social value" they found in their study of 33 higher-ambition CEOs (Foote, Eisenstat, & Fredberg, 2011).

State of
**CURRENT SHARED POSSIBILITY**

**O**

**Understanding of
Probabilities**        *Thinking*
                       *Cognition*        **Understanding of
                                          Possibilities**

**Committment to
Contribution**         *Relation*
                       *Emotion*          **Values &
                       Feeling*           Contributions**

**Action**             *Intention*        **Deepest Shared
                       *Willing*          Purpose**
                                          *

**U**

State of
**CURRENT SHARED REALITY**

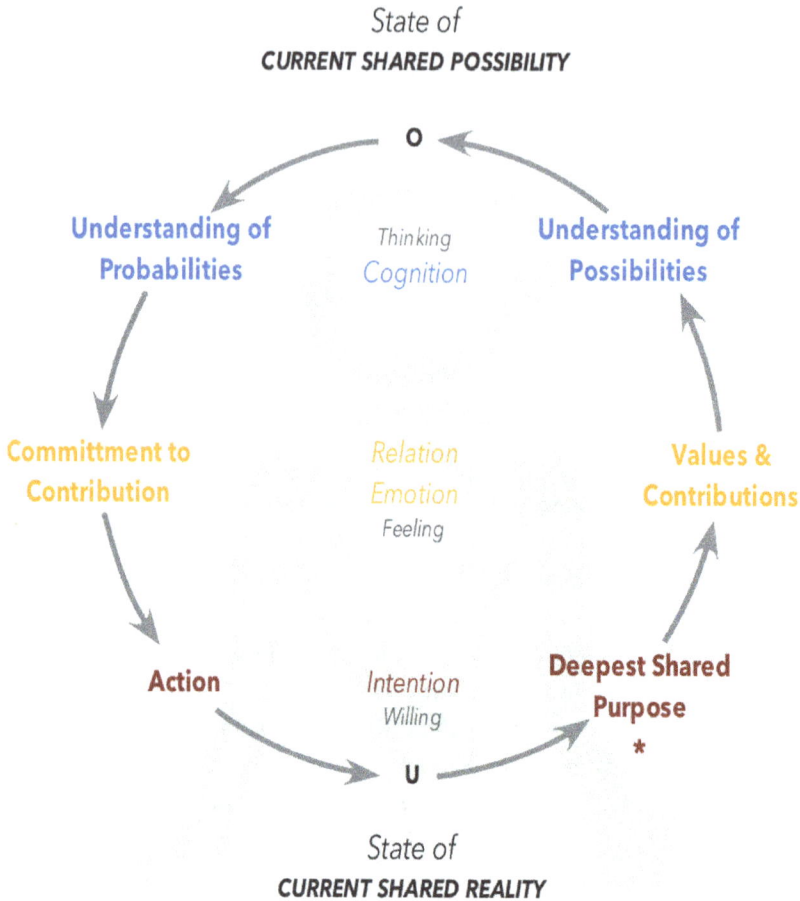

*Figure 37: O Process for Collaborative Alignment*

### Values and contributions

Sharing this deeper purpose allows everyone the freedom to contribute his or her creative best, like the individual players in a jazz group.[141] As in a jazz group, so in any group with a shared purpose, each person can make a unique contribution. In most situations, people tend to value only their own contributions, believing that others are wrong-headed, a waste of resource, or secondary in importance at best. Building alignment around values and

141    See Barrett's exploration of collaboration through the metaphor of jazz (Barrett, 2012).

contributions involves helping people see each other's unique contributions. This validates the other's existence, builds appreciation and strengthens the trust that comes out of seeing a shared deeper purpose.[142]

### Understanding of possibilities

Similarly, each group member brings a unique perspective on what is possible. Given the specific knowledge and experience of each group member, no two will see the same possibilities. When I remind the group that the different perspectives in the room are unique and necessary to address the shared deeper purpose, everyone comes to recognize the distinctions each person makes as valuable. They can see the different textures they each contribute to the picture of the "whole" possibility that emerges for them as individuals and as a group when they are addressing the shared deeper purpose. Alignment around seen possibilities highlights how these are different perspectives on the same future reality.[143] From this recognition emerges an awareness of the *state of current shared possibility*.

### Understanding of probabilities

When there is alignment on these first three areas—shared purpose, values and contributions, and shared possibilities—something incredible emerges: shared probability. This is the fourth alignment. When it occurs, everyone involved sees the same future, and that future begins to become "real." This happens when people begin to dedicate resources to something, way before it shows up physically. Many processes support the putting together of possibilities into forms that make the probabilities easier to see.[144]

---

142    Tools that align the values and contribution of others focus on: (1) the ability to see and appreciate another human being; and (2) the designer's ability to see how different parts fit together. The broad fields are inquiry and systemic design. For more on emotional and social intelligence, see (Goleman, 1995). For more on appreciative approaches to inquiry, see (Cooperrider & Whitney, 2005; Torbert, 1994). For more on systemic approaches to design, start with the classic treatise that influenced many schools of design (Alexander, 1964). To see that each individual has his own values and plays a functional role, the distinction of part versus whole is useful, best described in systems language as a functional part and a whole (Ackoff, 1993) and in integral language as a holon (Koestler, 1967; Wilber, 2000).

143    The broader category of tools that align possibilities focuses on collaborative idea formation. De Bono provides two classics on appreciating different perspectives (De Bono, 1971, 1999).

144    The conversion of possibilities to probabilities deals with different forms of sense-making—How can I know what I think until I hear what I say?—characterized by the social psychologist Karl Weick (Weick, 1995).

### Commitment to contributions

As the new reality seen with others begins to sink in, it comes into the relational space where people begin to make commitments to contribute what they can to this shared future reality in alignment with the deeper purpose they share.[145] Part of the commitment to being in the group is the commitment to participate, in both the seeing of possibilities and the manifesting of the probabilities. Since this is the work of the group and the individuals in the group, everyone is looking for what they can contribute to making the probability a reality. "What can I do?"

This part of the O Process focuses on what is required for taking on action items. It is about what the individual sees as the unique contribution his or her voice can make to the realization of the shared probability. "What part of this is mine?" This step engages the relational-feeling dimension we invited into the process in the second step of *Values and Contributions.* Now, however, we are calling on this dimension to play a part in moving people to take up the manifestation of what they have envisioned together.

### Action

Having made commitments for specific contributions, it is time for action. To act in alignment requires alignment around the will to go back to one's own world and do something. When the culture "back home" supports these actions, because they fit with what is already being done there, taking on actions and completing them is relatively easy. In many cases, though, the new collaborative probabilities seen require commitments to action that are not consistent with the existing culture back home. For people to take these actions, then, they require support from the group.

As individuals in the group move to action in support of their shared probability, they experience that they are all working in the same *current shared reality.* As one member of THORLO's CULICC put it, "We are all working, in our own way on our own actions, towards the common thing. We are in the same, shared reality, right now." This experience is very different from the feeling of action taken when everyone's action item emanates from a separate reality and serves a separate purpose. But, as in the THORLO case, there can be an experience of working in a shared reality. When the O Process creates

---

145    Most good processes have some form of commitment making, following some form of the RACI (responsible, accountable, consulted, informed), or the "atom of work" by Flores, which provides processes for making and keeping commitments ("Using the Methods of Fernando Flores, an Interview of Jack Reilly," 1997). Also see (Connolly & Rianoshek, 2002)

alignment within and amongst each of the six elements, people experience this higher state of current shared reality. This is a powerful motivating force.

Some people I have worked with say, "We do that," meaning that they work through the O process. Yet, when I explore what they actually do, I often find that they start at the cognition level of possibility and wonder why nobody shows up at the relational level of commitments or the intention level of action. They are missing the point that they need alignment on the right-hand side of the O in order to convert the possibilities into probabilities that people will commit to and take action. When I have seen the full O process engaged, however, it releases extraordinary power.

It seems that people shy away from alignment on all six elements, because they think it will take longer. Yet this alignment actually accelerates the process, leading to much greater efficiency, effectiveness and innovation. The efficiency comes from the fact that people are pursuing probabilities they have co-created in the service of a goal they think is important. There is no need to waste time and energy pushing them into doing things they do not want to do; they move willingly to action. Greater effectiveness comes about when people align on the purpose they share and on what they each uniquely contribute to that shared higher goal. Innovation shows up because everyone present saw and contributed their unique perspective, providing a richer environment of possibility in which the probability emerged. Greater efficiency, effectiveness and innovativeness from a bit more alignment would seem to be a great investment.

\* \* \* \* \* \*

CHAPTER 12

# MAKING A MOVE WITH DIVERSE STAKEHOLDERS

We have now followed the Harmonic Vibrancy Move processes of several individual lives, a small team and a small company. I suspect that many people have experienced or can imagine working toward positive change at those levels of scale and complexity. In contrast, the story I will share in this chapter describes a societal-level change effort, an initiative to bring about a radical shift of energy policy and behavior at the state level, in Vermont, USA. Change at this scale and complexity is something relatively few people are likely to have contemplated, much less experienced firsthand. Yet there are many such initiatives taking place around the world today in communities of all different sizes.[146]

These may be called dialogue processes, conflict transformation, public deliberation or many other things. However, they all involve bringing together representatives of all the people who have a significant interest in an important issue—"the stakeholders"—to share their different perspectives and figure out a way to address that issue together. The facilitators of such processes may see their work in terms of building society's capacity for collaborative problem solving; while the people who organize, support, participate in, or are just aware of these stakeholder processes tend to define them primarily in terms of the particular problems or issues they address. This was certainly true of most of the people who participated in the initiative in Vermont. From an

146    For information on the many stakeholder processes around the world, see Pruitt and Thomas (2007); the website of the National Coalition for Dialogue and Deliberation, www.ncdd.org; and the United Nations Development Program website, www.democraticdialoguenetwork.org.

Ecosynomics perspective, however, every problem-solving effort is at heart an effort to move out of the inner circle of scarcity, and the capacity to solve problems collaboratively is part of a larger set of characteristics of groups operating in the outer circle of harmonic vibrancy. In other words, all of these processes are essentially Harmonic Vibrancy Moves.

This is not to say that participants in the Vermont energy initiative or other stakeholder processes thought of what they were doing in Ecosynomics terms, nor that they rigorously followed the four-step process I have presented in this book. They did not. Nevertheless, a basic assumption of all stakeholder processes is that people can agree to act differently and produce different outcomes. Stakeholder processes also, more or less intentionally, engage participants in working with the five relationships and the three levels of perceived reality. We can therefore place them within the Ecosynomics framework and learn a great deal from studying and comparing them in those terms, even though they may be radically different in terms of the issues addressed and the specifics of the processes followed.

At the time I became engaged in supporting the Vermont initiative, in the fall of 2009, the work at THORLO I described in Chapters 10 and 11 was in its early stages. My thinking about the four steps of the Harmonic Vibrancy Move process was still evolving. Scott Spann and I had recently developed and used the O Process in a stakeholder initiative in Guatemala with the humanitarian organization CARE, and I was holding the question of how the O Process and other tools could contribute to a Harmonic Vibrancy Move.[147] Vermont was an important learning laboratory for me.

## SEEING A DIFFERENT POSSIBILITY

In 2009 Anne and Arthur Berndt, co-trustees of the Maverick Lloyd Foundation, and Jennifer Berman, the foundation's executive director, asked themselves a question: "can we develop much more systemic responses to our most challenging issues in Vermont?" In Ecosynomics terms, as they pursued this question, they took the first two steps of a Harmonic Vibrancy Move. This was the origin of the Vermont energy initiative, which became the Energy Action Network.

One of the larger philanthropies in the state, Maverick Lloyd was a leading force in a network of hundreds of not-for-profit organizations working to

---

147    You can read more about the CARE work in Guatemala in great detail (Ritchie-Dunham, 2008b), in the context of business strategy approaches to poverty alleviation (Ritchie-Dunham, 2008a), or as a learning history (Waddell, 2005).

address social, economic, and environmental challenges. As the result of a myriad of independent initiatives undertaken by these organizations, Vermont led the country – and the world – on many fronts, especially in next-generation responses to energy efficiency and renewable energy. For example, Vermont created the first energy efficiency utility, which makes money by taking watts out of the system through increased efficiency rather than by providing more and more energy to the system like most utilities. Vermont also led the nation in the percentage of its electricity coming from renewable energy sources, in part because of its aggressive regulatory policies. Yet, while these relatively large steps had moved Vermont ahead of the pack, Anne, Arthur and Jennifer felt that much more was possible. To them it seemed that a small state like Vermont, with fewer than 700,000 inhabitants, should be able to undertake a more coordinated, collaborative effort aimed at more aggressive goals for more radical solutions. They saw a gap between the current state of renewable energy and what they believed was possible. What would it take to move the state to the next level?

Holding this question, they searched nationally for groups that had done the kind of large-scale change effort they envisioned for Vermont. The search led to RE-AMP, an initiative that started in 2005 with a multi-stakeholder process, designed and led by Scott Spann, my colleague in work with CARE Guatemala. RE-AMP had produced a regional network involving more than 100 non-profit organizations and foundations across eight states in the upper Midwest. This network was pursuing a variety of projects in the areas of clean energy, coal, energy efficiency, global warming solutions, and transportation, with the ambitious goal of reducing regional global warming pollution by 80 percent by 2050. In short, RE-AMP was the kind of process Maverick Lloyd wanted to see in Vermont.

Through this connection, in the fall of 2009, the foundation found me and my colleagues, Mary Day Mordecai and Ned Hulbert, at Growing Edge Partners.[148] Our task was to support Maverick Lloyd in bringing the diverse, competitive, and sometimes fractious group of stakeholders in Vermont's energy system on board with the vision of stepping up to a new level of collaboration in order to achieve much more dramatic results.[149] One of my chief lessons from the Guatemala initiative, reinforced by my ongoing experience at THORLO, was the necessity of having a strong core group to

148    For more on the systems process that led to RE-AMP, see ⟨http://innatestrategies.com/docs/REAMPFinal.pdf⟩. For the current status of RE-AMP, see ⟨http://www.reamp.org/⟩. For more on the Growing Edge Partners process, see ⟨http://growingedgepartners.com/⟩.
149    Vermont's strong tradition of independence and mutuality is well documented in many statewide processes and surveys. For example, see the reports "Imagining Vermont: Values

host others in making this kind of shift within a large stakeholder system. I had learned this lesson in Guatemala by experiencing the problems associated with not having such a group in place. Fortunately, Mary Day and Ned brought lots of experience in the formation of a hosting leadership group that could sustain itself over many years.

## HOSTING THE PROCESS

As we began working with Maverick Lloyd, we quickly discovered that the task of forming a leadership group that could sustain an effort to define and realize a long-term, state-wide aspiration required tackling head-on the widely-held assumption within the state that certain individuals and groups of Vermonters would simply never be able to collaborate. We needed to start somewhere, however, and the convening power of Maverick Lloyd within the small circle of large philanthropic organizations in the state made it possible to do so. Initially the foundation assembled a handful of people from other leading foundations to consider what the goal of a possible project could be. This was a group that, if it decided on a change initiative, would be able to raise the funding necessary to underwrite it and, possibly, to convene a larger leadership group to carry it forward.

Over the next couple of years, three key elements would enable this small planning group to succeed in bringing in more leaders and stakeholders, and in moving the project to definitive action steps. The first was the audacity of the goal they defined–making Vermont's energy sources 100-percent renewable by 2030. The second key success factor was the ability to convene and form a diverse set of people into the leadership and stakeholder groups. Confounding all the assumptions about the impossibility of getting key actors to work together, they were able to include all of the voices that needed to be part of the conversation. The high level of harmonic vibrancy in the quality of leadership that the convening group provided was the third success factor. As the process unfolded, Ned, Mary Day and I witnessed a growing energy and capacity for collaboration, based on a growing alignment among people who started out highly skeptical that they would ever be willing to work together.

---

and Vision for the Future" at the Council on the Future of Vermont (http://futureofvermont. org/). Vermont's state motto is "Freedom and Unity" (see http://www.leg.state.vt.us/statutes/ fullsection.cfm?Title=01&Chapter=011&Section=00491).

## DEFINING THE GOAL

The small planning group convened by Maverick Lloyd reviewed the challenges facing the state. Focusing on the economic wellbeing of Vermonters, they considered which issues were sufficiently large-scale and required a systemic approach for significant change to occur. They decided on energy production and use, focusing on renewable energy.

To get specific about the goal, we used an exercise of looking at the degree of change required and the time horizon for that change. This exercise helped the planning group understand the gap between where they thought the state was headed and where they thought it needed to be. It was in this conversation that the group realized that, despite all of their hard work, a huge outlay of resources, and incremental progress in each of their areas on the advancement of renewable energy, they were not achieving their desired goals. They saw clearly that seriously addressing renewable energy issues in the state would require a fundamental shift across all the efforts in the state. Their current, independent activities would not change Vermont's energy supply and demand sectors fast enough.

The change-over-time exercise helped clarify this realization, by helping the group specify the degree of change needed and the degree of urgency. The group realized that it wanted to see a complete shift, which had to happen within the next generation in order to realize their goal. This led to the goal of making Vermont's energy portfolio 100-percent renewable by 2030. Some members of the planning group felt this goal was too audacious, but other members said, "We need to suspend disbelief, choose the boldest goal we can, and explore what it will take to get there." While there was much conversation about the political liability of such an aggressive goal, the group came to the agreement that it made a bold statement and pointed the initiative in a very specific direction. In this way the goal could serve as a rallying point for change, around which the group could invite others into the process.

## INVITING IN DIVERSITY

Next, the planning group set about building a leadership team that could convene a larger stakeholder process and carry an initiative forward over the period of years that would likely be required for success. The group selected carefully. All of the key energy sectors needed to be part of the mix. This included government agencies dealing with environmental and energy issues; elected government officials at the local, state and federal levels; non-profit organizations working on energy issues in the state; the electric utility industry; groups involved in developing renewable energy; the state's large employers; and the state university. Somehow the group also had to reflect the full political spectrum. The individuals representing the different sectors had to be prominent enough within their sectors to be able to influence opinion, and if necessary, bring others into the process. Finally, all the participants needed to be able to agree to be part of a multi-year process.

We formed a list of a dozen candidates whom the planning group members agreed to contact, often in pairs. For the most part, they chose to contact those people with whom they already had some connections or personal experience. At the next planning group meeting, they reported the findings from their interviews with the candidates, and we had the ten members we wanted for the leadership team. All ten members knew each other well, since they were all active leaders at the state level in different aspects of renewable energy in Vermont. They welcomed the chance to pool their efforts towards the shared audacious goal of "100 percent by 2030."

Many people had told us that it would be difficult or impossible to get the amount of time we wanted on these busy people's calendars. Yet once they saw who else was to be on the team, they made the time, often telling us something to the effect of, "I wouldn't miss working with a team of this caliber for anything." We also found out as the process moved forward that, for many of the ten individuals who eventually joined the leadership team, the goal of 100 percent renewable energy was a positive motivator, an indication that the conveners of this process were serious about achieving great things for Vermont.

## DEVELOPING HOSTING CAPACITY

With the official launch of Energy Action Now in 2010, the planning group passed the project on to the leadership team that would be responsible for carrying it through. The leadership team met a few times to build relationships among themselves, build their vision for the project, agree to the project design, and scope out whom to invite into the larger stakeholder conversations. Over the course of these meetings and the ensuing steps of inviting in the other stakeholders, the team came to see itself not so much as leaders but as hosts—the same transition the leadership team at THORLO had made the year before.

The team members realized that, unlike previous Vermont initiatives, they would not be individually leading a like-minded group towards fairly narrow and quite specific objectives. This time they were acting as a team to convene a diverse group of people, representing many conflicting perspectives, in order to pursue an extremely audacious goal. Through this realization, they came to see that they could not tell people what to do or even what they should try to achieve. Rather, they needed to invite people into a very broad exploration of possible pathways towards a shared future they would envision together.

The diversity of participants, each with a specific local perspective, strongly suggested the analogy of hosting a party, a party of very different people invited to figure out together what their future looked like and how to get there. When this connection was made, the leadership team realized it was hosting the broader stakeholder group more than leading it.

As the leadership team prepared to assemble a still larger stakeholder group, it did its own review of the goal. What did all the terminology mean? Was it doable? Were they willing to put their names on something like this? They agreed to stick with the 100-percent goal, but to make it tentative, pending conversations with a wider range of stakeholders.

## CONVENING THE STAKEHOLDER GROUP

The team was determined to be rigorous in its effort to ensure that all the key elements of Vermont's energy system were represented in the conversations on how to achieve the goal. This is a crucial step for any stakeholder process, and there are a variety of approaches to the task of "stakeholder mapping," which involves determining all the relevant actors in a situation, and as much as possible, the relationships among them. My colleagues and I supported the leadership team in taking a system-dynamics approach to this task. Through extensive discussions and a broad-ranging literature review, we helped them create a schematic map of Vermont's energy system (see Figure 38). Through many iterations of working with this map, they identified what perspectives had to be part of the mix and which individuals in the state could best bring those perspectives into the project.

(1) large-scale, (2) massively local

Supplier Shareholders

Supplier Satisfaction

National Security

Blockers and Drivers of Change

Venture capital Investors — Equity

Income

Affordability

Quality of Life

Home

Banks — Debt

Investment in Infrastructure

Demand Cycle

Community

Tax Incentives

Supply Cycle

Consumer Satisfaction

Large corporate

Rate

Reliability

Regulator Satisfaction

Education of Leaders and Population

Transmission

Land Use Same bldgs, new tech New bldgs

Distribution

Infrastructure

Supply of Renewable

Demand for Renewable

Political Influence

Efficiency

Energy Sources

Consumer Economic Activity

Economic job creation

Electricity

Heating

Transportation

Technology

Environmental Impact

Biomass Coal Fuel/Oil Geothermal Hydro Nuclear Solar Wind

Biofuel Woody Biomass Ag

Worldmarket Price Volatility

Distributed

Demand Management

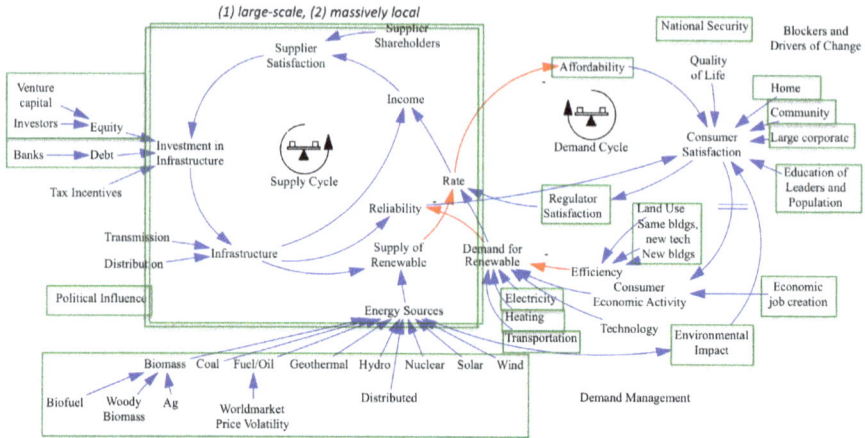

*Figure 38: Systems Process for Selecting Perspectives to Include*

Next, the team decided that each of its members would take personal responsibility for recruiting specific individuals into the stakeholder group. In the end, they surprised everyone, even themselves, with the diversity and comprehensiveness of the perspectives they were able to bring into the process—from conservative to progressive, small town to city, small to large business, civil society, government, bank and investment financing, local to national politics, electricity, heating, transportation, energy efficiency, and for and against renewable energy solutions. Many people whom we were told would not participate, because of old conflicts, rivalries or strong cultural differences, did in fact participate. In the later stages of the project, when new participants came in, more than one of them expressed amazement at joining people they never expected to see in a room together, much less collaborating on a change initiative. How did this happen?

What was clear to my colleagues and me as we observed this process was the importance of the hosting provided by the leadership team. The leadership team dedicated much effort and time to being clear, transparent, and open minded in working with the different stakeholders. They succeeded in creating a trusting environment in which very diverse and seemingly conflicting perspectives could be shared and integrated. This included inviting stakeholders who were long-term adversaries into the process and telling them how important it was to get their perspective into the group's understanding. This emphasis on the value of diversity helped shift the focus from warring perspectives to the richness and validity of different perspectives.

Many of the participants in the stakeholder group told us that it was the sincerity of the invitation that had brought them to the process, and the quality of leadership throughout a series of gatherings that kept them engaged and committed. It was also significant that the leadership team was open to redefinition of the goal by the larger stakeholder group. In this way, they established the principle of honoring all perspectives and set the stage for the emergence of strong alignment. When the full stakeholder group did its own analysis, it adjusted the goal to from 100-percent to 80-percent renewable energy by 2030. This was still audacious enough to make it clear the project would stretch the state's capacity to work collaboratively to address large, systemic issues and something everyone could fully embrace.

This is what leadership looks like at a high level of harmonic vibrancy. When sincerely hosted, people experience more of their own selves coming out, they experience more respect and support from and towards others, they experience a clearer contribution to the group, they experience the creativity in everyone, and they experience the grounding of inspiring possibilities. In Ecosynomics terms, they experience high levels of all five primary relationships and effectiveness at all three levels of perceived reality. They are functioning in the outer circle of the three circles of harmonic vibrancy.

The next phase of Energy Action Now would take the stakeholders through a collaborative inquiry into the details of the energy future they desired for Vermont, build on this early achievement, and move the group through all the steps of the O Process (Figure 39).

## SEEING POSSIBILITY TOGETHER

The shock people expressed at the diversity of the stakeholder group that assembled in September 2010 highlighted the challenge of getting the stakeholders to work together. The existing assumptions and agreements that sustained Vermont's small-scale, competitive-cooperative approach to addressing important issues facing the state would have to change. For this to happen, the process participants would have to start perceiving each other and talking to each other in new ways.

### SEEING THE SYSTEM AND EACH OTHER

As process facilitators, Mary Day, Ned and I supported this shift with a step that is common in stakeholder processes. Before the first stakeholder meeting, we conducted individual interviews with each of the twenty-four people who would be participating. The purpose of this exercise was to be able, when the group comes together for the first time, to reflect back to them a view of the whole that honored each person's perspective and uncovered areas of agreement that typically remained hidden behind the obvious disagreements. Providing this kind of feedback to a group is not unlike the hosting activity of "speaking the harmonic" that I described in Chapter 9. The mapping exercise also set the group up for embarking on the O Process, starting with a picture of the state of current reality.

In this case, we again took a system-dynamics approach. Our interviews focused on how the stakeholders perceived Vermonters' fundamental values, and the impact of energy on Vermonters as individuals, towns, and businesses. We also explored how the stakeholders thought about the environment, energy sources, regulation, and the funding of renewable energy projects, as well as how Vermonters were engaging with and learning about energy issues. Based on these interviews, we created a systems map of each stakeholder's perspective on Vermont's energy system; then we validated all of the maps with follow-up interviews with each stakeholder. Next we created a single map that integrated all of the perspectives, organized around five strategic considerations—goals, resources, actions, structure and people. Though not identified as such, the four Ecosynomic lenses were thus incorporated into this system map.[150]

The integrated map of Vermont's energy system was big, complex, and at first glance, quite impenetrable. Yet in the hands of the leadership team, it became a means of hosting the stakeholders through the O Process. To prepare for the first plenary session of the stakeholder group, the team examined this map of perspectives in depth. Then each member of the leadership team took responsibility for presenting one or more of the individual maps to the large group. The team made these assignments with the intention of creating some surprises for the stakeholder group. They made sure that each map's presenter was someone whom most in the group would see as unlikely to understand that stakeholder's perspective. As a map was presented, the "owner" of that perspective was invited to critique or expand upon the system captured in the map and the presentation of his or her perspective. This exercise was another way in which the leadership team set a clear example of open-minded inquiry and invited others to follow suit.

---

150    This is the GRASP framework, which has been applied in many strategic settings. For a detailed description of how to create a GRASP map, see (Ritchie-Dunham & Rabbino, 2001), and for many examples of its application, see (Ritchie-Dunham & Puente, 2008).

This format allowed everyone to hear what each stakeholder actually had to say about energy issues, rather than what they *thought* each other would say. We heard many times in this process, "I did not know that you and I cared about achieving the same goal, and I did not know what you were doing to contribute to that goal." It was through this mutual inquiry that people first began to see that they held similar values and a common aspiration for their state. They also recognized that each had a unique contribution to make toward achieving that aspiration. Once they agreed on the goal of 80 percent renewable energy by 2030, this understanding was critical for seeing the whole system and what could be done to shift it—in effect, for seeing what different agreements might be possible.

## MOVING TO THE TOP OF THE O

In processes such as this, there is often a discernable breakthrough moment, when the group makes a perceptible shift to a shared sense that something different is possible. For the Energy Action Now stakeholders this shift occurred midway through the second 3-day meeting. The stakeholders had broken into small groups by energy sector (i.e., electricity, heating, transportation, efficiency) to consider the feasibility of the 80-percent-by-2030 goal. As the groups reported their conclusions in a plenary session, one after another stated they could easily see how to reach the goal in their own sector, but could not see how other sectors could do so. The surprise and excitement in the room were palpable. Suddenly the stakeholders saw possibilities together that they had not seen before from their individual perspectives. They had moved to the top of the O in the O Process (see Figure 39).

From the first step of each stakeholder sharing his or her individual current reality, they had opened up to seeing all the separate realities and recognized a great deal of shared purpose underlying their separate perspectives and activities. With the guidance of the leadership team, they had become much more familiar with what other stakeholders brought to the system. This greater mutual awareness had opened their view to the possibilities in their own parts of the system and prepared the ground for the "ah-ha" moment of recognizing the much greater possibility existing in the system as a whole.

In Ecosynomics terms, the group had moved into a state of high harmonic vibrancy. From this position they could clearly see the limitations of the mid-level harmonic vibrancy agreements that had governed their prior efforts. They realized that they could come together with agreements at a higher level of harmonic vibrancy to achieve the more audacious energy goal they had defined, taking into account the state's renewable energy resources, how they could organize collaboratively, and the value Vermonters would experience from their success.

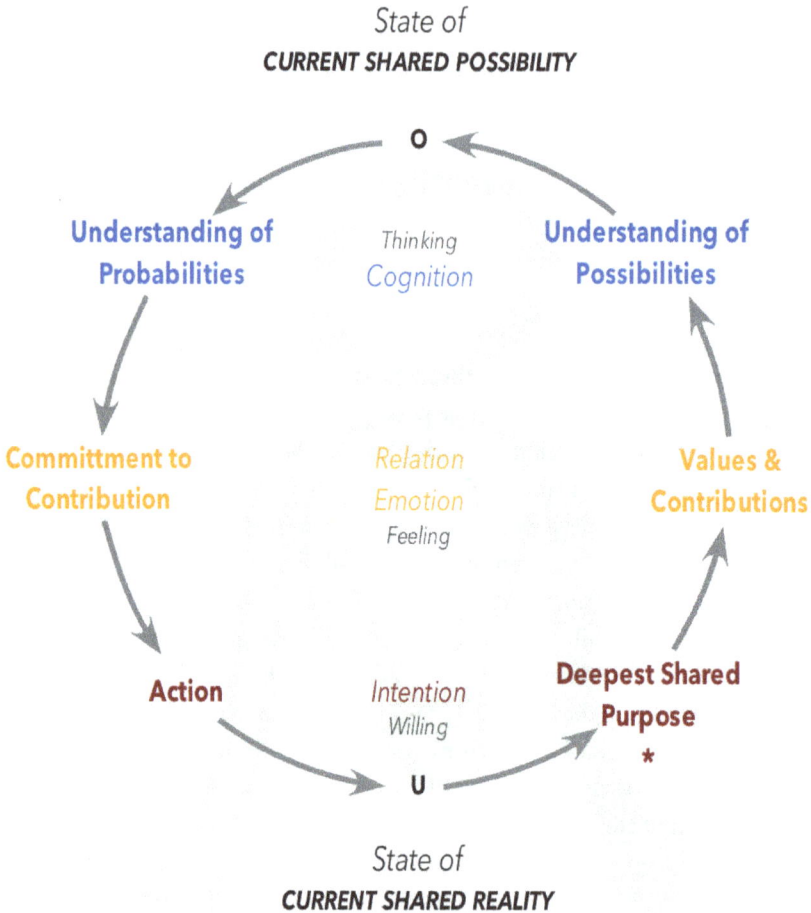

*State of*
**CURRENT SHARED POSSIBILITY**

O

Understanding of          *Thinking*          Understanding of
**Probabilities**          *Cognition*          **Possibilities**

**Committment to**          *Relation*          **Values &**
**Contribution**          *Emotion*          **Contributions**
          *Feeling*

**Action**          *Intention*          **Deepest Shared**
          *Willing*          **Purpose**
          U          *

*State of*
**CURRENT SHARED REALITY**

*Figure 39: O Process*

In the next step, the full group of hosts and stakeholders worked with the integrated form of the individual systems maps. They explored how the individual perspectives were interconnected, and how they influenced each other and the overall behavior of the system. It became clearer how they would each need to shift, in harmony with the others, to achieve the shift they envisioned for the whole system.

## MOVING FROM POSSIBILITY TO ACTION—THE GROUNDED POTENTIAL PATH

The move from possibilities to probabilities occurred in two steps. First, the stakeholder group worked through multiple iterations of analyzing and validating the integrated map of the energy system. Through this process, it identified a set of core system dynamics. Everyone agreed that these dynamics had to shift in order to move Vermont's energy system from its current, highly reliable and cost effective but "low renewable" portfolio of energy sources to a future, highly reliable, cost effective and "high renewable" portfolio. In Ecosynomics terms, having settled on a shared aspiration at the level of possibility-light, the stakeholders had begun to see what needed to happen at the development-motion level in order to produce outcomes at the things-matter level.

The group continued to work collaboratively with the integrated system map to identify the appropriate measures of overall health in Vermont's energy system. Next they agreed on which forces in the system most contributed to its health, and the points at which they could activate those forces to move the system in a positive direction. Based on this collective analysis, the stakeholder group converged on four leverage points for shifting the whole system. These were capital mobilization, technological innovation, regulatory and permitting policies, and public engagement.

Once it had clearly defined each of the four leverage-point areas, the stakeholder group took the second step, which was to launch four new stakeholder processes to develop initiatives in each area. It identified experts and key stakeholders in each area and created four teams to invite and convene the new stakeholder groups. Each team included hosting leaders, stakeholders, and experts in each leverage point area. When the expanded leverage-point teams came together in the spring of 2011, the hosting leaders shared the story of the project; how the original stakeholder group had moved through the first half of the O Process and the possibilities they had seen together. The hosting leaders then invited all the new participants into the exploration of how to convert these possibilities into probabilities and then move to action—the second half of the O Process.

In separate meetings conducted near Burlington, Vermont, the four leverage-point teams identified specific projects that could leverage Vermont's strengths and resources to achieve its audacious goal. This shifted the idea of a possibility, such as mobilizing capital or mobilizing public opinion, into a reality these experts and stakeholders could see as probable. Everyone worked to ensure that the recommendations from the teams were in alignment. Finally, the four leverage-point teams came together to share their recommendations and work out a unified action plan for the whole project.

## SHIFTS IN ASSUMPTIONS AND AGREEMENTS

Behind this seemingly straightforward process, there occurred many shifts in perspective and agreements; between individuals, between organizations, and across the state. The participants in the process saw, often for the first time, that they shared deep Vermont values. For example, two of the stakeholders who often went head-to-head in the state house saw that they shared the same "ends," they just disagreed on the "means." These ends were so important, and the means not so different, that they could agree to disagree—a shift for both of them.

Taking on the audacious goal of 80-percent renewable energy, across all four sectors, by 2030, was a galvanizing shift towards an aspiration they all had held yet none had believed possible. What was galvanized was a shift in agreements from working independently to working collaboratively toward that goal.

Many of the participants described the experience of that shift as moving from feeling responsible only for what they could directly impact, to feeling responsible collaboratively for all of the impacts across the state. As one participant described his shift, "I'm no longer just responsible for my results within the heating sector, rather for everything that influences our ultimate outcomes of sustainable sovereignty in deciding our energy future." Others talked about realizing that all four energy sources—electricity, heating, transportation, and efficiency—would be critical in achieving the goal, not just the one their own work addressed directly.

All participants agreed that accomplishing such an audacious goal would require systemic coordination across all four energy sectors and all four leverage points. The capacity for this kind of coordination did not exist in Vermont. Indeed, it could not exist under the old agreements by which change happened only through thousands of independent efforts. The stakeholders' committing to develop that capacity was a major shift. Towards the end of the process, it seemed that a new Vermont value became palpable in the group, expressed as "together we can and we must." While everyone held a deep appreciation of how this initiative built on all that had been accomplished before—innovative legislation and regulation, creative business innovation, an engaged civil society sector of non-profit organizations, and a committed citizenry—they also felt ready to move away from the previous mindset of "I will do what I can on my own."

## CONCLUSION

Energy Action Now concluded its work in June 2011, just as the governor of Vermont began the process of a new multi-year energy plan for Vermont, to replace the previous plan from 1998. Many of the stakeholders who had participated in our process were invited to help with this design. As they tell the story, they showed up to the governor's process with the recommendations from the four leverage-point teams, and were able to influence the state's new energy plan in a significant way. The Vermont Comprehensive Energy Plan was vetted in many public hearings and accepted in the late fall of 2011, after which the state created a system-wide coordinating body to support initiatives in the four leverage-point areas.[151]

From an Ecosynomics perspective, this stakeholder initiative sought to move Vermont from a medium level of harmonic vibrancy to a higher level, at which Vermonters could claim economic sovereignty over their own reliable, economic, low-environmental-impact energy future. Most people involved in the two-year project were clear that a move to a higher level of harmonic vibrancy was a move to a new game, and that this required playing the game by new rules, or new agreements. Moreover, all of the steps of the Harmonic Vibrancy Move process were part of this initiative, although I was not thinking of them in those terms at the time.

Identifying the gap took place at several key stages: at the outset, within the Maverick Lloyd Foundation; within the first convening group; and again, within the whole stakeholder group. In each instance, this activity provided clarity and inspiration in regard to the purpose of the initiative. Exploring the experience of others was also an important aspect of the process. This includes both Maverick Lloyd's initial search for models of large-scale collaborative

---

151    To see Vermont's Comprehensive Energy Plan 2011, visit (http://www.vtenergyplan. vermont.gov/).

processes, and the inclusion in the leverage-point teams of experts who could contribute knowledge of what was going on outside Vermont. All of the stakeholders' work with the system map was a deep dive into the third step of assessing their own experience, and this paved the way for the fourth step of defining and enacting a move, which was the convening and work of the leverage-point teams.

Most important perhaps, as the leadership team hosted the stakeholders through the O Process, they had a direct experience of the outer circle of harmonic vibrancy, working at all levels of perceived reality with all five relationships. As they moved around the O, the participants each saw their own unique contributions—past, current, and future—to a higher purpose. This gave them a positive experience of the relationship to self. By respectfully sharing each other's individual system map, they experienced supporting and being supported by other individuals, quite a different experience of the relationship to other from what they had been used to. Through their work with the integrated map, the stakeholders could each see how their individual perspectives came together and influenced each other within the larger system. From this integrated perspective, they could appreciate the value of each unique contribution to the whole, an experience of the relationship to the group that was far more powerful and positive than what they had experienced before. Moving along the grounded-potential path and seeing how possibility could move through development to concrete outcomes provided a strong experience of the relationship to nature. Finally, throughout this process, the hosting of the leadership team created an environment of abundant creativity, flowing from everyone in the group—a vibrant experience of the relationship to spirit.

My own experience with this stakeholder process helped me see how these steps fit together and contributed to a positive outcome in Vermont. In this sense, it helped me specify the Harmonic Vibrancy Move process as I have presented it in this book. More important, seeing the process work effectively at this scale confirmed for me the broad applicability of the principles of Ecosynomics. The processes that engage diverse stakeholders to work collaboratively on common issues represent an important phenomenon. They seem to show there is a pathway for moving society to higher levels of harmonic vibrancy. I believe societal change processes can be better understood—and perhaps become more successful—when placed in the Ecosynomics framework of agreements. I see the fact that there are so many stakeholder processes going on in such a wide range of situations as a sign, like the co-operative movement and the complementary currencies I discussed in Chapter 7, that people are already finding pathways to abundance and harmonic vibrancy. This makes me optimistic that our ability to shift agreements is growing.

# PART V

# AN ECOSYNOMIC VISION OF THE FUTURE

# CHAPTER 13

# COMING AROUND THE SPIRAL AND LOOKING AHEAD

## WHERE WE HAVE BEEN

We are approaching the end of this trip around the spiral. Starting with your own experience, you have become acquainted with the basic principles of Ecosynomics, seen how to apply them and shared in what others are learning from doing just that.

From the beginning of this exploration together, we have been clear that all human beings want to experience greater harmonic vibrancy in every aspects of their lives. In these pages we have uncovered what a Harmonic Vibrancy Move is, what it entails, and tools and processes for getting there. We saw that the critical starting point is the foundational assumption of abundance. This assumption changes everything.

From this starting point, we saw that we could shift our experience from scarcity toward abundance by shifting the underlying agreements. I showed you how to use the four economics-based lenses of resources, resource allocation, value, and organization to recognize the nature of agreements governing our experiences in the five primary relationships at three levels of perceived reality. With this perspective we saw we could identify the gap between our current reality and the level of harmonic vibrancy we aspire to, learn from the experience of others who have attained that level, and figure out how we could move there ourselves.

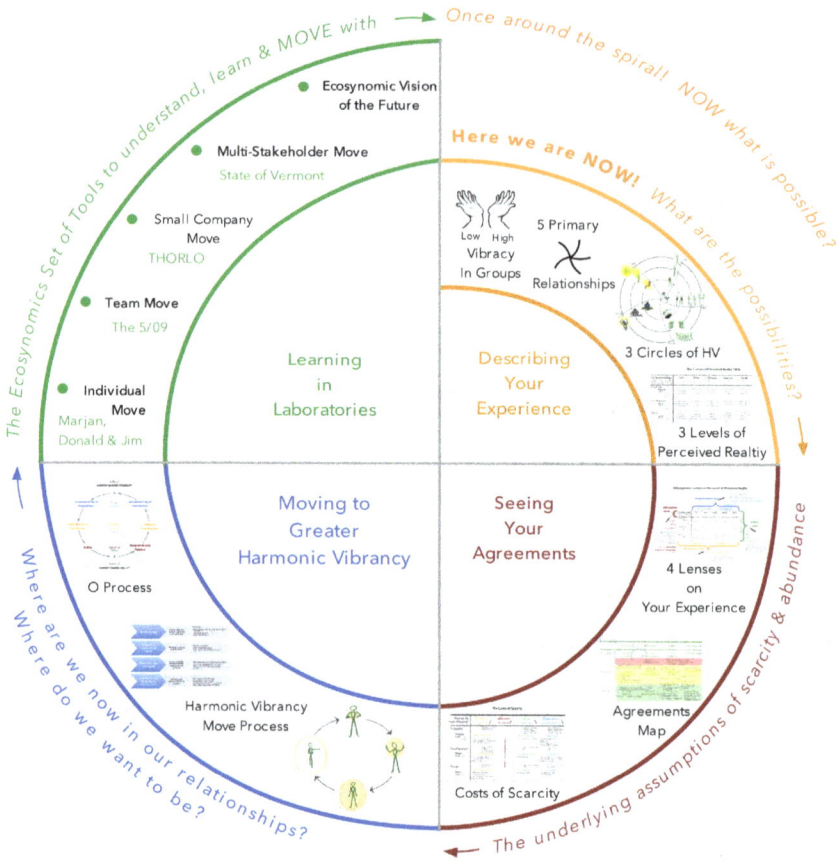

*Figure 40: The Pathway through the Book*

We looked at how the emergence of economics as a social science has helped bring tremendous material advances to millions of people over the past 250 years. We also saw how the pervasiveness of economics in modern societies has contributed to the scarcity so many of us experience in our daily lives. Just as important, we saw how the Ecosynomics framework enables us to recognize a wide range of seemingly unrelated innovations as Harmonic Vibrancy Moves, and to appreciate the large scale and broad scope of this movement toward abundance. As the social science of Ecosynomics continues to develop, we will gather the information needed to compare how these moves are made. We can then develop much greater understanding of what works under different conditions, so that more and more people can benefit from this process.

Now we are ready to embrace one of the highest principles of humanity—freedom, the freedom to choose the agreements we enter into. We can now see the why, what, and how of this choice. Why—because we want to experience greater harmony, vibrancy, and abundance. What—we will enter agreements based on what we see when we look through the four lenses at the five primary relationships and the three levels of perceived reality. How—we will shift agreements through the Harmonic Vibrancy Move. This means choosing the experience we know is possible in these relationships, learning from the experiences of others who are already living that possibility, and deciding how we will go about bringing the possibilities to the level of outcomes. Now we are ready to move.

## WHAT I SEE COMING

In presenting Ecosynomics, I have suggested that we know a great deal and are continuing to learn about choosing agreements that enable the high-vibrancy experiences we know are possible in our relationships. People often ask me what I see emerging in the future as more and more people take on these agreements. In the remaining pages, I will share my vision of what is possible as people apply Ecosynomics more broadly, and what needs to shift to facilitate this. I will also describe what I am doing to help realize this vision—and what you can do.

### WHAT IS POSSIBLE

The process of understanding and choosing agreements described in this book is something I have personally experienced and witnessed in a wide variety of groups. As a result, I now believe that every person born on this planet can have—and deserves—the experience of a greater level of harmonic vibrancy. I envision millions of people, within the next thirty years, recognizing their own experiences of scarcity and abundance, and seeing the agreements that underlie them. I see these people choosing abundance-based agreements and learning from others who are already figuring out how to create such agreements. Finally, I foresee all of this learning resulting in a massive shift in harmony, vibrancy, and abundance—a shift to a higher level of harmonic interaction, where people experience greater vibrancy in what they deeply value and greater abundance in the resources available.

Throughout this book, I have introduced you to many of the authors, leaders, organizations and citizens around the world who are already beginning to see and understand the scarcity and abundance in their lives. Many of these people, as they move into greater awareness of their own agreements, are starting to share their experiences. We are seeing self-reports of "what we did" as well as secondhand reports from scholars, who are noticing the broader patterns of what is emerging in these new agreements. Social media is greatly accelerating this sharing, allowing communications in text, audio and video to spread virally across virtual networks such as FaceBook and YouTube. Millions of people around the world can now witness the high-vibrancy experiences of others and begin to see how they might create similar experiences for themselves.

As developmental psychologists explain, people grow in maturity through their shift in perspective that such a recognition event can bring about. Conditions that previously went unnoticed, that were experienced subjectively as "the way I am" or "the way things are," now become visible through this framework. These conditions can now be seen more objectively and consciously acted on or chosen. This is the process I see happening when people recognize the agreements they have accepted and begin to engage their will, to shift scarcity-based agreements to healthier forms, or to take on new agreements.

I want to change the questions we ask when we wake up in the morning, from "How well can I do today relative to my neighbors?" to "How am I moving toward my own light-potential?" This will start to happen as more and more people begin to connect the dots between the Harmonic Vibrancy Moves that are already in progress, and to share their stories in a common language and framework of understanding. In the next thirty years, many expect the world's population to grow to more than nine billion. I suggest all of these people deserve the experience of higher harmonic vibrancy.

Given the extent to which people across the globe have become connected through electronic communication, I believe most of these people will have access to knowledge of what they need to do to make a move to a higher level, no matter where they are. The question here is how to support these moves for all people.

## WHAT NEEDS TO SHIFT

In order to support a global shift to higher harmonic vibrancy, a couple of changes in how we think about societal structures will be necessary. First, we need to redefine the criteria we use for evaluating the outcomes produced by human activity. In addition, we need to revise the charters of the institutions that provide structure for that activity. The existing standards and charters evolved under the influence of economic thinking. We can now rethink them from an Ecosynomics perspective.

### Standards for evaluating outcomes

In the world organized on economic principles, the "gold standard" for judging the results of human endeavor has three elements: efficiency; effectiveness; and innovation. In economic terms, these are typical indicators for assessing how successful people are in managing scarce resources, always with the goal of getting more out of those resources. As we move to organizing our activities on the principles of Ecosynomics, we will still need standards to help us know how we are doing. I suggest we can continue to use the economic concepts of efficiency, effectiveness and innovation; but redefine them as indicators of how well we are managing the transformation of possibility-light through development-motion to things-matter. In this case, the overarching goal is to create and sustain health in the five relationships, at all three levels of perceived reality. I propose this redefinition as a shift from a gold standard to a "light standard."

Efficiency is simply a ratio of outputs to inputs, what you get out for what you put in. Higher efficiency is better. If you can sell a cake for twenty dollars (the value of output), it is better to spend just ten dollars to make it (the value of inputs) than to spend fifteen. The gold standard for economic efficiency measures the units of value generated per unit of cost. This is an assessment of the amount of things in and the amount of things out—both at the things-matter level. To achieve greater efficiency, one either increases the value generated while keeping the costs the same or decreases the costs while producing the same value. This model of efficiency leads smart people, with the help of technology, to increase the size of their operations. This achieves competitive advantage through what are called economies of scale—the ability to produce many more units of output without increasing input. This drive for economic efficiency has contributed greatly to the predominance of large-scale businesses we see today. While this competitive focus is fine at the things-matter level, it is limited in its capacity to produce the relational health everyone wants at the development-motion level.

The Light Standard for Ecosynomic Efficiency measures the units of possibility-light transformed through development-motion into things-matter outcomes per unit of effort put into the transformation. This is an assessment of the transformation of light into motion into matter (the output) and the effort put into the transformation (the input). There is a direct analogy between this standard of efficiency and the way we measure the conversion of energy from light, in watts of power. In physics, power is the amount of energy, or work, per unit of time. The total energy available includes potential energy (a potential form) and kinetic energy (a movement form), both containing mass (a matter form). As opposed to the economic efficiency ratio of things-out/things-in, Ecosynomic efficiency is determined by the ratio of energy-out/energy-in. This shift highlights the efficiency of the effort to convert from the possibility level into the development and then outcome levels. Since this is a ratio, with the same units in both the numerator and the denominator, it is the energy-equivalent of work or effort.

In the Ecosynomic efficiency model an output would be the energy released from experiencing the value of seeing one's future potential, beginning to develop it, and seeing the early fruits of it. For example, you might experience a great degree of pleasure from imagining that you could play the flute, then practicing, and then hearing the music flow from your flute. This is the output energy, the value experienced, in all three levels.

The input is the effort put into it, in this case measured in terms of the number of hours or the degree of effort invested. Again, higher Ecosynomic efficiency is better. The pleasure-value experienced in seeing that you can indeed play the flute, enjoy developing your skills at playing, and enjoying the resulting music—is far greater than the energy released from simply playing, without perceiving the value in the potential and in the development.

Engaging in an activity in a manner that releases energy in its potential, its motion, and its matter forms is completely different from assessing value only at the matter level. Matter-level efficiency looks at just matter-to-matter conversions, missing potential and movement energy. This formulation allows you to assess the light-motion-matter energy realized from the energy put in. This is literally working with the power of possibility. Light-standard efficiency leads to organizational forms of interaction that seek to maximize the conversion of the potential already available in the resources at hand. Economic efficiency can now be recognized and used as a subset of Ecosynomic efficiency.

We can rethink the economic gold standard for effectiveness in much the same way. Effectiveness means the achievement of a goal. Economically, this is most often characterized in terms of the amount of stuff accumulated, for example, the money we get from wages, the car we may buy, or even the knowledge we gain in school or at work. This is things-matter focused effectiveness. In Ecosynomics, the Light Standard of Effectiveness focuses on the goal of closing the gap between the current level of harmonic vibrancy in the five relationships and the level we aspire to. To close the gap (defined in step 1 of the Harmonic Vibrancy Move process) one begins to work more consciously with agreements in the three levels of perceived reality for all five primary relationships (step 4 in the process). We saw how this can work in various examples in this book. Ecosynomic effectiveness is achieving the closing of the gap. Economic effectiveness—how much stuff is accumulated over a set period of time—can now be seen as a subset of Ecosynomic effectiveness, a step on the path to closing the gap.

The gold standard for innovation focuses on the inputs and outputs of economic efficiency. Innovation is coming up with new ways to generate value. Some innovations create value by reducing inputs relative to outputs, for example, through improved processes or technology. It takes far fewer hours of human labor to produce a million socks today than it did two hundred years ago, because of the technology. Other innovations create value by increasing outputs relative to inputs, for example, by developing new uses for an existing product. Your mobile phone used to be only for receiving phone calls; now it serves as a computer, a camera, a wireless network, and it receives phone calls. Whether innovating on the inputs or the outputs, the focus is on the outcomes level: fewer things in and more things out.

Ecosynomics suggests a Light Standard for Innovation, focused on increasing the value experienced in transforming infinite possibility through development into things, moving among the three levels of perceived reality. One form of light-standard innovation focuses on the range of value experienced. In addition to experiencing the value of innovations at the outcomes-things level, as in economic innovation, value can also be experienced in innovations that include light-to-motion-to-matter transformations, innovations in movement across the three levels of perceived reality. For example, like we saw in Chapter 11 at THORLO, the innovation in assessing a person's performance shifted to a dialog which included the person's potential, her development over time, and the outcomes she achieved: an innovation that interwove all three levels of perceived reality.

Another innovation, co-hosting, which I also described in Chapter 11, was an innovation in more efficiently presencing all three levels of perceived reality in a group, requiring far less time and effort than methods the group had tried earlier. Ecosynomic innovation gives a broader context for economic innovation.

### Institutional structures

From the Ecosynomics perspective, the purpose of any group is multi-dimensional. First, people come together as a group to generate greater value together than they can individually. To do this, the group grows its potential to develop its abilities over time and thereby increase the value it can generate. The group does this by building cohesion, both within the group and with other groups it interacts with. The group makes this effort because it desires to increase the wellbeing of the community it serves and the community in which it resides. Said another way, every group has a charter for growth, for social cohesion, and for social wellbeing.

These different dimensions of the group's charter depend on different processes within the group. The growth charter focuses primarily on the transformation of possibility into motion into matter, the grounded potential pathway. The choice of which pathway to use, among the three possible pathways defined in Chapter 2, is the terrain of the allocation mechanism lens ("who decides?"). The social cohesion charter focuses primarily on the value experienced in the five relationships in the organization of human interaction. This is the area viewed through the value lens ("by what criteria?"). The social wellbeing charter focuses mostly on the value experienced in the resources the group can access. This is observed through the lens of resources ("how much?"). Together, these three charters enable the group to manifest the potential seen at the possibility level, through development, as concrete outcomes at the things level.

All groups, to exist, inherently have this multi-dimensional charter. Yet most of the institutions we live with today define their purpose in terms of only one of the dimensions and minimize the value of the other two. Legal structures and regulations exist to define and control these one-dimensional institutions. All of this has created a starkly divided society.

The people who create and run organizations that have taken on the for-growth charter are often very entrepreneurial. They tend to be great at identifying and creating self-reinforcing structures that sustain the organization's ability to support its own growth. These self-reinforcing structures generate surpluses, which can be re-invested in the structure for its own (self generated) growth. A typical example is the reinvestment of a business's profits to sustain its own growth. Existing fiscal and regulatory systems support this seeking of self-growth mechanisms with incentives and controls that favor the business corporation. For example, organizations chartered as for-growth benefit from tax laws that promote profit maximization and reinvestment. They also receive protection from "excessive" liabilities through the legal structure of the limited-liability corporation. These rules focus on encouraging the growth of value generated over time, and give great latitude to whether or how business organizations deal with the dimensions of social cohesion and social well being which—most do not.

Other people want to build and work with organizations that take on the charter of social cohesion as a way to contribute to stronger relationships and community through their work. They try to create stabilizing structures that will promote balance amongst the five primary relationships and make them less vulnerable to shocks in the system. These stabilizing structures watch for behaviors that stray from the desired state, like a thermostat, and take action when the gap between the desired and actual states grows. For example, as the number of homeless people increases, the number of non-profit shelters also increases to give them a place to sleep, reducing the number of people sleeping on the street. When the number of homeless people decreases, so do the number of shelters serving them. In another example, many groups support long-term caregivers, like those caring for a spouse with Alzheimer's. To support these heavily burdened individuals, the caregivers, and to keep them from collapsing into the inner circle of harmonic vibrancy, many of these social groups provide an experience of healthy relationship in all five primary relationships, where the caregiver experiences being seen as a caring individual who is making an important creative contribution to the life experience of their spouse.

Some societies believe in the importance of these efforts and support them by offering a legal charter that honors the mission of social cohesion, while making few if any demands regarding self-supporting growth or societal well-being. Some of these charters restrict self-funding growth. For example, these organizations may be strictly audited in their sources and uses of funds to ensure that they are serving society and not the specific desires of the organization. Hence the organizations are identified as "nonprofits." The organizations that are chartered for social cohesion may also be called, collectively, "civil society." This means they are pursuing a society of and for all citizens, on an equal footing.

Another set of institutions consists of those chartered to serve the wellbeing of everyone in the group. They provide services that other groups want or need, but that fall outside the scope of the for-growth and for-social-cohesion charters. The people who want to build and work in these institutions tend to be those who want to focus on social wellbeing. The fiscal and legal structures supporting these organizations promote redistribution of resources for the purpose of the general welfare, while minimizing the focus on self-funding growth and social cohesion. For example, they can collect taxes and enforce the payment of those taxes by citizens. They can also regulate for-growth and for-social-cohesion organizations, usually through highly structured, bureaucratic organizations. This is the government sector.

Individually and together, the institutions operating with these single-focus charters do many things well. They do not, however, deliver the abundance and harmonic vibrancy we all want. Why? Ecosynomics suggests two reasons.

First, they are imbalanced in their focus on only one charter and inattention to the others. These current structures all require legal charters and strong regulation to make sure that their imbalanced structures do not hurt themselves and others. For example, for-growth business is regulated to control the negative consequences of its inattention to social cohesion and social wellbeing. Economists call these "externalities." Likewise, social-cohesion organizations are highly regulated to make sure they collect funds and use them only for charitable purposes, and not for their own growth or personal wellbeing. Government organizations are watched closely by outside groups to make sure the taxes they collect are used well, since they tax without the ability to support their own growth.

Second, the division of societal institutions into sectors with three distinct roles is based on an incomplete model for organizational forms. This multi-sectoral model suggests that society will be well served if corporations focus on growth of capital; civil society focuses on social cohesion; and government focuses on group health, through management of the commons. Ecosynomics suggests that every group should operate on a single charter, which encompasses all three areas: growth, social cohesion, and societal health. I call such a group the "Inspirited" organization. This name draws a clear contrast to the existing organizational form, called "Incorporated" in English, which signifies that the organization is legally a body (corpus) with specific rights and protections. The designation in-spirit means that the organization recognizes the deeper nature of being, including all three dimensions of perceived reality and serving all five primary relationships, through all three charters, as one: a move to a higher or sustained level of harmonic vibrancy.

CHAPTER 14

# WHAT WE CAN DO AND AN INVITATION TO YOU

To shift the experience everyone has to a higher level of harmonic vibrancy is going to take a lot of work by everyone. In the past few years, a group has formed to support this work—the Vibrancy Network. This network includes individuals and organizations working with Ecosynomic principles on research projects, in their consulting engagements with their clients, and in the articles they write. In some places, there are a few people working on these efforts together, like in Germany, Mexico, and the USA, and in other places they are still working alone. They are connected through conversations they have in groups over the Internet, and through project work where they get together in specific locations around the globe. For example, a few individuals and two companies just met in North Carolina to visit at THORLO, while others are meeting for a project this spring in Mexico, and others are meeting for a project in South Africa. This network is growing quickly, from just a few researchers, consultants, and companies two years ago in two countries, to thousands of people in dozens of groups today in six countries. I expect this will continue to grow quickly as this network's impact grows. In this section, I will describe what my colleagues in the Vibrancy network and I are doing to support a global shift, and how you can contribute too.

In thinking about how to support people making the shift, I see four distinct groups needing different kinds of support, based on four different orientations. The first group is composed of people who want to make the Harmonic Vibrancy Move on their own. For support, they just want some ideas on what to do and how to make the move, and they are most likely to look for this advice in books or courses. The second group is made up of individuals who want someone to do it for them or with them. They want an expert to guide them. These people will hire a consultant or expert to help guide them. The third group includes people who want to make the move with others who are like-minded. They are likely to seek learning partners, for example by joining communities of practice, joining societies, or going to conferences. The fourth group consists of people who want to learn about what we are learning and become involved in the continuing research. They are likely to seek out an academic expert or centers of excellence, where they can join others in researching the questions they have. Based on this analysis, our strategy is to develop the network and knowledge in each of these four areas, with specific Vibrancy meeting places for each, so that we can enable people across the globe to make the flip from unconsciously accepting scarcity-based agreements to consciously choosing abundance-based agreements.

## IF YOU ARE MAKING THE SHIFT ON YOUR OWN

My colleagues and I in Vibrancy Content, the meeting place in the Vibrancy network where we focus on content, want to help you in making this flip on your own by supporting you in the moment of realization that you can choose your agreements. To do this, we are contributing frameworks, such as those presented in this book, to provide the lenses through which you can see and shift your experiences, agreements and outcomes. We are also providing well-documented stories, illustrating how others have made the shift. Finally, we are using multiple content channels—the Internet and apps for mobile devices, as well as print media—to make this content accessible to everyone.

We envision that within ten years, there will be tens of thousands of people like you, sharing their stories of what they are learning and experiencing in books, blogs, and articles for popular magazines and scholarly journals. To support these content providers we find along the way, we have created Vibrancy Content, which has started by providing the *Ecosynomics* book and book-course, a short documentary, and my blog. We are also developing a mobile app that will support people in working through the four-step Harmonic Vibrancy Move process, allowing them to access the content they need for the questions that arise during the process.

You can contribute directly to this Content effort by sharing your story and your reflections about the ideas and applications in this book. You can do this through the Vibrancy community or other networks. However you choose to contribute, we invite you to let the global Vibrancy community know about your content contributions through harmonicvibrancy.com. There you can contact us, connect us to your blog, and use our Facebook page to post your vibrancy moments and case studies, and share articles you have written or found relevant.

## IF YOU ARE MAKING THE SHIFT WITH SOMEONE'S GUIDANCE OR WANT TO GUIDE OTHERS

If you want someone to guide you along the path, accompanying you as you take the steps toward the agreements that support a higher level of harmonic vibrancy, you would traditionally turn to the world of advisors and consultants—experts in the process. Or you might be interested in learning more about the Ecosynomics framework and how to guide others through making the shift.

To support the millions of groups that will be consciously choosing abundance-based agreements in the next decades, there will need to be tens to hundreds of thousands of such process experts across the globe. Whether or not they explicitly use the Ecosynomics framework, these experts will need to be working from an abundance-based perspective. And as a community of abundance-based practice emerges, it will need well-tested processes. Hence, it must be at the forefront of finding and developing the innovative practices that groups around the world are experimenting with in their new agreements, much like the ones I have highlighted throughout the book.

We have created a group called Vibrancy Process to support and encourage the development of this community of process experts. Within Vibrancy Process, we have developed tools for the Harmonic Vibrancy Move process, some of which I have shared in this book. You can find other processes on my blog at jlrd.me and at harmonicvibrancy.com. In those two websites, you can also find Vibrancy Process groups forming around the globe, including well-developed groups already working together in Germany, Mexico, and the USA. You can contact these Vibrancy Process individuals and groups for direct support in your own process, to meet and work with like-minded experts, and to participate in periodic learning circles.

In addition, to support Vibrancy Process people like you in your development of the Ecosynomics/Harmonic Vibrancy toolkit, we have created the Ecosynomics Certification program. This provides four levels of certification, each step of which offers a higher level of capacity development, access, and responsibility within the global network. You can learn more about this at harmonicvibrancy.com.

You can start with the tools I provide in this book, at the Ecosynomics.com book-course, and on my blog. You can adapt these tools to your own toolkit. You can also get certified as an Ecosynomist yourself. If you have worked through the Ecosynomics book-course, of which this is the last chapter, you are almost done with Level 1 of the certification (see harmonicvibrancy.com).

You can also contribute to the Vibrancy Process effort simply by supporting others in making the conscious choice to live in abundance-based agreements. Wherever you do that—at work, in your community, with your friends, or at home—you are doing the work of Vibrancy Process.

## IF YOU ARE MAKING THE SHIFT AND WANT TO MEET OTHER LIKE-MINDED PEOPLE

You may be like many people my colleagues and I have met in the past few years, who express shock when they discover, through the Ecosynomics framing, that they have discovered a pathway to higher levels of harmonic vibrancy and outcomes on their own. While they somehow knew it, this framing helped them see it more clearly. In most of these cases, the people have eventually asked us if there were others out there working at a similar level of agreements, experiences, and outcomes. You also may be interested in meeting these like-minded explorers, as you often have felt very alone in your persistent pursuit of abundance-based agreements. Meeting others like yourself provides you with both a "sanity check" (you are not crazy!) and a community of practice.

Within a few years, we envision hundreds of these communities of practice meeting all over the world to share both what they have learned in making their own shifts, and what they are learning in projects they develop together. Some of these communities of practice might be geographically centered, like the German, Mexican, and USA Sharing groups that are already forming. Or they might focus on industries (e.g., sustainable agriculture, textile, or banking). Or they might come together based on the level of harmonic vibrancy they experience.

You can engage in Vibrancy Sharing by creating your own community of practice where you live, or by joining one of the existing communities, which you can find at harmonicvibrancy.com/meet-like-minded-people. Either way, we would love to learn about what you are learning as you work together within your community of practice. Please share your stories by contacting us at harmonicvibrancy.com or posting on the Harmonic Vibrancy Facebook page at facebook.com/harmonicvibrancy.

## IF YOU ARE INTERESTED IN LEARNING MORE ABOUT WHAT WE ARE LEARNING

The fourth area of focus, or meeting place, is for people like you who want to keep abreast of what we are learning as we delve into the emerging field of abundance-based agreements. My colleagues and I want to engage with you as we broaden and deepen our understanding of the Ecosynomic framing of agreements, the experience of harmonic vibrancy, the outcomes achieved, and the shifts from one level of agreements and experience to another. Building on the frameworks, processes and cases presented in this book, we envision diving much deeper into the essence of human agreements, the character of humans as beings of light (*Homo lumens*) and the patterns emerging among the individuals and groups making the flip from scarcity to abundance.

We see thousands of case studies being shared in the coming decades, describing what all of us are learning. We envision millions of responses to the harmonic vibrancy survey, characterizing the broad trends emerging across the planet. We also see Ecosynomics applied to many different fields, as we are already doing in the area of money-currency-banking. Renewable energy, medicine, business models, sustainability, governance, education, aging, youth mentoring, and social-impact investing are all likely fields for this. To support this global effort, we foresee circles of researchers forming out of abundance-based principles, bringing the harmonic of their unique voices, so that we can more clearly see the emerging innovations.

As part of this research effort, we have created Vibrancy Insights, via the Institute for Strategic Clarity, a 501(c)(3) nonprofit research and education organization formed in 2003. Through Vibrancy Insights, we have developed the Ecosynomics framework you have explored in this book. We have documented what we have found in dozens of groups around the world and in the over 1,700 responses to the harmonic vibrancy survey. We share these Vibrancy Insights findings and related publications on my blog, jlrd.me, and at ISC's website, instituteforstrategicclarity.org. We are also working to integrate the work of Vibrancy Insights with that of Vibrancy Process, Vibrancy Content, and Vibrancy Sharing. These three other Vibrancy meeting places (Content, Process, Sharing) have data to share with the Insights group about what is emerging on the forefront and, in turn, they are platforms for sharing what is developed in Vibrancy Insights.

You can contribute to this part of the effort by reflecting on your own experiences and bringing the frameworks of Ecosynomics and Harmonic Vibrancy into your own research. Whether you do this research on your own or with Vibrancy Insights, we invite you to share what you are learning with the Vibrancy Insights group, by contacting us directly or posting to the Harmonic Vibrancy Facebook page, facebook.com/harmonicvibrancy. In addition, we, as researchers, will need to translate these abundance-based ideas, frameworks, processes, and examples into many languages, including the technical languages of specific fields such as banking, law or environmental science. You can play a huge role there, too. You can contact us at harmonicvibrancy.com.

To achieve this audacious vision of shifting the level of harmonic vibrancy for everyone on the planet, we need all of you to make the shift with us. Please take what you know and what we have shared with you into as many realms as you can, so that others can find access to this emerging field as well. Whether or not you choose to engage directly with the Ecosynomics framework, know that every choice you make based on an assumption of abundance is another step in the direction of higher vibrancy for us all.

# APPENDICES

# APPENDIX 1 – GLOSSARY

**Abundance.** Having plenty in life, including both tangible and intangible resources. The levels of reality one perceives also define abundance. Abundance-in-sufficiency means having enough right here, right now, as perceived at the things-outcomes level. Abundance-in-positive-net-flow means a net positive rate of flow, where more comes in than goes out, as perceived at the development-motion level. This is the United Nations definition of sustainability. Abundance-in-potential means infinite potential, as perceived at the possibility-light level.

**Agreement.** The word agreement comes from the old French agrément, which means, "pleasing." It is defined as: an arrangement between two or more persons as to a course of action; a mutual understanding; a covenant; concord; harmony. In other words, it is a social arrangement that people enter into willingly because they have had a hand in shaping it and it pleases them.

**Allocation mechanism.** A mechanism for allocating resources or productive assets. Allocation mechanism theory suggests optimal designs for allocating scarce resources, within a given political economy, in the most efficient way—the most value for the least cost.

**Collaboration.** People contribute their unique gifts toward a shared purpose that transcends operational effectiveness. Everyone is participating and contributing creatively to imagine future possibilities in all five relationships on a continuous basis.

**Competition.** The word competition comes from the Latin root for "striving," striving to be better than others. People strive to win something by defeating others who are trying to do the same.

**Cooperation.** People work together toward a similar outcome.

**Co-opetition.** Cooperative competition, where people work together on one level and compete on another.

**Economics.** From the Greek for the "laws of the household," or the "rules of relationship." It is the science of the allocation of scarce resources.

**Ecosynomics.** From the Greek for the "laws of relating together," or the "principles of collaboration."

**Harmonic vibrancy.** The experience of human well-being, simultaneously in the relationship to self, other, group, nature, and spirit.

**Harmony.** The degree of agreeable feeling or accord in how a group's agreements fit together.

**Nature.** The levels of perceived reality.

**Nomics.** From the Greek for "rules" or "laws." Rules determined at the whim of the ultimate leader.

**Organization.** A group of people with a specific shared purpose. It is a structure of processes with specific principles for how people interact with each other.

**Resource.** An accumulation of something that can be used for another purpose. The factors of production that are the input to the production process.

**Scarcity.** A state of lack, or not having enough. Restricted in quantity.

**Spirit.** The source of creativity.

**Value.** What something is worth to someone. Its importance or usefulness.

**Vibrancy.** The quality of being resonant. The sense of vitality in flourishing relationships.

# APPENDIX 2 – AN INTEGRAL VIEW OF ECOSYNOMIC AGREEMENTS

Many of the readers of this book might be familiar with the "integral" perspective of the American philosopher Ken Wilber. For those readers, there might be some confusion between the five primary relationships I present in Chapter 1 and Wilber's four perspectives. This appendix attempts to clarify the difference in the two approaches and how the "integral" approach provides an additional tool with which to understand the experience of the five primary relationships.

I consider myself a student of Wilber's brilliant work, and use it to deepen my understanding of what we are learning in Ecosynomics. In essence, Wilber has developed a perspective on the human experience, which shows that what may seem like divergent, conflicting perspectives of an experience are actually convergent, complementing perspectives. He does this through an "integral" framework that interweaves different perspectives and developmental levels in one framework, which has now provided deep insights in many fields of study.[152]

## RELATIONSHIPS AND PERSPECTIVES

You experience vibrancy in your relationship to your own self, to others, to the group, to nature, and to spirit. To understand more deeply the experience we have of these relationships, we need a very brief, slightly technical detour. We approach our experience of the five primary relationships we have to our self, the other, the group, nature, and spirit, from two very different angles.

These two angles, known as relationship and perspective, seem very similar, yet they are not. For simplicity, we will distinguish between what we *feel* in the experience of our heart, body, and awareness and how we *think* about that

---

152    The development and application of Ken Wilber's framework can be found in his many books (I recommend that you start with Wilber, 2000) and the Integral Institute that he founded (http://www. integralinstitute.org).

experience. We experience with relationship and we think with perspectives. While this is an oversimplification of the rich ways we make sense of our world, it is useful to distinguish relationships from perspectives. Relationships allow us to see that we experience, directly, our self, the other, the group, nature, and spirit. We are born with this capacity of direct experience; everyone has it, and everyone can tell us what he or she is experiencing in each of these relationships.

There are also multiple perspectives one can take on how to understand our experiences in each of these relationships. For example, we can start with the experience of the relationship you have to your own self. Let us look at the four overall perspectives on that relationship. First, we can look at your own inner, subjective experience—what you inwardly see that nobody else can see. This is the realm of your beliefs about your own potential and your ability to step into your own gifts. Next, we can also look at your behaviors: what is outwardly, objectively observable about you and your relationship to your self. This is the realm of seeing how you actually treat your self. These first two perspectives are those you have of your self, as an individual.

These perspectives are also interwoven with the group's perspectives. There is a cultural perspective, which is the inner, subjective perspective of how the group supports your relationship to your self. In this realm, the culture might be supportive of your continuous exploration of your own potential. Or perhaps, the culture might suggest that paying attention to your own self is a waste of time, and you should focus on others. And finally, there is an outwardly oriented, objective perspective of the structures and processes in the group that support or influence your relationship to your own self. In some groups, there exists a culture of developing your own potential that is supported by observable structures and processes, such as mentoring programs and training. However, in other groups, the structures and processes give incentives only to "get to work" and stop wasting time on frivolous navel-gazing. These are four perspectives, or four ways of making sense of your experience of the relationship you have to your self. We will now take an integral look at the agreements in all of the five primary relationships. We will start from an all-quadrants perspective, and then take a developmental, all-levels lens.

## AN "ALL-QUADRANTS" VIEW

There are multiple ways we tend to relate to our experiences of harmonic vibrancy, in general, and through the five relationships described above. Integral theory shows us that what may seem to be completely different experiences of each of the five relationships are indeed four different perspectives of the same experience. Here we use the word "perspective" to mean a way of seeing something. Ken Wilber suggests that we can look at human experience from: (1) either the individual's or group's perspective; and (2) either the inner, subjective or outer, objective perspective. By putting these two dimensions on two axes, he created the four quadrant model of perspectives (see Figure 41).

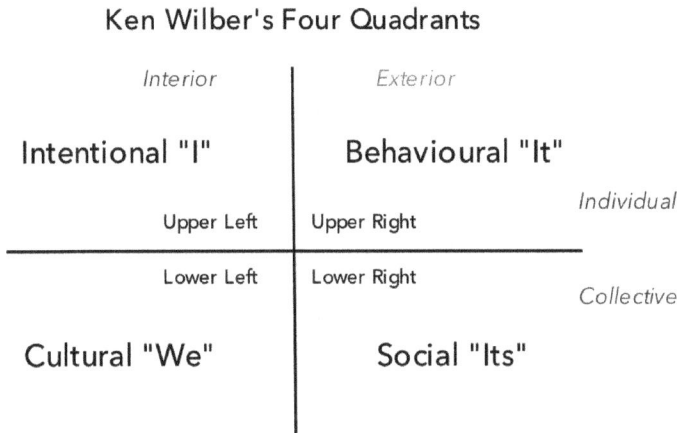

## Ken Wilber's Four Quadrants

| Interior | Exterior | |
|---|---|---|
| Intentional "I" | Behavioural "It" | *Individual* |
| Upper Left | Upper Right | |
| Lower Left | Lower Right | *Collective* |
| Cultural "We" | Social "Its" | |

*Figure 41: Ken Wilber's Four Quadrants*

Each of these four perspectives (ways of seeing or understanding an experience) has a long and well-developed field of inquiry supporting its practice; and thus we can learn from these perspectives, by showing what each brings individually and collectively to more richly describe the experience of each of the five relationships, as shown in Table 1, below.

In the first row, the inner-individual perspective sees the five relationships as different manifestations of the self: self-in-self, self-in-other, self-in-group, self-in-nature, and self-in-spirit. The outer-individual perspective, in the second row, is how an individual inwardly experiences the outer "it" of the five relationships: from one's own body/head-mind for the self; to the heart-mind for the other; the gut and group-will for the group; life-force-awareness, the sense of balance and movement for nature; and finally to the subtle to causal energies for spirit. The inner-group perspective, often referred to as culture, expresses the support for: liberty for the self; equality and pluralism for the other; solidarity for the group; eco-balance for nature; and transcendence for spirit. The outer-group perspective, where the social systems and processes in place are a reflection of the group's inner awareness, expresses itself as: free markets of creativity for the self; justice and rule of law for the other; cooperatives and central control for the group; ecosystems for nature; and religion-as-narrative for spirit.[153]

| Relation ship | Self | Other | Group | Nature | Spirit |
|---|---|---|---|---|---|
| UL Quad (Inner Individual) | self-in-self | self-in-other | self-in-group | self-in-nature | self-in-spirit |
| UR Quad (Outer Individual) | own body, head mind | heart mind | gut, group will | life-force awareness, balance, movement | subtle to causal energies |
| LL Quad (Inner Group) | liberty | equality, pluralism | solidarity | eco-balance | transcendence |
| LR Quad (Outer Group) | free markets | Justice, rule of law | Cooperatives central-control | ecosystems | religion-as-narrative |

*Table 1: Wilber's 4 Quadrant Perspectives as applied to the Five Relationships*

This integral perspective of the five relationships shows us that there are different perspectives or ways of studying each relationship. Each of these perspectives comes from a very different discipline and brings very different insights. What is interesting for us, right now, is to start to see how they show us different perspectives on the same experience. For example, when different expert perspectives describe the relationship to one self, they highlight different aspects. Psychologists and spiritual teachers might focus on the self-in-self, while doctors and physical therapists might focus more on one's own body, the mind as head, and specific behaviors. Sociologists might describe the same relationship from the culture of freedom that supports it, while economists might focus on the social structures and processes of free markets. These are all simply different ways of seeing, describing, and supporting the same phenomenon.

---

153    Through the four quadrant framework of perspectives, Wilber shows how the nature-nurture debate simply points at the nature (neurological, outer-individual) and the nurture (cultural, inner-collective) perspectives of the same experience (Wilber, 1998).

## AN "ALL-LEVELS" VIEW

The five relationships find very different expressions at different stages of ego-consciousness (see Table 2).[154] It remains an open question whether or not there is a direct correlation between a person's predominant stage of ego consciousness and the level of harmonic vibrancy they experience in a group. Observation suggests there are many people with access to later stages who reside stably in scarcity-based worldviews, and that there are many people who act from earlier stages who reside in stable forms of abundance. What seems to be clear is that actively and stably accessing later stages allows for the choice and subtlety of what can be observed. Nonetheless, this remains an open question for research. I thank Susanne Cook-Greuter for a multi-year, continuing dialog that has helped me explore this question of whether access to later stages of ego consciousness ensures the ability to express higher levels of harmonic vibrancy for oneself and in one's group, or whether it merely nurtures the possibility.

| Level of Agreement | Unitive Based Ironist (6th P) | Construct Based Alchemist (5th P) | Context Based Strategist (4th P) | Economic Based Achiever (3rd P) | Rules Based Diplomat (2nd P) |
|---|---|---|---|---|---|
| Relationship to Self | • I contribute by seeing the beauty of all opposing and interdependent poles and accepting things as they are<br>• I create original maps of time/space<br>• I embrace paradox | • I contribute by making fluid heretofore inflexible boundaries/definitions<br>• I create integrated maps for action | • I contribute from my creative self, my highest gifts to all sentience as deeply as I can see them now<br>• I create integrated maps for action<br>• I contribute by seeing the beauty of poles and accepting things as they are | • I do my best by working efficiently and effectively<br>• I learn from practice/study<br>• I contribute from what I know and can do<br>• I plan and receive feedback | • I give from what I have<br>• I will be given what I need to do my work<br>• I work hard |

---

154    These descriptions have emerged in work with Alain Gauthier, Terri O'Fallon, and Beena Sharma, to all of whom I am very grateful.

| Level of Agreement | Unitive Based Ironist (6th P) | Construct Based Alchemist (5th P) | Context Based Strategist (4th P) | Economic Based Achiever (3rd P) | Rules Based Diplomat (2nd P) |
|---|---|---|---|---|---|
| Relationship to the Other | • I see how you are me, I am you, and how we create each other, despite the uniqueness of our individual selves. We flow together in relationship<br>• I am aware instantaneously of the ground for community that arises between us | • I see the paradoxes and projections in our relationship and I learn about who I am by seeing you in me and me in you<br>• I am aware of how together, we construct community | • I accept and support your authentic expression in the world and expect you to grow and develop<br>• I am aware of how I, you, and we benefit when we are healthy as a community<br>• You and I grow through each other | • You also need to work effectively and efficiently according to the plan, bringing the skills and capacities you have developed<br>• I support you in your growth, and to contributing what you know and can do | • You need to give of your best, according to what you have been given<br>• You need to meet your obligations<br>• I support you in working hard |
| Relationship to the Group | • I see the perfection of the whole as it is, even in those parts that some might call imperfect,<br>• The success of the whole and consciousness will occur in its own way as each being finds their own way home in the company of others | • I see the limitations of the whole as a rigid entity and work towards a whole of one interconnected, though complex community on this earth<br>• The success of the whole depends on the integration of disparate parts of the human family. | • I believe the group is healthiest when you and I contribute from our best expression<br>• Our sustainable relationships generate sustainable value for our community | • Our group success depends on everyone contributing their part effectively and efficiently<br>• Our success is a function of how well we perform<br>• We can create the world | • We each do our part<br>• If we each take on a part, then there can be enough for all of us<br>• I trust that the whole will take care of all of us<br>• We will work hard together |
| Relationship to Nature | Nature is the expression of consciousness and comes in many forms; the natural beauty of a forest, cities, the ocean, tsunamis, and every part of the Kosmos | Nature is an expression of the paradoxical, complex and unpredictable; we can use it as a model for the whole, a great teacher | Humans are an integral part of nature, treating it with love and respect, protecting and restoring it for future generations | Nature is our servant, and as a resource, serves humanity's needs to improve our future | Nature is here to use up for our purposes and use is defined by my group |

| Level of Agreement | Unitive Based Ironist (6th P) | Construct Based Alchemist (5th P) | Context Based Strategist (4th P) | Economic Based Achiever (3rd P) | Rules Based Diplomat (2nd P) |
|---|---|---|---|---|---|
| Relationship to Spirit | I witness internal and external all-time/space and become the simple fluidity of life and the Kosmos as a free functioning human being | I witness the fluidity and complexity of self and Kosmos in the moment, as it relates to immanence | I witness my internal voices which lead me to my authentic deeper self | • I reflect on my internal self, and become aware of my patterns <br> • I choose the codes I live by | I follow the moral code of action of my identified community |

*Table 2: Stages of Awareness in Ecosynomic Agreements*

# APPENDIX 3 – THE HARMONIC VIBRANCY SURVEY

The Harmonic Vibrancy survey was designed to assess the level of harmonic vibrancy an individual experienced in a group through the five primary relationships, which are developed in Chapter 1. To further assess the context of the harmonic vibrancy being experienced, the survey asks questions about the quality of leadership and the group's outcomes.

The survey instrument as it exists below was developed over four iterations. In the first pass, the pilot version was designed in collaboration with Alain Gauthier, Terry O'Fallon, and colleagues of the Global Transformation Ensemble, to whom I am eternally grateful. We tested the pilot version of 89 questions with 91 colleagues in our immediate networks from 11 countries. From this initial dataset, we were able to use components factor analysis and feedback from our colleagues to reduce the survey to 61 questions. Essentially this process showed that some of the questions were unnecessary, unclear, or repetitive. We tested this second survey with 224 individuals in a strategy class I taught. With this data, we further refined the survey to its current form with 57 questions. We then began to translate the survey into multiple languages.[155]

> "The survey was a mirror for me. Through it I could
> see my self, and my other relationships more
> clearly."
> — Dr. Luis Paiz Bekker, Director, Doctors Without Borders Argentina

---

155    For translation of the survey into the different languages, we had native speakers familiar with the concepts translate the text and validate the translation. I thank Yufang Yin for the Chinese translation and Jiajia Schwede Assoon for validating it, Eveline Batenburg and Marije Hoeksema for the Dutch translation, Parisa Gholampour for the Farsi translation and Mostafa Nejati for validating it, Alain Gauthier for the French translation, Christoph Hinske, Fiona Wollensack, and their colleagues at IFOK for the German translation, Asami Helmlinger for the Japanese translation, Evgeny Pustoshkin for the Russian translation, and Luz Maria Puente for the Spanish translation.

A little more detail from the surveys highlights some of what we are finding. The survey data, as of January 27, 2014, includes descriptions of 1,748 experiences in 1,189 groups, from 89 countries. Of that, 31% of groups were smaller than 10 people, 49% were between 10 and 100 people, 12% were between 100 and 1000, and 8% were over 1000. Of the types of groups, 64% were work places, 34% were civic, church, or sports groups, and 12% were family groups. The survey takers were 46% female and 54% male. We have also described 81 teams, with all team members describing their experience of the same team.

The survey results (see Figure 42), which we have shared throughout the text, show a very strong relationship among the five primary relationships, and the level of leadership quality and group health outcomes.

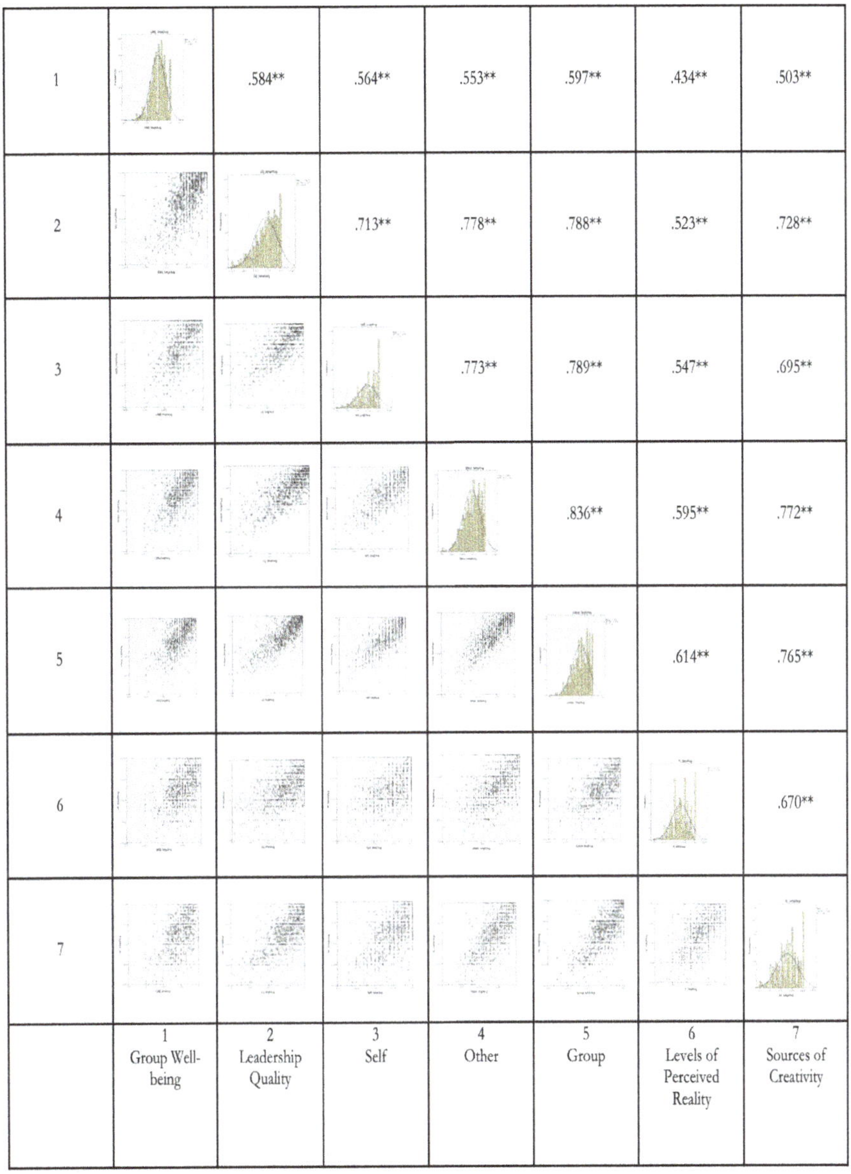

| | 1 Group Well-being | 2 Leadership Quality | 3 Self | 4 Other | 5 Group | 6 Levels of Perceived Reality | 7 Sources of Creativity |
|---|---|---|---|---|---|---|---|
| 1 | | .584** | .564** | .553** | .597** | .434** | .503** |
| 2 | | | .713** | .778** | .788** | .523** | .728** |
| 3 | | | | .773** | .789** | .547** | .695** |
| 4 | | | | | .836** | .595** | .772** |
| 5 | | | | | | .614** | .765** |
| 6 | | | | | | | .670** |
| 7 | | | | | | | |

*Figure 42: Statistical Representation of Survey Results*

The correlations of the main variables of group well being, leadership quality, relationship to self, other, group, nature (levels of perceived reality), and spirit (sources of creativity) are shown in Figure 42. All of the relationships are highly significant.[156]

## FINDINGS

In Figure 42 we see a very clear pattern. While it might be hard for some to "see" in the three-dimensional graphic, that the dots are clustered in a specific way is clear. The cluster has a technical description, which indicates that as the harmonic vibrancy in the relationship to the "self" increases, so too does the harmonic vibrancy in the relationships to the "other" and to the "group." This is depicted in the data from the surveys in the graphic on the left-side of Figure 42. The graphic in the middle of Figure 42 shows that this relationship holds also with the harmonic vibrancy experienced in the relationships to "nature" and to "spirit."

This means two things for us right now. First, it means that when someone describes their experience of the overall harmonic vibrancy in a group, they also report an experience of a similar level of harmonic vibrancy in all of their relationships. Specifically, if they report an experience of an overall high level of harmonic vibrancy in a group, they also describe each of the five relationships as being of high harmonic vibrancy, as well. The second thing the data tells us is that one experiences a similar level of harmonic vibrancy in all five relationships. The data is very clear. To move to an experience of higher levels of harmonic vibrancy, you need to increase the level of harmonic vibrancy experienced in all five primary relationships.[157]

---

156 For a complete statistical analysis of the data, visit the Institute for Strategic Clarity (http://instituteforstrategicclarity.org/take-the-survey/)

157 For the technically oriented, we now see a very different formulation of harmonic vibrancy, with the overall harmonic vibrancy being equal to the contribution of the harmonic vibrancy experienced in each relationship. Mathematically this is:

$$HV_{overall} = HV_{self}^{\frac{1}{5}} * HV_{other}^{\frac{1}{5}} * HV_{group}^{\frac{1}{5}} * HV_{nature}^{\frac{1}{5}} * HV_{spirit}^{\frac{1}{5}}$$

$$HV_{overall} = \prod_{n=1}^{5} HV_{n}^{\frac{1}{5}}, \text{ where n = one of five primary relationships}$$

1 = self, 2 = other, 3 = group, 4 = nature, 5 = spirit

We also see that the harmonic vibrancy possible in any specific relationship is closely related to the overall harmonic vibrancy, with a rough approximate being $HV_n = HV_{overall} \pm 1$. This means that overall progress to a higher level of harmonic vibrancy comes from inching forward in all five primary relationships at the same time.

# ACTUAL SURVEY

## WORD FORM

This survey takes approximately ten to twelve minutes to complete, addressing the experience of the five primary relationships, group outcomes, and the quality of leadership. It is available on-line in many languages at (http://instituteforstrategicclarity.org/take-the-survey/).

### ISC Experience of Relational Abundance Survey

*Welcome! Through this 12-min survey, you will describe your experience of a group. We will share your results with you at the end. We thank you for your time.*

*If you have been asked by a group to answer this survey, your group will benefit from your response by receiving information that can further enhance its effectiveness.*

*This survey is designed to explore the individual and collective experience of groups and their leadership. This survey is part of a more in-depth research inquiry to further understand the broad spectrum of today's leadership in the world. The goal is to understand how different groups and leaders show up in their level of vibrancy.*

*This survey consists of a series of statements, which you will be rating on a five-point scale. It may take 12 minutes to complete. The information you provide will be treated confidentially.*

Identification:
Please share some basic information about you and your group.

Group Code:
Please write your answer here:

| Name | |
|------|--|
| E-mail Address | |

Gender: - Please choose only one of the following:
- ○ Female
- ○ Male

Highest level of formal education - Please choose only one of the following:

- ·○ Primary school
- ·○ Some high school
- ·○ High school graduate
- ·○ Some college
- ·○ College graduate
- ·○ Advanced degree

Identify a group you are part of, where you spend time. It could be where you work, the community you live in, where you volunteer, where you go for relaxation, your extended family.

| Name of group/Org | |
| --- | --- |
| Country | |

General description of the group
Please choose only one of the following:
- ○ Work group where I am paid for what I do
- ○ Church group
- ○ Community, civic group, or network where I participate
- ○ Sports team
- ○ Family
- ○ Other

Which of the following best describes your usual role?
Please choose only one of the following:

- ○ Leader or primary organizer
- ○ Regular participating member
- ○ Occasional participating member

How many people are in this group?
Please choose only one of the following:
- ○ Less than 10
- ○ 10 to 50
- ○ 51 to 100
- ○ 101 to 1000
- ○ over 1000

How many years has this group existed?
Please choose only one of the following:

- ◯ Less than 1
- ◯ 1-3
- ◯ 4-7
- ◯ More than 7
- ◯ More than 7

How many years have you been a part of this group?
Please choose only one of the following:

- ◯ Less than 1
- ◯ 1-3
- ◯ 4-7

## Leadership Quality

In this section, we invite you to share your experience of the quality of leadership in the group you have selected.

What is your experience of the following dimensions of well-being of your group?
Please choose the appropriate response for each item

| | Almost never true | Rarely true | Often true | Usually true | Almost always true | I do not understand the question |
|---|---|---|---|---|---|---|
| Everyone has dignified work | ◯ | ◯ | ◯ | ◯ | ◯ | ◯ |
| Everyone makes enough money to provide for himself or herself | ◯ | ◯ | ◯ | ◯ | ◯ | ◯ |
| The group has enough money to do its work | ◯ | ◯ | ◯ | ◯ | ◯ | ◯ |
| We are considered top performers by our peers | ◯ | ◯ | ◯ | ◯ | ◯ | ◯ |

What is your experience of the quality of leadership in your group?
Note: Leadership can be exercised formally or informally, and by one or more individuals.
Please choose the appropriate response for each item:

| | Almost never true | Rarely true | Often true | Usually true | Almost always true | I do not understand the question |
|---|---|---|---|---|---|---|
| Our leadership recognizes the gifts of all of the members of the group, and invites each of us to express them in fulfilling our greatest individual potential | ○ | ○ | ○ | ○ | ○ | ○ |
| Our leadership inspires us to see the gifts and differing points of view of other groups we know | ○ | ○ | ○ | ○ | ○ | ○ |
| Our leadership inspires us to value our differences | ○ | ○ | ○ | ○ | ○ | ○ |
| Our leadership cares deeply for the quality of relationships within the group | ○ | ○ | ○ | ○ | ○ | ○ |
| Before making decisions, leadership reaches out, listens, reflects deeply, and invites us to do the same | ○ | ○ | ○ | ○ | ○ | ○ |
| Our leadership demonstrates its willingness to learn from what happens in the group, and to change the group structures and processes when appropriate | ○ | ○ | ○ | ○ | ○ | ○ |

| | | | | | | |
|---|---|---|---|---|---|---|
| Our leadership helps us clarify our shared intentions | ○ | ○ | ○ | ○ | ○ | ○ |
| Our leadership inspires us to see the gifts of the other members of the group | ○ | ○ | ○ | ○ | ○ | ○ |
| Our leadership helps us take into account all the stakeholders in what we do | ○ | ○ | ○ | ○ | ○ | ○ |
| Our leadership invites us to be aware of where we are in the present, and to be audacious and persistent in closing the gap between our aspirations and current reality | ○ | ○ | ○ | ○ | ○ | ○ |

Does your group have a specified or designated leader or is leadership of this group a shared or rotating responsibility?

Please choose only one of the following:

- ○ We have one specific or designated leader
- ○ Leadership is a shared responsibility
- ○ Leadership rotates
- ○ Other leadership model

Make a comment on your choice here:

Overall, what is your experience of the quality of leadership in your group? Please choose only one of the following:

- ○ Extremely poor
- ○ Below average
- ○ Average
- ○ Above average
- ○ Exceptional

## In-depth assessment of relational well-being

In this section we invite you to assess the experience you have of your relationship to your own self, to others, to the group, to the process of innovation, and to the source of creativity.

Describe your experience of yourself, in this group
Please choose the appropriate response for each item:

|  | Almost never true | Rarely true | Often true | Usually true | Almost always true | I do not understand the question |
|---|---|---|---|---|---|---|
| I step further into my aspirations and gifts because of this group's support | O | O | O | O | O | O |
| My work in this group is highly satisfying | O | O | O | O | O | O |
| I share who I really am with this group | O | O | O | O | O | O |
| The members of this group encourage me to grow my talents and deeper gifts, to the achievement of this group's purpose | O | O | O | O | O | O |

What percentage of your potential do you bring to this group?
Please choose only one of the following:

- O 0%
- O 25%
- O 50%
- O 75%
- O 100%

Assess your experience with other individuals in this group
Please choose the appropriate response for each item:

| | Almost never true | Rarely true | Often true | Usually true | Almost always true | I do not understand the question |
|---|---|---|---|---|---|---|
| I look for opportunities to help other members contribute their best | O | O | O | O | O | O |
| I am aware of talents and deeper gifts other members can contribute | O | O | O | O | O | O |
| Members in this group believe that hearing different points of view is valuable | O | O | O | O | O | O |
| Each member's point-of-view is considered in most decisions and processes | O | O | O | O | O | O |
| The methods and processes we use enable each member to make a unique contribution | O | O | O | O | O | O |

In your experience, what percentage of their potential do others bring to the group?
Please choose only one of the following:

- ○ 0%
- ○ 25%
- ○ 50%
- ○ 75%
- ○ 100%

Assess your experience of the whole group
Please choose the appropriate response for each item:

| | Almost never true | Rarely true | Often true | Usually true | Almost always true | I do not understand the question |
|---|---|---|---|---|---|---|
| I am clear about my purpose in this group | ○ | ○ | ○ | ○ | ○ | ○ |
| I experience lots of positivity and possibility when this group meets | ○ | ○ | ○ | ○ | ○ | ○ |
| All members actively engage when the group meets | ○ | ○ | ○ | ○ | ○ | ○ |
| I am clear about who we are as a group, and why we do what we do | ○ | ○ | ○ | ○ | ○ | ○ |

| | | | | | | |
|---|---|---|---|---|---|---|
| There is a high degree of trust among members | O | O | O | O | O | O |
| Our group clearly acknowledges, in many ways, my unique contributions | O | O | O | O | O | O |

Assess your experience of the process of innovation in this group
Please choose the appropriate response for each item:

| | Almost never true | Rarely true | Often true | Usually true | Almost always true | I do not understand the question |
|---|---|---|---|---|---|---|
| I experience high vibrancy when I am in the place of this group | O | O | O | O | O | O |
| In this group, we see new ways of doing things, and we do them, learning along the way | O | O | O | O | O | O |
| Our group spends time imagining new solutions that we never develop or deliver | O | O | O | O | O | O |
| Our group's incentives focus mostly on outcomes | O | O | O | O | O | O |
| We focus on results and developing our ability to deliver better results | O | O | O | O | O | O |

| "Be realistic" is a common statement to creative people in our group | ◯ | ◯ | ◯ | ◯ | ◯ | ◯ |
|---|---|---|---|---|---|---|

Assess your experience of the source of creativity in this group
Please choose the appropriate response for each item:

| | Almost never true | Rarely true | Often true | Usually true | Almost always true | I do not understand the question |
|---|---|---|---|---|---|---|
| Anything is possible in this group | ◯ | ◯ | ◯ | ◯ | ◯ | ◯ |
| Our group looks for inspiration in everyone, in everything, all of the time | ◯ | ◯ | ◯ | ◯ | ◯ | ◯ |
| We each bring our own creative ideas to the group | ◯ | ◯ | ◯ | ◯ | ◯ | ◯ |
| We do things the way they have always been done | ◯ | ◯ | ◯ | ◯ | ◯ | ◯ |

How would you rate the overall effectiveness of this group in meeting its purpose?
Please choose only one of the following:

- ◯ Extremely poor
- ◯ Below average
- ◯ Average
- ◯ Above average
- ◯ Excellent

When you consider all of the groups you are currently a member of, how would you rate this group?
Please choose only one of the following:

- ○ Unquestionably the worst functioning group I am currently a member of
- ○ Not the worst functioning group, but clearly it falls well below the average of all the groups I am currently a member of
- ○ Neither near the top nor the bottom, more in the middle of all the groups that I am currently a member of
- ○ Not the best functioning, but one of the better groups I am currently a member of
- ○ Unquestionably the best functioning group I am currently a member of

Is there any aspect of the way your group works that seems to be missing from this survey?
Please write your answer here:

Submit your survey. Thank you for completing this survey.

# REFERENCES

Ackoff, R. L. (1993, November). *From Mechanistic to Social Systemic Thinking.* Paper presented at the Systems Thinking in Action Conference.

Agrast, M. D., Botero, J. C., & Ponce, A. (2010). The World Justice Project Rule of Law Index 2010. Washington, D.C.: The World Justice Project.

Alexander, C. (1964). *Notes on the Synthesis of Form.* Cambridge, MA: Harvard University Press.

Amato, N. (2013). The Leadership Cycle: How to Effectively Lead and Develop Talent. *Journal of Accountancy* (June).

Arefi, M. (2008). Asset-based Approaches to Community Development. In X. Q. Zhang (Ed.). Nairobi, Kenya: United Nations Human Settlements Programme (UN-HABITAT).

Argyris, C. (1993). *Knowledge for Action: A Guide to Overcoming Barriers to Organizational Change.* San Francisco: Jossey-Bass.

Baggott, J. (2011). *The Quantum Story: A History in 40 Moments.* New York: Oxford University Press.

Barkley Rosser, J., John, & Rosser, M. V. (2004). *Comparative Economics in a Transforming World Economy* (Second ed.). Cambridge, MA: MIT Press.

Barnard, C. I. (1968). *The Functions of the Executive* (Thirtieth Anniversary ed.). Cambridge, MA: Harvard University Press.

Barrett, F. J. (2012). *Yes to the Mess: Surprising Leadership Lessons from Jazz.* Boston: Harvard Business Review Press.

Barry, D. (2007, February 25). Would You Like That in Tens, Twenties or Normans? *New York Times,* p. 1.

Bentham, J. (1988). *The Principles of Morals and Legislation.* Amherst, NY: Prometheus Books.

Berman, M. G., Jonides, J., & Kaplan, S. (2008). The Cognitive Benefits of Interacting with Nature. *Psychological Science, 19*(12), 1207-1212.

Bhatnagar, D., Rathore, A., Moreno Torres, M., & Kanungo, P. (2003). Participatory Budgeting in Brazil *Empowerment Case Studies.* Washington, D.C.: The World Bank.

Bohm, D. (1992). *Thought as a System.* New York: Routledge.

Boroush, M. (2010). NSF Releases New Statistics on Business Innovation (D. o. S. R. Statistics, Trans.). In B. Directorate for Social, and Economic Sciences (Ed.). Arlington, VA: National Science Foundation.

Brandenburger, A. M., & Nalebuff, B. J. (1998). *Co-opetition.* New York: Currency

Doubleday.

Bratton, W., & Tumin, Z. (2012). *Collaborate or Perish!: Reaching Across Boundaries in a Networked World*. New York: Crown Business.

Burchell, M., & Robin, J. (2011). *The Great Workplace*. San Francisco: Jossey-Bass.

Churchman, C. W., & Ackoff, R. L. (1950). Purposive Behavior and Cybernetics. *Social Forces, 29*(1), 38.

Coase, R. H. (1973). The Nature of the Firm. *Economica, 4*(16), 386-405.

Cole, G. D. H. (2011). *Socialist Economics*. New York: Routledge.

Collins, J. (2001). *Good to Great*. New York: HarperCollins.

Connolly, M., & Rianoshek, R. (2002). *The Communication Catalyst: The Fast (but not stupid) Track to Value for Customers, Investors, and Employees*. Chicago: Dearborn Trade Publishing.

Cook-Greuter, S. R. (2002). A Detailed Description of the Development of Nine Action Logics Adapted from Ego Development Theory for the Leadership Development Framework (pp. 36). Cambridge, MA: Harthill USA.

Cooperrider, D. L., & Whitney, D. (2005). *Appreciative Inquiry: A Positive Revolution in Change*. San Francisco: Berrett-Koehler.

Cox, B., & Forshaw, J. (2010). *Why Does E=mc2? (And Why Should We Care?)*. Boston: DaCapo Press.

Cox, B., & Forshaw, J. (2011). *The Quantum Universe*. Boston: DaCapo Press.

Damasio, A. (2010). *Self Comes to Mind: Constructing the Conscious Brain*. New York: Pantheon Books.

De Bono, E. (1971). *Lateral Thinking for Management*. New York: Penguin.

De Bono, E. (1999). *Six Thinking Hats*. New York: Back Bay Books.

Dubin, R. (1978). *Theory Building* (Revised ed.). New York: The Free Press.

Dweck, C. (2006). *Mindset: The New Psychology of Success*. New York: Random House.

Easterly, W. (2006). *The White Man's Burden*. New York: Penguin Books.

Edmans, A. (2011). Does the Stock Market Fully Value Intangibles? Employee Satisfaction and Equity Prices. *Journal of Financial Economics, 101*(3), 621-640.

Eisler, R. (2007). *The Real Wealth of Nations*. San Francisco: Berrett-Koehler.

Erdman, D. V. (Ed.). (1988). *The Complete Poetry & Prose of William Blake*. New York: Anchor Books.

Fairbairn, B. (1994). The Meaning of Rochdale: The Rochdale Pioneers and the Co-operative Principles. In C. f. t. S. o. Co-operatives (Ed.), *Occasional Paper Series*. Saskatoon, Saskatchewan, Canada: University of Saskatchewan.

Fenn, D. (2005). *Alpha Dogs: How Your Small Business Can Become a Leader of the Pack*. New York: Collins.

Ferguson, N. (2008). *The Ascent of Money: A Financial History of the World*. New York: Penguin.

Foote, N., Eisenstat, R., & Fredberg, T. (2011). The Higher Ambition Leader. *Harvard Business Review, 89*(9), 94-102.

Forrester, J. W. (1971). Counterintuitive Behavior of Social Systems. *Technology Review, 73*(3), 52-68.

Forrester, J. W. (1990). *Principles of Systems*. Portland, OR: Productivity Press.

Frankl, V. E. (1986). *The Doctor and the Soul: From Psychotherapy and Logotherapy*. New

York: Random House.

Fredrickson, B. L. (2009). *Positivity: Groundbreaking Reswearch Reveals How to Embrace the Hidden Strength of Positive Emotions, Overcome Negativity, and Thrive.* New York: Crown Publishers.

Galbraith, J. K. (1975). *Money: Whence It Came, Where It Went.* Boston: Houghton Mifflin Company.

Gelleri, C. (2009). Chiemgauer Regiomoney: Theory and Practice of a Local Currency. *International Journal of Community Currency Research, 13,* 61-75.

Goffee, R., & Jones, G. (2013). Creating the Best Workplace on Earth. *Harvard Business Review, 91*(5), 98-106.

Goleman, D. (1995). *Emotional Intelligence.* New York: Bantam.

Goleman, D. (2010). *Ecological Intelligence.* New York: Broadway Books.

Goold, G. P., Page, T. E., Capps, E., Rouse, W. H. D., Post, L. A., & Warmington, E. H. (Eds.). (1997). *Xenophon IV: Memorabilia. Oeconomicus. Symposium. Apologia.* (Vol. LCL 168). Suffolk: St. Edmundsbury Press.

Graeber, D. (2011). *Debt: The First 5,000 Years.* Brooklyn, NY: MelvilleHouse.

Greene, B. (2003). *The Elegant Universe.* New York: Vintage.

Greene, B. (2011). *The Hidden Reality: Parallel Universes and the Deep Laws of the Cosmos.* New York: Random House.

Greenwald, D. (Ed.) (1983) *The McGraw-Hill Dictionary of Modern Economics* (Third ed.). New York: McGraw-Hill.

Groysberg, B., & Slind, M. (2012). Leadership Is a Conversation: How to Improve Employee Engagement and Alignment in Today's Flatter, More Networked Organizations. *Harvard Business Review, 90*(6), 76-84.

Hallsmith, G., & Lietaer, B. (2011). *Creating Wealth: Growing Local Economies with Local Currencies.* Gabriola Island, BC, Canada: New Society Publishers.

Hammond, K. R. (1996). *Human Judgment and Social Policy: Irreducible Uncertainty, Inevitable Error, Unavoidable Injustice.* New York: Oxford University Press.

Harter, J. K., Schmidt, F. L., Agrawal, S., & Plowman, S. K. (2013). The Relationship Between Engagement at Work and Organizational Outcomes: 2012 Q12® Meta-Analysis. Washington, D.C.: Gallup.

Hartig, T., Evans, G. W., Jamner, L. D., Davis, D. S., & Garling, T. (2003). Tracking Restoration in Natural and Urban Settings. *Journal of Environmental Psychology, 23*(2), 109-123.

Hawking, S. (Ed.). (2011). *The Dreams that Stuff Is Made of.* Philadelphia: Running Press.

Heilbroner, R. L., & Milberg, W. (2002). *The Making of Economic Society* (11th ed.): Upper Saddle River, NJ: Prentice Hall.

Heslin, P. A. (2010). Mindsets and Employee Engagement: Theoretical Linkages and Practical Interventions. In S. Albrecht (Ed.), *The Handbook of Employee Engagement: Perspectives, Issues, Research and Practice* (pp. 218-226). Cheltenham, UK: Edwin Elgar.

His Holiness The Dalai Lama. (1996). *Beyond Dogma: Dialogues & Discourses.* Berkeley, CA: North Atlantic Books.

His Holiness The Dalai Lama. (1999). *Ethics for the New Millennium.* New York:

Riverhead Books.

Jantsch, E. (1980). *The Self-Organizing Universe: Scientific and Human Implications of the Emerging Paradigm of Evolution*. New York: Pergamon.

Kahneman, D. (2011). *Thinking, Fast and Slow*. New York: Farrar, Straus and Giroux.

Kaku, M. (2008). *Physics of the Impossible*. New York: Anchor Books.

Kaluza, T. (1921). Zum Unitätsproblem der Physik. *Sitzungsberichte Preußische Akademie der Wissenschaften, 96*, 69-72.

Kaplan, S. (1995). The Restorative Benefits of Nature: Toward an Integrative Framework. *Journal of Environmental Psychology, 15*(3), 169-182.

Keeney, R. L. (1992). *Value-Focused Thinking: A Path to Creative Decisionmaking*. Cambridge, MA: Harvard University Press.

Kegan, R., & Lahey, L. L. (2009). *Immunity to Change: How to Overcome It and Unlock the Potential in Yourself and Your Organization*. Boston: Harvard Business Press.

Khadka, R. (2012). Switching Gears: From Needs To Assets Based Approach To Community Development In Nepal. *OIDA International Journal of Sustainable Development, 3*(11), 81-88.

Kleindorfer, P. R., Kunreuther, H. C., & Schoemaker, P. J. H. (1993). *Decision Sciences: An Integrative Perspective*. New York: Cambridge University Press.

Koestler, A. (1967). *The Ghost in the Machine*. London: Arkana.

Kretzmann, J. P., & McKnight, J. L. (1993). *Building Communities from the Inside Out: A Path Toward Finding and Mobilizing a Community's Assets*. Evanston, IL: Institute for Policy Research.

Langer, E., & Piper, A. (1987). The Prevention of Mindlessness. *Journal of Personality & Social Psychology, 53*(2), 280-287.

Langer, E. J. (1989). *Mindfulness*. Cambridge, MA: Perseus.

Langer, E. J. (2009). *Counterclockwise: Mindful Health and the Power of Possibility*. New York: Ballantine Books.

Leaf, A., & Hulbert, N. (2010). An Assessment of Ecosynomics at THORLO, with Implications and Possibilities. Harrisville, NH: Institute for Strategic Clarity.

Leaf, A., Hulbert, N., & Throneburg, J. (2010). *THORLO: An Entrepreneur's Vision of Sustainability*. Institute for Strategic Clarity. Harrisville, NH.

Lietaer, B. (2003). A World in Balance? *Reflections: The SoL Journal of Knowledge, Learning and Change, 4*(4), 6-16.

Lietaer, B., & Dunne, J. (2013). *Rethinking Money: How New Currencies Turn Scarcity into Prosperity*. San Francisco: Berrett-Koehler.

Lietaer, B. A. (2001). *The Future of Money*. London: Random House.

Magretta, J. (2011). *Understanding Michael Porter: The Essential Guide to Competition and Strategy*. Boston: Harvard Business Review Press.

Mankiw, N. G. (2008). *Principles of Economics* (Fourth ed.). Mason, OH: Thomson.

Marshall, A. (1890). *Principles of Economics*. New York: MacMillan and Co.

McKnight, J., & Block, P. (2010). *The Abundant Community: Awakening the Power of Families and Neighborhoods*. San Francisco: Berrett-Koehler.

Metcalf, M., & Palmer, M. (2011). *Innovative Leadership Fieldbook*. Tucson, AZ: Integral Publishers.

Mullainathan, S., & Shafir, E. (2013). *Scarcity: Why Having Too Little Means So Much*.

New York: Time Books.

Nash, O. (1953). *You Can't Get There From Here*. New York: Little Brown & Co.

Navratilova, M. (2006). *Shape Your Self: My 6-Step Diet and Fitness Plan to Achieve the Best Shape of Your Life*. New York: Rodale.

Needleman, J. (1991). *Money and the Meaning of Life*. New York: Currency Doubleday.

North, P. (2010). *Local Money: How to Make It Happen In Your Community*. Dartington, Totnes, UK: Transition Books.

O'Neil, G., & O'Neil, G. (1990). *The Human Life*. Spring Valley, NY: Mercury Press.

Ortega y Gasset, J. (1962). *Man and Crisis*. New York: W.W. Norton & Company.

Pascale, R., Sternin, J., & Sternin, M. (2010). *The Power of Positive Deviance: How Unlikely Innovators Solve the World's Toughest Problems*. Boston: Harvard Business School Press.

Peattie, L. (1983). Realistic Planning and Qualitative Research. *Habitat International, 7*(5/6), 227-234.

Pruitt, B. & Thomas, P. (2007). *Democratic Dialogue – A Handbook for Practitioners*. 2007. New York: United Nations Development Programme.

Ritchie-Dunham, J. L. (2008a). A Collaborative-Systemic Strategy Addressing the Dynamics of Poverty in Guatemala: Converting Seeming Impossibilities into Strategic Probabilities. In C. Wankel (Ed.), *Alleviating Poverty through Business Strategy* (pp. 73-98). New York: Palgrave Macmillan.

Ritchie-Dunham, J. L. (2008b). *The End of Poverty – The Beginning of Self-determination: An Integral Systemic Exploration of Self-determination in Guatemala*. Wilton, NH: Institute for Strategic Clarity.

Ritchie-Dunham, J. L. (2009a). The Dynamics of Our Relationship with Money: Social-Political-Economic Drivers of the Agreements that Guide Human Interactions [Working Paper]. Wilton, NH: Institute for Strategic Clarity.

Ritchie-Dunham, J. L. (2009b). *Strategy for Initiating GANs — Interview Research with Leading GAN Founders*. In iScale Strategy Community of Practice (Ed.). Boston: iScale.

Ritchie-Dunham, J. L., & Puente, L. M. (2008). Strategic Clarity: Actions for Identifying and Correcting Gaps in Mental Models. *Long Range Planning, 41*(5), 509-529.

Ritchie-Dunham, J. L., & Rabbino, H. T. (2001). *Managing from Clarity: Identifying, Aligning and Leveraging Strategic Resources*. Chichester: John Wiley & Sons, Ltd.

Ritchie-Dunham, J. L., Throneburg, J., & Puleo, M. (2010). *Living Ecosynomics: Brand Stewardship at THORLO*. White Paper. Institute for Strategic Clarity. Harrisville, NH.

Robbins, L. (1945). *An Essay of the Nature & Significance of Economic Science* (Second ed.). London: Macmillan and Co.

Robbins, T. (1990). *Jitterbug Perfume*. New York: Bantam.

Roncaglia, A. (2006). *The Wealth of Ideas: A History of Economic Thought*. New York: Cambridge University Press.

Rosser, M. V., & Rosser, J. B. (2003). *Comparative Economics in a Transforming World Economy*. Cambridge, MA: MIT Press.

Russell, B. (1969). *The ABC of Relativity*. New York: Mentor.

Russell, C. (2009). Communities in Control: Developing Assets (First European ABCD Summit ed.): Carnegie Foundation.

Sachs, J. D. (2005). *The End of Poverty: Economic Possibilities for Our Time*. New York: The Penguin Press.

Sachs, J. D. (2011). *The Price of Civilization: Reawakening American Virtue and Prosperity*. New York: Random House.

Samuelson, P. A., & Nordhaus, W. D. (1995). *Economics* (Fifteenth ed.). Boston: Irwin McGraw-Hill.

Schumacher, E. F. (1973). *Small Is Beautiful: Economics as if People Mattered*. New York: Harper & Row.

Seligman, M. E. P. (2011). *Flourish: A Visionary New Understanding of Happiness and Well-being*. New York: Free Press.

Sheehan, G. (2003). *Building the Mercado Central: Asset-Based Development and Community Entrepreneurship*. In ABCD Institute (Ed.). Chicago, IL: ACTA Publications.

Shorter Oxford English Dictionary. (2007) (Sixth Edition ed.). New York: Oxford University Press.

Simon, H. A. (1997). *Administrative Behavior* (Fourth ed.). New York: Free Press.

Sisodia, R. S., Wolfe, D. B., & Seth, J. N. (2007). *Firms of Endearment: How World-class Companies Profit from Passion and Purpose*. Upper Saddle River, NJ: Wharton School Publishing.

Spann, R. S. (2008). Some things are impossible-until they're not: Solving 'intractable' business and social problems. http://innatestrategies.com/docs/Impossible. pdf

Spann, R. S., & Ritchie-Dunham, J. L. (2008). The Promise of Systems Thinking for Shifting Fundamental Dynamics. *The Systems Thinker, 19*(7), 6-10.

Spence, M. (2011). *The Next Convergence: The Future of Economic Growth in a Multispeed World*. New York: Farrar, Straus and Giroux.

Sterman, J. D. (1989a). Misperceptions of Feedback in Dynamic Decision Making. *Organizational Behavior and Human Decision Processes, 43*, 301-335.

Sterman, J. D. (1989b). Modeling Managerial Behavior: Misperceptions of Feedback in a Dynamic Decision Making Experiment. *Management Science, 35*(3), 321-339.

Sterman, J. D. (1994). Learning in and about Complex Systems. *System Dynamics Review, 10*(2-3), 291-330.

Sterman, J. D. (2000). *Business Dynamics: Systems Thinking and Modeling for a Complex World*. Boston: Irwin McGraw-Hill.

Sterman, J. D., & Booth Sweeney, L. (2002). Cloudy Skies: Assessing Public Understanding of Global Warming. *System Dynamics Review, 18*(2), 207-240.

Strickland, B., & Rause, V. (2007). *Make the Impossible Possible*. New York: Currency/ Doubleday.

Sullivan, J. W. (1892). *Direct Legislation by the Citizenship through the Initiative and Referendum*. New York: True Nationalist Publishing Company.

Throneburg, J. L. (2011). *THORLO Leadership and Employee Handbook: The Structure-Process of Integration*. Statesville, NC: Second Registry Leadership Academy Press.

Torbert, B. & Associates. (1994). *Action Inquiry: The Secret of Timely and Transforming Leadership.* San Francisco: Berrett-Koehler.

Twist, L. (2003). *The Soul of Money: Reclaiming the Wealth of Our Inner Resources.* New York: W.W. Norton & Company.

Umer Chapra, M. (2000). *The Future of Economics: An Islamic Perspective.* Leicester, UK: The Islamic Foundation.

Using the Methods of Fernando Flores, an Interview of Jack Reilly. (1997). *Center for Quality of Management Journal, 6*(1), 15-20.

van den Bergh, J. C. J. M. (2001). Ecological Economics: Themes, Approaches, and Differences with Environmental Economics. *Regional Environmental Change, 2,* 13-23.

von Bertalanffy, L. (1950). An Outline of General System Theory. *British Journal for the Philosophy of Science, 1*(2).

von Bertalanffy, L. (1975). *Perspectives on General System Theory.* New York: George Braziller.

Waddell, S. (2005). A Learning History: The CARE-LAC – Institute for Strategic Clarity Guatemala Poverty Project (pp. 32). Wilton, NH: Institute for Strategic Clarity.

Waddell, S. (2011). *Global Action Networks: Creating Our Future Together.* New York: Palgrave Macmillan.

Wampler, B. (2009). *Participatory Budgeting in Brazil: Contestation, Cooperation, and Accountability.* University Park, PA: Pennsylvania State Univ Press.

Weick, K. E. (1995). *Sensemaking in Organizations.* London: Sage Publications.

Wheatley, G. (2006). *Complementary Currency and Quality of Life: Social and Economic Capital Effects on Subjective Well-Being.* (Masters Thesis), University of Calgary, Calgary.

Whitehead, A. N. (2007). *The Concept of Nature.* New York: Cosimo.

Whitehead, A. N. (Ed.). (1978). *Process and Reality: An Essay in Cosmology* (Corrected ed.). New York: The Free Press.

Wiener, N. (1954). *The Human Use of Human Beings.* Cambridge, MA: Da Capo Press.

Wilber, K. (1998). *The Marriage of Sense and Soul: Integrating Science and Religion.* New York: Random House.

Wilber, K. (2000). *A Theory of Everything.* Boston: Shambhala.

Williamson, O. E. (1981). The Economics of Organization: The Transaction Cost Approach. *The American Journal of Sociology, 87*(3), 548-577.

The World Factbook 2011. (2011). Retrieved from https://http://www.cia.gov/library/publications/the-world-factbook/index.html

Zajonc, A. (1995). *Catching the Light: The Entwined History of Light and Mind.* New York: Oxford University Press.

Zander, R. S., & Zander, B. (2002). *The Art of Possibility.* New York: Penguin Books.

# Index

Thank you for your interest in Ecosynomics. The following resources are available to help you and your group better understand your current agreements and see the next level of agreements available to create more effective, innovative and vibrant results.

To get an initial idea of your group's level of vibrancy go to:
www.instituteforstrategicclarity.org/take-the-survey/

To learn more about Ecosynomics go to:
www.ecosynomics.com

To buy the book and learn more about the live or online courses, workshops & certification courses available on the Ecoysnomics Framework, go to:
www.vibrancyisachoice.com

# A NOTE ABOUT THE AUTHORS

### Jim Ritchie-Dunham

Jim is president and founder of the Institute for Strategic Clarity. ISC is a non-profit 510(c)(3) research and education group focused on understanding the foundations and effects of human agreements. After 20 years of teaching, research, consulting, and coaching he combines a comprehensive academic framework with practical applications to support high-success groups in understanding the underlying foundations of their success. Jim has shared the work in courses, workshops, and speaking engagements in 15 countries - so far. Jim is also president of Vibrancy Insp., a company dedicated to using ISC's research and the resulting Ecosynomics framework to find, support and bring together high vibrancy groups from around the world to share knowledge and, with Ecosynomics, to gain a clearer understanding of what it is they are actually doing that works! Jim has a PhD in Decision Sciences from UT Austin and two masters in international management from Thunderbird and ESADE. He is also the author of *Managing From Clarity* (1999) with Hal Rabbino. He lives in western Massachusetts with his wife and children. You can contact Jim at: info@ecosynomics.com and follow his blog at jlrd.me.

### Bettye Pruitt

Bettye assisted in the writing of this book and has made it much more accessible to the reader. A PhD in history, she is the author/co-author/editor of six books, including most recently *Democratic Dialogue—A Handbook for Practitioners* (2007) with Philip Thomas.